CHALLENGING YEARS
My Life in Chemistry

Karl Spinoto.

Karl Winnacker

CHALLENGING YEARS

My Life in Chemistry

*

Translated by
DAVID GOODMAN

SIDGWICK & JACKSON
LONDON

I.S.B.N. 0.283.97900.3

Printed in Great Britain by
Morrison and Gibb Limited, Edinburgh
for Sidgwick and Jackson Limited
1 Tavistock Chambers, Bloomsbury Way
London, WC1A 2SG

To my wife

Foreword

by the Right Honourable The Earl of Longford, K.G.

IT IS a great pleasure to write a short foreword to Professor Karl Winnacker's most interesting book. It can be read and appreciated on at least three levels. In the first place, it is a first-class account of how modern science and technology can be applied to the development of a great business under very varied conditions. Secondly, much light is thrown on the social, economic, and psychological conditions which brought about the tragedy of Nazi rule and yet enabled Germany to achieve her fine moral and material recovery. Thirdly, it provides a fascinating human and, in many places, humorous story from one who was at the centre of the storm and survived to give such a creditable account of it all. Whether occupying an important position in industry or relegated to the life of a gardener, or restored to still greater heights in business, he appears before us always the same man, friendly, tolerant, scientific, 'tried by both extremes of fortune and never disturbed by either'.

His book inevitably has a special interest for me as one who was Minister for the British Zone of Germany in 1947 and 1948. I often wondered how the German industrialists, for example, felt when their businesses were taken over by the British, or in this case, American authorities, and they themselves were reduced to a humble role. Professor Winnacker gives us a fascinating picture of this, among many other aspects of Germany, in recent times. It will long be invaluable as an industrial, social, and personal history.

LONGFORD

Prefaces

To the English Edition

SINCE THIS book was first published, many major events have taken place in the world. In the economic field, one of the most important developments has been the impending entry of Great Britain and some other countries into the Common Market. This will take the integration of Europe a decisive step forward.

Such closer economic ties will also promote amongst the peoples involved a greater interest in each other. To succeed in the common venture, it will be necessary to acquire an even deeper knowledge of and understanding for the roots, traditions and development of the partners in Europe.

Nor will such efforts be limited to the partners in the Common Market. In today's fast-changing world, the interdependence between national economies and industries is becoming increasingly important everywhere. There is a clear trend for multi-national corporations not only to sell but also to produce in many countries throughout the world. This cannot be done without getting thoroughly acquainted with the local background. Since overseas ties of this kind are most advanced between the United States and Europe, I like to think that this book will also be of interest to American readers.

I hope that the English version of my autobiography may provide a small contribution towards the general aim of mutual understanding, if only in a special, but nonetheless rather important industrial field. Although the experiences related in this volume are largely concerned with the German chemical industry, I should like to think that some of the lessons to be drawn from them may be of relevance to international chemistry as well.

It is with this in mind that I commend the English version of my book to my many friends throughout the English-speaking world.

I should like to thank David Goodman for his help in preparing the English version of this book and also the publishers, Messrs Sidgwick and Jackson, for the very great trouble they have taken in its presentation and production.

KARL WINNACKER

To the German Edition

WHEN IN 1968 and 1969, the generation change was being prepared in Hoechst, friends and colleagues suggested to me that I should write down my recollections of a significant chapter of German chemistry.

The decisive impulse was provided by the publisher, Erwin Barth von Wehrenalp, who has taken a great deal of trouble over this book.

Ernst Bäumler, who has been in charge of public relations in Hoechst since 1963, in continuous discussion with me elicited many personal reminiscences and thoughts which, I hope, have helped to make the text a little less dry.

As I often used to talk to my children of my experiences, they were able to contribute sound advice and valuable criticism from the viewpoint of the younger generation.

KARL WINNACKER

Contents

List of Illustrations

CHALLENGING YEARS
My Life in Chemistry

1

Two Encounters with America

IN OCTOBER 1969, as every year, I flew to the United States with a number of my colleagues for discussions. The regularity with which these visits had taken place since 1954, and the 'Hoechst Evening' that formed part of them, where we met many of our colleagues in the U.S.A., have caused these visits to become known amongst ourselves as the 'Oktoberfest'.

The number of Hoechst people in America, the number of our companies, and the number of guests had again increased in 1969. Even more than in previous years, the programme took up every minute of our stay. Board meetings with our companies, discussions with the American partners of joint ventures, press conferences and interviews with daily and trade press, and above all many talks with friends in American chemical companies followed closely upon each other.

These annual visits had become almost indispensable once the huge American market with its highly developed technology and superior living standards, unmatched by Europe, had again become accessible to us. We had been cut off from the world for almost twenty years, and we no longer had any kind of yardstick for a development that had taken place free from all state intervention and that could draw on almost inexhaustible resources of raw material.

During two victorious wars, an industrial potential had developed in the United States that could readily be applied to the needs of a peaceful economy. American agriculture had rationalized its production methods at considerable cost and was producing a considerable surplus of food which helped to feed a large part of the world, even during the Second World War. In comparison to the immense human sacrifices of the European nations, the destruction of their cities and industries, American losses had been small.

The consequence of the Second World War was, of course, deep involvement of the United States in the vital political questions that were now confronting the world. America was not able to return to isolation, as she had in 1918, but had to take on the role of leader of the western world. Life as practised in America became the standard of the modern way of life. In addition, she became involved technologically and economically in all parts of the world to a far greater extent than ever before.

Any country intent upon re-developing its industry after the destruction of the war, and determined to participate again in international competition, obtained generous American support – for example as part of the European Recovery Programme – though later it had to compete with the powerful American industry which was rapidly establishing itself in the free part of the world. As Europe recovered from the holocaust of the war, and as its economy improved, it had to contend increasingly with the highly developed technology of the Americans, the immense power of the dollar and their ingenious marketing approach. This applied particularly to the Federal Republic of Germany.

For these reasons, my visits to the U.S.A. always provided invaluable lessons. I once calculated that, in all, they accounted for more than a year of my life. Many customs were, of course, quite strange to begin with. Above all, this young nation, unlike Europe, was not weighed down by tradition, and was thus able to approach each problem with a sober and practical attitude. In a compressed Germany, where so many values of the past were lost through the war, this pragmatism taught us much that was of value in our reconstruction problems. For this reason, if for no other, I cannot support the reserve, and certainly not the negative attitude, of many Europeans towards the United States.

Thoughts in 1969

In 1969, my American journey was of particular significance. It wasn't my last visit to the United States, but I no longer came as chairman of the board of management. During the annual general meeting in June of that year, I had laid down my office and had become chairman of the supervisory board. I therefore experienced the U.S.A. more fully than ever before.

I particularly valued the great friendship offered to me by so many Americans. In more than fifteen years of collaboration and reciprocal visits, a community of thought and of understanding had developed that would have been unthinkable before then.

Many difficulties, everywhere vociferously discussed, beset this rich country. They arise from the world-wide political responsibilities of the Americans, the race problems and the poverty that is still rampant in the slums of the large cities. But these problems should not obliterate the imposing generosity and open-mindedness of the United States. The large majority of Americans continue to be filled with an indestructible self-confidence, coupled with an inborn optimism and an unshakeable belief in progress. We in Europe have lost this self-confidence. And that is why we are so surprised by the frankness with which everything, whether pleasant or unpleasant, is discussed in America.

The Americans conduct their industrial activities abroad with the same informality and self-confidence that they display at home. Indeed, their whole mode of life abroad is a reflection of their society at home. But in America itself, there is a strict set of commercial rules. Rigorous cartel prohibition, anti-trust laws, the need for public disclosure and, in certain cases, powers of state intervention all set certain limits to the independence of industrialists in America. German companies that want to operate in the States have to grow used to this economic system and they do not always find it easy.

Moreover, the American market is protected by high tariff barriers. At the present time, the Americans are not very anxious to adopt the more liberal forms of European economy, particularly since they were for a long time hardly interested in exports or economic activities overseas. This meant that they lacked a proper understanding of the related problems.

However, as they increasingly realized the opportunities in other countries, they seized them with their typical nonchalance. As their activities multiplied during the sixties, they provoked, at times, considerable antipathy abroad. Perhaps the sharpest reaction was that of General de Gaulle who fiercely opposed the economic influence of the Americans in France and even banned NATO headquarters from the country. In view of the close historical relationship between France and the United States, going back as far as Lafayette, this was a deep disappointment.

It was also France that gave currency to the slogan of the 'American challenge' which produced a great deal of quite un-justified indignation in Europe. In contrast, during my many con-versations with Americans, I again and again found a genuine respect for European culture and the technical and economic achievements and opportunities of Europe.

European Initiative Needed

The answer to any American challenge must surely be progress in the integration of Europe and the achievement, at long last, of a united economic structure. The threat from American competition would be far less if European integration proceeded less slowly and less tortuously. The common tariff policy so far realized can be but a small beginning.

If we had a common economic structure extending from London to Paris, and Bonn to Rome, with standard measures and monetary systems, uniform industrial safety standards and identical corpo-rate law, we would find it far easier to resist the power blocs that represent our competitors in both east and west.

Europe can maintain its strong economic position only through the unwavering pursuit of a unification policy. It does not reveal a great deal of self-confidence to criticize the Americans without meeting the alleged 'American challenge' with an initiative of one's own.

In the summer of 1969, I had a special opportunity of thinking along these lines. Together with Lord Plowden, the president of Tube Investments Ltd, I had to prepare a report, on behalf of the Action Committee for the United States of Europe – the Monnet Committee – on the industrial aspects of an integrated Europe. With the support of a small commission that we had set up for this pur-pose, we worked out a review of the considerable technological and economic possibilities that would open up after European integration. At this time, incidentally, I undertook my first extensive trip to Russia where I gained some insight into the powerful integrated economy that faces us in the east.

My trips through the United States convinced me again and

again that a unified Europe ought to be possible, in spite of the different traditions of its individual peoples. America showed me clearly the power of the melting pot, though, of course, it would be futile to deny that a mixture of peoples and nationalities does not bring with it many difficulties, whatever integrating forces may be at work.

Nevertheless, it remains an overpowering experience to see how strongly national characteristics have developed in more than 200 million Americans in a comparatively short period of time. Many Americans are engaged in the great problems of the future from which we in Europe seem to shy away because we are not capable of the unprejudiced collaboration that is needed to finance them. Space exploration is perhaps the clearest example.

It is this sort of activity which provides proof of the creative power of the many ethnic groups in the United States. It yields impressive results because, through voluntary integration into a uniform state system, Americans of varying origin are held together more effectively than those subject to authoritarian systems in many other parts of the world.

In contrast to their normal attitude, the Americans were fairly pessimistic in October 1969. The war in the Far East remained unsolved and sapped not only the economic but also the moral reserves of the nation. The industrial situation, especially in the chemical industry, was in part very unsatisfactory. The balance of payments situation was daily worsening. Internal conflicts threatened to assume explosive proportions.

On the other hand, the boom in the Federal Republic of Germany had reached its peak. Foreign currency flowed into Germany in such large amounts that revaluation of the Mark became, for the second time, a subject for discussion. The result of the elections to the German Parliament in September 1969, and the imminent change in government, made it likely that a number of changes would be made in respect of both internal and foreign policy. It had to be assumed that the new government, in disregard of a good deal of contrary advice, would soon carry out revaluation of the Mark. The troubles in France in May 1968, caused by leftist workers and students, were at that time still very much in the mind of all those concerned with the future of Europe. The economic situation in Britain seemed depressing.

Great Interest in European Chemistry

At the New York press conference of 1969 and during my many conversations in the United States, there was much discussion of these European problems. Since the German chemical companies had become so strong, particularly in the last few years, concern about a German or European superiority was voiced repeatedly. People appeared to have forgotten that we in Europe, in return, had long been concerned with American economic power.

As on previous occasions, I was continually asked by the Americans whether there would again be a fusion of the large chemical companies in Germany. Memories of the economic power of the I. G. Farbenindustrie, which had been dismembered in 1945, still weighed heavily upon the Americans. These questions were, of course, prompted to some extent by the large number of mergers that were taking place in Europe at that time. This was especially true in French, Swiss, and Italian industry, while in Germany there had been only a few major mergers since the dismemberment of the I. G.

In reply to such questions, I always expressed the conviction that I did not regard a return to the old collaboration as feasible. The German chemical companies formed after the dismemberment of the I. G. have in the meantime become so large, and have developed in such fundamentally different directions, that a renewed merger would not only be extremely difficult but serve little purpose.

In fact, European developments point to collaboration with the chemical industries of other countries. Such supranational associations, in whatever form, would help to strengthen European economic power so that it could maintain itself between the two great power blocs in the world. But in order to render such supranational mergers within Europe possible at all, integration efforts would have to be pursued with far greater intensity than at present, especially in the field of corporate law.

Now and Then

During the weeks following this American visit, my thoughts often went back to 1945, as I considered the contrast between the friendly relationships in 1969 and my first encounter with the Americans at the end of the war. At that time, the people who came into our factories were in uniform and our talks were more in the nature of interrogations. In those days, America, which we did not know from personal experience, confronted us with the toughness of the victor.

The army of occupation had an incomplete understanding of the European customs and habits with which it now had to concern itself, and it was filled with bitterness over a war conducted with unusual cruelty. The subject of the interrogations was the I. G. Farbenindustrie whose fate I had shared from 1933 to 1945. One of the war aims of the Allies had been to destroy this economic force.

Because of the contrast between the two encounters of 1945 and 1969, I was confirmed in my resolve to record my memories of this disputed and contradictory period, and to report also on the reconstruction and reconstitution of Farbwerke Hoechst as one of the successor companies to the I. G. Farbenindustrie.

These memoirs may also provide a small contribution to the history of the German chemical industry after the war. Perhaps, too, they will help to arrive at a better assessment of the fate to which my generation was subjected in a period of change.

Interrupted Career

I occupied a responsible position in the I. G. Farbenindustrie for only a comparatively short period of time. I had started in the Hoechst works in 1933. During my twelve-year career I had been employed as a chemist in the dyestuffs laboratory, as a process engineer, as departmental manager of inorganic production, and as divisional director. That I never reached the last milestone, the technical direction of Hoechst and thus probable promotion to the board of management of the I. G., could be regarded only as a piece of luck in 1945. Had I got that far, then, like my colleagues and superiors, I would have had to face the Nuremberg tribunal.

My more modest career ended far less dramatically. On 16 July 1945, an American officer simply told me that I was dismissed immediately.

I had expected this ever since the Hoechst works had been occupied in March 1945. We all knew that the dismemberment of the I. G. Farbenindustrie was one of the declared aims of the Allies. When I was dismissed, I was forty-two years old. I was not the only one to suffer this fate. I shared it with millions of other people in Germany.

There were at that time few optimists amongst us. Almost everyone had to fight for his existence and the survival of his family. My wife and my sons, aged three and four, were quartered only a few kilometres from the Hoechst works, in the little Taunus village of Hofheim. After much difficulty, I was able to find a job as a gardener. This is one of the reasons why even today I can join discussions about market gardening and fruit growing without appearing entirely ignorant. I shall never forget how difficult a vocation it is, requiring one to work hard in all kinds of weather.

This hard physical work left me with ample time to think. Every one of us at that time was thinking about his own future, many conceiving the oddest notions. We were always being told that perhaps we might never be able to practice our profession again. But I could not accept that all the things that had moulded my life thus far could simply be brushed away at a stroke. Attendance at the humanist high school during the German Imperial period, study of chemistry in Brunswick and Darmstadt, my years as assistant under a greatly revered teacher and, finally, a not entirely unsuccessful period with the I. G. Farbenindustrie – was it really conceivable that a big black line would be drawn through all this?

It was a time of reckoning. We had to ask ourselves over and over again where we had been right in the past and where we had gone wrong. This applied equally to our national and our private fates which had led us into the cul-de-sac where we now found ourselves.

2

Adolescence in Yesterday's World

MY PARENTS' house in Werléstrasse 75 in Barmen was probably a fairly faithful example of the bourgeois middle classes at that time. I was born there on 21 September 1903 and was the fourth child. Both my parents were teachers. Coming from modest homes, they had raised the family with thrift and diligence. In this home, I, my sister Martha, and my brothers Ernst and Fritz found security and had access to all the educational facilities available at that time. Through spare-time earnings, my parents had succeeded in acquiring their own, even if modest, house and garden after only ten years of marriage. The house had two and a half floors and, being the youngest, I was assigned to the top floor.

A stroke of fate fundamentally changed our world in the Werléstrasse. In January 1914, shortly before the First World War, my father died of cancer at the age of fifty-three. From then on, life in the family was directed by my mother. After twenty-five years of marriage, she had lost her support, and she now tried to carry out our father's intentions on her own. What I know about my father probably owes very little to my own impressions. Most of it has been related to me by my mother.

One of my most vivid memories, in fact, is the funeral. My eldest brother, then a twenty-four-year-old clergyman, performed the consecration. This was not easy for him but my father had expressly stipulated it in his will.

Following the quiet exequies at home, we went on foot to the cemetery. It was a cold winter's day. In addition to ourselves and the neighbours, the entire high school attended the funeral.

The boys wore their blue school caps and were led by the school band, a conventional institution in Barmen.

Again, all the knowledge I have about my family and my ancestors has been passed to me by my mother who has written down the history of her life in a little diary. Incidentally, the last event recorded there concerns my entry into the I. G. Farbenindustrie.

My mother had been friendly with my father ever since childhood. She taught French and music and was a sensitive, cultured woman. Her own father, my grandfather, had taught mathematics, and my grandmother music.

During and after the war, I was at home a great deal with my mother and she attempted to calm the impetuosity of her growing young son with her quiet intellect devoted to literature and art. She would read to me from the classics for hours, and sometimes to my friends, too, giving preference to Goethe and Lessing. From her father's side, she had inherited a knowledge of the Mecklenburg dialect and was able to familiarize us with many of Fritz Reuter's works, particularly his *Franzosentid* and *Stromtid*.

She played Beethoven sonatas even in old age, displaying a great deal of concentration and conciseness. She was also very fond of Mendelssohn's music. When she died in 1934, aged seventy-one, she had fulfilled a life full of worries but, in many respects, one rich in experience, too.

My father appears to have had a very strong personality. His father in turn was a modest customs official who was moved about much of the time. Each one of his six children, therefore, was born in a different place. It was due to my energetic grandmother that of the five sons three went to university, and the two youngest eventually became prosperous merchants.

My father had studied in Marburg in the early eighties. In 1888, he became head teacher at the high school in Barmen. In addition to mathematics and physics, he also took physical training classes. After some years, as usual at that time, he was awarded the title of professor. School left him with sufficient time to participate in the cultural and social life of his native town.

Barmen and Elberfeld, joined into Wuppertal since 1930, were towns with an outlook quite out of character with the area around them. Enterprising merchants and industrialists had developed a fairly active economic life which did not fit properly into the world of large-scale industry and the Ruhr. Nevertheless, the towns made a name for themselves throughout the world because of their successful small textile and iron industries. Many a family was able to accumulate a great deal of wealth.

As a result of a school friendship, I came into contact with such a Wuppertal family. I experienced its life, with its spirit of enterprise and yet modest style of living, its firm adherence to the reformed church and its warm hospitality and helpfulness, in the home of the building contractor Samuel Schutte who had five children, all about my age. I am pleased that my friendship with this family has survived to this day.

On the other hand, in this narrow valley of the Wupper between the gay Rhineland and the more serious Westphalia, there ruled a puritanical, almost narrow-minded spirit. In the novel *The Wiskottens*, Rudolf Herzog, whom my mother knew personally, has aptly described this area's social and intellectual climate. It was a world of bigotry, a strict protestant religiousness in which grandmother Wiskotten, during the breakfast break, read from the Bible to the girls in the knitting mill in the firm conviction that 'God is in work'. But in spite of this orthodox regime, there were many protests as early as the middle of the last century. Even quiet grandfather Wiskotten admonishes his uncompromising wife when she judges the young generation rather too harshly: 'I wonder whether, during our married life, we have not thought too much about the acquisition of earthly possessions and not enough of the treasures in heaven.'

It is probably not surprising that revolutionary ideas found so much fertile ground in this restrictive atmosphere. Friedrich Engels, one of the founders of German socialism, was born in Barmen in 1820, as the son of a manufacturer. Seventeen years after his death, the Social Democrat delegate, Friedrich Ebert, first President of the Weimar Republic and moderate politician, who thought in terms of reform, rather than revolution, was elected in 1912 to represent the constituency of Barmen and Elberfeld.

The important leaders of the German Social Democrats were no longer dreaming of world revolution according to Marxist precepts. By patiently working through parliament, they were attempting to bring up to date the outmoded feudalistic institutions of which there was no shortage in imperial Germany. Their work, the foundations laid by Bismarck in social policy and the general urge for more knowledge and better education, facilitated the advance of more and more workers and artisans into bourgeois society.

Overture to World War

Strictly speaking, my childhood fell in a world of revolution in which forty-four years of peace had produced a superficial feeling of security. The Kaiser, it is true, was fond of sabre-rattling speeches. With the outspokenness so typical of him, he granted numerous but not always wise interviews, and upset his English cousins with a provocative naval policy. But basically, he was not nearly as martial as he wanted many to believe. In any case, there were the Chancellor and Parliament in which the Social Democrats had an important say, particularly as far as the defence budget was concerned. The glamour of the soldiers and their weapons was, apparently, intended more as a colourful patriotic spectacle than as a preparation for serious war.

In any case, was there not sufficient reason for being satisfied with what had been achieved? The founder years towards the end of the last century had provided industry with great prosperity. The working classes, too, were at long last reaping the fruits of their labours. Science had yielded discoveries that had hardly been thought possible. The bacteriological achievements of medicine began to conquer age-old diseases and epidemics, technology conjured up more and more sophisticated equipment and promised an incomparably more comfortable and more enjoyable life for the future. Everything seemed to be in the best of order. But underneath the smooth surface of Europe, the pressures of the approaching social revolution were beginning to build up. Political and literary seismographs predicted enormous social and military eruptions. A new world began to form. Not a beautiful world, but a world of hatred and genocide.

At that time, of course, only a few anticipated such a development. The flashes of lightning that lit up the literature and art of the expressionist era frightened only the unusually sensitive. Most people dismissed them as a deviation of eccentric artists. Similar phenomena in the political arena, such as the anarchistic and revolutionary slogans of Russian emigrants in the capitals of western Europe were airily written off as 'coffee shop communism'.

Since the foundation of the Reich, the strong loyalty to both

Emperor and Reich had become a bond that held the nation together in spite of its heterogenous trends during the first serious reversals of the war and the immediate post-war period.

My father had carried out his military duties, although at considerable financial sacrifice. As an officer of the reserve, he had advanced to the rank of captain. I still have in my possession the official appointment signed personally by the Kaiser with his enormous, 15 cm. long signature.

Intellectually, my father was a freemason in outlook in his younger years. Later he abandoned these beliefs and adopted the liberal trends of protestantism. He became the founder of the 'Friends of Protestant Freedom' in Barmen, the followers of the protestant vicars Karl Jatho and Gottfried Traub.

The start of the war in 1914, following my father's death, came as a serious blow to the family. My father's pension was small and the children's education had by no means been completed. My eldest brother Ernst, the clergyman, on the other hand, had married early and left home. He was a quiet man, somewhat shut off from the world, who took after my mother. Deep pessimism and melancholia alternated with sparkling wit. He was very musical, a passionate violinist and organist, and well known throughout the Ruhr as an impressive speaker. Humorous poems and witty after-dinner speeches made him greatly in demand at social functions. During the National-Socialist regime, he remained a sincere clergyman of the professing church.

But he did not know how to cope effectively with the problems of life. In particular, he could not master material problems and was, therefore, rarely in a position to help me, his younger brother, in the early years of my expensive studies.

My sister Martha, twenty-one years old when war broke out, left home in 1915 to teach. She was clever, busy and enterprising. She looked after me in a most touching manner and made many sacrifices for me. But she, too, was not of a strong nature and not quite up to the heavy demands of life.

In total contrast to 1939, the outbreak of the 1914 war was greeted with enthusiasm and delight. The opening of the Reichstag by Wilhelm II was accompanied by the masses singing *Heil Dir im Siegerkranz*. In his memorable speech to the crowd, the Emperor had emphatically affirmed: 'I no longer recognize parties, I know only

Germans. And as a sign that you are firmly resolved to keep together and to follow me through thick and thin, through privations and into death, without differences of party, class or religion, I ask the leaders of the parties to step forward and confirm it by shaking my hand.'

At that time, such words were designed to overcome all objections, particularly as everyone was convinced that this war had been forced upon Germany. Even the Social Democrats, so often described in the past as characters without a fatherland, caught the general enthusiasm. 'In this hour of danger, we will not forsake our fatherland,' proclaimed one of the Social Democrat leaders in the Reichstag. The Social Democrat faction voted unanimously for war credits.

But war enthusiasm was not confined to Germany alone. In other European countries, too, there was an immense surge of national consciousness. There, too, the members of the socialist parties became ardent patriots. This applied particularly to France where the humane, pacifist socialist, Jean Jaurès, had been murdered on 31 July 1914 by the nationalist, Raoul Villain. The old Europe was breaking apart into two worlds filled with hatred. Nobody was listening to the voice of reason any more.

For weeks, we schoolboys marched every day to the railway station from which the troops were leaving for the front. We distributed soup and cheered the young, smart soldiers. We were convinced that they were leaving for a short, victorious campaign.

The young and the healthy all wanted to join, like my second brother Fritz, who was only seventeen. My mother however, recently widowed, had no sympathy with his intentions. She declared categorically: 'First I want to see you pass your exams.'

At the back of her mind, of course, was also the worry that she might lose him altogether. But one day, in the first weeks of the war, my brother left home secretly to volunteer. In the evening, he came back demoralized and depressed because he had not been accepted. There was an excess of volunteers. Later, however, this gay, strong man had his wish fulfilled. He died in Flanders in 1918 as leader of a company.

The popular enthusiasm that swept Germany in 1914 could not, of course, continue at the same pitch. As the war dragged on, against all expectations, as the men at the front froze in trench warfare and the big material battles unfolded, there was a change in public feeling. Rapid victory by German arms looked more and more improbable. The sacrifices demanded from the soldiers and those at home became increasingly exacting. Few had any doubts about the justification of this defensive war and there was still hope of victory. But more and more people questioned the price that would have to be paid for it. When finally, in 1917, the Americans entered the war and the first troops under General Pershing landed in France, public morale deteriorated rapidly. Now only a few die-hards continued to cherish the hope that a war against half the world really could be won.

During these war years, my mother and I were at home alone and came to depend on each other more and more. I tried to replace my father as best I could. My childhood came to an early and abrupt end. I carried out the necessary repairs, looked after the garden and helped organize our food which was daily becoming scarcer. Queueing outside shops and the art of hoarding soon became second nature to me.

Conditions in Germany looked bleak. The British naval blockade began to bite deeper and deeper. Turnips became the main food and the winter of 1916–17 saw a great deal of starvation. Not without reason it has become known in history as the 'turnip winter'.

The many sacrifices, the concern for her son and for day-to-day existence further affected the already impaired health of my mother. During my first years at college, she spent many months in hospital. As my father had died so early, his pension was hardly sufficient for the bare necessities. There was not enough money for anything beyond this, let alone the medical bills.

In order to improve our situation a little, I was forced to undertake private coaching in a number of subjects. This left me with very little time for my own homework. Nevertheless, I was a good pupil, though somewhat strong-willed and difficult at times. I never became a shining star who could boast of outstanding achievements in every subject – indeed I never tried. Still, I did manage to stay near the top of my form, which was just as well because I was able to go to college only on a municipal scholarship which depended on class performance.

German literature and history were my particular interests. My teachers therefore fully expected that I would choose them later on as my subjects for university study. Naturally, they were very surprised that in the end I chose to become a chemist.

The end of the war in November 1918 lives vividly in my memory; I was then fifteen and rather more mature than one would have expected from a boy of my age. The revolution, the Emperor's abdication, and the proclamation of the republic by the Social Democrat leader Philipp Scheidemann marked the beginning of the Weimar era which was to be characterized by inflation, party squabbles, enormous reparation debts and, finally, the worldwide economic crisis.

With some astonishment, the students in the town watched the workers' and soldiers' councils that had assumed power. Sailors patrolled the streets of Barmen, rifles pointing downwards. In the newspapers, we read of the activities of the 'Spartakists' in Berlin, a group of fanatics who had not been satisfied with the proclamation of the republic and were bent on converting the country into a communist-bolshevik state.

Barmen was fermenting, too, with riots and looting. Fortunately, our quiet family life remained unaffected and, in any case, the whole episode only lasted a short time. But while it went on, we were huddled together in the evenings, shivering in the dark. There was neither coal nor gas and the electricity supply was totally inadequate.

Following the armistice, the troops under Field-Marshal Hindenburg arrived. They quickly restored order. Workers, and soldiers, councils, spartakists and communism disappeared like phantoms.

Once again, we students ran out to greet the soldiers and to supply them as best we could. But the atmosphere was rather more restrained than four years ago. The returning soldiers had become different people too. Their faces reflected the frightful experiences of the murderous battles in northern France, of the unrelenting trench war, and of the desperate realization that it had all been in vain.

'Undefeated on the battlefield' – how eagerly we seized on this slogan which soon spread around Germany. In spite of the misery at home, it seemed, indeed, as though no clear-cut military defeat had been suffered. After all, had our troops not stood deep in enemy territory right up to the time of the armistice? Was it not true that in 1918, only a few months ago, the high command had launched

My parents

My parents' home

offensive after offensive and gained great tactical advantages? Certainly, it could not be denied that the people back home were tired of war and longed for an early peace. But wasn't the same also true of the other side? Hadn't there been mutinies in the French army affecting whole divisions?

In endless discussions, we tried to understand the reasons for our defeat and to arrive at a proper assessment. Brought up nationalistically as we were, we tended, of course, to be prejudiced in favour of the German case. We were, therefore, filled with deep detestation of the Treaty of Versailles which had clearly been governed by the retributive intentions of the Allies, placing the guilt for the war solely at Germany's door. We were particularly disappointed at the attitude of President Wilson of the United States who was unable to impose his views on the Allies, especially the French. His formula of the right to self-determination of people was practised only in favour of the victors. The Germans from the Sudetenland and the Austrians enjoyed no such rights. Although this has been claimed – and denied – I remain convinced that Hitler and his movement might never have happened if the injustices of the Treaty of Versailles had not provided them with so effective a platform.

School life was only slightly influenced by the bitter end of the war and the immediate post-war period. Occasionally there were 'coal holidays' and we had to help during the harvest and in the unloading of transport. There were no physical training lessons because the gymnasium was used to store potatoes.

In the main, however, everything continued as before and only a few facts from the outside world penetrated the thick walls of our old humanistic high school. Discussions on topical political subjects took place only rarely. There was a students' council which, historically, may be regarded as the forerunner of our modern student participation schemes. Our particular council, however, did not flourish and was soon dissolved.

Most of our teachers were far too old for their profession but as there was a general shortage of teachers, they could not be retired. Of course, young people always regard their teachers as old, but in my class, for example, we had the same teachers as my brother had had fifteen years before. We could not expect from these people clear and convincing answers to the burning questions of the day. They probably faced those times with even more despair than we young people.

Until a few years after the war, the high school of Barmen was administered by an extraordinarily conservative and much-feared man. Both his sons had fallen in the war. As a result, he had completely withdrawn into himself. Unjust as children and young people often are, we learned of his death with a certain amount of relief. His successor will never be forgotten by his pupils. Wolfgang Paeckelmann was a scientist and only thirty-six years old. He displayed a great deal of understanding and tried to train us to develop clear judgements and independent views. He also protected us from the exaggerated conservative attitude of many a teacher who was more concerned with authority than his subject. Young people today cannot imagine the narrow and regimented world in which we lived. We weren't even allowed to go to the cinema. In the whole of Barmen there was only one restaurant that we were allowed to visit in the evening now and again to drink a glass of beer. But even then, a master from the school was always present to watch carefully over our behaviour.

Paeckelmann at long last introduced a great deal more freedom and life into this rigid and cobwebbed school. He was also one of the first teachers to take his pupils on working holidays, and to organize sports trips and theatre visits. Neither our respect for him nor our scholastic performance suffered as a result.

Later, Paeckelmann was entrusted with the management of the German Educational Foundation in whose creation he had played a significant part. After he retired, this enthusiastic educationalist became director of the Hermann-Lietz schools. He died in 1970 in Wasserburg on Lake Constance near Salem castle. Only a few years previously, the old gentleman had visited me in Hoechst for the last time.

Study of Chemistry

In 1922, four years after the painful transformation of the empire into a republic, I took my final examination at the Barmen High School. Only now did I begin to think more seriously about a career. I have been asked many times why I became a chemist. My answer has always been that I don't exactly know, a reply which usually causes surprise. But it is a fact that my choice of vocation had nothing whatsoever to do with any inner calling.

I think that I probably developed a certain preference for science because of my home background. In the humanistic high school in Barmen there was no course in chemistry as such. We learned mathematics and even physics, Paeckelmann being our teacher in the last few years. The physics lessons were sound and solid and dealt with the fundamental principles that a chemist has to know. This preparation proved sufficient later on to enable me to pass the preliminary examination in physics. But there were big gaps in mathematics. We did not, for example, learn differential or integral calculus, and chemistry remained a book with seven seals for all of us.

School, and in particular the humanistic high school, did not at that time provide vocational preparation. On the other hand, the lessons provided a remarkably broad level of general education and formed a firm base for later specialization. I was able to fill in the gaps later on without much difficulty. At university, no specialized knowledge was required. You started practically from nothing. This was possible only because there were relatively few students in the laboratories and lecture rooms, a fact which facilitated personal contact with the university professors.

Perhaps my decision to study chemistry also had something to do with the fact that this industry had become the centre of public interest since the war.

We had learnt as children how important chemical products could suddenly become. My little library included a small volume called *The Journey of the Deutschland* which described how this unarmed merchant submarine had broken through the English blockade of the North Sea and the Atlantic early in the war, to take certain chemicals and pharmaceuticals to the United States, still neutral at that time. These products were urgently needed, and Germany held a scientific and patent monopoly in the field.

Following this success, the German Admiralty planned the construction of a whole fleet of such unarmed submarines but the tragic fate of the U-boat *Bremen* probably caused these plans to be dropped. The *Bremen* had set out on 26 August 1916 on its risky journey across the Atlantic filled to the last corner with valuable chemicals. Nothing was ever heard again of either the ship or its crew.

Barmen provided us with another interest in chemistry. Close by, in Elberfeld, were Farbenfabriken Bayer, where more than 10,000 people were engaged in the manufacture of chemical products and world-famous pharmaceuticals such as Aspirin. Carl Duisberg, Bayer's chief, came from Barmen.

My decision to study of course raised the delicate question of how these studies were to be financed. My mother could help only a little. Therefore, in 1922, at the age of nineteen, I worked for six months in a mine and coking plant.

It was an encounter with a world completely strange to me and, to begin with, I was very depressed. Because I had been forced from an early age to help support the home, I had been left very much to my own devices after school. The class differences at that time were far more pronounced than they are today. I suddenly found myself pitched from the comparative shelter of home and school into the rough world of the Ruhr workers. Only then did I discover that there was, in fact, a proletariat conscious of its class. It was not a very pleasant experience for a high school pupil. I suffered the same rude treatment as a recruit to the forces; the language was very coarse and new to me.

I found a great deal of difficulty in coming to terms with this environment. Certainly, the mental and emotional adjustment involved a far greater strain than the hard physical requirements. Nevertheless, this confrontation with the robust world of the miner also had its good sides. My narrow view of the world was greatly broadened, if a little roughly at times. Also, later on, I was able to learn a few useful tips in the mine's laboratory.

After this six months' interlude, my actual studies began. What I had saved out of my wages was sufficient to finance the beginning. The choice of university was decided more or less by accident. A relative who was taking some interest in me at the time advised me to go to the university in Brunswick where he was a lecturer in engineering. Then, as now, there was little to choose between the various academic institutions as far as the quality of their chemical teaching was concerned. Brunswick was one of the oldest German technical universities and had a good name, especially in chemistry, electrical engineering and architecture.

At the beginning of the winter term I arrived in the old residential town, where the retired Grand Duke still played a limited role. Although he was no longer prominent in the politics of the country, his intellectual and social position remained unaffected, especially in the fairly conservative circles of Brunswick State.

At that time, Brunswick was still very much the famous old Guelph town, relaxed, and rich in historic monuments. At first, industrial and economic life played only a modest role. There were, of course, famous industrial companies like Voigtländer, the camera people, Büssing, the commercial vehicle builders, and Grotrian-Steinweg, the piano manufacturers. In the main, however, Brunswick was the centre of an agricultural area in which sugar and canned goods factories were of far greater importance. Few foresaw the development of large-scale industry in Wolfsburg and Salzgitter which was completely to change the landscape. Brunswick was a typical north German residential town. It had a large garrison, a good theatre and, of course, the university which had grown out of the Collegium Carolinum in 1877 and which, by 1922, boasted almost a thousand students.

University and student life of that period had a unique character. After the end of the war, students who had been in the trenches, whose outlook had been moulded by the experience of war, poured into the German universities. They were far more mature for their age than one might have expected. The universities had survived unharmed and were ready to receive this young generation that had returned thirsting for knowledge.

The arrival of my generation, younger than these war-veterans, at first changed little in this situation. We, too, were more mature than our age might have suggested. So far as the formalities of life were concerned, we made few demands. Hardly any of us had a decent suit, and we were happy with the obsolete uniforms of our fathers or brothers. We shared a desire for comradeship, pleasure, and sociability with the former soldiers from the front. Fraternity life, therefore, experienced a renaissance under totally different circumstances than in the Imperial period before the war. The exclusive and feudal style of the students was a thing of the past. Perhaps it lingered still in the memory of the old guard.

Like the majority of the students, I enthusiastically joined one of these fraternities. Membership of the Guestphalia Society and then of the Normannia Fraternity in Darmstadt was a vital factor in my later life. I was suddenly pitched into a form of comradeship quite unknown to me until then, and I lived my first term at university in a community that loyally shared its meagre resources. Of course, we were full of the high spirits generated by freedom and student life with its duels, but we also imposed upon ourselves the necessary discipline for fifty to sixty young people to live together harmoniously.

During this period, lifelong friendships were formed of a kind much more difficult to make when one is older. One of my surviving friendships of this time is with Heinrich Vorkauf, who was also with me in Darmstadt. Unlike me, he became an independent manufacturer and owned a small, but world famous, engineering company whose *La Mont* boiler enjoys a very high reputation in chemical engineering even today. Another of my friends of that period was Werner Schultheis. He was my age, and came from Hesse. Although our careers frequently diverged, we both eventually sat on the board of Hoechst for many years.

Student life offered few opportunities for extravagance. I had hardly entered university when inflation broke out. The money so painfully earned from my work in the pit melted like snow in the sun. Devaluation gained increasing momentum. By November 1922, a loaf of bread weighing 2·2 kg. cost 300 marks and a litre of milk 140 marks. In the following year, prices reached astronomical proportions. By May 1923, a pound of butter cost 8,400 marks and by July 210,000 marks. In August of the same year, the officials of Brunswick State received a daily salary of between 3 and 4 million marks. In November, at the height of the inflation, their basic income was multiplied by about 11 million marks.

Inflation also affected student fees. In 1922–3, the fee at the university was 30 marks and the enrolment fee was about the same. Only a year later, the situation was completely out of control. The prospectus of the university stated: 'In view of the varying currency conditions, the fees and other dues to be paid will be announced only at the beginning of the winter or summer term.' Prior determination of the fees had become simply impossible because of the steadily climbing prices.

The situation was stabilized only in December 1923 when the famous Rentenmark reform was introduced, and it was again possible to plan expenditure. After the euphoria of the paper millions, the mark had suddenly become a rare commodity. The strictest housekeeping became necessary, and not only for us students. In 1924, manual workers received a weekly wage of between 16 and 22 marks. This was just about enough for a pair of shoes of medium quality or for the rent of a simple flat. But by far the most serious consequence of inflation was that the savings of the middle classes and of the pensioners had evaporated, and hundreds of thousands of people were now in dire straits. The serious political consequences of the situation were to manifest themselves a few years later.

Patience in the Laboratory

I worked mainly under Karl Fries, ordinary professor of chemistry, who was also the head of the chemical institute. In summer, he gave a six-hour lecture on inorganic experimental chemistry and in winter a five-hour dissertation on the organic aspect of this subject. He also supervised the work in the chemical laboratory and conducted private oral examinations free of charge. The chemistry curriculum provided for thirty-two hours a week in the first summer term, and twenty-three hours a week in the first winter term.

Like the university itself, chemistry at Brunswick had a long tradition. The university had been founded in 1745 as the Collegium Carolinum by Abbot Johann Friedrich Wilhelm Jerusalem. During extensive journeys in Holland, Jerusalem saw the high standard of ship and dyke building, of milling and road construction, and recognized the outstanding importance of technology for the future. At that time chemistry was already being taught in Brunswick, and further facilities for it were provided when the Collegium Carolinum became the 'Herzögliche' Polytechnic in 1862 and finally the university in 1877. Brunswick, however, had always remained a relatively small university and even at the beginning of my studies there, the number of students was probably below a thousand.

Incidentally, Fries worked for a time at Farbwerke Hoechst. When he later took up a position at the university of Marburg, he continued his links with the company. It was thanks to him that many of his pupils joined Hoechst in the succeeding years.

In those years, chemical instruction at the German universities was purely preparative and analytical. First of all, one had to study for one and a half to two terms the chemical relationships involved in inorganic chemistry, using the techniques of qualitative analysis. This was followed by a similar period employing quantitative analysis in which qualitative and visual identification was replaced by isolation, weighing and titration.

Depending upon one's work or diversions, the study period up to the preliminary examination took four to five years. Extreme accuracy was demanded in quantitative analysis. This required a methodical and neat approach which a chemist has to acquire for life because as works manager, for example, he has to carry out exact observations every day. During these terms, therefore, lessons were taken up almost completely with pure laboratory work. Lectures accounted for no more than one or two hours a day. When I started my studies in Brunswick, I knew nothing whatsoever about chemistry. It therefore happened quite frequently that Fries, during his morning rounds of the laboratories, asked me about some chemical process and I had to admit openly: 'Herr Professor, I don't know this yet; I never studied chemistry at school.'

During my later years in Brunswick, all my interest in chemistry nearly evaporated when it came to quantitative analysis which demands such infinite patience. In addition to chemistry, we also had to study physics and applied mathematics, and to draw simple machinery components.

In spite of all its gaiety, student life was simple, and at times even frugal. Most of us had to work during the holidays to earn money to pay for our studies. As there was already a certain amount of unemployment, this was by no means easy. During the critical months of the inflation, we worked night after night in the sugar factories, even during term time. It was, of course, unavoidable that our studies were affected as a result, just as it was unavoidable that we should develop our own views about the universities and politics. With our professors and teachers, we defended the independence of the universities and reacted sharply against any attempt at state intervention. By far the greatest majority also wanted to keep the universities free from any party influences.

The north German milieu preserved us from the extreme trends of National Socialism which had its roots in the south. Sound advice from older comrades also prevented us from getting involved in the adventures of the Freikorps. Instead, large numbers of us joined the official Reichswehr in Wolfenbüttel headed by Otto Gessler. Our company commander was Major Wilhelm Keitel, who was to play such an unhappy role as a field-marshal later on. Fortunately for us, we never saw active service.

Nevertheless, this interlude was a sign of the unsettled year of 1923 which saw French troops march into the Ruhr to be met by the passive resistance of the populace, communist attempts at revolution in central Germany, and many other dramatic events.

The doctrinal fight between the parties became more and more bitter. The differences between left and right were magnified by the argument between old and young concerning the monarchy and especially the Emperor. Our parents and the 'old boys' of the fraternities were convinced monarchists, mainly because this was the form of government under which they had lived all their lives. But we young students recognized the weaknesses of the monarchy and no longer supported it. The dismal demise of the Hohenzollern family, and the flight of the Emperor to Holland, were hardly calculated to generate any enthusiasm among us for the restoration of the monarchy.

On the other hand, the weak Weimar cabinets, with their lacklustre politicians and their sometimes excessive eagerness to comply with the requests of our former enemies, did not endear us to this system either. We had neither the patience nor the foresight to realize that discreet persistence can be a political virtue and that, in the long run, it may often be more successful than noisy and spectacular political gestures. A modest and non-heroic man like Friedrich Ebert, the first President of the Weimar Republic, was therefore not our idol. We had rather more sympathy for Gustav Stresemann who had made a determined attempt to rebuild Germany's position step by step, and to consolidate this position by the pact of Locarno.

Although I was much occupied with these questions in Brunswick, politics did not play any part at all at home. My ailing mother, whom I saw regularly, had become even more introverted and took no interest in such matters. Of course, she could never have understood why I duelled, so I always waited until any cuts had disappeared before I visited her. If she had seen me in Brunswick during the duels, she would have been horrified.

I had hardly any personal links with my teachers in Brunswick. In any case, I was not over-anxious to foster close relationships with my professors, for my performance as a chemical student was hardly outstanding. Of course, there were many different factions among the student bodies. The fraternities and other student societies, to which a large part of the student population belonged, pursued a great variety of aims. These were also reflected in such bodies as ASTA[1] which already existed at that time. There were considerable differences also between the duelling fraternities, the nationalistic Burschenschaft[2] being the most active politically. In addition, there were scientific, religious and, of course, political student societies. The majority of students participated in discussions and in academic life to a far greater extent than today, largely, no doubt, because their fraternities obliged them to do so.

The present topic of university reform was not very much in our minds. As a result, there were fewer conflicts between professors and students than there are today. Instead, the universities had to defend themselves against state attempts to subject them more firmly to the aims of the new republic. In contrast to the majority of its professors and students, the town and country of Brunswick were comparatively left-wing. The Minister-President of Brunswick, Heinrich Jasper, belonged to the German Social Democratic party. Another young member in Brunswick was also gaining increasing attention: Otto Grotewohl who became Minister-President of the German Democratic Republic in 1949 and Deputy Chairman of its State Council in 1960.

It should not be forgotten that this period was characterized by class differences of a kind that we have properly overcome in Germany only in the last few decades. Students were regarded as academics and as members of a privileged class whether they had any money or not. When we marched in our coloured caps with our rapiers from the university to the old castle of Henry the Lion and thence to the cathedral to celebrate our rituals, the roads were lined with hundreds of people distinctly unfriendly towards us.

I devoted myself to academic life with great enthusiasm. After my sheltered upbringing, this demanded a fundamental change on my part. Perhaps, as so often in my life, I performed this with rather more enthusiasm than the occasion demanded. For three terms, I was even spokesman or principal delegate of my fraternity and in 1924 I became chairman of ASTA. In consequence, I had to appear in public, argue my point of view with a group of people of the same

[1] *Allgemeiner Studentenausschuss*, the General Students Committee.
[2] *Burschenschaft*, a student fraternity.

age and make speeches. This was valuable experience for my later career and, I believe, a profitable form of training.

Today's judgement of these student associations and their past is in many respects unjust and wrong. They were neither a hotbed of reaction nor of favouritism and social prejudice. And one should not forget that soon after Hitler came to power they were banned because the regime feared their aims of political education and personal character training.

This turbulent student life, however, did not do much good to my scientific studies. The training of a chemist requires regular presence in the laboratory and lecture-hall. Thus, I omitted much in these first terms that was essential for my preliminary examination. Eventually, during the summer term of 1925, I was able to pass in at least some subjects, though with only average results. I recognized that in view of my financial situation, I could not allow my affairs to drift further in this manner and eventually decided to change my university. Together with my friend, Heinrich Vorkauf, I left the familiar Brunswick to go to Darmstadt. I put an end to student life and fraternity activities and resolved to devote my time exclusively to the laboratory and to chemistry.

3

A Great Teacher

ANYONE VISITING Darmstadt today will find a town full of self-confidence, bustling with commerce, and obvious well-being. The town is crossed by broad thoroughfares and the houses reflect modern, rather conformist, post-war architecture. Present-day visitors might well regard Darmstadt as a town constructed only a few decades ago and they would not be all that wrong in fact. Darmstadt has been largely rebuilt following its almost complete destruction in 1944. Only a few houses in the old town and some streets in the north and south then survived. Reconstruction began in 1947 when some of the few remaining architectural buildings from the court period were pulled down as well. Nevertheless, even modern Darmstadt has retained much of the flavour of the period when it was under the liberal and gentle rule of the Grand Dukes of Hesse and Rhine.

I was fortunate enough to have known Darmstadt during the period 1925 to 1933. It then presented a most attractive mixture of old capital, university town, and home of revolutionary and artistic impulses. Everywhere the influence of Grand Duke Ernst-Ludwig could be detected. Like all the other German dukes, he had lost his throne in 1918 but, because of his pleasant and distinguished manner, continued to enjoy the respect and sympathy of the people of Darmstadt.

Ernst-Ludwig was not one of those German provincial rulers whose horizons coincided with the frontiers of their small state. More than any other German duke, he was closely related to almost every important European ruling family. His mother Alice, whose monument in front of the theatre we frequently passed as students, was the second eldest daughter of Queen Victoria. Princess Alix, the

38

youngest sister of the Grand Duke, was married to the later Czar
Nicholas II whom she had met as a twelve-year-old in Petersburg
while attending the wedding of her sister Princess Elizabeth of
Hesse to the Russian Grand Duke Sergius. Ernst-Ludwig therefore,
like Kaiser Wilhelm II, was both a nephew of the Queen of England
and a brother-in-law of the Czar. The Darmstadt populace, therefore, sadly remembered the tragic end of the royal family in Ekaterin-
burg in 1918. Many of the older Darmstadt residents had often seen
the Czar and his Czarina during their frequent visits to Darmstadt
and the castle of Wolfsgarten. Away from his capital, Nicholas II
had proved an open-minded, happy young man.

Even if one did not follow the history of the European ruling
houses with any consuming interest, in Darmstadt it was difficult
not to feel sympathy for the fate of the rulers of Hesse, characterized
as it was by so much splendour and so much misery. These events
also provided my landladies with an inexhaustible subject for discussion. I had a room in the flat of two unmarried ladies, daughters
of a gunsmith at the grand ducal court. As in almost every Darmstadt home, their front parlour was full of photographic reminiscences
of this unforgettable period.

Even after his death, the tall, art-loving Grand Duke Ernst-
Ludwig was greatly respected by all sections of the population.
Following the early death of his father, he had succeeded to the
throne of Hesse at the age of twenty-three. He probably never had
any big political ambitions but made up for this by a considerable
enthusiasm for the theatre and the arts. At the beginning of this
century, he founded an artists' colony which made Darmstadt a
household name throughout Europe. He displayed great interest in
the court theatre and supported many composers, particularly Max
Reger.

There was also no shortage of literary events in Darmstadt, which
is closely linked with the name of the powerful dramatist Georg
Büchner. After the First World War, the magazine *Das Tribunal*
(The Tribune) became a focal point for much of the literary and
political activity in the town. It had been founded by the Social
Democrat Carlo Mierendorff who became one of the most active
resistance fighters in Germany during the Hitler period. Mierendorff
was later joined by Kasimir Edschmid and Carl Zuckmayer. Grand
Duke Ernst-Ludwig also called Count Keyserling, the philosopher,

to Darmstadt where he founded the 'School of Wisdom' and gathered his disciples around him. Keyserling was not universally admired, however, and was subject to a great deal of cynical comment.

Culture in Small Doses

Darmstadt, therefore, offered many cultural attractions and temptations. But however strong these may have been, we yielded to them only to a limited extent. As young scientists and technicians, we had, in fact, little inclination for such pursuits. Moreover, I was anxious not to repeat the follies that had kept me away so much from my studies in Brunswick. Only later on, when I had become an assistant, did I allow myself more cultural enjoyment but even then only on a modest scale, going mainly to concerts and the theatre. Karl Böhm and Hans Schmidt-Isserstedt gave concerts in Darmstadt while I was there. Of the outstanding actors whom I saw in those years, I particularly remember Paul Wegener as Wallenstein and as Mephistopheles in *Faust*.

On the whole, however, we enjoyed student life more. The 'Normannia' fraternity, which was close to us and with which I still have many links today, provided pleasure and companionship.

My real world during my eight years in Darmstadt, however, was the university which had developed from a building school founded in 1812. Twice during its history the school was threatened with closure because too few students had enrolled. After the First World War, however, it gained considerable popularity, and by the time of my enrolment in 1925, it boasted some 2,400 students. There were forty-one ordinary professors and forty-three other professors, thirty private lecturers and a total of seventy-two assistants.

I firmly resolved to devote myself completely to my work for I had a great deal to catch up on in the shortest possible time. In Brunswick, I had passed only half my preliminary examinations. Without these it was fairly difficult to get a job in the laboratory for advanced students. The universities conducted their teaching according to a strict curriculum. Fortunately, the chemo-technical institute in Darmstadt dealt with such problems in a non-bureaucratic way and no certificates had to be produced.

I completed the first stage of my practical work quickly and satisfactorily. We had a generous assistant who was very sympathetic towards us and who gave me, in particular, a great deal of help. He also made it possible for me to complete the work that was outstanding, which should have preceded the preliminary examination, in the evening and on Sundays. After seven terms I finally passed my preliminary examination, although only with the mark 'satisfactory'.

The decisive event of my time in Darmstadt was my encounter with Ernst Berl, the director of the chemo-technical institute. His school, which I left at the age of thirty, has left its mark upon me for all time. When I think of the current heated debates about university reform, I frequently recall Berl. No reasonable person will deny the need for a new form of collaboration between students, assistants and professors at our high schools and universities. But we should never forget that an academic system does not simply depend upon abstract statutes and equality of representation but, in the final analysis, upon the personality of the individual teachers. Many problems could be solved more readily if the study of chemistry could be carried out by the methods that Berl and many other famous tutors of that time employed during my Darmstadt years.

Berl had no time for the comradely intimacy that many students today proclaim as their professorial ideal. He was a small, neat person who, at first sight, gave an impression of being unapproachable and tense. Indeed, in his relations with us students, he always insisted on keeping a certain distance. While he firmly maintained his authority, he also displayed complete impartiality so that any injustices, which could not be avoided altogether, were less painful to bear.

Berl was a teacher completely dedicated to his work who put his science above everything else. His concern for students and colleagues was not always immediately obvious. But there were many occasions when he dipped into his own pocket to help us along. Such a relationship between teacher and pupil cannot be defined and guaranteed in statutory paragraphs. But it was the sort that frequently could be found in German universities during the years when these acquired their world fame in the natural sciences.

The small number of students facilitated close contact, but, probably in special subjects one personality will always stand out from all the other professors. In my Darmstadt days, when the large chemistry faculty was well-staffed, such a personality without doubt was Berl, with his chemical technology which was then becoming a focal point of general interest in chemical industry.

Berl came from Freudenthal in Moravia. He had studied chemical engineering in Vienna and was, therefore, closely involved with both technology and the natural sciences. He perfected his knowledge in Zurich under Alfred Werner and Richard Lorentz, and he finally became assistant and collaborator of Georg Lunge, one of the out-standing technologists of his time. Richard Willstätter, who gained a Nobel prize in chemistry, described him as Lunge's best and most loyal pupil. Berl also took his degree in Zurich. When Lunge retired prematurely, there was talk of Berl becoming his successor. But instead Berl decided to go into industry. He believed that he was not yet ready for such an important academic position. He always said that chemical technology had to be learned from industrial experience. For the same reason he also rejected the chemistry professorship at the newly-founded technical university in Trond-heim, Norway.

Berl became chief chemist of the large and well-known Tubize artificial silk factory in Belgium. When war became imminent in the summer of 1914, Berl, who had married in the meantime, returned to Vienna. He was called up, and served initially in the heavy artillery. Soon, however, the war ministry sent him to manage the gunpowder factory at Blumau, south-west of Vienna. Sub-sequently, he took over the war direction of the whole chemical industry in the Austro-Hungarian monarchy. In April 1919, Berl accepted an appointment as professor of chemical technology and electro-chemistry at the university of Darmstadt.

At that time, chemical technology consisted mainly of the description of plants and chemical manufacturing processes. Chemistry had changed greatly during the immediate pre-war years and during the war itself. The splendid developments of the founder period, with the great successes in synthetic organic chemistry, appeared to have come to an end. Together with all its patents and trade marks, German industry had also lost its export opportunities. The war had enforced much technical improvisation but the era of organic synthesis had not yielded any fundamental innovations in the technological sense. In general, the laboratory equipment with which the important earlier inventions had been made had not

My thesis

Beiträge zur
Kenntnis der Oxydationsvorgänge
von Motorbetriebsstoffen.

———

DISSERTATION

zur Erlangung der Würde eines Doktor-Ingenieurs

der

TECHNISCHEN HOCHSCHULE ZU DARMSTADT

vorgelegt von

DIPL.-ING. KARL WINNACKER

aus

BARMEN

———

Referent: Prof. Dr. Berl
Korreferent: Prof. Dr. Schöpf

———

Tag der mündlichen Prüfung: 28. Mai 1930.

My teacher – Ernst Berl

*My first job in Hoechst with Fritz
Osterloh and foreman Philipp Bauer*

Alizarin laboratory A4

been improved upon. True, they had been enlarged in scale, but technological development was far behind. Physical chemistry and electro-chemistry, which had such modest beginnings, recorded great successes only in the last years before the war when they excited tremendous interest and were greatly developed. Catalysis and high pressure techniques were milestones on the road of this development.

All this epoch-making progress had now to be adapted for a peacetime economy. Anyone in industrial or university research looking for a new career was forced completely to re-orientate his previous work – economically, methodically and even scientifically. This might have been tremendously attractive – as in fact it was – but it took place against the backdrop of a hopeless political and economic situation.

The artificial silk industry, from which Berl had come, had also to be placed on a new technical basis. Artificial silk and explosives were closely related in both their chemistry and technology. Thus Berl had been able to apply his experience in Tubize to Austrian explosive technology without much difficulty. Now he pursued this technological approach in Darmstadt. In Berl's time, technological practice was based more frequently on a craft than a scientific basis. He used to tell the story, only half meant as a joke, of the foremen in the old days who used to spit into acid containers as a method of analysing fuming sulphuric acid. If the contents hissed, the acid was more than 90 per cent. I don't believe the story was much exaggerated.

This example shows how necessary it was to convert the experience of industrial practice into reliable and measurable methods and processes. Much that we now take for granted had not even been developed in rough outline in those days. Exact scientific observation had to replace the current empirical modes of observation. As a result, a large part of Berl's early work was devoted to the investigation of methods that he had employed in the artificial silk and explosives industry. He also took up once more the work of his teacher Lunge and prepared an entirely revised version of *Chemo-Technical Methods of Analysis*, a standard work running into many volumes. These analytical methods remain an important basis for all chemical technology. Particular attention was paid to the analysis of the nitrating acids – sulphuric acid and nitric acid. The work was centred on the relationship between the concentration of the acid and the nature of the nitrates.

The preoccupation with sulphuric acid confronted Berl with the problems of its manufacture in lead chambers, a subject into which his teacher Lunge had already conducted extensive scientific investigations. This lead chamber process, and thus the catalysis of the nitrous gases, had once given rise to passionate discussion amongst inorganic chemists at the beginning of the century. Berl also became interested in the cellulose derivatives used in the artificial silk industry and the attendant solvent recovery problem. This led him on to the investigation of explosive mixtures and work on the technology of absorption on large surface area substances. He also took an interest in the production of activated charcoal and silica gel.

All these problems required modern physical measuring methods which Berl took over from the optical and electro-technical industries. He was a close friend of Fritz Löwe, the scientific chief of Zeiss, who came to Darmstadt with his new instruments, spectrometers and interferometers, and who invited us to a holiday course to be held regularly in Jena, the Zeiss headquarters. About this time, Berl also became interested in structural X-ray analysis which later was to become so vitally important for cellulose chemistry. He had connections with H. F. Mark, at that time scientific chief in Ludwigshafen, who used to come to Darmstadt to give invitation lectures.

As a result, and on the basis of examples with which he was familiar, he created the preconditions for more modern chemical processes.

Berl carried out all this work himself with the help of his pupils. Apart from the new analytical methods, he investigated the progress of the processes and at the same time compiled the required data in tables and nomograms. In this way, he became one of the founders of the new chemical technology. Because he occupied himself so intensively and successfully with the problems of technology, his advice and assessment were greatly esteemed in circles outside the polytechnic. He provided expert testimony for patent litigation, and his services were always sought when industrial catastrophes had to be investigated. His love for the chemistry of cellulose brought him into a field that was then exciting the interest of many important chemists. This was the era in which the constitution of plastics was being investigated and there was considerable dispute over the structure of cellulose until, finally, Hermann Staudinger developed his ideas concerning the structure of high polymers which remain valid today. Berl also met Friedrich Bergius who was investigating coal hydrogenation in conjunction with BASF. A great deal of thought was given in Darmstadt to the formation of coal from cellulose and other natural substances, and much work was done on this subject.

Later, Berl extended his work far beyond these initial areas and devoted himself to a great variety of technical problems. One of these, for example, was the behaviour of boiler feed water which was investigated by a study group under his direction. As boilers were now operating at far higher temperatures, the boiler feed water, in order not to give rise to corrosion, had to be of a quality quite unknown until then.

All of us at the institute participated in these investigations. Berl had his own methods of teaching and research. Either he or his assistant gave each of us a specific problem to work on. During the course of this work, it was usually found that relevant references hardly existed in the literature. Nevertheless, Berl made us search and investigate until we had arrived at our own result and evaluation. Only then did he intervene himself and help us to find the most successful route to a solution. Sometimes he quite forgot the qualification of the student he was dealing with. But that, too, had its positive side for even the most junior saw himself as a small but significant part of a chain that led to an important economic goal. This provided a great deal of enjoyment and helped us acquire a more balanced view of the value of our own personality.

Berl also operated a private laboratory in Darmstadt. This concerned itself with evaluations and patents for industry. We had the impression that Berl was earning a great deal of money in this laboratory although a large part was pumped back into the institute. His peculiar and certainly unconventional method of working was criticized at times. This type of research did not yield far-reaching or even epoch-making results benefiting natural science. On the other hand, the profit to technology was enormous.

Berl applied his keen intellect to specific problems. First of all he would always find the core of a problem and then try to resolve the difficulties obstructing a solution, using every method available to him on the strength of his industrial experience. Frequently, he used knowledge from disciplines allied to chemistry. There was hardly an institute in Darmstadt to which we were not sent to get advice.

Such a method of working was not likely to result in the Nobel prize. But it did provide an extraordinarily fruitful basis for the area of science which we call today chemical technology or process engineering. The contents of Berl's numerous patents did not in the main refer to new substances but more generally to new processes. To the outsider, and in the first years that applied also to me, a good many things seemed to be jumbled up. In the course of time, however, a more orderly picture evolved. Judging from my present experience, I feel that Berl's method of thinking and teaching could not have been more appropriate to my later career. At the start of an investigation, few of us knew the larger context and even fewer had any idea of the result at which we would arrive.

Even those who had been with Berl for a longer period of time rarely knew what his exact intentions were. It was not easy to determine whether he liked you or not. Many were uneasy, and some felt distinctly unhappy in his presence. When Berl suddenly appeared next to you at the laboratory bench, he could be very critical. I remember a very able and senior colleague who always made a practice of operating a burette and carrying out titration during Berl's rounds because he then felt less susceptible to Berl's criticism.

It was absolutely necessary to acquire a high degree of self-assurance in this institute without, however, succumbing to vanity. This, too, was an important lesson for later life. Berl was usually impatient and rather terse when making the rounds of the large institute. If you had nothing new to announce, he immediately moved on. When a student once said in answer to a question by Berl, 'Thank you, professor, I am satisfied'. Berl replied sharply: 'Never be satisfied until the coffin lid has been closed over you.'

There was no need to take such remarks tragically. I remember once, when I was trying for my diploma, standing in front of a successful experimental arrangement and trying it out in a whole series of tests so as to get material for my lecture. Suddenly Berl was standing behind me. He said abruptly: 'My dear colleague, there is little point in standing in front of your apparatus with your hands in your pocket to confirm to yourself that you are a big man after all.' This continuous urging, which was not allowed to give rise to doubts or insecurity, was a most useful feature of the institute. Berl's teaching could be very hard but it did equip you adequately for your later career. To be honest, I only fully appreciated this in later years.

It was not easy to feel at home in this laboratory. Personally, however, I established close contact with Berl fairly quickly. In the first months I worked there late into the night and every weekend to make up for what I had missed while I was enjoying myself as a student in Brunswick. This was particularly important because funds were short during those bad times and everyone was anxious to start earning money at the earliest opportunity. There were no distractions; we lived almost like monks. I threw myself into my work with great enthusiasm. Berl, who had a habit of visiting the institute at any time of the day, saw me often. This gave me enough courage to ask him for my diploma thesis in 1927. He put me in a group that was studying oxidation processes in hydrocarbons. There was considerable interest at the time in the knocking of carburettor engines. The problem had become acute because the car industry was constructing engines with far higher compression than before. Lead tetraethyl was already in use as an anti-knock agent and the I. G. Farbenindustrie was trying to introduce ferric carbonyl for the purpose. A group of students under Berl was, therefore, engaged in investigating oxidation processes, for example the determination of self-ignition temperatures. My particular task was to examine the catalytic action of anti-knock agents.

Private Assistant to Berl

I was engaged in these activities, which included work for my diploma and doctorate, for three years. Shortly after my diploma examination in 1928, Berl said to me out of the blue, 'Would you like to become my private assistant?' And how! Without a second's hesitation, I agreed, and henceforth considered myself the luckiest man on earth. I was to start the job in six months' time. The offer was particularly valuable because we were approaching the great economic crisis in which chemistry graduates could rarely look forward to a job.

So six months later I moved into Berl's private laboratory. It was fairly small and its equipment comparatively primitive. Normally, no more than two or three chemists were working there. One of these was the assistant who, apart from scientific work, was concerned with lectures and the administration of the institute. Although he had the title of private assistant, he was in fact no more than an ordinary assistant. The salary wasn't very high, but on the other hand it provided a regular income. After four years, when my Darmstadt period was coming to an end, I was earning about 300 marks. The monthly cheque of a student was then between 100 and 150 marks. As assistant, one was financially over the worst. The salary was enough for food, clothing and accommodation. It was very important to me that I now no longer needed to rely on help from home. My modest, but comfortable, apartment wasn't far from the institute. It consisted of two large rooms and the rent was 50 marks a month. The apartment was in a three-storey, reddish-yellow, brick-built house, very much in the style of suburban architecture at the period. It was destroyed by bombs in 1944.

I didn't spend much time in my apartment. Anyone who was really interested in his profession preferred to go and work in the institute, especially because of the friendly atmosphere there. In view of the ever-growing army of unemployed, we were conscious of our good fortune in being able to do this. Later on, many qualified chemists worked at the institute without being paid a fee, getting only their expenses, simply so as not to be idle during those years. Our conversation used to concentrate on work, even during the occasional relaxations that we allowed ourselves and on our joint excursions. After all, we were still young, and the seriousness of the time did not weigh so heavily with us.

I remember the publication at that time of a novel by Vicki Baum. The famous author had once been a harp player in Darmstadt where she married Johannes Richard Lert, the court band master. The peculiar title of her novel *Stud. chem. Helene Willfüer* – a science graduate – caught our attention. Working with us in the private laboratory was an attractive young woman whom we jokingly identified with the heroine of Vicki Baum's novel. Unfortunately, the reference in the novel to the premature maternity of its heroine was not altogether appreciated by our lady colleague.

As assistant, I continued for quite some time to work on my thesis. Later, I was entrusted with additional tasks. One of these was to become the turning point of my life. Berl got permission to build a gas institute in the former barracks adjacent to us. This meant that to begin with I had to look after the design and equipment of this institute. Then I had to determine its field of work. In this connection we developed a syllabus for engineers, and also developed the idea of a fuel institute. It was to be the beginning of my academic career.

Berl always maintained the closest possible contact with the world outside the university. He travelled a great deal in Germany and the neighbouring countries and during my assistantship he also visited the United States once or twice. A great number of lectures had to be prepared for these trips and these he corrected, sentence by sentence, with painstaking accuracy. It caused us a great deal of work and we often complained about the infinite care that he demanded. His university lectures, too, were continuously revised in the light of new experience.

It was from Berl that I heard the first description of the exciting industrial developments in the United States. It was almost a quarter of a century before I was able to go and see for myself. Many friends and acquaintances of Berl came to listen to his lectures at Darmstadt. These included a number of Nobel prizewinners such as Fritz Haber (chemistry 1918), Richard Willstätter (chemistry 1915), and Friedrich Bergius who had been awarded the Nobel prize for chemistry together with Bosch in 1931. Fritz Haber had become a close associate of Berl's during the war. Basically a pacifist, he had not hesitated any more than Berl to place his chemical abilities at the disposal of his country.

The leaders of the chemical industry around us were popular speakers in our lecture hall. Sometimes they engaged in passionate scientific arguments of a kind seldom experienced today.

Wherever the introduction of a new technical method in the chemical field appeared to promise success, or whenever new measuring or analytical methods became available, Berl had them installed in the rapidly expanding process engineering complex.

Berl had a weakness for the history of science; he never forgot that the roots of science are in its past. Because of this, he devoted much energy to the restoration of Liebig's birthplace in Darmstadt. In the institute itself, he set aside one room for memorabilia of August Kekulé whose pupil Richard Anschütz came to see us regularly.

As Berl's private assistant, I was also frequently engaged in historical work. Sometimes, however, this activity seemed too antiquarian and too little related to topical scientific problems. In those moments, Berl managed to make clear to me the inseparability of past and present. Today, I understand this much better. Indeed, I now sometimes suffer strong pangs of conscience when I see how little we are concerned with the history of the natural sciences. We ought to have had a comprehensive history of the sciences long ago. So far as I know, no one has yet tackled this task on the required scale.

First Contact with Industry

The Darmstadt Institute was in close contact with industry both at home and abroad. We young people had the good fortune of being able to profit from these connections. They also enabled Berl to arrange many excursions, a rarity at that time. Berl used to choose a group of twenty to twenty-five students whom he then thoroughly prepared in his lectures for these industrial trips through Germany. I have taken part in many such trips and excursions with him, first as student, and later as assistant.

In this way, I was able to visit the works of the I. G. Farbenindustrie. Later I was reminded often enough that the I. G. works had afforded me the first view of industrial practice. These trips generally made a deep impression on us, and participation was greatly sought after. Berl provided part of the costs from his own pocket, just as he used frequently to give financial assistance without the recipient being aware of it. Few people realized how well he knew the personal situation of each one of his pupils. The quietly-paid bill for chemicals or the 100 mark note just before Christmas were part of his generous, and only superficially distant, character. Close contact soon developed between Berl's institute and the German Society for Chemical Apparatus (Dechema), then in the course of development, which organized the Exhibition and Conference for Chemical Apparatus (Achema). The Dechema, which is dealt with in greater detail in a later chapter, was the particular work of Max Buchner who recognized the need for close collaboration between chemist and engineer. As a result of his efforts, a section on chemical apparatus was founded in 1918 as part of the Society of German Chemists. Dechema grew out of this section in 1926, again as a result of Buchner's efforts. In its statutes, Buchner expressly laid it down that chemists and engineers, experts from research and industry should be represented in equal numbers in this society.

We visited, together with Berl, all the Achema exhibitions that fell into my Darmstadt period. Compared with today, they were on a small scale. Berl walked with us from apparatus to apparatus. He knew every development and he was known on every exhibition stand. We were deeply impressed by the conciseness and the tremendous amount of knowledge with which he explained the larger principle and the smallest detail of each piece of apparatus. In this way, he introduced us to process engineering and the allied fields of interfacial physics, flotation and many other problems. Later on, Berl sent one or other of us as assistant and adviser to Achema.

During my time with him, Berl also carried out the basic work for a new technology which was to be quite different from anything else that had been published before in this field. The three-volume work was called the *Chemical Engineering Technology*. I worked on it from the very start and was privileged to include a significant contribution of my own. These volumes represented the first successful attempt to progress from descriptive technology to modern technical chemistry. The discussions with Berl on this subject often extended far into the night but they were extremely instructive to me.

A new aspect of the *Chemical Engineering Technology* were the practical and mathematical principles to which the Darmstadt mathematician Alwin Walther made an important contribution. I was to come into close contact with Walther again many years later when we set up our computer at Hoechst.

Political Upheaval

Before all our plans could mature, the National Socialists came to power in 1933. Paul von Hindenburg, who had been elected President of the Reich for the second time in 1932, defeating Adolf Hitler and the communist Ernst Thälmann, now entrusted the chancellorship to the 'Bohemian corporal', whom previously he had so vigorously rejected. Before Hitler's appointment, Germany had been ruled by emergency decrees. Franz von Papen and General Kurt von Schleicher, the last Chancellors before Hitler and without doubt the men who indirectly paved his way, had no longer been able to count on a parliamentary majority. The National Socialists celebrated their accession to power with a vast torchlight procession through the Brandenburg Gate, cheered by huge crowds.

Although in Darmstadt we were almost totally preoccupied with our work and had little time for political engagement, we naturally followed these events with great interest. Indeed, we could hardly escape them, for ever since we had been pupils, we had lived from one crisis to the next. Although after the currency reform of 1923, the internal unrest and the occupation of the Ruhr had come to an end, the overall prospect for our generation remained grim. We struggled through university and experienced the divisions of the people, fragmented into innumerable parties. Election followed election, each one accompanied by the shrill cries of dema-gogues from both the left and the right, and by fights between the armed units of the extremist parties. The once peaceful celebra-tions of 1 May ended in unimaginably bloody and ferocious battles.

The reason for Germany's difficulties was its unhealthy economic situation and the continuous plight which produced a feeling of utter hopelessness among the war and post-war generation. The young Weimar Republic did not endear itself to us because we felt that a fragmented parliament would be unable to find a way out of the confused situation. The victors in 1918 did not realize, as they did in 1945, that even a former enemy must be given a reasonable chance of building a decent life. It is, of course, true that after the introduction of the Rentenmark and with the aid of American credits, the economy had begun to recover. Indeed, 1927 marked the height of the new boom. The trend was then suddenly interrupted by the worldwide economic crisis triggered off by the famous Black Friday of 25 October 1929 on the New York Stock Exchange. Germany was hit all the harder by this because the only country that had helped us with loans and credits now found itself in an almost fatal crisis. A situation that had rocked the wealthy United States under President Herbert Hoover was bound to spell disaster for an unstable Germany. In December 1930, Germany had 4·4 million unemployed. By the beginning of 1932, the number had grown to 6 million. Bank scandals and bankruptcies involving millions intensified the misery and undermined industrial and social morals. The result was political apathy or radicalism in the people.

Emergency Decrees

People began to look to the strong men of the right and the left since, after the death of Gustav Stresemann in 1929, the success of a moderate policy had become doubtful. The National Socialists on the one hand and the communists on the other were mercilessly squeezing the ruling centre parties out of office.

Heinrich Brüning, Chancellor since 1930, ruled by emergency decrees. He tried to balance the economy and to get extensions for Germany's foreign credits. He cut wages and salaries and introduced many other drastic economy measures, all of them highly unpopular. In 1932, he even wrested a moratorium for the reparations payments from the Allies.

It has never been clearly established whether Brüning, as has so often been claimed, was really at the point of breakthrough when Hitler came to power. Brüning's autobiography does not provide a clear answer either. It is a fact, however, that even wealthy America managed to weather the crisis only very slowly under Roosevelt who displaced Hoover as President in 1933. Brüning had already resigned the year before. He had not succeeded in getting his policy across to the broad masses of the people. He was relying solely upon the grey-haired, eighty-five-year-old President of the Reich. When Hindenburg withdrew his support, Chancellor Brüning's fate was sealed. His successor, Franz von Papen, who dismissed the Prussian government under the Social Democrats Otto Braun and Carl Severing by way of a bloodless *coup* and who lifted the ban on the stormtroopers, provided the final stepping-stone for Hitler, whether he intended to or not.

There will never be a final answer to the question of how widely the German people welcomed the appointment of Hitler. The election of July 1932 gave the National Socialists some 230 out of a total of 608 seats. This meant that they were the strongest party, and as a result Hermann Göring became President of the Reichstag. Many historians maintain that at this time Hitler's star was already setting and that the party would soon have collapsed because its financial resources had been practically used up by the many elections. Be that as it may, many of the younger people were tired of coalition governments who went from crisis to crisis, largely because of the uncompromising attitude of the victors. They were tired of the eternal economic crises, and of the bloody street fights.

Even Hitler's cynical view of the Reichstag did not seem entirely unjustified if one followed the debates which were dominated by party political quarrels and sectional interests and remarkable only for their wearisome pettiness. The Weimar Republic did not offer young people, who were certainly not interested in a restoration of the monarchy, a way out of the misery to which they had been condemned since childhood.

Frankly, I felt the same. I had never seen Hitler and I had never heard him speak. Lost in my work, and used to precise thinking, what I heard of his demagogy, his fanaticism, and his racial prejudices, was anathema to me. Thanks to my position under Berl, I did not suffer any immediate need although I saw it daily among the people around me. Berl discussed the political events with his pupils. He was a 'Prussian' Austrian, a man who liked order and whose thinking was strongly patriotic. Neither he nor we ourselves could possibly have opted for the communist alternative. Thus, together with many of my colleagues at the institute, I joined the S.A. stormtroopers in Darmstadt in the spring of 1933 and belonged to it until about 1936. Fortunately, because of my fading interest, I did not achieve any distinction in the S.A. so that eventually I could quietly take my leave of it.

Because of the political developments, there was a radical change in the institute. Only now did we become conscious of an aspect that had seemed unimportant to us until then. Berl was a Jew and a convinced and proud follower of Judaism at that, although he had never manifested this in his attitude. Amongst his pupils there were hardly any Jews. I myself had never been given to anti-semitism. My parents were progressive humanists, my father and grandfather freemasons. Through a friend on my father's side, I had seen a great deal of the culture of the Jewish citizens of Frankfurt. On the other hand, we young people liked many facets of National Socialism such as its decisiveness and its courage to tackle complicated political and economic problems. Whenever we spoke about this, Berl fell silent. He clearly foresaw that the harmony of our collaboration would be endangered. After 30 January 1933, nobody was at first prepared to believe that Berl's position at the polytechnic was in any danger. He was well known amongst the students for his patriotic attitude. Who was going to attack him? Indeed, the National Socialist Student Federation soon invited him to lecture on his experience in the field of armaments during the First World War. This he did and, in fact, appeared to enjoy his reminiscences.

But the truce between the new regime and the generally respected professor did not endure for long. A circular was issued in April 1933 according to which all 'racially undesirable' members of the teaching profession were suspended with immediate effect. On that particular morning, Berl, as always, arrived shortly before eight o'clock. We could hear the rattling of his keys. A few minutes later he left his office, never to set foot in it again. In his office, the circular, about which we knew nothing, lay opened on his desk. There were excited discussions amongst ourselves. I called him up at home in the evening and he allowed me to come and see him. I have thought of that hour many times since. Thereafter, his closest collaborators often visited him at home.

Following Berl's departure, a great many things had to be sorted out. First of all, there were the theses of the doctorate and diploma candidates. We collected signatures and submitted petitions to the government of Hesse, pleading for Berl to be allowed to take the doctorate examinations. I myself paid a visit to Ferdinand Werner, the new Minister-President of Hesse. Our intervention was successful. Racial discrimination was as yet in a preliminary phase; the Nuremberg laws of 1935 and the final inferno of the extermination camps were yet to come. Our pleas for the reinstatement of Berl were, however, firmly rejected.

Berl obviously was one of the few Jews who even at that time realized what the new masters would really be capable of. I suppose the only thing that really surprised him was the early date of his dismissal and the ruthlessness with which it was carried out. However, he was not entirely unprepared. He very quickly settled his personal affairs and left for the U.S.A. three months afterwards.

As a result of his lectures and scientific contacts, he had a good many connections in the States. He therefore soon found a position in the Carnegie Institute in Pittsburgh, Pennsylvania, which was then the centre of American mining and its allied industries. The Carnegie Institute was the leading authority on coal research in the United States. Here Berl pursued his ideas for some years. But he was hardly able to start any fundamentally new work. At the age of fifty-six, and after the brutal uprooting from his life's work in Darmstadt, it was scarcely to be expected.

Berl never saw Germany and Darmstadt again. He died in exile in 1946.

My Way into Industry

When Berl's dismissal was ordered, it became clear to me that this meant the end of my Darmstadt days although I could, of course, have remained for a time. But we all realized that with Berl's departure, life in the institute would change completely. Our work had been dominated too strongly by Berl's indefatigable spirit, his ideas and his hard work, to say nothing of his infinite experience. Indeed, the entire institute had revolved around him. It seemed unthinkable to be there without him, and only a few stayed after Berl's departure. Most of us preferred to find another field of activity.

Berl had only a few months before he emigrated. Nobody would have criticized him if in the circumstances he had no longer concerned himself with the problems of his former colleagues. But his behaviour was perfect, even in this respect. He looked after every one of us. In my case, it took some time, but he always assured me that I need not worry. First of all, I had to help Berl with winding up his work. This involved the *Chemical Engineering Technology* in particular, which was then half-finished.

Eventually, the hour of departure from Darmstadt arrived for me too. Shortly before he left, Berl told me that he had spoken on my behalf with Farbwerke Hoechst and that I should apply to join them. This application was purely a matter of form as Berl had already arranged for my employment. I discussed my letter of application with him. It sounded slightly proud and self-confident. Berl had always taught us not to hide our light under a bushel, though we should avoid becoming conceited. A few days after my letter of application had been sent off, there was a quiet farewell party for Berl and his assistants before he left for the United States. I maintained contact with him for a long time, especially as the *Chemical Engineering Technology* was nowhere near completion. Many letters were exchanged between us during that time. Texts had to be revised, and the proofs read before the first volume appeared in 1935. By that time, I was already trying out chemical engineering technology in practice. The scene was the Hoechst works of the I. G. Farbenindustrie which I had joined in September 1933.

4

___

At I. G. Farben

I HAD not seen the laboratory for many years. Described as Building A4, it was a long, dark, fairly antiquated building that looked like a fossil among the modern surroundings in which it stood. It was here that I had begun my career with Hoechst in September 1933. In spring 1969, this career was coming to an end. The old laboratory had been chosen as a backdrop for a short film on television that recalled my years with Hoechst.

Hoechst had started in 1863 with dyestuffs – with five workers, a bookkeeper, a chemist and a small steam engine with an output of 5 h.p. – as a much-quoted chapter in the company's chronicles recalls. I, too, had started with dyestuffs, in this very A4 building which housed the alizarin laboratory.

The history of alizarin is one of the most fascinating episodes of the German dyestuffs industry, and fairly familiar to me. After fuchsin, alizarin was the second great dyestuff in the as yet limited Hoechst range. Originally obtained from plant roots, it has secured its place in history because of the red trousers of the French soldiers in the 1870–1 war.

Carl Graebe, who had joined Hoechst as its second chemist in 1864, played a decisive role in the synthetic manufacture of alizarin. Graebe, Carl Liebermann, who was professor at the University of Berlin, and Heinrich Caro of BASF, had fairly quickly developed a synthesis based on anthracene, a component of coal tar. These three were able to submit their patent application twenty-four hours before William Henry Perkin who had been the very first man to produce a synthetic dyestuff. Quite independently of this development, Ferdinand Riese discovered another method in

57

April 1869 which Adolf Brüning, one of the founders of Hoechst, had patented on 18 May of the same year.

Shortly afterwards, Hoechst started up production. Together with fuchsin, rosaniline blue, methyl green and methyl violet – the triphenylmethane dyestuffs – alizarin remained an important product for a long time. Following intense competition between a variety of manufacturers, it was eventually replaced by improved dyestuffs. In 1921, alizarin manufacture in Hoechst ceased altogether. When I joined Hoechst in 1933, the plant was still there at the back of our laboratory as though mothballed for some future use. Nothing had changed since it had been abandoned.

In the thirties, there were many such obsolete or partially obsolete plants in Hoechst. They had been abandoned after the end of the First World War, or during the world economic crisis, or as a result of the rationalization measures that followed the merger of the German dyestuffs factories in December 1925 to form the I. G. Farbenindustrie.

The history, size and scientific importance of the I. G. was once generally known throughout the world. For many of the older generation, the I. G. remains a vivid concept for its fate also represents a significant part of German industrial history. The scientific and technical achievement of this complex influenced the development of chemistry as a whole for many decades. Today, I feel, few young people know much about the I. G. or what it stood for.

Let me, therefore, give a brief description of the formation and organization of this undertaking to which I belonged from 1933 to the end of the war in 1945. In the company chronicles and the biographies of its leading people there is a lot of information covering this period. But no detailed account of the I. G. has ever been written. The I. G. enjoys singular and varying reputations in industrial history. Some looked upon it as a shining example of scientific and economic efficiency. Others have regarded it as a dark secret plot to gain control of the economy, if not of the state as a whole. The trial of the I. G. by the American military tribunal in Nuremberg in 1947–8 hardly made a contribution to a more objective assessment of its real significance.

How the I. G. was formed

The central figure in the foundation of the I. G. Farbenindustrie was Carl Duisberg who was born in 1861 in my native town of Barmen. At the age of twenty-two, he joined Farbenfabriken Bayer in Elberfeld as a chemist. After he had proved himself in the laboratory, he was entrusted with the establishment of a new works in Leverkusen near Cologne which went on stream towards the end of the nineties and has since formed the centre of Farbenfabriken Bayer. The masterly design of this huge complex became the proto-type for later large-scale plants. The memorandum in which Duisberg wrote down his ideas of the building presents a mine of valuable information for works planning even today.

In 1903, during the construction of Leverkusen, Duisberg went to the U.S.A. where he witnessed the imposing growth of American industry that had resulted from the successful concentration of parallel production facilities. He regarded it as a model that could be usefully applied also to the German dyestuffs industry. While on his way back to Europe, Duisberg formulated his first thoughts on this subject. He was reinforced in his intentions by Gustav von Brüning, the former director of Farbwerke Hoechst and son of one of the founders, who also knew conditions in the U.S.A. from personal experience. He moreover held the view that such a merger would also find the interest and agreement of BASF. Finally, Duisberg wrote down his ideas on fifty-six typed pages and this document was sent in January 1904 to the other major German dyestuffs producers. Its most important suggestion was an 'association for certain dyestuffs classes'. Although this was a bold proposal, the recipients did not reject it out of hand. Indeed, first discussions with the larger companies proved most encouraging.

But then Farbwerke Hoechst applied the brakes. The company believed that the time for such a merger had not yet arrived. Brüning feared above all that the incentive generated by keen com-petition might well evaporate within such a large organization. He wrote to Duisberg: 'If you are working under fairly comfortable conditions, it is only natural that tension slackens, that one person relies upon another and that artificial incentives will fail to induce employees to work nearly as hard as they do today under the pressure of competition.'

Probably the negative Hoechst attitude was governed by even

more decisive factors. There seemed to be no overriding economic need for a merger. True, the German dyestuffs industry was facing great problems but it was by no means in such desperate straits that pooling of all its resources had become indispensable. The existing difficulties were due more to vigorous competition and rapid growth which required enormous investments. In the end, therefore, only partial solutions were arrived at during the period 1904 to 1907. Hoechst joined with Cassella in 1904 and with Kalle in 1907. Bayer, BASF and Agfa merged in 1904.

The situation changed completely with the outbreak of the First World War. Overnight, the extensive international connections of German industry were severed. Just as suddenly, the Reich was cut off from many important raw materials such as saltpetre from Chile, cotton, rubber and many other products. Now it was up to chemistry to overcome these problems through the development of new processes.

Of course, Germany's enemies also suffered from the interruption in trade. They particularly missed German dyestuffs and pharmaceuticals. Before the war, no less than 85 per cent of the world requirements of synthetic dyestuffs, and a similar percentage of pharmaceuticals, had been produced by German companies.

Even in the highly industrialized U.S.A., no significant organic chemical industry existed until the outbreak of the war. The inorganic chemical industry had been well developed and the munitions industry was also flourishing. But organic chemistry, at that time essentially the chemistry of organic dyestuffs and pharmaceuticals, had been neglected. Only 10 per cent of the dyestuffs needed for the home market were produced by American companies. But even these purchased some 90 per cent of the necessary intermediates from Germany.

In Great Britain and the other Allied countries, the products of Germany chemistry were also missed. Here again, dyestuffs and pharmaceuticals had largely been bought from Germany. Nobody had expected that world trading would stop overnight.

The inevitable result was the rapid establishment of dyestuffs industries in those countries. Particularly in the U.S.A., where all the important raw materials were available with the exception of nitric acid, new chemical plants shot up everywhere with state support. Even the erection of five plants for the production of nitrogen from air was planned because the U.S. government expected the war to last until 1920.

The Americans simplified the establishment of new chemical plants by confiscating all German patents and the subsidiary companies of German firms in the U.S.A. The newly-created chemical foundation, which had bought the patents from the custodian of enemy property, offered these results of German science and technology to American firms and private persons. There was no shortage of buyers amongst the chemical companies in the U.S.A.

In Great Britain, France, Italy and Spain, too, new chemical factories were built during the war.

The German chemical industry soon realized the likely consequences of this development. Whatever the outcome of the war, one thing was certain: Germany's predominant position as a supplier of synthetic dyestuffs and pharmaceuticals to the international market had been shattered for ever.

In the face of such a sombre outlook, the questions of a merger once more became acute. The companies involved were still hesitant to agree to an unconditional merger, to the irreversible 'plunge into the unknown', as Gustav von Brüning called it. Nevertheless, they did decide upon an association that comprised all the important dyestuffs companies. This 'small I. G.' was set up in August 1916, right in the middle of the war.

By the end of the war it was obvious that this had been the right decision. The issue was no longer simply over the number of new dyestuffs factories that had been erected abroad. Now competition had been rendered almost impossible because most of the enemy countries had taken steps to protect their young chemical industry through high protective tariffs, particularly in the U.S. These ensured that the German chemical industry could no longer function as a dangerous rival. Britain even prohibited all imports of any dyestuffs that could be manufactured in the country. In such cases, a committee made up of manufacturers and users had to issue a special permit. This dyestuffs bill remained in force until after 1930.

German companies that wanted to export the products of their own research had to reckon with patent litigation and prohibitions. The same applied to German trade marks. In addition, there were the effects of the high reparation sums that Germany had to pay to the Allies

Large-scale Chemistry Under One Roof

In view of this situation, Duisberg, in a new paper, advised the foundation of a joint holding company. For most concerns, however, this was now no longer enough: they wanted a complete merger. As a result, there came a momentous day in the history of German chemistry. On 9 December 1925, Bayer, Hoechst, BASF, Chemische Fabriken Weiler-ter-Meer, Chemische Fabrik Griesheim-Elektron and Agfa merged to form the I. G. Farbenindustrie AG.

The new organization also included Cassella and Kalle whose major shareholding was already in the hands of the I. G. members. In addition, the I. G. had large shareholdings in many other companies including several mining concerns, the Aktiengesellschaft für Stickstoffdünger, Knapsack, the Duisburger Kupferhütte, Ammoniakwerk Merseburg, Aluminiumwerk Bitterfeld and Alexander Wacker GmbH in Munich. Dynamit AG in Hamburg, Rheinisch-Westfälisches Sprengstoff AG in Cologne, the artificial silk factories in Bobingen, Rottweil and Premnitz and a number of other small concerns also joined the I. G. In fact, the major part of the German chemical industry had been brought under one roof.

The management of the new concern originally consisted of all the board members of the founder companies, making a total of eighty-three. This was not, of course, an effective decision-making body.

A working committee was therefore set up to which only part of the ordinary board members belonged. Moreover, no successors were appointed for any board members who retired. As a result, only about twenty people belonged to the working committee by the beginning of the thirties. A few years later, in 1938, the slimming-down process had progressed to such an extent that the working committee could be dissolved. Its functions were taken over by the board of management which by the end of the Second World War consisted of only twenty-two members.

Duisberg became head of the supervisory board while Carl Bosch, who was thirteen years younger, became chairman of the board of management. Bosch had previously been chairman of BASF. In 1931, two years before I joined the I. G., he had been awarded the Nobel prize for chemistry. Carl Bosch was, without doubt, the outstanding figure of the I. G. Karl Holdermann has written a very instructive and detailed biography about him, called *Under the Spell of Chemistry*.

Bosch had joined BASF in Ludwigshafen in 1899. Shortly afterwards, he was to enter the field in which he was later to record his
greatest achievement – ammonia synthesis. Ammonia was the starting material for valuable fertilizers required in increasing amounts
to ensure sufficient food for the world. For this reason, the chemical
industry was intensively engaged in developing processes for obtaining ammonia from atmospheric nitrogen.

Such a process was offered to BASF in 1908 by Fritz Haber,
the director of the Institute of Physical Chemistry and Electro-
Chemistry at the University of Karlsruhe. In this process, ammonia
was produced catalytically from atmospheric nitrogen and hydrogen.

It was Bosch's task to perfect this process on an industrial scale.
In view of the level of technology at that time, this was easily one
of the greatest achievements of chemical industry.

Developments required a great deal of time. The enterprise of
the BASF management and its confidence in Carl Bosch were
tested to the extreme. But in May 1912 the breakthrough came.
The erection of a large-scale plant was begun in Oppau, near
Ludwigshafen. It went on stream in 1913 with an initial annual
output of 36,000 tons of sulphuretted ammonia.

In Bosch and Duisberg, neither of whom I knew personally, the
I. G. had two extraordinary men at its head. They had many
features in common, both of origin and career, but, according to
their close colleagues and biographers, their personalities differed
widely. Duisberg was sanguine, loved extended discussions and
enjoyed good company. Bosch was quieter and of a much more
placid temperament. He was probably a lonely man who found it
difficult to communicate with others. He did not regard loquacity
as a virtue. Every conference or conversation with him had to
confine itself to the absolute essentials. Problems had to be submitted to him ready for a decision, without doubts or reservations.

A large number of vital decisions had to be taken, especially
during the first year, when the I. G. had to lay its plans for the future
as a result of the adoption of new technical developments. These
made considerable demands on Duisberg, Bosch and the I. G.
management generally. The merger into one single company had
created a vast potential that economically had to be deployed as
effectively as possible.

During these years, Germany recovered surprisingly quickly from war, from inflation and its consequences. Although the technical innovations of the I. G. were not yet bearing fruit – on the contrary they called for large and risky investments – the company was able to increase its sales from slightly more than 1,000 million Reichsmark in 1926 to 1,400 million in 1928. Then, the I. G., too, started to slide down the dangerous slope of the international economic crisis so that by 1932 its sales had dropped to 871 million Reichsmark. The German coal tar dyestuffs industry had been hit especially hard by the economic crisis because more than half of its output – some 57 per cent – was exported.

My First Salary: 300 Marks

When I joined Hoechst in September 1933, there were early signs of a slight recovery, but the situation remained serious for some time. Short-time working, which meant a free Saturday even then, albeit without pay, continued until the end of 1936.

No reductions had been achieved in the army of unemployed in Germany which by 1932 had risen to more than 6 million. The number of employees in Hoechst had been reduced from 11,660 in 1929 to 7,300 in 1933. Every day, there was an endless queue of unemployed stretching from Hoechst railway station, past the labour exchange to the gates of the company. I will never forget the faces of these people, reflecting resignation and poverty, or the occasional hope that seized them when a few were able to land a job in the factory. Those who had been lucky enough not to lose their job gladly accepted short time in the hope that the day of dismissal might never come.

Hoechst had not engaged a single chemist for the past four years and so, when I made my tour of introduction on the first day, my colleagues regarded me as something like a world wonder. In the end, half a dozen new chemists joined the company in 1933. The older colleagues regarded this as an encouraging sign. Perhaps it was the end of the slope.

My starting salary of 300 marks was comparable to my income in Darmstadt, and enabled me to rent two rooms in Hoechst, in the Königsteiner Strasse, which had been inhabited by whole generations of chemists. It was quite a comfortable flat. There was even a small cooker on which I could prepare an evening meal. I needed this slightly larger retreat because in the evenings and at weekends, after Berl had left Germany, I had to work on the *Chemical Engineering Technology*.

Work in Farbwerke Hoechst began at quarter past seven in the morning. I had a walk of about twenty minutes. Practically the only form of transport were bicycles; cars were hardly ever seen. My first chief in the alizarin and vat dyestuffs department, Hans Tampke, was production manager. He, in turn, was answerable to the departmental head, Georg Kränzlein, who was also responsible for a large scientific laboratory. I was soon to find that a deeply-entrenched departmental federalism flourished in Hoechst. The individual departments operated fairly independently even in scientific respects. In the final analysis, they were, of course, responsible to the joint works management. It was not easy for a newcomer to absorb the organization and working methods of this giant undertaking. And, of course, Hoechst was only a part of the far more comprehensive I. G.

Nobody made any particular effort to explain the internal relationships. In any case, the whole of industry was at that time not very publicity-minded in terms of either internal or external communication. You had to ask your colleagues for the essential information.

The moulding of the I. G. Farbenindustrie into a homogenous structure passed through many painful stages during those years. When the Allies dismembered this industrial complex after the Second World War, its component parts had by no means grown together completely.

A number of technical members of the board were responsible for each large works and they had their headquarters there. The board members ruling in Hoechst when I joined were Ludwig Hermann, Friedrich Jähne, and Carl Ludwig Lautenschläger. Several works were always joined into regional groups. For example, Ludwigshafen-Oppau was the centre of the Upper Rhine group, Hoechst of the Central Rhine, Leverkusen of the Lower Rhine, Bitterfeld and Wolfen-Farben of the Central German and Agfa of the Berlin group.

This regional arrangement was complemented by vertical responsibility for coordination throughout the concern. A technical commission ruled over all technical questions. It took all the necessary decisions and these needed approval only from the main board of management. This technical commission was omnipotent throughout the entire technical field of the I. G., as was the department to which I belonged when I joined Hoechst.

Fritz ter Meer, who headed the technical commission from 1933 until the collapse in 1945, was one of the leading industrial personalities of his time. His father, Edmund ter Meer, was a typical self-made man who had developed an important chemical company from very small beginnings in Uerdingen in the Rhineland. Understandably proud of his achievements, he fought bitterly to the last minute against the I. G. merger.

His son, on the other hand, who had enjoyed a comprehensive, modern education, recognized quickly that a merger of the German dyestuffs concerns was unavoidable. Apart from chemistry, he had also studied law and he took a deep interest in the commercial problems of his father's company. Extended journeys abroad deepened his understanding of international commerce. He fully realized that the future would require a research effort by the chemical industry of which companies of the size of Weiler-ter-Meer were simply not capable.

Soon after the merger in 1929, Fritz ter Meer had taken over Division II, the most important of the three great divisions that had been formed during the first phase of reorganization. Its most important traditional products were dyestuffs and pharmaceuticals. It also included organic intermediates, pesticides, solvents, plastics, synthetic rubber, detergents and inorganic chemicals.

Division I comprised ammonia synthesis and the entire field of high pressure technology. Its chief from 1929 to 1938 was Carl Krauch who came from BASF and who was one of the closest technical collaborators of Carl Bosch. When Krauch was given a special assignment under the four-year plan, he was succeeded by Martin Müller-Cunradi. In contrast to ter Meer's division, Division I was controlled very closely, with far fewer commissions than the organic division. Its management had its headquarters in Ludwigshafen-Oppau.

Division III looked after numerous special fields. These included the photographic products from Agfa, cellulose, artificial silk and fibres and the processing of plastics. Its chief was Fritz Gajewski who, like Krauch, was a pupil of Bosch.

Naturally, to ensure a continuous exchange of experience, rather more than the technical commission was needed. A large number of commissions was therefore set up covering science, manufacture, application technology and process engineering. In my division alone, there were more than thirty such commissions, including an analysts' commission, a physics commission and a packaging and storekeeping commission.

In addition, there were four sales groups which enjoyed a rather independent existence. The dyestuffs and chemicals sales groups were housed in the 'Grüneburg' in Frankfurt. This skyscraper, built by the Berlin architect Hans Poelzig in 1929 in Grüneburg Park in Frankfurt, was at that time probably one of the most beautiful and certainly one of the best known administrative buildings in the world. It also housed all the management offices of the company. The pharmaceutical sales group had its headquarters in Leverkusen. Berlin was the headquarters of the photography and artificial silk sales group.

In 1933, the I. G. was still a fairly young organization. Complete integration had not been achieved even by the end of the war in 1945. From each one of the various works, whose right to independent decision was still fairly extensive in spite of the merger, there emanated a quite distinct *esprit de corps*. True, one belonged to the I. G. and was proud of it. But one was also, and sometimes even more so, a man from Hoechst, from Leverkusen or from Ludwigshafen. Each works had its own life and its own problems, often based on many years of history. Not infrequently, there were differences of opinion when management appointments were involved or the spheres of influence of the former independent works were discussed. In the first years, bitter disputes occurred also over the rationalization of production, involving, as it often did, the shut-down of existing plants.

The final arbiter in such disputes was the main board of management of the I. G. Its chairman from 1935, following Carl Bosch, was Hermann Schmitz from BASF, a financial expert rather than a scientist.

Dyestuffs Chemistry in Hoechst

Our department in Hoechst, which was devoted mainly to vat dyestuffs, was only a small part of the comprehensive I. G. organization. In the post-war years, the I. G. Farbenindustrie had managed to create a wide range of very fast vat dyestuffs which were based on the classic Indanthren of René Bohn and which were successfully sold under the trade mark Indanthren. The range had been supplemented in Hoechst with valuable new additions by Kränzlein and his collaborators. But even so, it was still being developed and was by no means complete.

Leaving aside these new beginnings, dyestuffs production was still being affected by the consequences and complications of the merger even though this had taken place more than seven years earlier. Consolidation and re-organization of the dyestuffs business had been its prime purpose. Their realization was the great priority of the administration. After all, the company was not called the I. G. Farbenindustrie for nothing. After many intermediate solutions, a final arrangement was arrived at in 1930. Rationalization of the dyestuffs business meant that out of more than 50,000 dyestuffs produced by the founder companies before the merger, only 10,000 remained. For their production, some 2,500 different chemical substances were needed. Each one of these substances, in turn, required several preliminary stages. A great deal of knowledge and experience was needed to supervise and control this large variety of products.

All these dyestuffs were the result of a long and successful development period. They served the dyeing of a large variety of materials. Originally, textile dyeing commanded the greatest interest, the natural fibres such as cotton, wool and silk being joined by more and more synthetic fibres. Later, pigments for the production of printing inks and paints played an increasing role.

For many decades, dyestuffs chemistry was one of the large domains, if not the foundation, of organic chemistry. German research and development were able to record notable successes so that by the thirties, some 42 per cent of world production was again manufactured by Germany, that is to say I. G. Farbenindustrie.

As was usual for all the fields of I. G. Farbenindustrie, the entire dyestuffs planning was controlled by a central coloristic commission. It decided on new products, prices and investments. There were sub-commissions for the various dyestuffs classes both for the coordination of research and for production.

The central coloristic commission was at that time headed by Hans Walter, a member of the board of management. Walter was a chemist and had originally been employed in Leverkusen. Because of his extraordinary knowledge and his tendency to sharp criticism, he was much feared. I was present once when he chaired a world coloristic conference of the I. G. in the restaurant at Hoechst. I admired his enormous factual knowledge and keen intellect.

The commissions had great influence. Even board members in charge of the groups found it very difficult to contest decisions by a commission. This well thought-out democratic system proved highly successful on the whole, and without doubt, I. G. Farbenindustrie owed a large part of its success to it. Of course, it was not an ideal system. Like every human organization, it engendered certain injustices and a degree of arbitrariness.

The manufacture of the dyestuffs and their starting and intermediate products was so organized that each of the four groups – Leverkusen, Ludwigshafen, Central Germany, and Hoechst – was allocated a section of the vast range. Every effort was made to take traditional fields into account. Attempts were also made to maintain an element of competition by allocating the various dyestuffs always to two of the groups. Naturally, such a new arrangement, which had to take into account more than sixty years of tradition, was subject to rivalries, disputes and injustices.

In such conditions, the strength of the leading personalities – amongst whom Carl Duisberg and Carl Bosch were outstanding – was the decisive criterion. After the early death of Gustav von Brüning in 1913 and after that of Herbert von Meister in 1919 – both were sons of the founders – the management of Hoechst no longer had sufficient unity, particularly in its cooperation with Griesheim and Offenbach. Cassella, which belonged to the Central Rhine group, also maintained a separate role for a long period of time under the direction of its famous founders, especially the Weinberg family. It was integrated only very slowly into the new organization.

Fragmented Production

When the reckoning began during the various phases of rationalization, the outlook for the Hoechst group became extremely bleak. Technical conditions at Hoechst were much less favourable than at Bayer or at BASF. Transport and power costs, indeed every item that had to be included in the calculation, were far higher than in any of the other works. The reason was the fragmentation of the antiquated production.

I remembered from my Darmstadt days that the papers had then carried reports that the works of the Maingau were to be closed down altogether. This would, however, have been so unjust that the I. G. management finally decided to leave Hoechst with sufficient products to ensure its existence. It was probably also as the direct result of these considerations that Friedrich Jähne was sent from Leverkusen to Hoechst as chief engineer with instructions to do something about the technical equipment at Hoechst which had been so greatly neglected.

In the end, however, Hoechst fared rather badly. It kept indigo production and a few of the old triphenylmethane dyestuffs. It lost however all the azo dyestuffs, in so far as they were used for textile applications, and, perhaps even more serious, the starting products for these dyestuffs. The only consolation was the group of azo pigments which had been specifically developed at Hoechst and of which it could hardly be guessed that they would eventually play such a significant role. Finally, Hoechst was also left the alizarin and vat dyestuffs department, but again as a torso from which many important end and starting products had been amputated. A large part of the sulphur dyestuffs was now manufactured at Cassella.

A new dyestuffs business was to be built up on the basis of an organization arranged in four research and production groups. The wounds and scars produced by such ruthless surgery might have healed fairly quickly if a period of prosperity had guaranteed continuous development. Instead, a world-wide economic crisis arose which hardly favoured a new start. By the time this had been overcome, interest had shifted to new fields. These included synthetic rubber and plastics, rayon staple, petrol from hydrogenated coal and the light alloys.

Dyestuffs chemistry, including the chemistry of aromatic carbon compounds, therefore remained a cinderella during the succeeding years, and certainly during the war, because it could contribute only very little to the developments of that time.

Those of us who had entered industry in 1933 had been optimistic and enthusiastic. But, talking at lunch or over a cup of coffee with our older colleagues, we encountered a great deal of pessimism. Many of these people could boast of long experience and an impressive record of achievements. But the reorganization that followed the merger, and the lethargy produced by the economic crisis had robbed them of much of their creativity.

In the alizarin department under Kränzlein, however, conditions were different. I really had been fortunate to end up there. Kränzlein possessed enormous enterprise and no reverse could discourage him.

At first, the type of chemistry involved in the department was a closed book to me. I had entered the world of the condensed ring systems, of aromatic chemistry, where new colours with surprising fastness properties were continuously being discovered by increasingly sophisticated molecular manipulation. These products were manufactured as soon as the coloristic commission had given its blessing.

These dyestuffs were heterogenous mixtures of aromatic compounds. Their shade, in fact, was often based on this very chemical heterogeneity. This meant, of course, that production was extremely difficult. Each works manager had a small scientific laboratory in which he tried to determine the manufacturing conditions with the help of a few laboratory assistants and usually also a second chemist who at the same time acted as plant assistant. A simple thing like damage to an enamel kettle could result in an iron content that changed the shade to such an extent that it no longer conformed to the intended colour.

These dyestuffs were often quite valuable. The particular pride of the alizarin laboratory was Brilliant Orange GR, a vat dyestuff, which cost 80 marks per kilo. This was about a quarter of my monthly salary at that time. Fortunately, the works management realized that because of my special technological training, I could contribute little to such traditional research; in any case we were soon faced by new problems. As competition increased, so the requirements made upon our dyestuffs also became more stringent. Conventional ideas of organic chemistry and coloristic routines were no longer adequate to carry us forward. Shade and fastness properties ceased to be the sole criteria. In the United States, where large production units were operated because of the high salaries and the huge domestic market, economic production was now the prime requirement.

Henceforth, dyestuffs had to meet the highest demands. They had to be suitable for high speed printing machines and continuous dyeing apparatus. To achieve this, it was necessary to render them into a form, either paste or powder, which ensured a rapid reaction during printing or dyeing. This was a new problem for the organic chemists on whose solution they worked with a great deal of flair and eventually considerable success. The so-called finish had become almost a secret science.

What could be more appropriate than engaging a young chemist to bring a little light and method into this darkness? Significant successes were unlikely at first. Colloid and interfacial chemistry was a little known and rarely practised science. Dyestuffs were impure substances which altered their surface characteristics during grinding, drying and mixing and which, moreover, caused unpredictable changes in the flow properties of starch-containing printing pastes. In addition, these products were often subject to considerable temperature differences during transport and storage. In powder form, they sintered together during drying, could not be suspended in water and lost their tinctorial strength.

Although this was a strange field for me, it was not entirely outside my experience for I had learnt how to combine various technical possibilities and how to apply methods from other fields of science. In the alizarin department, I met Siegfried Kiesskalt with whom I was to work for the rest of my life. Kiesskalt was one of the collaborators of Jähne, the new chief engineer. He was supposed to pave the way for a modern process engineering and physics approach in Hoechst. Like me, Kiesskalt had spent a long time at different universities working on a variety of problems. We formed a working partnership that was only interrupted in 1945 by the end of the war.

In collaboration with the plant managers of the alizarin department, we did in the end build up a systematic picture of the factors that governed dyestuffs finishing. Additives and characteristics like flow properties and viscosity were standardized, and manufacturing specifications derived from these standards. In this way, dyestuffs with specified characteristics could be produced by standard methods.

Since the subject was so obscure to start with, it was the occasional flash of inspiration and the perfect understanding with my colleagues, which included my university friend and later Hoechst management colleague Werner Schultheis, that gradually illuminated the scene. In recognition of my work, I was eventually presented to the appropriate dyestuffs commission and in the course of time given many further jobs.

For example, shortly after my joining the department, I was asked to supervise the re-building of the powder grinding shop. It was a fairly large project for those days and I regarded it as an expression of considerable confidence in me. Kiesskalt had developed a vibrating ball mill which was capable of such fine grinding that the dyestuffs could be crushed until they lost all tinctorial strength, that is to say down to below the wavelength of light. With the aid of this mill and an atomization dryer, and providing suitable wetting and dispersing agents of a tannin-like character were added, powders could be prepared which dissolved in water to give an ink-like dyeing, passing every normal filter.

It was, of course, not quite as simple as it sounds. Nevertheless, it did result in a principle that could be used uniformly for all Hoechst vat dyestuffs, provided that changes were made in the additives. As far as I know, the process is still in use today. Construction and operation of the mill were a modest initial success which I greatly enjoyed and which helped to spread my 'fame', at least in Hoechst.

The First Patent

I was also engaged in problems from other coloristic departments, for example the triphenylmethane dyestuffs. The Americans had marketed a product for paper printing which, given the same amount of dyestuff, was far more intense than the old Hoechst product. The physicists had rightly concluded from the quite different grain character that this product had been dispersed in linseed soil without intermediate drying. In Hoechst, this drying caused far greater grain coarseness. How could we get round the drying problem?

I found that analagous to phenomena during ore flotation, small additions of organic amines suffice to separate the Reflex Blue, present as an aqueous paste, from the water by combining it with linseed oil. This principle is now used worldwide and known as flushing. It was my first patent. So far as I know, it was withdrawn because it could not be defended.

There were numerous applications for our techniques of grinding and dispersing pigments and large surface area substances, particularly for their subsequent behaviour in hydrophilic and hydrophobic liquids. This work eventually led me beyond the actual dyestuffs field. We tried to embed finely-ground pigment in viscose as a method of dyeing artificial silk in the mass before spinning. This brought us into contact with the artificial silk factory in Dormagen near Leverkusen where intensive work on this subject was already being carried out.

My horizons as an industrial chemist were greatly widened in this way. The strict, rather conservative rules of the dyestuffs division no longer applied. I still remember the horror on the faces of the coloristic commission when we presented samples of mass-dyed rayon staple to them. It transpired that we had replaced the expensive black dyestuffs by ordinary carbon black, on the advice of a chemist from Dormagen at that. It was tantamount to damaging business. Still, the carbon black turned out to satisfy the Indanthren standard of fastness. Even today many synthetic fibres are dyed black in this way, when it is desirable to carry out preparation prior to spinning. The good old horsehair brooms, too, are now produced mainly from synthetic fibres dyed with carbon black.

Meanwhile, I had attracted the attention of Ludwig Hermann, who was then director of the Central Rhine group. In quiet Hoechst, it was still possible for the chief to meet each newly-engaged chemist and personally follow his fortunes.

After Berl, Hermann was the second person to have had a decisive influence on my career. He had become chief of the Central Rhine group in 1933 in spite of a great deal of opposition and after many changes in the management and the departure of many members from the board.

Hermann had been trained as an electro-chemist. His first industrial activity took him into the potash works at Aschersleben where, together with the Viennese Jean Billiter, he set up a chlorine-alkali electrolysis. He then went to Hoechst and subsequently to Gersthofen where he made a vital contribution to the development of electrolytic chrome oxidation and Billiter electrolysis as well as to the start of wax production. Eventually, he returned to Hoechst where he took over the management of the indigo department which was finding it very difficult to cope with the competition from BASF.

This, too, had been a question of continued existence. Hermann had successfully fought against the shut-down of this large part of the works which, with its complex starting products and enormous sales, remained an important pillar of Hoechst production for a very long time. There was fierce competition from BASF until the end of the war. Every three months, the prime costs of Hoechst and Ludwigshafen were carefully compared. After the war, indigo finally lost its importance and manufacture was not resumed in Hoechst.

With his jovial Bavarian manner and his open character, Hermann quickly gained the goodwill of the people in Hoechst. Of course, he did not find it easy at first to persuade the many powerful 'crown princes' and old-established departmental heads to fall into line. We young people were particularly impressed that he took no notice of bureaucracy, or the camp followers of which there was no shortage in the I. G. Fortunately, Hermann got on well with chief engineer Jähne so that Hoechst, after a long period, once again possessed a united leadership.

Friedrich Jähne came from Neuss in the Rhineland and had been moved from Leverkusen to Hoechst in order to modernize the largely antiquated plant. He was in his middle fifties and a totally different type from Hermann. This is, no doubt, why the two got on so well together. Jähne, whose desk was always immaculately tidy, was a man of decision but also extraordinarily calm and relaxed. When we once urged him during an argument with some high-ups from the I. G.: 'Mr Jähne, you will have to get involved for once; you will have to get excited', he replied calmly: 'No, gentlemen, you should never do that on principle.' Normally, the chief engineer of a works did not belong to the management but Jähne was spokesman for all the chief engineers of the I. G. and he was therefore made a member of the board of management in 1934. He played his part in Hoechst magnificently.

The Central Rhine group was represented on the I. G. board at that time by Carl Ludwig Lautenschläger who, as scientist and manager of the pharmaceutical department, tended to keep rather in the background. Another group representative on the board was Constantin Jacobi, but as he lived mainly in Mainkur and Griesheim, we saw him only rarely in Hoechst.

As an electro-chemist, Hermann found little of personal interest in Hoechst. Prodded by Kiesskalt, he therefore frequently visited our modest laboratory. He would suddenly turn up amongst us and take part in our discussions to which he contributed a great many facts and examples from the I. G. life and his wide personal experience.

He also encouraged us to take up questions that were far beyond our terms of reference.

One day in 1935 we were able to show him how simple it was to dehydrate lignite and de-ash it at the same time. As mined in Germany, lignite contains about 50 per cent water and 10 per cent ash. If it is mixed with tar oil and if the ph value is properly adjusted, then, as in our dyestuff experiment, phase reversal occurs. Lignite and tar oil combine to give a hydrophobic paste. The water is displaced from the coal and carries the hydrophilic ash components along with it. A coal/oil mixture practically free from water and ash is obtained.

After we had repeated this simple and, to us, familiar experiment with a variety of lignite grades, we showed it to Hermann and Jähne, suggesting that this phenomenon might possibly be applied to coal hydrogenation. This was then a subject of considerable interest not only to the I. G. but to the world at large.

Hermann and Jähne quickly accepted our ideas and made contact with Ludwigshafen where the work on coal hydrogenation was concentrated in the hands of Matthias Pier. BASF, and later the I. G. Farbenindustrie, had invested large amounts of money in processes for the production of synthetic fuels. Following the outstanding achievement of the Haber-Bosch synthesis, the methanol process had been developed after the war by Matthias Pier who thus earned his first spurs in the chemical industry. The shortage of crude oil in Germany and increasing motorization once more highlighted the fuel problem, particularly in view of the ambitions of that era to be self-sufficient. Carbon oxide syntheses, for example that of methanol, which could also be extended to other oxo compounds, did not seem quite suitable for this purpose to the people in Oppau. When Franz Fischer from the Mülheim Institute for Coal Research returned to carbon oxide synthesis using new types of catalyst, there were sharp controversies concerning the potentialities of the process.

BASF followed another route which had been mapped out by the experiments of Friedrich Bergius. BASF acquired the know-how from Bergius who had carried out important investigations into the hydrogenation of coal, and who was later engaged in wood saccarification. Bergius had obtained liquid fuels by reacting hydrogen and coal, i.e. through coal hydrogenation. However, the development of the simple autoclave experiment, which we had repeatedly carried out in Darmstadt, into a continuous, large-scale process was found to be extremely difficult. Under the patronage of Bosch, who had almost unlimited authority throughout the entire I. G. because of his outstanding successes, further development work was taken up with great energy in Oppau and Leuna.

It was comparatively easy to convert liquid hydrocarbons with high boiling point, such as lignite tar, into low viscosity hydrocarbons through pressure hydrogenation. Almost insuperable difficulties arose, however, if solid coal, i.e. lignite or ordinary coal, was used. Apart from the fact that it took much longer to obtain fuel-like products from these materials, the solid coal had to be introduced into the high pressure chamber and then discharged from it again. The mineral components, the coal ash, remained in the reaction product, and this ash, together with the hydrogenation products, formed a residue that could be processed only with great difficulty.

The work in Oppau and Leuna met with tremendous success. But for a long time, it did not yield an economically useful result, in spite of an investment of many millions of marks.

There have been numerous descriptions of the dramatic circumstances under which further development work had to be stopped during the world economic crisis of 1929 when the resources of the I. G., too, started to dwindle. Nevertheless, the fame that these processes, like all high pressure syntheses, enjoyed was so great that Bosch and Bergius were jointly awarded the Nobel prize in 1931. A large experimental plant had been started up in the Leuna works as early as 1927. In the succeeding crisis years, however, petrol prices almost completely collapsed and the Leuna production was several times in great danger of being shut down altogether. Its continued, if modest existence, was due solely to the anxiety of the I. G. management to maintain jobs for the workers.

The Americans also showed great interest in this development. The I. G. concluded comprehensive contracts with Standard Oil of New Jersey, the present-day Esso. The Americans were interested in the reactions and hydrogenation processes with which the quality of inferior crude oils could be improved. They were also concerned, as they always had been, with the prospect of their crude oil resources soon becoming exhausted. In 1929, Standard Oil and the I. G. formed Standard Oil I. G. which took over the patents for the hydrogenation of oil, coal and tar. The I. G. acquired approximately 2 per cent of the share capital of Standard Oil valued at approximately 35 million dollars. The contract resulted in an active exchange of knowledge. Up to the outbreak of war, it yielded many interesting results that could, however, be fully realized only after 1945, when petro-chemistry developed.

When I paid my first visit to the U.S.A. in 1954, I met some people at Esso who still remembered this period with enthusiasm.

In 1933, the I. G. resumed work on coal hydrogenation. The new regime had an understandable interest in providing its own fuel if it was to realize its ideas of autobahns and Volkswagen cars. An even more important aspect later on was rearmament. An agreement with the economics ministry at the end of 1933 ordered the I. G. to expand its production of petrol from lignite to 350,000 tons per year. Other companies later erected production units on the basis of I. G. licences. In 1944, the total annual capacity of the German hydrogenation plants was 3·5 million tons of petrol and fuel oil.

In 1936, Matthias Pier came to Hoechst to have a look at our de-ashing experiments. I immediately developed a great sympathy for this vital and active man who throughout his whole life remained faithful to physical chemistry in spite of all his industrial diversions. This combination of industrial technology and natural science made him one of the most valuable friends of the Dechema in whose work he played an active part right up to his death in 1965.

I often went to Oppau to see Pier and his colleagues at work and to learn something of their particular style. Sufficient funds were now available, and the price of petrol was no longer so decisive. The important thing was to solve the innumerable technical details whatever the cost.

Pier radiated boundless optimism. A short vivacious man of mercurial temperament, he bubbled over with new ideas and enjoyed a wonderful relationship with his colleagues. In Oppau, I got to know all the people who later became managers of hydrogenation plants: Albert Pross, Wilhelm Urban, Carl Müller von Blumencron and Kurt Wissel, with whom I had a great deal to do in Wesseling after the war.

The hydrogenation plant in Leuna was already under construction. It was a bold undertaking in view of the fact that a number of process phases had not yet been resolved. One problem in particular was ash removal with which I was so closely concerned. In the gay Oppau district, which liked to celebrate at the least provocation, a rather appropriate story used to make the rounds: 'At the end of the plant in Leuna there is a white dot on the map. Here a Doctor X has to remove an unknown quantity of a residue of unknown composition using an unknown process.'

It was a situation often encountered in chemistry. Everything threatened to fail over a residue problem. On the other hand, we knew how to grind the pre-dried lignite with an oil obtained from the process itself and to hydrogenate it in the presence of a catalyst, unaffected by sulphur, in a first, semi-solid phase. The product was dried on centrifuges yielding a volatile oil which was then further hydrogenated in the gas phase. The centrifuge residue had a consistency like shoe polish and was composed of the ash and the asphalt-like oil particles adhering to it. This was the Achilles heel of the process. The residues had to be removed by an expensive and technically unsatisfactory method because the process could not wait for the results of my work.

In 1936, Pier made lignite and the so-called grinding oil available to me. I was able to demonstrate after a short time that phase reversal occurred in the aqueous coal if oil was added and that the coal was transformed into the oil phase practically without ash. Water and ash remained together and could readily be separated. A seductive success! We were asked to develop a continuous process. The necessary staff was made available to us and we worked in a happy atmosphere of inventiveness.

But first, we had to overcome organizational obstacles. The Hoechst dyestuffs department, which was pursuing other goals, had little sympathy for work done in its laboratories, and probably at its expense, which had nothing to do with its own products and which in any case was hardly a delectable subject. No doubt we progressed too impetuously. Therefore, one day in March 1936, a very serious complaint was levelled against us. A personal, at times vehement, interview with Hermann took place. I am afraid I cannot pretend to be the soul of meekness. In any case I had to defend myself. I had worked hard and I had had some success, if not to the benefit of the dyestuffs factory, certainly to the advantage of the company as a whole. As a result of the discussion, I was allowed to continue, and, moreover, the establishment of my own scientific technical department was approved. This was to be divorced from production and dyestuffs interest and directly responsible to the chief engineer. It was christened 'Process Engineering'.

This, my first big row in Hoechst, took place on 19 March. I remember the date so precisely because in the evening I celebrated my engagement. Soon afterwards I married Gertrud Deitenbeck, a daughter of the protestant minister in Frankfurt – Sossenheim. In August 1936, I moved with my wife into an attractive company flat situated in the middle of the factory. My salary at that time was 500 RM. This was supplemented at the end of the year by a personal annual bonus of 1,000 to 2,000 marks. Nevertheless, it was only a modest foundation on which to build a family life.

Of course, I was allowed to, and indeed had to, continue with the problems of the dyestuffs division in spite of my new position. But the important thing was that I was now in charge of an independent scientific department. It included the physicists who, with their laboratory, happily joined the new department, as well as some additional assistants. My immediate boss was Jähne, the chairman of the engineering commission of the entire I. G. Farbenindustrie. This meant that our process engineering department had a direct line to the I. G. management and we, in turn, had some idea of and access to the problems of other I. G. works. This was not only proof of confidence in us but also afforded an opportunity to map out our field of activity as we saw fit.

The creation of the new department was in line with a trend noticeable in many other areas. It was a time when Jähne, Arnold Eucken, and others, were engaged in the development of process engineering as a new branch of science. We played a considerable part in this development. The present Society for Process Engineering within the framework of the Society of German Engineers is the final result of these efforts. The description 'process engineering' was coined deliberately to distinguish it from the Anglo-Saxon 'chemical engineering' which did not seem to be appropriate to German conditions.

The first priority was to pursue the coal de-ashing process. Kiesskalt constructed a twin extruder in which the process, hitherto performed discontinuously in a kneader, could now be operated continuously. We now also learnt what every chemist has to learn in the end: One needs infinite patience to ripen scientific discovery into technical maturity. Numerous plant experiments on a scale of many tons, using a variety of coal grades, became necessary. But a chemist in the laboratory simply has to display endless perseverance.

During this work, additional applications emerged for our de-ashing process. In the vicinity of Halle, there were large deposits of salt-containing lignite which, precisely because of the high salt content, was totally unsuitable for coal hydrogenation. The deposit of evaporated common salt also presented difficulties during combustion. We found that salt coal could also be completely de-ashed by our method since the salt was discharged with the water. Moreover, we found that the de-ashed and dehydrated coal pulp could be converted into a high-grade coke by heating to approximately 1,000° C, the tar oil being largely recovered. In view of the rapid development of lignite hydrogenation, however, this work came too late.

In the new Buna works in Schkopau, which were being erected in the immediate vicinity of Leuna near Halle and Leipzig, a new problem arose. Several hundred thousand tons of coal-coke, which had to be transported from the Ruhr or from the Lausitz, were needed for carbide production. It was therefore decided to produce our 'colloidal' coal for the first time at the rate of about 10,000 tons a year at Schkopau. The plant went on stream towards the end of 1942 and performed fairly satisfactorily. It was a tragedy that the able young chemist Erwin Strohfeld, whom I had managed to have exempted from military service so that he could do this work, was killed during the last days of the war in a bomb attack on Halle.

Slowly our young department became known throughout the I. G. More and more problems were passed on to us. In the processing of coal, which was almost our only raw material in Germany, there arose the problem of electrode coke which might be useful as a starting material for the manufacture of graphite electrodes.

Gustav Pistor, chief of Bitterfeld, who was known as the father of industrial electro-chemistry, had taken up this question at the beginning of the war. Petroleum coke was not available in adequate amounts. Lignite coke could not be graphitized even in our improved form. Finally, we found entirely new ways of largely de-ashing coal and processing it into a coke that could be readily graphitized. A large scale experimental plant being erected in the Ruhr could not, however, be started up in time.

The importance of this work, for which considerable funds were available, can be understood only if it is remembered that Germany wanted to be self-sufficient in raw materials. Of course, we were able to make only a small contribution to the extensive efforts undertaken at the time. The end of the war and free access to the crude oil of the western world have now rendered these efforts uneconomic, so they have been stopped. Since crude oil is now available in unlimited amounts, the chemical industry has lost much of its interest in coal. Moreover, its price in Europe has risen so steeply that it will probably remain of little interest as a chemical base material for a long time to come.

On the other hand, there are moves afoot, particularly in the United States, to take up these German efforts once more, using new processing technology. Although there are enough crude oil residues available for the oil-coke needed in electrode coke production, our experience of the graphitizing properties of coke continues to be invaluable and should be of interest even today for the central German lignite deposits. The processing of lignite has become interesting again also in the Federal Republic now that cheap energy at high temperature levels is available from the waste heat of the high temperature reactor.

Synthetic Rubber Problems

The new process engineering department was soon concerned with questions of rubber synthesis. Unfortunately, Hoechst itself had been pushed very much in the background in the field of acetylene and plastics chemistry which are involved in the production of synthetic rubber. This had happened in spite of the fact that Hoechst, through its collaboration with Knapsack and its 50 per cent interest in Wacker-Chemie, had provided the I. G. with practically everything of any significance in the field of acetylene chemistry.

But then Hoechst had failed to look properly after its connections with Wacker and Knapsack. The interest in Wacker, established in 1920, had not resulted in any real collaboration. The serious economic situation and the standstill of all major developments during the immediate post-war period had given rise to much jealousy. In the later I. G. period, therefore, many disputes had to be resolved by a neutral source, particularly by Bosch and, on his behalf, by Gajewski.

Relationships with Knapsack had been equally unsatisfactory. An extensive acetylene chemistry had been developed with the help of Hoechst but when the group was merged in the I. G., repeated disputes broke out between Knapsack and Hoechst. The result was that the acetone and acetic acid department in Hoechst was without a carbide basis and had to manage as best it could. When rationing was introduced, Hoechst was completely cut off from its raw material source in this field. Hoechst's research, too, had been able to earn only few laurels during the I. G. period after the departure of Paul Duden who was scientist and technical manager in Hoechst until 1932.

Suddenly, the I. G. interest centred once more on synthetic rubber. Before the First World War it had been recognized that the fundamental unit of natural rubber was isoprene whose chemical manufacture did not, however, appear rewarding at that time. But it was known that the synthesis of rubber required a substance which had to have a carbon chain with four carbon atoms and two double bonds, similar to isoprene. This substance is butadiene

$$H_2C = CH - CH = CH_2$$

which today can readily be separated from cracking gases. According to the prevailing knowledge of acetylene chemistry, to which Hoechst had made such a significant contribution, butadiene was produced from acetylene in four stages via aldol, butylene glycol and the latter's dehydration.

This procedure was followed in Schkopau and later in Hüls for the large-scale manufacture of synthetic rubber. But even in this field, in which we had achieved such a considerable success, Hoechst suffered a disappointment. In 1935, a serious fire broke out in the aldol condensation department and three people were killed. As a result, there was a clamour for the closing down of the entire department in Hoechst. Eventually, a less dangerous continuous process was developed for Schkopau.

In competition with Du Pont in America, Hoechst tried to design a different butadiene process. Using considerable manpower and material in the search, an attempt was made to add together two molecules of acetylene to give vinyl acetylene and then to hydrogenate this to form butadiene. Everyone realized that a lead of only a few weeks could win the race against Du Pont.

This two-stage method via vinyl acetylene appeared to be the quicker one. Both stages, particularly the second stage, were dangerous because of possible side reactions, and in fact they resulted in fatal accidents. When yet another chemist and his assistant were killed at Hoechst in 1935 carrying out these experiments, they were finally stopped. Human life was regarded as too high a price to pay for chemical progress.

There remained the possibility, initially pursued by Du Pont as well, of adding hydrochloric acid to the unstable vinyl acetylene instead of hydrogenating it. This was a far less dangerous route to chloroprene, a chlorine-substituted butadiene. Polymerization to give the corresponding rubber was investigated in Leverkusen. There, however, the chemists had arrived at the correct conclusion that chloroprene was not suitable for the production of car tyres. As a result, the work was not pursued. In addition, there was also a patent situation which was highly unfavourable for Hoechst. Du Pont, on the other hand, continued to work on chloroprene and developed it into an interesting material outside the actual tyre field.

Hoechst had rather more luck in the field of plastics. Starting from the earlier experiments of Fritz Klatte in Griesheim in 1912, Kränzlein, at the end of the twenties, attempted the polymerization of vinyl acetate. This work resulted in polyvinyl acetate and later polyvinyl alcohol, although always in competition with Wacker.

Until the war ended in 1945, these were the only successes that Hoechst was able to score in this field. Unfortunately, the importance of vinyl chloride, which had also been investigated by Klatte, had not been recognized in time. Perhaps permission to do such work in Hoechst had not been granted by the relevant commission. Be that as it may, these developments were certainly continued in Ludwigshafen, Bitterfeld, and by Wacker.

Hoechst had thus been excluded once more from a promising field of research. It also became more and more obvious that Knapsack and Wacker were drifting further and further away from us. The younger ones amongst us in particular realized that this was rather more serious than just an opportunity slipping away from Hoechst. Fundamentally, this development was also wrong from the larger viewpoint of the I. G. A strong and independent management should have ensured that such proud Hoechst traditions did not remain unexploited.

Our process engineering department came into contact with the

Buna problem in a totally different way. Buna had become the name for synthetic rubber because originally butadiene had been polymerized with sodium whose Latin name is natrium. As early as 1936 it had been obvious that the Buna plant being erected in Schkopau would not yet yield a satisfactory result.

It was found once again that manufacture according to the processes developed in only a few years with the help of many I. G. works presented difficulties. Basically, a great deal was still lacking. The Buna S produced by the emulsion process in Leverkusen was not suitable for car tyres without the addition of natural rubber. Its inferior plastic deformation caused difficulties when the large amounts of carbon black, which continued to be a prime condition for the adequate strength of synthetic rubber, were added on the roller mills.

The same problems arose during conversion of Buna into tyres. If the synthetic rubber had not been mixed previously with the natural material, it could be processed only with the greatest difficulty. We were asked to have a look at this situation. At the beginning, Leverkusen did not like this very much, regarding it as an unwarranted interference. But eventually we managed to establish a satisfactory relationship with our Leverkusen colleagues. In Hoechst, our first efforts were directed at incorporating the carbon black during the precipitation of the rubber emulsion, using our familiar method of phase reversal. In fact, we were able to produce a carbon black coagulate in this way. For the moment, it seemed as though we had solved the problem. Subsequent plasticization, however, was not facilitated by this process, and the initial success did not result in any further progress. Leverkusen then invented a process of degrading the brittle and hard polymer through heating.

We then turned to the fundamental problem of polymerization kinetics. Franz Patat, who had joined us in the meantime, contributed his excellent physico-chemical knowledge which he had gained under Hermann F. Mark in Vienna and Arnold Eucken in Göttingen.

Patat and I first worked on chloroprene whose polymerization could be carried out more simply than that of a mixture of butadiene and styrene. We found that polymerization was inhibited by molecular oxygen and accelerated by reduction agents like hydrosulphite. We deduced from this that the reaction could be controlled by a redox potential. In this way, a much more plastic and much more sticky polymer could be produced at far lower temperatures.

When we filed this invention for patent announcing it internally, many pursued the further development of this method for controlling Buna polymerization. In the ensuing excitement, the copyright became rather doubtful. Perhaps this was not surprising in view of the rapid progress that was being made. Eventually, this work resulted in cold rubber which could be produced at temperatures of around 5°C. Comprehensive accounts of this work have always acknowledged our invention of which we were quite proud even then. We continued to occupy ourselves with chloroprene and its processing, a subject that had been little pursued in Germany until then. We finally obtained an excellent polymer with high solvent resistance that we intended to try out in practice.

This resulted in a lively argument. Gustav von Brüning, Kränzlein and I were called one day to ter Meer who complained that we had taken it upon ourselves to send samples of the polymer to customers. He said that this was interfering with his licence negotiations with Du Pont concerning the Buna complex. The charge was, in fact, quite unjustified but for some time ter Meer did not give us any opportunity of rebutting it. It was only when his anger had subsided that he brusquely demanded to see what we had produced. When I then calmly showed him my samples and my data, his mood completely changed. He became friendly again and said: 'If your results are right and if you can confirm them I shall negotiate with Du Pont about it.'

That was my first encounter with ter Meer with whom I was to have such close dealings later on. These and similar incidents were typical of my career. It was possible to risk serious disputes in the I. G. as long as right was on your side and you were prepared to fight for your point of view. Later on, I often tried to imbue my young assistants with this principle. This practice can only be successful, however, if a company is managed expertly, honestly and loyally.

Further work on chloroprene during the war did not produce any other practical results because the need for rubber tyres claimed everybody's attention. Collaboration between Knapsack and Leverkusen was realized only after the Second World War, the former producing the monomer, and the latter making and selling the polymer.

1938 – Year of Fate

The year 1938 began sadly in Hoechst. Karl Staib, barely forty years old, suddenly collapsed at a meeting from the delayed results of a war injury, probably gas poisoning. He had come to Hoechst from Bitterfeld only in 1934 and many hopes had rested on him. In a very short time, this active, experienced man had succeeded in fusing together all the inorganic departments at Hoechst which had been leaderless for so many years. He had initiated a promising reorganization in which the inorganic factory, the solvent department, the pigment factory, the intermediate department and the pharmaceutical department worked alongside each other within well-defined spheres of activity. Only a few years previously, Hoechst had been suffering from aimless decentralization in this respect.

Staib had enjoyed everybody's respect because he was endowed with the progressive intellect that was so characteristic of life in the modern central German plants. He had probably been quietly selected as Hermann's successor.

When we gathered round his coffin in early January that year, Hermann delivered the final farewell. Many of us were conscious of the double tragedy of this event for it had become known that Hermann, then fifty-six years old, was seriously ill. His hoarseness betrayed the disease involved – cancer of the throat.

Soon afterwards, on 11 January, Hoechst celebrated the seventy-fifth year of its existence. Since the company no longer existed as an independent concern, it had been decided to forego extensive festivities. Instead, an internal celebration took place in one of the halls of the works. Hermann was only able to say a few words, and those with the greatest difficulty. The jubilee speech was made by Gustav von Brüning, the grandson of the founder, who thus presented himself as the coming man.

Shortly afterwards, in May 1938, Hermann succumbed to his disease though he continued to come to the factory right to the very end. A few days before his death, I was allowed to see him for the last time. He was probably seeking diversion and wanted to speak once more with his young colleagues. I had just been to Berlin to listen to a lecture by Bodo von Borries about the new electron microscope. When I suggested to Hermann that we should get one for the physicists in the process engineering department, he was immediately interested. Although he could hardly stand up, he at once gave instructions for the purchase of the first electron microscope for industrial use. It cost about 150,000 marks, a considerable amount of money for those days.

When the brothers E. and H. Ruska received the Paul Ehrlich prize in the Frankfurt Paulskirche in March 1970, they reminded the audience of this first order which meant so much to them. They also mentioned that this historic instrument, after more than twenty years of valuable service, could now be seen in the German Museum in Munich.

After the deaths of Hermann and Staib, a certain amount of confusion apparently reigned among the I. G. management. The view seemed to be that management recruits should come from within the big groups. No doubt, the links of the founder families with the old works also played a part as they extended far beyond their shareholding. For example, Walther vom Rath, who came from one of the Hoechst founder families and who was a deputy chairman of the supervisory board of the I. G. Farbenindustrie, still came regularly to Hoechst.

At the beginning of August 1938, I was called to see Gustav von Brüning who had taken over the inorganic factory after Staib's death. He revealed that within a year he would become the new chief at Hoechst. He also told me that I had been selected to take charge of the inorganic factory after him. This came as a complete surprise to me. I had never set foot in that part of the factory and I hardly knew any of the people who worked there.

As I was very happy in my job as manager of a department of my own creation, I don't think I put too cheerful a face on this revelation. It was decided that I should use the next twelve months to familiarize myself with inorganic production. Until the end of that time, I would have the option of returning to process engineering.

A New Loss for Hoechst

It only gradually became clear to me that I should have to abandon my scientific and technical career and join the management echelon. As usual in such cases, summer leave, which I had been about to take, was cancelled. I began to participate in meetings of the inorganic department.

Von Brüning was well equipped to lead Hoechst. He had graduated as a chemist in Heidelberg and thereafter, as grandson of the founder, had passed systematically through all the important departments of Hoechst. But on 4 October 1938, the news suddenly spread round the factory that von Brüning, in a fit of depression, had taken his life the night before in the old castle of Hoechst where he lived as a bachelor. Understandably, the I. G. management now faced a most serious problem. Three people, in the prime of life, could not easily be replaced on the management of such an important company. As a result, many weeks passed before a solution was found.

In the meantine, I had taken over the inorganic department and I soon decided that I would stay there.

A long interregnum began at Hoechst. Rumour was rife and one speculation chased another. We young people were of course vitally interested in who was to be the new Hoechst chief. We urged Jähne, with whom we had a close relationship, to make himself available. After all he had been the balancing and calming influence in Hoechst for years. He enjoyed a fine reputation throughout the entire I. G Farbenindustrie and, at fifty-nine, seemed the most suitable candidate to bridge this intermediate phase.

Because of my close relationship with him, I, too, often tried to influence him. But he rejected all my arguments. He accepted our intervention gracefully but with distinct reserve. He used to say: 'Firstly, it is none of your business and secondly, the manager of Hoechst, in view of today's complex chemistry, has to be a chemist. But, as you well know, I am an engineer.' Nevertheless, I think he would have been appointed if he had agreed to take the job.

Instead, to everyone's surprise, Carl Ludwig Lautenschläger became head of the Central Rhine group. This was surely not an easy decision for the I. G. administration and probably not for Lautenschläger either. As his closest collaborator, I was able to see for myself how difficult it was for him to carry out his duties, particularly as the Second World War was about to break out.

Carl Ludwig Lautenschläger had come to Hoechst in 1920 and had joined the I. G. management board in 1931. He had made a name for himself because of his important work in the field of diabetes. He was fifty in 1938 and had had a wide education as apothecary, chemist and doctor. He was the embodiment of the professor type engrossed in his work. Even as works manager, he was always surrounded by his books and always seemed rather unhappy when the complexity of the organizational and administrative tasks weighed down upon him and kept him away from his scientific interests.

He had been responsible for the entire pharmaceutical division in Hoechst, not an easy task. The fame of the big old pharmacy, as Hoechst was described throughout the world, threatened to pale into insignificance. As a result of the I. G. Farbenindustrie merger, Hoechst had also had a raw deal in the pharmaceutical field. All the pharmaceuticals had been assigned to the Bayer cross, and central sales had been transferred to Leverkusen. There was no real reason for this at all. It was probably one of the concessions agreed upon by the main negotiators in the I. G. merger.

The management of the world-famous pharmaceutical division, which was responsible to Division II and thus to ter Meer, included a commercial man and two scientists, one in Leverkusen and the other in Hoechst.

In view of this organization, it was inevitable that the centre of pharmaceutical activity should shift to Leverkusen. The pharmaceutical advertising of the I. G. was also largely orientated towards the Bayer cross. This meant that after the war, and after dismemberment of the I. G., the world knew very little about Hoechst and its pharmaceutical achievements. All the major pharmaceutical discoveries of the I. G. period were credited to Bayer Leverkusen.

The pharmaceutical position of Hoechst was weakened still further by the increasing estrangement of the Behringwerke. Even as far back as 1912, there had no longer been complete harmony between Hoechst and Emil von Behring. After the contracts with Hoechst concerning diphtheria sera had expired, Behring had founded his own company in Marburg. Following his death in 1916, and certainly after the end of the First World War, the Marburg factory was no longer able to continue independently. On the initiative of Leverkusen, it was absorbed in the I. G. in 1929. Hoechst was supposed to look after Behringwerke but the people who worked in Marburg preferred to look towards Leverkusen where their products were being sold.

Thus, the great Hoechst pharmaceutical tradition, which had achieved its highest attainment in the collaboration with Robert Koch, Paul Ehrlich and Emil von Behring, came to an end for the time being.

My three children in 1956 (left to right) *Ernst-Ludwig, Lotte, Albrecht*

Our house in Hoechst until 1945

Annual general meeting

The transfer of pharmaceutical sales to Leverkusen was not of benefit to the entire pharmaceutical business of the I. G. The relationship between the two world-famous pharmaceutical research establishments at Leverkusen and Hoechst was never a very happy one and the two never truly worked together. The situation did not serve their joint interests in world pharmaceutical trade in which the I. G. still had a 40 per cent share at the beginning of the Second World War.

In addition, the pharmaceutical division, because of the peculiarities of its research and development, will always be an independent domain which has little in common with the other activities of a great chemical company. Lautenschläger, who was very introverted and loath to get involved in any kind of conflict, had never been able to cope satisfactorily with this situation and was certainly not prepared to face up to it. However, then as now, such a large complex simply had no room for men afraid to fight for their position.

I am sure that I am not being unjust to Carl Ludwig Lautenschläger but I do not think that he was very happy. When he was accused at Nuremberg together with the other members of the board, it seemed that fate was pursuing him. During his detention before the trial, his only son died from a malignant disease and he was unable to do anything for him.

Lautenschläger was acquitted at Nuremberg but he soon withdrew from the world's stage. I am happy that I was able to meet him once more before he died, although he had declared after 1945 that he would never set foot in Hoechst again.

The Inorganic Empire

In October 1938, at the age of thirty-five, I finally became chief of the inorganic factory. Once again, Hoechst did nothing to smooth my path and I had to rely entirely upon my own initiative. It simply did not occur to anyone that a new manager should be properly introduced to all concerned. Hoechst's efforts in this respect were confined to a circular letter. It was left to me to make myself known in the inorganic field of the I. G. Farbenindustrie.

I waited two years for my appointment as 'procurist' [a title which under German law confers the right to a legally valid signature], because at Hoechst nobody bothered with the matter although, as manager of such a large department, I had a great many

C.Y.—7

dealings with the outside world. The chiefs of the inorganic groups in the other large companies were by then members of the board. My appointment as 'procurist' came through only when, for the first time in my life, I resorted to the ultimate protest, and asked, in writing, to be transferred from Hoechst to another of the I. G. works.

Sometimes it was almost impossible to accept the conditions in Hoechst. You simply had to fight for everything and usually seek your own salvation. But, at the end of the day, it proved a most useful experience, and when I took charge of Hoechst, I tried to bear these lessons in mind. I did all I could to promote young people in good time so that they did not waste their energies worrying over titles and honours. Many less thick-skinned people than me failed in Hoechst at that time or simply got themselves transferred to another I. G. factory.

Leaving aside these internal complications, my job was satisfying and full of interest. The inorganic factory of Hoechst consisted of the nitrogen department and the general inorganic department, with a central inorganic research laboratory. From my process engineering activities, I added coal de-ashing to the department because it fitted well into my new sphere. Walter Geisler was put in charge of this work. He was an experienced chemist who held the job until the end of the war.

The nitrogen department in Hoechst had been formed during the First World War. Like BASF, Hoechst had investigated the synthesis of ammonia and the production of nitric acid. Calcium cyanamide production was started up in Knapsack using the continuous furnace process of F. E. Polzeniuss. Ammonia was produced from the cyanamide by saponification with calcium hydroxide. At the suggestion of Wilhelm Ostwald, work had been done in Gersthofen on ammonia oxidation using platinum grids even before the First World War. This work was resumed at the beginning of the war and formed the basis of present-day processes for the oxidation of ammonia.

Ammonia production from calcium cyanamide was stopped during the war after Leuna had taken up its manufacture. Incidentally, at the end of the forties, I discovered the autoclaves rusting on a site in Knapsack. As part of the so-called Hindenburg programme, a fairly large ammonia oxidation plant with many absorption towers had been erected at Hoechst during the First World War using platinum grids with a diameter of only 50 cm. The plant provided highly concentrated – 99 per cent – nitric acid for the production of explosives.

By the end of the war, Hoechst had reached a monthly output of approximately 5,000 tons of concentrated nitric acid. This was a very large amount indeed for those days. After the war, Hoechst had turned with some success to the production of fertilizers. This involved the manufacture of large amounts of calcium nitrate which required ammonium nitrate as the mixing component.

Organizationally, the nitrogen department did not really belong to Hoechst. It was the only manufacturing activity of Division I which had been set up as a result of the development of the Haber-Bosch synthesis. During my time, this was directed by Carl Krauch. Its organization was entirely different from that of the other divisions. All the nitrogen plants were controlled centrally and fairly dictatorially from Oppau. Since everything depended upon one product – ammonia – its production dominated the activities of Oppau and Leuna. The processes were kept fairly secret even in the thirties, particularly as considerable competition had arisen throughout the world.

The processing plants, including Hoechst, were allocated their quotas of ammonia from the divisional office in Oppau. Internal competition was fierce. We knew the manufacturing techniques and the processing costs, but we did not know the price of ammonia and were thus in the dark about the total costs of our products. Costing had been separated from Division II and was carried out according to entirely different principles. Sales were in the hands of a nitrogen syndicate of which 90 per cent were owned by I. G. Farbenindustrie.

This special position of Division I dated from the time when the nitrogenous products were the pioneering substances of a new technology and, therefore, highly profitable.

Through confidential channels, I was able subsequently to get some idea of the real costs which were kept absolutely secret. They were incidentally of roughly the same order as in the companies today, after their conversion to petro-chemistry. This shows what an extraordinary degree of rationalization the new processes and the vastly increased capacities had made possible. The Leuna works, by far the largest ammonia plant in the world during the thirties, produced approximately 1,200 tons per day. Now installations are being erected throughout the world, that produce a thousand tons a day each.

A Visit to Leuna

As manager of the inorganic factory, I was in a sense involved in another world in which I came into contact with the leading men of the I. G. although, with my small Hoechst nitrogen department, my opinion did not command much weight. But Leuna was the scene of a tremendous technical development – high pressure technology and its allied fields.

My work on coal de-ashing gave me an opportunity of getting to know the imposing Leuna works rather closely. It was a wholly-owned subsidiary of I. G. Farbenindustrie, known as Ammoniakwerk Merseburg GmbH. The factory was, however, administered completely by Oppau. It took quite some time before Leuna, constructed during the First World War, achieved an independent existence. However, when coal liquefaction was added to its programme, Leuna developed a special type of chemistry. One of its major aims was the production of high grade fuel oils and lubricants. For example, starting from ethylene, which had been obtained through the hydrogenation of acetylene, Leuna eventually produced a high-grade lubricating oil.

The other major activity concerned Mersolates, detergent raw materials which were sulpho-chlorinated by ultra-violet radiation. In the Second World War, these products were to play an important role as a soap substitute sparing us a renewed encounter with the clay soap of the First World War. The Mersolates represented a pioneering development that has retained its significance to this day. Sulphoxidation, a modification of this process, again employing ultra-violet radiation, which we are now beginning to use on a technical scale, was discovered by Hoechst at that time. The actual inorganic chemistry side of my department was no less important to Hoechst. It consisted mainly of the manufacture of sulphuric acid and many of its derivatives, and also a sodium chloride electrolysis.

With the heavy chemicals, I again experienced an unhappy situation at Hoechst. Because of the inadequate technical facilities, everything was much dearer. Since the sulphuric acid plant was not located directly near the river, the materials had to be transported to and from the Main. In fact, we overcame this particular drawback only a few years ago, when we established a new sulphuric acid plant directly on the southern bank of the Main.

In the thirties, however, a great deal of ingenuity had to be used to enable us to compete with the more fortunate sites, especially Leverkusen. The roasting of pyrites in rotary furnaces, developed by Bayer, was also eventually employed at Hoechst and led to the construction of two large plants. An important product during the war was a smoke-generating acid, a mixture of chlorosulphonic acid and sulphur trioxide, that was widely used for covering military bases with a smoke-screen.

The New Electrolysis

The most interesting development was the new sodium chloride electrolysis which Hermann and Staib had acquired for Hoechst before I joined. The electrolysis of common salt on mercury anodes, originally discovered by Hamilton Young Castner in England, had been operated by Gersthofen at the beginning of the century without proper success. Essential improvements were then developed in Leverkusen. These related mainly to decomposition of the sodium amalgam on graphite.

The main advantage of this process resided in the quality of the caustic soda solution which was free from common salt and of a degree of purity suitable for rayon staple production. The amount of caustic soda needed for this cotton substitute governed the capacity of the electrolysis plant. Unlike today, in 1938 chlorine was simply a by-product obtained in excess amounts. At one time, a competition was arranged among chemists for suggestions as to how to use it.

The first large-scale plant in Hoechst to operate by the amalgam process suffered from many teething troubles which kept us busy day and night for a long time. A by-product of the process was hydrogen which, amongst other things, was used to fill airships. It was carefully freed from mercury with the aid of activated charcoal to avoid corrosion of the aluminium casing of the airships. The hydrogen was delivered to the airport through a pipeline that passed underneath the river Main. In this way, we had a close connection with the Zeppelins which, until the disaster of Lakehurst in 1937, made regular flights to Frankfurt. When the Second World War began, the hangars containing the Zeppelins were blow up.

War Economy

In September 1939, I experienced the outbreak of war for the second time in my life but this time with totally different feelings. The atmosphere in Germany was generally depressed. There was no real enthusiasm anywhere. After the danger of war had passed in 1938, because of the agreement with Chamberlain in Munich, people confidently expected that war would be averted once more in 1939. Peace in our time – these hopeful words of Chamberlain had found unreserved acclaim not only in Britain. At the age of thirty-six, I was too old to become a soldier just as I had been too young at the end of the First World War. In any case, I was occupying a responsible post in industry. In the commercial field, little changed at first. Complete material rationing had been introduced long before. It affected not only production but also repair materials, power and many other things. There was a mobilization plan at Hoechst that had been kept in a safe. When we opened it, the contents hardly surprised us.

Basically, all that was produced in Hoechst, and indeed throughout the I. G. Farbenindustrie, was necessary for the general economy both in peace and in war. Of course, there were a number of urgent priorities decreed by Berlin. The most important of these were the big new developments such as petrol from coal hydrogenation, Buna, and the light alloys.

In my sphere, only highly concentrated nitric acid was given a high priority classification. Fertilizers, on the other hand, were pushed into the background. For priority production plants, everything required was readily available. As a result, production of nitric acid in Hoechst was eventually increased to 10,000 tons per month.

The control and approval system according to which all these decisions were made, was, as in all planned economies, bureaucratic and inadequate. Anyone in a managerial position had continually to travel to Berlin to pursue his claims with the numerous officials involved.

The Hitler regime had little understanding of the need of scientific and technical endeavour, except, of course, in the fields of aeroplanes, tanks, and the like. It was therefore tremendously difficult, at any rate in the first years, to get the skilled people needed in Hoechst.

Throughout the Hitler era, including the war, this government attitude had one particular result. Hardly any building was possible in Hoechst. The site looked as antiquated as it did at the time of the I. G. fusion and during the economic crisis.

Our laughing gas enterprise in Hoechst is a good illustration of the dilletantism with which war tasks were occasionally handled. Hoechst had long been producing small amounts of laughing gas from ammonium nitrate. Used primarily as a dental anaesthetic, its output was only about ten tons per year. One day, I was asked to come to Berlin to the army ordnance department which had conceived the idea of injecting liquid laughing gas into the cylinders of aero engines. The hope was that this would significantly increase the acceleration of planes, particularly at great heights.

The ordnance department requested several hundred tons of laughing gas per month. This was many times the amount that we could produce in this short period of time. The Luftwaffe was greatly interested in the project, although there were certain justified doubts as to whether the hoped-for effect might not be achieved more readily by another route. Be that as it may, we got the order to erect four large plants. Overnight, we received contract numbers, approval for the iron, and whatever else was needed to push through a crash programme for this not entirely harmless factory.

After about six months, we were proud to be able to report the completion of the first plant. At first we didn't even get an answer from Berlin, and the amounts we had produced stayed in Hoechst. When we queried the matter, we learned eventually that doubts had arisen in the meantime concerning the use of the gas. It had been found that the containers with liquid laughing gas were not bullet proof. Laughing gas is an endothermic compound and decomposes explosively if suitably ignited.

Subsequently, the plant was never properly used. A great deal of valuable material and scarce labour had been wasted needlessly. This example made it clear to us how inadequate and bureaucratic the German war machine really was.

In my former process engineering department, much work was being done on the protection of U-boats against discovery by radar which had caused grave losses to the German U-boat fleet. But in this sphere, too, scientific and technical knowledge did not bear proper fruit.

Unexpected Turning Point

In September 1941, in the midst of the war, an unexpected and decisive turning point occurred in my career. Throughout my life, all the big events that had a personal significance, both the pleasant and unpleasant, have always happened suddenly.

One morning, Lautenschläger said to me: 'Ter Meer wants to see you at half past twelve in the Grüneburg.' Remembering my first, somewhat stormy, encounter with this man, I tried to get out of Lautenschläger what it was all about. He was evasive and the whole matter was obviously embarrassing to him. But he finally admitted that he had known for some days that I was to visit ter Meer. 'The management has taken a certain decision concerning you,' Lautenschläger said, adding that he himself had actually been against it because at the age of fifty-three, he would like to manage the works a little longer. Gradually I guessed the nature of the message that Lautenschläger was to give me. 'You see, Mr Winnacker,' Lautenschläger finished, 'I don't regard it as necessary but Mr ter Meer is going to tell you . . . and, well, you'll have to see how you can cope with it.'

I was still not a hundred per cent certain whether I had understood Lautenschläger properly but in any case, it was clear to me that nothing unpleasant would be involved.

I therefore drove to the administrative building of the I. G. Ter Meer came straight to the point: 'You are to become the technical manager of the central Rhine group after about four to five years.' That, of course, meant that I would also join the board of management. To prepare me for the new job, I was to deputize for Ulrich Haberland in the management of the Uerdingen works. Haberland had long since been selected as chief of Leverkusen and spent most of his time there. The job was to take effect immediately. After one and three-quarter years, I was to spend three months in Schkopau in order to study the operation of the new and steadily expanding Buna works.

After the two years, I was to return to Hoechst in September 1943. At that moment I would be appointed a director of the I. G. Farbenindustrie and would assume responsibility for a well-defined but far larger field. At the same time, I would become a member of the technical commission and several other important commissions of the I. G.

It was obviously a decision taken in detail by the management some time ago. Ter Meer regarded the matter as extremely urgent, and fully expected that I should start my new job in Uerdingen in a few days. When I telephoned Haberland immediately afterwards, he was surprised that he hadn't heard from me before then.

Nothing was said about my current activities in Hoechst. Deputies were appointed but basically it was taken for granted that I would also retain the management of the inorganic plant. For me Uerdingen meant an intimate acquaintance with the German railways. I travelled to Uerdingen every Monday morning, and back to Hoechst every Friday night. Saturday and Sunday were reserved for my inorganic factory. As ter Meer said to me in his dry manner: 'Herr Winnacker, you can always make sure at the weekend that things are going all right at Hoechst.'

My wife, of course, was not at all pleased with my continuous absence but in those days family life did not command a very high premium. In any case, Ernst Ludwig, my first son, was born in July so that my wife was fully occupied. Private life consisted of carrying on with your job – after all I lived in the middle of the factory – and of trying to meet the basic needs of the family. There was no leave. That was taken for granted in wartime.

Cordial Relations with Ulrich Haberland

When I came to Uerdingen the first time, Haberland had planned a minor sensation by announcing: 'My successor will arrive at eleven o'clock today.' It can readily be imagined what a guessing game this started in a factory where other people had also nursed hopes of getting my position. Haberland had asked me for an undertaking never to mention that I would be in Uerdingen only temporarily.

So, once again, I had to jump in at the deep end. It wasn't easy and would hardly be thinkable today. However, sudden and surprising personnel decisions were then the order of the day. Thanks to the support of ter Meer and Haberland, I found my feet fairly quickly. I developed most cordial relationships with the people at Uerdingen, and many of these continued for many years afterwards.

Shortly after I went to Uerdingen, Leuna celebrated its twenty-fifth jubilee. Because of the war, no official ceremonies were held. The I. G. management met in Leuna for a conference at which I represented Hoechst. The lectures were followed by a factory tour which provided an exciting impression of the site which was then still totally unaffected by war. Finally, there was an extended party in the restaurant. The guests included a large number of board members, especially the older ones who had witnessed the erection of the plant in 1916. The works was given a swimming pool as a present from the company.

There was much for me to learn in Uerdingen. The site employed some 3,250 workers and staff and belonged to the Lower Rhine group. This meant that I now also had dealings with Leverkusen and took part in the meetings of the departmental heads. I found the atmosphere totally different from Hoechst.

Bayer was still very much ruled by the spirit of Carl Duisberg who had died in 1935. He had built this giant complex from scratch, first in Elberfeld and then in Leverkusen. He lived like a patriarch in the middle of the works opposite the administration building and had imprinted his gay, sympathetic Rhineland character upon everything around him. Carl Duisberg was born near my birthplace in Barmen in 1861, the same year as my father. I had seen him only from afar as a student at conferences.

For more than forty years, Leverkusen had been fortunate enough to enjoy a homogenous leadership and, under Duisberg, its future had been assured for a long time in both technical and human respects. This meant that it had a great lead over Hoechst.

Uerdingen represented the domestic power of the ter Meer family, for it was the senior ter Meer who had sold out to the I. G. in 1926. The plant was fairly antiquated and its facilities were limited. However, it weathered the merger well, especially as it could offer some highly interesting products which commanded considerable interest during the Hitler period including the war.

Haberland's special achievement was the development of the iron oxide pigments from the by-product of the reduction of nitrobenzene to aniline. He had built up a whole pigment range and followed it with a wide range of iron oxides and certain other pigments. It was a typical feature of this I. G. circle that every leading technician had to qualify with some technical invention that could be firmly linked with his name. Connections alone did not serve advancement in the I. G.

A manager at Uerdingen, which was very much smaller than

Hoechst, was faced with a whole barrage of problems. Because of the position for which I had been selected, it was very important for me to learn how to master these problems. I was faced with many social and administrative issues which had been rendered even more complex by wartime conditions. The provision of our employees with food and clothes presented considerable difficulties. In addition, we employed many civilians from the occupied territories. In short, though not yet forty years old, I had become the father of a large family that found it hard to make ends meet.

My life at Uerdingen was demanding. Apart from the weekly railway journey, there were my responsibilities in Hoechst. The heavy air attacks on the Ruhr had begun and Düsseldorf did not escape them. I spent many hours in emergency air raid shelters at home, on stations or even in the factory. The home of ter Meer's parents in Uerdingen, where I lived, was hit by bombs, but fortunately nobody was injured.

As always in war, people drew closer together. Haberland, born in 1900 and only three years older than I, was an energetic and dynamic man. In the cellar of the administrative building, where there were a few guest rooms, or during bowling in the Uerdingen restaurant – an activity that simply had to continue even during the heaviest air attacks – a close personal relationship soon developed between us. It survived the war and, indeed, when ten years later we headed our respective companies, Farbenfabriken Bayer and Farbwerke Hoechst, it became even closer.

We were not, of course, then expecting any such development, although we forged many common plans. We envisaged the same position for ourselves after the end of the war, albeit with a few years difference because Haberland had a lead over me careerwise.

As the 'crown princes' of our two groups, Leverkusen and Hoechst, we were critical of much that was happening. Conditions in Germany were edging us closer and closer to the abyss. We were also concerned with many aspects of the I. G. and we agreed that when the war was over it would require fundamental reorganization. It seemed to us totally wrong, and it hurt us deeply, that the policy of transferring important manufacturing activities, with which we had historical links, to central Germany or even the east, was, if anything, intensified.

In view of the course that the war was taking, the military reasons that were advanced carried little conviction with us.

In any case, Berlin forged many plans that were total nonsense from both a technical and a scientific point of view. A striking example was the removal of chemical plants underground. Such a measure was doomed to failure from the start because the resulting effluent and waste air problems simply could not be solved. What might have been acceptable for mechanical plants was not reasonable for chemical processes, fusion electrolyses and other manufacturing activities.

Fortunately, most of these plans were not realized. Nevertheless, we were greatly concerned that for many years almost all investments were placed in central and east Germany while our valuable works, with their great scientific and technical potential, began to go to waste. During the dismemberment of the I. G., when we had to accept complete responsibility for the I. G. interests of our shareholders, we found clearly, and in detail, how after only a few years the assets of the old parent companies had been transferred to the east.

It was in the nature of things that Haberland and I became protégés of ter Meer, but he did not make this privileged position easy for us. The closer you came to him, the more he demanded. Ter Meer often came to Uerdingen because he still had family connections there. He would then sit in his old office which had been occupied by his father before him. Here, in his home town, he could be so pleasant that it was difficult to believe that you were sitting opposite the same man. Being the offspring of a founder family, he was a wealthy man. Intellectually, too, he radiated superiority and was not easy to get on with. Tall and slim, he often appeared unapproachable and, in fact, often was. He was undoubtedly one of the outstanding personalities of the old I. G. for which, in Nuremberg, he was ready to accept a large part of the responsibility. He was also the man to write the only concise history of the I. G. era. His family misfortune – his two grown-up children died in tragic circumstances – probably intensified his severity. Nevertheless, on close acquaintance he revealed many pleasant human characteristics.

When I returned to Hoechst after the war, our relationship had, of course, changed from the I. G. days and there was cordial friendship between us. On the other hand, ter Meer's views of past events or matters outside his jurisdiction remained inflexible and uncompromising. So far as Hoechst was concerned, he could be very unjust in his opinions. On the evening before our centenary celebrations in 1963, to which ter Meer, then a member of the Bayer supervisory board, had of course been invited, we met in the house of Leisler Kiep who had died in 1962.

Ter Meer had never been very fond of the old Hoechst hierarchy or its politics and even now, over a glass of wine, he repeated his charge that all had not been well during the negotiations preceding the I. G. merger. He probably meant that Hoechst had glossed over its real situation. The exchanges that evening became more and more heated. They ended only when the lateness of the hour forced us to break up.

When I met ter Meer in the beautifully decorated centenary hall next morning, he asked with a chuckle: 'Was it very bad last night?' which I confirmed with a frank, 'Yes, it was very bad.' This is how we all remember him – a fighter, full of character. He simply could not bear to sidestep a confrontation.

'Crown Prince' in Hoechst

In June 1943, my Uerdingen period came to an end. I moved to Schkopau for three months and lived in the 'Goldene Kugel' in Halle, where air raids were now almost a nightly event. Under the direction of Carl Wulff and Wilhelm Biedenkopf, the first Buna works in the world had been erected in record time in Schkopau. The first plants went on stream in 1938. Even from today's point of view, the production of synthetic rubber was probably one of the finest technical achievements ever accomplished in chemistry. To have experienced part of this story personally will always remain one of my most cherished memories.

When it was started up in 1938, the plant had no parallel anywhere in the world. All the various stages of the process, which had been developed in different I. G. works, were assembled here and had to be started up and maintained by the experts from these works. Schkopau was in a way the offspring of the joint efforts of all the big I. G. works. As time was a vital factor, vast sums of money and huge amounts of material were poured into the project. It was a tremendous achievement, whose full extent people can have little idea today. It must be remembered that Schkopau did not have available the petrochemical basis that the Americans were able to adopt later on. Schkopau produced the first usable material from lime and coal alone, through many intermediate stages.

My return to Hoechst was as strange as my departure in 1941. Nobody had spoken to me in the past two years about the appointment mentioned to me earlier. No matter how often I met ter Meer, no matter how many I. G. problems we discussed on trips to Berlin – even, when too tired for serious talking, we simply played cards – he never spoke a single other word concerning my personal future. At times, I found this strange but one had learned to accept these things. I folded my tent in Schkopau and returned to Hoechst in the middle of September 1943.

After I had completed my tour of inspection on the first morning of my return, ter Meer asked me to come and see him and handed me the appointment as director of the I. G. Farbenindustrie, promised two years previously to the very day. At the same time I was appointed a member of the technical commission whose meetings I now attended until the end of the war.

During the turbulent war years, this technical commission was the key body in the I. G., apart from the board of management. The investment programme had reached thousands of millions of Reichsmark, almost as much as the entire share capital of the I. G. Farbenindustrie. This is, of course, again the case with the major German chemical producers. Technical problems were the main preoccupation then, and questions of finance and economy were hardly discussed. For this reason, the position of the three divisional heads was extremely strong. Hermann Schmitz, the chairman of the board, who came from the financial side, only acted as 'primus inter pares' in the truest sense of the word.

It was, of course, a happy feeling to be appointed a director of the I. G. one week before my fortieth birthday – no mean achievement. But pleasure in my new position was increasingly overshadowed by the course of the war. Germany was being driven remorselessly to defeat. It wasn't only the big military defeats such as the lost campaign in Africa, the end of the 6th Army in Stalingrad, or the landing of the Allies in Italy which clearly showed that the Allies were moving closer to victory. The situation at home provided an equally clear pointer to the coming German defeat. The total air supremacy of the Allies and the destruction of Germany's industrial potential showed even more clearly than the battlefront that the Allies held the key to victory firmly in their hands.

Our plants had suffered heavily. The petrol plants, in particular, had been subjected to continuous attack and were partially destroyed. They could be repaired only with the greatest difficulty.

True, plans for the future were still being forged. But for what future? Nobody knew the answer to this. All of us round the conference table knew only that the situation was becoming daily more and more hopeless. In reality, the industrial leaders no longer enjoyed any freedom of decision. Normal, commercial activities no longer existed so that all the trade initiatives were paralysed. What was to be used and what was to be manufactured rested mainly with the German armaments chief, first of all Fritz Todt and later Albert Speer and his huge organization. But they, too, were enmeshed in the hopeless economic situation in which we found ourselves in those last few years. Only matters assisting the hectic war economy were of any interest to the authorities.

A large part of the effort concentrated on the production of Buna, petrol and light alloys for aeroplanes. The decisions concerning location and capacity, as well as the provision of the vast amounts of money needed, no longer lay in our hands. The huge investments in Upper Silesia and in Auschwitz must be judged against this background. No reasonable man could possibly have assumed that a viable industry could be maintained in the long term in these remote areas.

Management of German industry was greatly hampered by exaggerated secrecy. Everyone engaged on a particular project was obliged to maintain the strictest secrecy towards his chief and even towards the board of management. When we looked like meeting similar problems in the fifties, the management decided that none of our employees had the right to accept such obligations of secrecy on behalf of third parties. How can you discharge your responsibilities properly to a large company if you do not know all that is going on?

In the western works of the I. G., operations gradually came to a halt as the air attacks increased in intensity. The meetings of the technical commission now took place in the deserted Villa Bosch in Heidelberg. Only rarely were all the members present. Some were absent because their works had been bombed one or two days before, others because they were sitting in railway trains that had been delayed for half a day or more. But anyone who could, came to Heidelberg in those last months of the war.

The Heart Stops

At these conferences, the sobering figures of capacities and output clearly showed the economic collapse. They revealed how successful the bombing of Leuna, Ludwigshafen, and eventually of Leverkusen had been. These must have been particularly bitter moments for the older members, for Schmitz, ter Meer, Gajewski and even Krauch, when they saw their proud industrial empire inexorably reduced to rubble and ashes. Perhaps this is how a general feels when the situa-map tells him with brutal frankness of the defeat of his armies and divisions.

In the end, the meetings of the technical commission became farewell meetings in the true sense of the word. Ulrich Haberland was not present at the final meeting. American troops had already entered Uerdingen. Each one of us was henceforth concerned only with his own works and with the fate of the people in his charge.

I also had to think of my own family. When in March 1944, during an air attack on Frankfurt, a few bombs fell on Hoechst almost by accident, I thought the time had come to evacuate my wife and the children – Ernst-Ludwig born in 1941 and Albrecht born in 1942 – to Hofheim at the foot of the Taunus where my wife's family had a place of refuge.

Strangely enough, the Hoechst works did not suffer any extensive damage. While all around large parts of Darmstadt, Wiesbaden and Frankfurt were being destroyed, Hoechst remained almost untouched. Massive air attacks would have caused untold damage for, apart from a few small bunkers, the air defence measures for the employees and the people of the town and its surroundings were totally inadequate.

The plants along the Rhine had in the meantime also ground to a halt after the destruction of the Rhine bridge at Mülheim near Cologne, in the spring of 1944, which finally blocked shipping on the river. We now had to rely on the coal trains from the Ruhr which were allocated to us, wagon by wagon, from Berlin.

In February 1945, I visited my friends in central Germany for the last time. We drove in a big old Mercedes equipped with a gas generator and a supply of charcoal. We travelled once more to Berlin

Centenary celebration 1963 (left to right) *Carl Wurster, Fritz ter Meer, Hermann J. Abs, Richard Kuhn, Otto Hahn, the Bavarian Minister of Economics Otto Schedl*

Decision to found Buna-Werke Hüls in 1955 (left to right) *Hermann Richter, Ulrich Haberland, Hans Werner von Dewall, Karl Winnacker, Carl Wurster*

Above: *Inauguration of the American Hoechst Office in Bridgewater, New York, 1970 (left to right) Rolf Sammet, Kurt Lanz, the governor of New Jersey William T. Cahill, John G. K. Brookhuis*

Below left: *Work begins on the swimming pool in the young people's home Oberaudorf, Bavaria, 1959 (foreground) Erich Bauer (back right) Hans Bassing*

Below right: *Friedrich Müller, personnel manager, with a group of young apprentices*

via Leuna and Bitterfeld. Actually, there was little to do and even less to discuss. But I felt I wanted to see everything just once more. The Soviet armies were to the east of Berlin. Every night, the sirens wailed and bombs rained down on the metropolis, already extensively devastated. We realized it would be our turn soon. Nobody had any idea of how the military occupation would turn out. As Theodor Heuss said then: 'We do not expect mercy or benevolence from the victors.' We knew that war was a hard business and that we had not been earmarked for particularly friendly treatment. That much, at any rate, was clear to us from the little information which had reached us about the Allied conferences at Teheran and Yalta. For the rest, we tried not to think too hard about the details of what would soon enough be bitter reality. One of our greatest worries was that the commands of the retreating German army might set up their headquarters in the factory and then blow it up at the last minute.

Fortunately, we were spared this fate. We were also able to prevent, though only just, the dynamiting and other senseless measures that had been planned. Our employees held together in those days. Everyone wanted to avoid additional destruction at this late stage.

During the night of 23 March 1945, the final hour arrived. In accordance with the rota, I was in charge of the command post. The order from the I. G. headquarters in Frankfurt to shut down the factory arrived. With a heavy heart, I gave the instructions drawn up for this eventuality.

It took some hours before the heart of the factory stopped. Only a single boiler, which provided the necessary power and steam, was allowed to operate. Next morning we learnt that the first American tank units had broken through from the south and the north and were rapidly approaching the Frankfurt area.

A few days later, the victors marched into Hoechst. The history of the I. G. had come to an end.

5

From Gardener to Board Member

THE AMERICANS soon appeared. Two of them, an officer and a private, stood suddenly in my office, one of the traditional director's offices in the Hoechst administrative building. The officer threw his automatic pistol on the old mahogany desk and tore the Hitler picture, obligatory since 1933, off the wall. He then asked me to accompany him on a tour through the factory.

Silently we drove in a jeep through the intact, but lifeless, plant, past the old laboratories, factories, and the large fertilizer silos. After about an hour, the officer deposited me once more in front of my office. During the whole of the journey we had hardly spoken a word. It would not have made much sense if we had for I had great difficulty in understanding his peculiar English. The purpose of this tour never did become quite clear to me.

This first encounter, in strict accordance with the rules of non-fraternization, had taken place at the end of March. Afterwards, not a single American seemed to take any interest in either the plant or the people. Until a few days previously, everybody had still been busily at work. But now there was an unusual, strange silence. Everyone was left to his own devices. The workmen were standing about doing odd jobs but mainly waiting to find out what was to become of them and the factory. Nobody had any idea what the next day would bring. Nobody knew the American plans. Most of us, I'm sure, did not even want to think about the prospects that were facing us. The American military commander in Frankfurt resided in the headquarters of the Metallgesellschaft near the opera house where the military offices responsible for Farbwerke Hoechst were also located. These people made only occasional appearances. The Americans simply confiscated the administrative building and the restaurant. The management moved into the old factory offices where, at first, it was left entirely alone.

During the first days after the arrival of the American troops in Hoechst, public order broke down completely. The last representatives of the city's administration quietly disappeared. Nobody took their place. After a while, some men arrived in the factory and declared that they had taken over the administration of Hoechst. We didn't know any of them. Similarly, our visitors did not have any clear idea of what they were supposed to do. They disappeared again fairly quickly and were eventually replaced by a proper administration.

In the shops, the last food on the now largely empty shelves was being sold. Spontaneous looting was at first confined to the railway goods station where there were still a few wagons of food and other commodities. While the fair distribution of the meagre rations had been reasonably maintained until just before the cessation of hostilities, an unrestrained black market now developed on a scale unknown throughout the entire period of the war. Most people lived from hand to mouth, without having any idea as to where the next day's food was coming from.

The factory and surrounding parts of Hoechst had remained practically intact. To this day, there is no reasonable explanation why Hoechst and Griesheim and also the headquarters in the Grünepark, unlike all the other I. G. works, were never bombed. Talks that we had with the Americans about this much later threw no light on the matter.

There were, of course, many rumours to explain this really remarkable fact. I myself seem to remember that on the maps of the arriving troops, Hoechst had been marked as a special area. Perhaps, so we surmised, the big plant with its workshops, railheads and loading ramps had been earmarked as a kind of major rear base in case the advance of the Americans met strong German resistance.

At one time these suspicions seemed quite justified. About a week after the occupation we were ordered to evacuate the entire works and all the flats in the adjoining western part of Hoechst. We were given only a few hours. As quickly as possible, therefore, we packed our things, left the doors open as ordered, and removed what we thought was essential and what we were able to transport on carts and wheelbarrows. The faithful Belgians who had lived with us for the past three years were a great help. They obviously had experience in how to behave towards an occupation army. I myself took rather more interest in the factory which was now totally empty.

I was one of the last to leave the factory late in the afternoon, and I cycled to Hofheim where my family had been installed for some time in the pharmacy which formed part of the inheritance from my mother-in-law's family. There, my wife and the two young boys were far enough away to be safe from any interference and yet I could reach them quickly at any time of the day.

The future appeared darker than ever before. But in spite of all the hopelessness, I was not afraid. I think you feel fear only if you have time to think and, mercifully, time to think was a commodity that we did not have in the midst of the prevailing confusion. Everyone was fully occupied in ensuring that life went on the next day.

Next morning, at about five o'clock, I risked cycling once more into the empty factory, with a rucksack on my back, and made my way to my home. My reason for this was to collect a few bottles of wine which I had forgotten during our hurried departure. They were still there behind the open door. With this most valuable cargo on my back, I cycled past the lone military sentry, through Hoechst and to the house of a colleague of mine in Unterliederbach with whom I deposited my treasure.

None of us had any idea what the sudden evacuation order was supposed to mean. Once again, all kinds of rumours started to circulate. One of them claimed that Hoechst was to become the headquarters of an army on the move. This may well have been correct because the war was by no means over. Both in the east and in the south of Germany heavy fighting was still going on. Berlin had not yet fallen and more than a whole month was to pass before the armistice was finally concluded on 8 May.

Our homes were empty but nothing happened. There was no sign of the Americans. After waiting for two days, we crept back carefully and hesitantly to the factory and to our flats. At first, we did not feel very secure and behaved as though we were committing a crime. We feared that at any moment the Americans would come rudely to eject us. But nothing of the kind happened, and we gradually began to feel a little more secure within our four walls. Perhaps the Americans had realized that Germany was not able to offer prolonged resistance and that further fighting was unlikely, so that Hoechst was no longer needed as a major base.

Life in Hoechst and Frankfurt became turbulent. Thousands of former prisoners of war and workers from the occupied countries roamed through the streets. The occupation forces described them as displaced persons. They were pitiful creatures who had been forcibly removed from their native countries and made to work mainly in the armament factories.

When the Hitler regime collapsed, these displaced persons, for whom the hour of liberation and triumph had come at last, congregated in the major American administrative centres where they hoped for help to return to their homeland. The American troops looked after them as best they could, particularly as far as food was concerned. But beyond that, the soldiers could do little for them. The Americans, too, we were soon to find out, could boast of a surprisingly cumbersome bureaucracy.

Repatriation got under way very slowly. It was not surprising therefore that many displaced persons filled in this waiting period with profitable deals. It was also psychologically understandable that they wanted to pay back in kind the German people whose government had forcibly removed them from their own homes and had treated them as inferior people.

The foreign labour that had been working in Hoechst behaved with exemplary discipline. These people came and discussed their problems with us. Unfortunately, apart from good advice, we could not offer them any concrete help. Our Belgian lodgers had found refuge in the vicarage in Sossenheim. They would have liked to have stayed with us because at home they had lived under far less favourable conditions. Eventually, however, they were transported back to their homeland. We maintained contact with them until quite recently.

The main assembly point of the displaced persons, many of whom were half-starved and near collapse when the Americans arrived, was the I. G. building in Frankfurt which the military authorities had released specifically for this purpose. At first, these displaced men and women from all over the world were left largely to their own devices. It is not difficult to understand that under these circum-stances life in the I. G. building was not as sedate as in a four-star hotel, with the result that in a short period of time the furniture and entire equipment of the multi-storey building had been extensively damaged.

One day, the Americans put all these displaced persons on lorries and transported them to Hoechst within the space of a few hours. Carl Ludwig Lautenschläger and myself, who still belonged to the official works management, had been asked to go to Frankfurt at very short notice. There, the Americans gave us laconic instructions to provide all these people with beds. Nobody told us how we were to carry out this almost impossible order. Therefore, we were forced to set up emergency quarters in whatever factory building was remotely suitable.

Then our workmen were put to work repairing the considerable damage to the I. G. building. We learnt that it was to become the headquarters of General Eisenhower. To carry out this renovation, we needed Mowilith which we used to produce as a vehicle for paints. In a somewhat complicated, and doubtlessly not entirely legal manner, we obtained permission to resume production of Mowilith.

This was the first manufacturing permit that we were granted after the arrival of the Americans. We were overjoyed. Was this the first gleam of hope on the horizon? Would new production be approved soon?

We did not realize then just how greatly such hopes were divorced from reality. At that time, the American military authorities still had strict orders to prevent any resumption of work in the factory. Non-cooperation between Americans and Germans was to continue for a very long time.

During the first weeks and months of the occupation, we did not know much about what was happening in the world outside. On our people's radio, all we could hear was the news from an occupa-tion forces transmitter. There were no newspapers, as the first, and for a long time the only newspaper – the *Frankfurter Rundschau* – did not appear until 1 August 1945. On the notice boards, which had previously been filled with Hitler announcements, there were now the proclamations of the occupying power, such as the Four Power Declaration of 5 June 1945 in which it was laid down that Germany should accept all demands that might be made upon it now or later.

We also heard little about the capitulation on 8 May. So far as we were concerned, the war had finished some time ago. The blackout had been lifted in the first days of April after almost six years of war. Indeed, that was the only redeeming feature of those dark days. It is difficult to realize today how little the German population, with a few exceptions, was informed about the major events in the world outside. Only a few knew anything about the signing of the United Nations charter at San Francisco on 26 June 1945.

The arrival of thousands of displaced persons quickly changed the quiet atmosphere of Hoechst. There was an increasing number of incidents and riots. The tall American military policemen watched all this with understandable, though sometimes frustrating, equanimity. They confined themselves to controlling the almost non-existent traffic, and to ensuring absolute observance of the nightly curfew.

A number of crimes were committed during this period. A factory guard was beaten to death; two sons of a Hoechst lawyer were murdered. Compared with the far more numerous crimes elsewhere, and the general misery all around, these events, however terrible they were for the families concerned, might have appeared comparatively insignificant to the outsider. But they caused a considerable sensation in Hoechst because its inhabitants had hardly suffered during the war years. Only a few had died as a result of bomb attacks. Just before the fighting stopped, there had been a few casualties from dive-bombing and the senseless use of the Volkssturm ['people's army' of children and old people equipped with rifles and makeshift anti-tank weapons]. Mainly, however, Hoechst was a part of Frankfurt that, externally anyway, had hardly been affected by the war. This was why its inhabitants felt so deeply about what was happening now.

On 30 April 1945, the large number of displaced persons housed in Hoechst prepared to celebrate 1 May. While the D.P.s were thronging through the town in groups, some of them discovered a neglected tanker in the Hoechst railway goods station. It contained fuel for V2 rockets. The fuel was a violet mixture of methyl and ethyl alcohol. News of the discovery spread like wildfire. More and more people arrived at the station in order to get some of the liquid which was mixed with sugar of which large amounts had been stored in Hoechst. It was with this drink that the D.P.s celebrated the eve of the first peaceful May after six years.

When 1 May dawned, the camp at Hoechst was a dreadful sight.

Its occupants were convulsed with the agonies of methyl alcohol poisoning. Rapid medical aid, in which Lautenschläger personally participated, helped to save the majority but even so more than a hundred died a painful death. They were buried in a common grave in the cemetery at Sossenheim.

This disaster at long last alerted the American military police who, until then, had been distinguished by their passivity. As suddenly as they had arrived, the D.P.s were carried off again to another destination. Fortunately, the works management of Farbwerke Hoechst was able to establish beyond doubt that the rail tanker had not been their responsibility. Otherwise there might well have been serious consequences for the company.

Gradually, demoralization also became evident at the Hoechst factory. Until then employees had been fairly disciplined, but the collapse of the state now engendered an understandable breakdown of the social order. Accepted moral values had lost their validity and sacred ideals and principles had been dishonoured with the result that conventional concepts of property and ownership became blurred also. People felt betrayed by the state and its leadership which had collapsed so dismally and they felt justified in seeking recompense for what they regarded as legitimate private claims.

It was every man for himself, and people simply appropriated what could not be obtained normally and legally. In order to confine theft and looting to tolerable limits, we organized an unarmed works patrol which covered the site day and night.

The settling of accounts with the vanquished Hitler dictatorship did not halt in front of our factory gates. Actually, there was little cause for such inquisitions within the Hoechst factory. Even when National Socialism was at its zenith, the management had largely succeeded in keeping party politics out of the company's affairs. Many people who were politically or racially at risk were able to work in Hoechst until the end of the war. Those in power did not succeed in laying their hands on them. Moreover, Hoechst had not taken part in certain types of particularly important war work.

Nevertheless, there was a great deal of human disappointment in those days. The temptation to woo those who had always been against the National Socialist state was overwhelming. Suddenly we found in our ranks many a resistance fighter whose opposition to the regime had, until then, been precious little in evidence.

I found it particularly unjust that soldiers returning from the front or from the prisoner of war camps should be treated as though they had always been passionate adherents of National Socialism. This attitude, which affected many innocent people, caused a great deal of bitterness. Later, it cost a great deal of time and effort to erase these memories.

Anyone who had joined Hitler's party before 1933 was dismissed on the spot at the direction of the military government. Such steam-roller methods not infrequently affected those who had long since been cured of their illusions about National Socialism because of developments since 1933. Many of them had recognized the true character of the regime, the road to disaster, far more clearly and far earlier than others who joined the party at a much later date. Therefore, this measure hit many who had already turned back. In addition to their dismissal, they also fell victim to looting and humiliation.

The management, too, succumbed to much human weakness and disunity in those days. Unpleasant and sterile discussions, which seldom sprang from true political motives, suddenly developed. Sometimes they served only to settle personal scores. In addition, of course, the older and younger generations reacted completely differently to the collapse and its consequences.

Understandably, the older generation found it all much harder to take. For many of them, the world was no longer in its proper place. Their reactions frequently reflected total helplessness, often border-ing on despair. Many of the older generation in Germany sought release from their anguish in suicide. We younger people were, of course, faced by the same uncertain future but, still, we felt that our lives were ahead of us. Certainly, we were not prepared to resign so readily.

Anyone who had occupied a leading position in the Hoechst works of the I. G. Farbenindustrie was subject to many investigations and interviews. The questions mainly referred to conditions and happenings in Hoechst. Such cross examinations were unpleasant but harmless so long as they remained factual. After all, Hoechst had not played any role in the National Socialist war economy. On the other hand, it was not easy to convince the suspicious Allied investigation officers of this. In particular, they could not understand the German practice of describing all sorts of measures as a 'secret command matter', which prevented even the management of a company from knowing what was going on.

The cross examination also probed into the activities of the remainder of the I. G. Farbenindustrie which had nothing to do with Hoechst. For example, right at the beginning, we were cross-examined individually for days on end by four officers – American, French, British and Russian – about our contribution to the preparation of a gas war. This is how we learnt for the first time about the work on phosphates carried out by Gerhard Schrader and his collaborators in the main scientific laboratory in Leverkusen. Apart from the plant protection agents, now indispensable and manufactured throughout the world, this work had also yielded compounds that could have been used as poison gases and agents of mass destruction.

As the war was still going on, the Allies were looking feverishly for people who knew about these activities, particularly about production and storage. They told us during these interviews that Germany had planned to use these gases in the last desperate phase of the war. Even now, the danger still existed. Fortunately for all of us, the gas was never used.

This explains why, towards the end of March 1945, Germany toyed with the idea of clearing out everybody from the entire area east of the Rhine. Perhaps the German leaders really did have the intention of starting such a gas war at the last moment. But probably it would never have come to this because the troops of both sides were far too intermeshed by then.

Many people visited Hoechst during this time. The military government had instructed us to provide all visitors with whatever information they required. They did not even have to identify themselves. Very often there were foreign technicians, including chemists and industrialists, in the uniform of one of the armies of the Allies. Some were rather arrogant, others excessively affable. But all wanted to profit as much as possible from our technical knowledge.

There were, however, a few pleasant exceptions and these I like to recall even today. There was, for example, the former president of the American Hooker company, R. Lindley Murray of Niagara Falls. He took from his briefcase a whole batch of drawings, spread them across my table and asked me to agree to a detailed exchange of knowledge about the electrolysis cells of Hooker and Hoechst. In fact, we did come to a friendly arrangement about this. During an American trip that I undertook ten years later as chairman of the board, I paid a visit to Murray. We both recalled with pleasure the fair discussion that we had in 1945. Murray's company eventually operated an electrolysis plant constructed by Uhde and based on our principle.

When the final boundaries of the occupation zones had been fixed, the Americans vacated the central German I. G. works which they had conquered. The people in charge there were allowed to escape to the west with their families. Many colleagues from Bitterfeld, with whom we had been on such friendly terms, therefore suddenly arrived at Hoechst. Unfortunately Erich Bauer, who had just taken over the works management of Bitterfeld and had felt it his duty to stay with his employees, was absent. He had to pay for this attitude with almost two years in prison, having been arrested shortly after the Russians occupied the factory. When he was released, he managed to escape to the west. He was a member of the Hoechst board from 1956 until his death in 1969.

We were glad to have these reinforcements from Bitterfeld for we all nurtured the hope that we might soon start producing again. The Bitterfeld electrochemists were the prodigal sons returned in more than one sense for they had originally left Griesheim near Frankfurt, the cradle of electrochemistry, to work in Bitterfeld. We forged many optimistic plans with them. We discussed, for example, the possibility of a phosphorous plant which was eventually realized in Knapsack, as this offered a more suitable site.

All our ideas, however, remained wishful thinking. The American occupation forces had no intention of granting us permission to carry out any kind of production.

This would, of course, also have contradicted the secret instruction JCS 1067, which had been imposed upon the American commander-in-chief for Germany. According to this instruction, Germany was to be treated not as a liberated but as a conquered, hostile nation. This document, which was valid up to 15 July 1947, stated: 'You should not undertake any steps that (a) aim to restore the economy of Germany or (b) would help to maintain or promote the Germany economy.'

We did not then know anything of these harsh war aims of the

Allies and continued to ask ourselves every day what tomorrow would bring. In July 1945, all these uncertainties ceased.

Dismissal

On 5 July, the works management was ordered into one of our conference rooms. The doors were flanked by American guards and the conference room had been decorated with the stars and stripes. An American colonel was seated in the centre. When we were all assembled, he rose and read a document: 'Law No. 52 for the freezing and control of assets: The general specification No. 2 of this law states: "The entire management of the I. G. Farbenindustrie, including the supervisory board, board of management, directors and other office-holding or non-office holding persons who alone or jointly are empowered to act on behalf of the I. G. Farbenindustrie, or to sign in its name, are herewith dismissed from their positions and relieved of their entire powers regarding the company or its assets." '

The whole ceremony did not last longer than twenty minutes. The regulations were to come into force at once. The military government took over control of the I. G. Farbenindustrie. We were asked to remain in office for the time being, but we realized that this was only an act of grace.

Subsequently, the handover of the Hoechst works was re-enacted for the American newsreels. As we left the room, American troops marched into the works once more and hoisted their flag. The film production of the occupation was beautifully stage-managed.

Although we had all been dismissed, once again, nothing seemed to change at first. On 15 July, I was even driven to Ludwigshafen in an American military vehicle in order to talk to Carl Wurster, the manager of the Upper Rhine group, concerning possible supplies of BASF ammonia to Hoechst. This was my first opportunity after the collapse to meet one of my colleagues from the I. G., and it was highly welcome.

Apparently, the Americans had little idea of the exact occupation zone boundaries. The instructions that I carried were addressed to an American authority in Ludwigshafen. In the meantime, BASF had been occupied by a French unit because the town belonged to the French zone of occupation.

While I was at Ludwigshafen, the Americans finally dismissed the entire management of Hoechst. I learnt about this only when I arrived in my office next morning. It was 16 July and I remember this date so well because it was my father's birthday, an event that we always celebrated in our family.

At the entrance to the works, people were crowding in front of the notice announcing the dismissals. My name was on the list. Because I had been at Ludwigshafen, nobody had been able to inform me personally. At first, my inclination was to leave the factory without a murmur. But then I thought better of it. It might well be that this dismissal could have some legal consequences in the future and I therefore insisted on getting a personal notification as well.

Max Bockmühl, until then the leading scientist in the pharmaceutical division, had been appointed chief of the factory. I telephoned him and asked him to try and get me an official note of dismissal. Bockmühl, who clearly was unhappy in his new office and who occupied it only for a short period of time, responded only gingerly to my request. He did, however, promise to see what he could do for me. In fact, I was called to the American control officer in the coloristic department a few minutes later, and was personally dismissed on the spot. German chemists, who had earlier been responsible to the dismissed management, now acted as interpreters for the new rulers.

I protested against my dismissal both verbally and in writing. Of course, this served little purpose and I did not really expect that my protest would change my position in any way. After the brief dismissal ceremony in the office of the control officer, I went into my office in the inorganic department. Here I took leave of my close collaborators. My secretary, Tilly Dörr – she was later to work for me again when I became chairman of Farbwerke Hoechst – and Adam Blum, my personal assistant, both accompanied me to the door. Then I jumped on my bicycle and rode home.

These were the days of the Potsdam conference between Churchill (and later Attlee), Stalin, and Truman who had succeeded President Roosevelt after his death on 12 April 1945. We knew little about this conference which took place from 17 July until 2 August and which determined the future of Europe for a long time to come. Only later did we learn that the Allies had by no means been united at this meeting.

We Germans were surprised and alarmed at the decisions that

had been taken at Potsdam. The implications of these decisions only dawned on us slowly. In the Allied newspapers produced for us, there were few hints of the Allies' real intentions or of the differences of opinion that had arisen in Potsdam. One day before the Potsdam conference began, the first atomic bomb was exploded in the desert in New Mexico. On 6 August, an atomic bomb was dropped on Hiroshima and three days later another on Nagasaki. It precipitated the end of the war in the Far East five days later.

All Connections Severed

The American control officers and the new works management were not satisfied with just my dismissal. I soon received a letter, signed by two of my former colleagues, in which I was given notice to quit my works flat immediately. In contrast, however, to the practice applied to other directors, my bank account was not immediately blocked. Some time previously, the Americans had somehow got hold of the staff lists but apparently they were not up to date. As I had been appointed a director only in 1943, my name was obviously not on the list. I was therefore able to withdraw my money from the bank and hide it in the damaged ceiling of our flat in Hofheim. House searches and a great deal of other chicanery caused us many anxious weeks. The vicarage in Sossenheim, however, my wife's home, remained a welcome sanctuary because on its door was the 'off limits' sign, a much coveted distinction at that time. The Americans always observed this injunction scrupulously.

With my dismissal, all connections between Hoechst and myself were severed. My last days at Hoechst had already been marked by unhappy events but the news that now occasionally reached me from the factory did not fill me with any enthusiasm to return. As always at such times, those who could be manipulated, or who were prepared to fawn and court the favours of their new masters, rose to the top. Frequently you discovered that people with whom you had worked for many years no longer recognized you in the street.

Internal disputes and jealousies in the factory increased. At first, the dismissals had been confined to leading members of the works management. Later, many hundreds of ordinary employees also got the sack. This first wave of de-nazification was initiated by the American military government who intended it to be a punishment and a necessary lesson to the vanquished German people. It is now well known that no particular distinctions were made during this action. In this period of general upheaval, the desire for retribution hit not only the genuinely guilty but also numerous people who, though they had nominally been party members, had never derived any advantage from this fact.

Later, the German authorities pursued de-nazification. The result was a large number of trials in which there was no shortage of either denunciations or injustice. Consequently, the first months after the war caused a great deal of internal dispute in Hoechst and destroyed all mutual confidence. All these events are deeply ingrained upon the memory of both my wife and myself. At the same time, however, we remember thankfully that both inside and outside the factory, but particularly in our immediate personal neighbourhood, there were many people who loyally stuck by us in those days even though it was hardly a wise thing to do in the atmosphere of the time.

Perhaps one of the hardest measures for the population was the requisition of houses and flats. Evacuation orders arrived daily in the houses around the I. G. building in Frankfurt and also in parts of Hoechst. Sometimes people weren't even given enough time to collect their most essential belongings.

In a few weeks, a serious housing shortage developed in Hoechst. In comparison with the miseries of the German-occupied areas during the war, this was perhaps insignificant but even so, it was felt to be an unnecessary piece of chicanery. Incidentally, the requisition orders were issued at random and without regard to the personal situation of the families involved and irrespective of whether they were members of the party or not.

Only many years later, when during my travels I got to know the United States with its generous, if rather robust, people, did I begin to understand that many of the measures enforced at that time did not appear particularly harsh to the Americans. I found, for example, that instantaneous dismissal of leading industrialists is still practised in America today. Similarly, when a new administration is elected, it is not unusual for some of the previous employees to be replaced from one day to the next. Moreover, many of the orders issued rather nonchalantly by the American military government were then carried out by subordinate German offices with truly teutonic zeal. This trait and the curious German enjoyment of a kind of self-destruction unnecessarily increased the effect of many of the regulations issued by the occupation authorities.

In the first days following my dismissal, I felt that the most important thing would be to find some kind of job. It would have been intolerable for me to sit about in our small flat doing nothing, particularly as this was the wrong moment to worry about the future. I was forty-two, in good physical condition, and did not consider myself one of the old brigade. I also took some comfort from the fact that I was sharing the fate of millions of other Germans.

It was difficult to look at the future with imagination and optimism. Indeed, it was some time before I was again in a position to make serious plans. It was, therefore, a good thing that the problems of everyday life fully occupied us for the time being.

Fortunately, the military government in the American zone took no further interest in those whom it had dismissed from companies and offices. I could look for a new job without constraint. Since my wife and the two boys had found refuge in my grandfather's pharmacy in Hofheim, I joined them there. Through the help of some friends, I found another job only a few days after my dismissal: I became a gardener at Marxheim near Hofheim.

My new employer was Heinrich Wichmann, a wonderful man. About my age, he came from Holstein in north Germany, and had once worked for a short time in Hoechst. He later opened a small nursery garden which flourished after the war when fruit and vegetables were very much in demand.

Wichmann, a devout protestant, had belonged to the professing church which had strongly opposed Hitler. As a result, there were many animated discussions in the nursery, as everywhere else in Germany. Who was to blame for what had happened? Could we have prevented it if we had taken a greater interest in politics? Many questions were asked, many answers given.

I continued to work as a gardener for almost two years until the spring of 1947. With me was another former I. G. employee who had also been dismissed from the headquarters in Frankfurt. From morning till evening, summer and winter, we worked in the beautiful Taunus countryside, whatever the weather. The salary was not very much, but in any case that was not important. I still had a little bit of money, which then finally lost its value after the currency reform in 1948.

During my days as a gardener, I acquired a considerable respect for the gardening profession, which calls for stout characters and has a great deal in common with farming. But unlike farmers, who can retreat to the stable or the barn when the weather is bad, a gardener must work in the open, whatever the weather. Anyone who knows what to look for, will recognize in old gardeners the rheumatism acquired over many years of outdoor work. In spite of the heavy physical work and the many domestic worries, I couldn't really complain as I was so very fortunate to be able to live with my family, which meant I was spared many of the anxieties that additionally burdened many of my friends.

Herr Wichmann once came to visit my house in Königstein. He inspected all the fruit trees very carefully and eventually said: 'I think Farbwerke Hoechst has planted some very bad trees here.'

In view of the Allies' intention of preventing us from ever again carrying out our profession, I seriously thought at that time of setting up my own nursery and market garden. It was by no means clear whether the Allies would allow us ever again to carry out industrial chemistry. Every day we were reminded of the danger that Germany presented to the peace of the world. Eager proponents of re-education, both from home and abroad, spent a great deal of energy in producing evidence to show how nasty and undemocratic we Germans had always been. Our whole history showed, so they claimed, what little faith could be placed in us. Frederick the Great, Bismarck, and Hitler were all lumped together for the purpose of this argument. Because of Germany's responsibility for the outbreak of the Second World War – which is not disputed – the old legend of Germany's sole guilt for the First World War was also resuscitated although it had long been disproved by neutral historians. In the long run, many of us began to lose confidence and asked ourselves seriously whether everything in our history and our culture, extending over so many centuries, had really always been only negative and damnable.

The I. G. is Requisitioned

In November 1945, the control council set up in the meantime by the four occupying powers issued law No. 9 concerning the confiscation and control of the property of the I. G. Farbenindustrie. The preamble made it clear what the aims of the victor powers were: 'In order to eliminate any future threat by Germany to its neighbours or to world peace, the Allies decree the dismemberment of the I. G. Farbenindustrie.' The decree provided for the handover of industrial plant and property by way of reparations; the destruction of all plant used exclusively for war purposes; the distribution of ownership rights in the remaining industrial plants; the liquidation of all cartels; and control of all research work and the entire production programme.

The Allies followed entirely different methods in the treatment of the I. G. in their respective zones. The Russians immediately attempted to convert the very modern I. G. works in their zone into nationalized industries, as was the custom in the east. The British and the French subjected the works in their area to strict control but did not interfere with their uniform structure.

The Americans, on the other hand, completely reorganized the I. G. works in their zone with almost missionary zeal. These works mainly involved those of the Hoechst group – Hoechst, Griesheim, Offenbach, Cassella, Kalle, Behringwerke and the entire I. G. complex in Bavaria. The American officers and civilians devoted themselves to this task in the firm conviction that the I. G. Farbenindustrie, too, had been an unreserved supporter of Hitler. Many Americans also regarded the administration of enemy property as a suitable field for economic experiments intended to result in the destruction of German economic power.

The London Agreement of 8 August 1945 concerning the punishment of people who had committed war crimes and crimes against peace or humanity, formed the basis of the war trials held from November 1945 to October 1946 in Nuremberg, as a result of which some twelve of the main actors in the Hitler drama were sentenced to death. The trial was reported in full detail in the press and on the radio. The German people were given a sombre picture of the brutality and moral decrepitude of the leading men of the regime. All of us who heard these terrible details for the first time were deeply shaken by the dreadful crimes that had been committed in our name. At the same time, there was almost daily news of the terrible consequences of the unconditional surrender. I remember, for example, the extradition of German prisoners of war to the

Soviets, the dismantling operations in the occupation zones, the confiscation of German property and finally, and probably worst of all, the expulsions from the eastern territories.

The unusually cold winter of 1945–6 further intensified the plight of our occupied country. For most of us it was a sad Christmas. Nevertheless, in spite of all the bitterness of the situation, we experienced a feeling of liberation. War and dictatorship were ended for ever. Unlike many Germans, I was lucky enough to have a roof over the heads of my family. Also, most of my relations lived in the west, so the random division of Germany hardly affected us.

In the following year, there was a certain change in the occupation policy, at any rate so far as the Americans were concerned. The American Secretary of State, James F. Byrnes, made an important speech in Stuttgart on 6 September 1946 in which he declared: 'Peace and prosperity are inseparable and our peace and our prosperity cannot be bought at the price of the peace and prosperity of another country. We shall oppose harsh and revengeful measures that are an obstacle to true peace.' Byrnes further stated that the Americans would not extract reparations from current production and would not agree to reparation payments that exceeded the conditions agreed to at Potsdam.

This speech probably gave expression to the voice of those numerous Americans who found it incompatible with the liberal ideals of their country to exploit a defeated people for all time and to destroy its economic power. Byrnes did not gain the sympathy of the east with his speech, particularly as he expressly stated that the eastern German territories had been handed to the Soviet Union and Poland for administrative purposes only until affairs were finally regulated in a treaty. Incidentally, Byrnes came from the southern states of America. He lived in Spartanburg, South Carolina, where our Trevira factory was erected in 1965.

We felt that Byrnes's speech was a ray of light in a situation whose apparent hopelessness can hardly be imagined today. It heralded a historic turning point which finally led to the merging of the American and British zones of occupation.

Although the circumstances of my life in those first few months were reasonably tolerable, particularly as I was busy working, I was beginning to feel that I wanted to get back to work in my own field. During the long winter evenings, and the days when the weather was simply too bad to go out, I started to occupy myself once more with chemistry. As all my books and data had been lost, I wrote down whatever I could remember from my past activities. I described processes and prepared sketches of chemical processes with which I had become familiar during the interesting years of the I. G. era. Now and again I met friends and colleagues who had experienced the same fate as I, and we refreshed our memories of these exciting chemical activities.

At that time I acquired the habit of writing a great deal by hand. I filled hundreds of sheets in this way, adding to the information all the time. Later on, I drafted by hand all the important lectures and speeches that I had to give. The same applies to this book.

I was always grateful when I met people who had not forgotten me. Shortly after my dismissal, I was visited by Wolfhart Siecke of Lurgi, the well-known company which is engaged in the construction of chemical plant. I knew Siecke from my days in Hoechst and we spent much time both in his home and in his offices at Lurgi discussing plans for the future construction of chemical plant. Siecke suffered from chronic arthritis, which soon rendered him bedridden. He died long before the beginning of the reconstruction to which he could have made such an enormous contribution.

My contact with Siecke was the result of a suggestion from Alfred Petersen of the Metallgesellschaft, with whom I was later to enjoy a close friendship. Petersen had suffered racial persecution; from 1945 to 1949 he officiated as president of the Frankfurt Chamber of Commerce. During those difficult weeks and months, he proved a real tonic to me, although the talks with Lurgi at so early a date were not likely to lead to any concrete results.

My former colleague Ernst Weingärtner put me in touch with the Hanser publishing house in Munich. Carl Hanser suggested the publication of a work on chemical technology to us. The resulting long association with him and the continuous exchange of ideas was one of the most positive gains of the immediate post-war period.

At first, we had few facilities for the preparation of such a work. We had no access to German or foreign literature and as we had practically no contacts, it was almost impossible to find authors for the individual subjects. Nevertheless, we painstakingly created the concept of a five-volume handbook in which contributions from forty to fifty experts were to be amalgamated into a comprehensive description of chemical technology.

Such a handbook presents a great deal of work for little material reward. Nevertheless, work on this handbook on chemical technology, started under such unusual circumstances, has provided me with a great deal of pleasure throughout the whole of my life. It meant that I had to occupy myself continuously with technical details and that my knowledge was always up to date.

I worked on the handbook in the only living room available to us at Hofheim. The remaining part of the comfortable but overcrowded apartment was lived in by a related family. All family life took place around my desk. But this did not worry me in the least – nor did my two little boys who manoeuvred between my desk and chair legs with their wooden train.

When the first volume of the handbook of chemical technology appeared in 1949, I experienced all the feelings of an author – from pride in a work finally completed, to the anxious anticipation of both the critic's verdict and the echo of the scientific world. In fact, both were remarkably positive, especially since I thought certain chapters rather incomplete. Ten years later, when the second edition was published, conditions were far more favourable. Extensive journeys and a thorough reading of all the relevant literature had once again brought us up to date with the latest advances in chemical technology. Since Weingärtner, the co-editor, had gone abroad long before the first edition was completed, I enlisted the services of Leopold Küchler, the manager of the laboratory for applied physics in Hoechst.

In those first years after the war, my work on the handbook was like a lifeline and helped to restore my self-confidence and professional existence. I frequently return to it because the rapid change and progress in technology mean that a reference work of this kind is never completed. New fields are continuously being opened up and new possibilities are for ever being discovered. Now, when I am moving from active professional life into retirement, I am greatly looking forward to the publication of the third edition.

Excursion into Food Chemistry

Heinrich Vorkauf, my student friend from Berlin, suggested that rapeseed, of which a great deal was being cultivated in agriculture and in gardens, might be used for nutritional purposes. An engineering friend and I constructed an extruder and we used this to help the peasants to extract the oil from the rapeseed. It was highly suitable as an edible oil. As a reward, we were given some of the substance we had helped to produce.

We were allowed to retain the rapeseed cake because the peasants had no use for it. After a few experiments, we soon found out how to remove the bitter elements from the cake by washing it with hot water at a given pH value. The result was a highly palatable protein product which could be used for the preparation of sweets and other foodstuffs and also as a meat substitute.

Anyone who has experienced the calorie shortage during those years can readily imagine the eagerness with which we pursued this excursion into foodstuffs chemistry. The first products were manufactured in the washhouse and they greatly enriched our menu. My wife, with her immense culinary ability, was able to turn our rapeseed protein into a succession of exciting, if unconventional, dishes.

I wondered whether our discovery could not be used on a larger scale. I turned to Willibald Diemair, the manager of the food inspectorate in Frankfurt-Niederrad, whom I had known from the war. He had helped us improve our works canteen by means of deep-freeze and preservation procedures. Diemair established a contact for me with Lacroix, the delicatessen firm, which was not far away. At Lacroix, there was considerable excitement at the prospect of obtaining valuable protein from rapeseed. I was able to conduct large-scale experiments in the bottling plant, and these finally resulted in a small production unit. In the spring of 1947, I gave up my gardening activities and joined the company for a short time.

Eugen Lacroix, head of the company, was not only an internationally famous cook but also an educated and much-travelled man. He taught me a great deal about culinary enjoyment and the significance of international cooking. I remained in close contact with him even after I had become chairman of the board of management of Farbwerke Hoechst. We celebrated his seventieth birthday in 1956 in the Park Hotel in Frankfurt when he himself took over the management of the kitchen.

Protein production from vegetable residues was a profitable

business. We carried on with it until well after the currency reform and we even interested in it an oil mill in the lower Rhine area. The only difficulty was that rapeseed protein, because of its chemical constitution, deteriorated fairly quickly. Nevertheless, rapeseed chemistry made a considerable contribution to solving our personal nutritional problems. Since then, the production of meat-like foodstuffs from vegetable protein has become a large-scale industry in the U.S.A.

After my dismissal, I had no kind of contact with Hoechst. I therefore made increased efforts to maintain a link with my friends in Leverkusen. Ever since 1945, I had visited them at short intervals, whenever the occasion arose. At first, I travelled in empty goods trains or on lorries. Later I used the overcrowded passenger trains.

The situation in Leverkusen was far more encouraging than in the American zone of occupation. With only a few exceptions, the British control officer had allowed the old management to remain in office and he did not interfere much in production matters. He lived in Leverkusen and was, therefore, accessible to the German works management at any time. Ulrich Haberland had remained as head of Leverkusen. All the I. G. works in the British zone had been integrated in the Leverkusen administration so that they could continue to maintain their economic links.

I was always received cordially in Leverkusen and allowed to stay in the restaurant which had not been destroyed and, for those days, offered an extraordinary degree of comfort. Each guest was given a bottle of wine and was able to have a bath, something that we had had to abandon in our crowded home in the Taunus. I met up with old colleagues and friends and returned laden with gifts of sweeteners, drugs, and even a new bicycle tyre – then articles of rare value.

In Leverkusen, I learnt something about the fate of the I. G. Farbenindustrie and its management. The members of the former I. G. board had gradually been arrested. With remarkable tenacity, the Americans were preparing trials against the leaders of German industry in which the other Allies did not participate. The first of these three industrial trials began in Nuremberg in August 1947. The I. G. Farbenindustrie, the Flick Group, and Krupp of Essen were in the dock. We followed the trial of the I. G. with passionate interest. After all, it was our own affairs that were being thrashed out there, even if I personally had had the good fortune not to be among the accused. The procedure followed in these trials did not conform to German justice since both the charge and the sentence were based on retrospective legislation.

The most serious charge was the preparation of aggressive war. Much to our satisfaction, all the accused were declared innocent in this respect. The other charges were theft and plunder and the employment of forced labour. Some of the accused, including Fritz ter Meer, were sentenced to long periods of imprisonment although these sentences were later commuted. A large number of the accused were declared innocent on all counts. The sentences were promulgated at the end of July 1948.

At the Duisburger Kupferhütte

By 1948, I had been living for more than a year in the British occupied zone where, in May 1947, I had accepted a position of chemist at the Duisburger Kupferhütte. My eighteen-month stay at the Kupferhütte was extraordinarily important to me. However humble my position, and however restricted my activity compared with earlier days, I was at long last back in the chemical industry after my years as gardener, author, and private inventor. Much of the uncertainty that had hung over my life disappeared. I felt that I was back on firm ground, able to build a new career on this basis with comparative peace of mind. On the lower Rhine, the scientific world was re-forming.

In Leverkusen, we listened to Max Planck who was ninety years old and unable, because of a circulatory collapse, to complete his lecture. He died soon afterwards. Otto Hahn, who had received the Nobel prize in Stockholm in 1946 for the discovery of nuclear fission visited us in Duisburg. In his jocular manner, he told us how he had been received at the Swedish royal court as a British prisoner of war.

Ulrich Haberland, Otto Bayer, the scientific manager of Leverkusen, Karl Ziegler, the manager of the Mülheim Coal Research Institute, Burckhardt Helferich and Theo Goldschmidt formed the core of a reconstituted Society of German Chemists. It held its first annual meeting in Bonn in 1947, an event greatly welcomed by all of us.

My wife and I had been right to avoid any fundamental decision in these first stormy years. Although I was not exactly overwhelmed by offers of jobs, now and again somebody from home or abroad did solicit my services. Many of these approaches were quite tempting in the circumstances of the time. But we had agreed at home that I should not commit myself so long as housing problems, a shortage of the necessities of life, and financial difficulties clouded my proper judgement.

The situation in the Duisburger Kupferhütte induced little optimism. I was welcomed in Duisburg with open arms. The works management provided me with a tiny room in a worker's flat in Hochfeld where a woman with a little daughter waited in vain for her husband's return from Stalingrad.

Even in pre-war years, Hochfeld, a suburb of Duisburg, had been a dark and forbidding place. Soot and smoke blocked out the sunshine. The people had to work especially hard to earn their living with the result that social conflict in this area had always been vigorous and intense.

The Kupferhütte had been badly destroyed and was cut off from its raw material sources and customers. It was also threatened by dismantlement. The supply of one of the main raw materials, pyrites from Spain and Norway, had been interrupted. The traditional link with a number of sulphuric acid producers along the Rhine, on which the economic existence of the Kupferhütte was based, appeared endangered by the I. G. dismemberment. To believe in the future under such circumstances required a man with the energy and optimism of Ernst Kuss, the director of the Kupferhütte. He was surrounded by an excellent team which was applying all its energies to the reconstruction of the factory.

At the Kupferhütte, there was plenty of work for a chemist. The company had always tried to find a way of processing pyrites waste obtained from the sulphuric acid factories, before it was smelted in the blast furnace, so that as many components as possible were isolated and refined. Kuss, who had been a pupil of Alfred Stock in Karlsruhe, had achieved great advances in this respect during the I. G. period. Sodium sulphate, lead, cobalt, silver and gold had become important by-products together with copper and zinc. Most of the metals, however, could be sold only as crude and impure starting products which, of course, depressed prices. We therefore attempted to produce a pure zinc oxide that could be sold as a filler and solved this problem through wet precipitation. Later, the process was replaced by a more modern one.

Another problem to which we devoted a great deal of attention was the utilization of the lead from the salt solutions of the leaching plant. We were attempting to produce a new rust protection agent through precipitation with calcium cyanamide to replace the conventional red lead. The process was very successful for a time and, in fact, pursued a development that had been started in Hoechst during the war.

This also applied to efforts to obtain elemental sulphur from pyrites, an important problem during the war because of the shortage of sulphur. The large present-day sulphur deposits had either not yet been opened up at that time or were not accessible to us. The management of the Kupferhütte attempted to buy additional sulphur pyrites waste from Belgium and Holland because the German sulphuric acid factories were only slowly getting back into production. This measure later on greatly increased the profitability of the Kupferhütte.

From today's point of view, my tasks at the Kupferhütte were neither original nor chemically very exciting, and, with a few exceptions, the work had no significant consequences. The most important thing about it was that I gained a valuable insight into the actual problems of the Kupferhütte and its relation to metal smelting generally. I therefore acquired a subtle knowledge of the characteristics of this company which stood me in good stead when, after the reconstitution of Hoechst, I joined the supervisory board of the Kupferhütte to represent Hoechst's 30 per cent interest. I remained a member of the supervisory board until 1969, eventually as chairman.

Adequate supplies of sulphur and sulphuric acid are the basis of the existence of the Kupferhütte. For many years, the interlinking of west German chemistry, which also included the nitrogen industry on the Ruhr, ensured an internationally competitive raw material basis. Continuous intensive work in this field was of extraordinary economic importance for all those involved in it. It ensured that the Spanish and Norwegian as well as the other European pyrites mines were able to sell their products abroad because there was no sulphuric acid market in their own country. The metals present in the waste, especially copper and zinc whose separation was steadily improved by the Kupferhütte, have remained important starting materials in a country like Germany which is so short of raw materials. The special grades of pig iron developed by the Kupferhütte are of vital importance for foundries.

Today, the extensive deposits of elemental sulphur that have been opened up throughout the world represent serious competition. Cheaper transport from all parts of the world and the increase in the price of coal and coke have presented the Kupferhütte with new and difficult problems that it will hardly be able to solve on its own.

Unfortunately, at Duisburg I had to live away from my family. I was only able to travel to Hofheim every second Sunday; the trains were always overcrowded, and I usually had to stand all the way. Sometimes I was lucky and got a lift in a car.

Food was particularly short in the Ruhr. Sometimes the meagre rations were unobtainable in the shops for days. The British, who were themselves suffering from similar difficulties at home, could help little, with the best will in the world. Anyone who was not able to find extra rations in the countryside around the Ruhr simply went hungry.

Now and again I was able to supplement my rations, of which we were allowed to take home a special portion, through occasional visits to my relatives in Westphalia. Moreover, both coal and coke were available in Duisburg and they could be sent home in chemical drums. Officially, of course, this was strictly prohibited.

I was not a member of the Kupferhütte management and did not therefore shoulder any particular responsibility. It was in any case clear from the beginning that I would stay there for only a short time because possibilities were limited. Thanks to the friendliness of my colleagues, however, I was never regarded as an outsider. I was allowed to participate in everything and I was thus able to learn much that was later useful to me at Hoechst.

Changes in the Social Climate

For the first time after the war, I was also made aware of the new mood amongst employees. I remembered, from my own experience, the disunity and the class war of the Weimar period. I also recalled the uniformity and enforced collaboration between management and employees during the times of the German labour front.

Now I was to experience what could be achieved if management and staff collaborated without reservation, on a basis of equality. The needs of the moment had created a new social climate in which the class divisions were beginning to vanish. To our great satisfaction, this trend is continuing today and, indeed, most of us now accept it as a matter of course. It was one of the decisive criteria for German reconstruction.

The closer social contact during those years revealed sharply the quality of the individual. As yet, there was no confrontation between separate organizations. People cared about each other and co-operated in mastering everyday problems. Just as we conferred together to find ways of obtaining materials and tools for the reconstruction of the factory and how to avoid dismantling, so we also attempted to devise means of improving our standard of living. Every possibility was explored. The young Heinrich Schackmann, later successor of Kuss, was usually the ringleader of such enterprises.

A memorable one was the ghost ship which everyone who then worked at the Kupferhütte will remember. As the result of barter deals with foreign companies, we had been able to lay our hands on potatoes, flour, lemons, and oranges. The ship containing this precious cargo was anchored in the free port of Duisburg, its main cargo being pyrites waste from Belgium. The Duisburg municipality threatened to confiscate all the foodstuffs if the ship attempted to leave the harbour. We therefore arranged that the ship would sail on Christmas Eve, when the officials tended to be less wary, and move down to the quayside of the Kupferhütte where many of the employees had lined up to discharge the goods and distribute them as fairly and as quickly as possible.

Families lived in overcrowded conditions in the company estates which had been partially destroyed. These estates, built by the Kupferhütte long before the war, were to serve as a model in many respects when Hoechst set about providing houses for its people. A small apartment was prepared for me in one of the houses, and I moved in with my wife and two young boys in May 1948. Shortly afterwards, in July, my daughter Lotte was born in Duisburg hospital.

The social work of the Kupferhütte provided me with many ideas for my later work. The company chief, Ernst Kuss, was a far-sighted man with an outstanding social conscience, who realized his ideas with vigour and exceptional single-mindedness of purpose. For example, he introduced a profit-controlled bonus. His idea was that the usual Christmas bonus, awarded in addition to wage or salary, should be pegged to the declared profit of the company. In this way he hoped to raise the interest of employees in the success of the company. In principle, this scheme had already been operated in the I. G. Farbenindustrie although only inadequately. Unfortunately, these ideas of the Kupferhütte had to be scaled down and finally abandoned altogether because they had been calculated on the wrong basis and were unsuitable in this form for the Kupferhütte.

Naturally, this failure gave rise to criticism and derision. It would, however, have been much better if German industry, both large and small companies, had taken these experiments seriously and discussed them thoroughly. They related to problems that are of vital relevance today. Our social landscape would offer a far more pleasant view if German industry then had shown rather more initiative.

When I returned to Hoechst, I pleaded for such a profit-sharing scheme and I quickly gained the assent of my colleagues. As a result, Hoechst became one of the first companies to grant its employees a comparatively high dividend-related bonus.

The Birth of the D-Mark

On Sunday, 20 June 1948, the long awaited currency reform was announced. The Reichsmark, which had become almost valueless as a result of war and inflation, was taken out of circulation and replaced by 500 tons of new paper money printed in America and Britain. Every German received a capitation payment in two instalments of 40 and 20 marks each. All cash had to be surrendered and any bank or savings account was reduced in the ratio of 100 to 6·5.

Temporarily, we had all become equals, even though this material equality did not last for long. Overnight, the windows filled with goods that we had not seen for many years. On my way home I could not resist the temptation to buy an electric train for my two boys, with part of the 'capitation' money. They had never had a proper toy in their life. In the bakery shop tempting sweets, not seen for many years, reappeared. After eight years, my wife and I enjoyed a butter cream gateau once more.

The currency reform made deep inroads into everyone's life. For the second time in our life, any assets that had not been invested in real estate were lost. Share values, particularly of confiscated industries, remained uncertain for many years. Similarly, no dividends could be paid for some time to come. In addition to the misery of the millions who had forfeited almost everything in central Germany and the east, there was the added deprivation of the old people who had lost their last savings.

On the other hand, the currency reform did represent a turning point for the economy. Now that it was worthwhile once more to produce and to sell, the range of goods available increased daily. This also applied to agricultural products, so that the food situation improved immeasurably. The alleged world food crisis, which had hit the headlines of the newspapers for so long, had suddenly passed. Overnight, foreign countries were interested once more in supplying the German market even if only strictly against cash.

To start with, money was short. Salaries and wages increased only slowly. According to the wage agreements made at the time, the basic wage of a worker was approximately 1 DM per hour. The initial enthusiasm soon gave way to the need for careful management. On the other hand, controls had to be maintained for some time to facilitate an orderly return to normal conditions. Slowly, the last food rationing cards disappeared from the British and American zones but raw materials like coal and many other commodities remained rationed for a very long time afterwards.

Next Stop: Knapsack

In the summer of 1948, the management of Knapsack offered me the position of departmental head. I accepted, and during the middle of September I moved with my family to Hürth near Cologne. I had made it a condition of my employment that I would have to have a flat, however modest, as I had been separated from my family for long enough. We were therefore given a five-room flat which by the prevailing standards was fairly comfortable. A new phase of my life had begun.

I had readily agreed to this move to Knapsack in spite of a bad conscience vis-à-vis my family. The lignite area to the west of Cologne had become an important industrial area during the first half of this century and because of its cheap lignite and electric power it had gained tremendously in importance.

To live in this area, however, was not nearly as tempting a

proposition; this much I remembered from my many pre-war visits. The pits, the briquette factories, and the power stations, to say nothing of the industrial plants, daily emitted vast volumes of smoke and ash. Nothing had been done to integrate the large tips into the countryside. Living at Hürth therefore meant living in a world of fog and smoke, hardly an ideal atmosphere for a young family with children.

The last time I had visited Knapsack had been in June 1945 when I was driven there from Hoechst in a military vehicle along heavily damaged roads and over makeshift bridges. We had to make many detours before we reached Cologne where all the crossings of the Rhine were impassable. Eventually we crossed in an improvised ferry near Deutz. Before then, all our papers had been carefully checked in a military barracks and we had also been sprayed with some indefinable delousing agent. We drove to Knapsack through Cologne which was nothing but one vast ruin. Knapsack itself had been almost completely destroyed during an air attack in 1944. The management of Knapsack had always striven for comparative independence within the I. G. Farbenindustrie, and was now paying the price of isolation as apparently nobody knew after the attack what should be done next, or how the reconstruction of the factory could be brought about. Some leading people left the works even before the war ended. Our visit in 1945 therefore made it clear to us that Knapsack was in no position to provide starting products for Hoechst, particularly as the two plants were situated in different zones.

When I returned to Knapsack in 1948, the situation had greatly improved. Nevertheless, unexploded bombs were still buried underneath the wreckage that covered a considerable part of the plant.

In Cologne itself, reconstruction proceeded only slowly. Streets were re-built very gradually and each step of progress was celebrated as if it were a major triumph. I was deeply moved when I stood with my children in Cologne cathedral which, as though by divine intervention, had escaped complete destruction and had been partly restored for its seventh centenary celebrations in 1948.

The suburbs, where most of the Knapsack workers lived, presented an equally depressing picture. The area beyond, right up to the Eifel, had suffered greatly as a result of the German Ardennes offensive in January 1945. Many mines were still buried in the forests so that roads and paths had to be used circumspectly for a long time to come.

The limeworks were situated in the area of Düren and Aachen where damage was particularly severe. We were keenly interested in repairing them because their output was vital for Knapsack. The employees, together with a few managers who remained, had begun reconstruction work on their own initiative. A proper works management was appointed only much later by the British control officer.

Throughout this difficult early period, Frederik William Arnet was a tower of strength. A Norwegian, he had stayed in Knapsack during the war with the express approval of his government. Way back in the twenties, he had introduced the Söderberg electrode, invented in Norway, into the Knapsack furnaces. I quickly became friendly with Arnet and later made my first trip to Norway in his company.

The new works management was able only slowly to regain the confidence of the employees. For this reason, the social situation was particularly difficult at the beginning. The staff at Knapsack had always proved robust and critical. But, as these difficult times showed, they were extremely fond of their homes and their work.

The people around Knapsack are a frontier people. Many come from the Eifel, whose barrenness offers few opportunities to its inhabitants. These people with their Rhineland temperament are gay, full of self-confidence, and extremely vivacious. Once you have made a friend of one of them, you can rely on him for life. During my three years at Knapsack, and also later on, I was able to see how efficient these reliable people are.

I was cordially received in Knapsack, though not entirely without reserve. I subsequently learnt that many people thought that a former I. G. director had now come from Hoechst to take over Knapsack once more. The earlier difficult relationship with Hoechst had left vividly unfavourable memories.

I soon formed a good relationship with the leaders of the works council, Karl Schmitz and Johann Müller, as well as with their colleagues. They were confident and powerful representatives of the Knapsack employees. One could not help liking them in spite of, or probably because of, the tough but honest way in which they conducted their negotiations. When management problems arose in Knapsack, during the re-organization of the Hoechst group, the employees, and their works council in particular, showed a tremendous understanding of the difficulties that faced us.

For the first time since the war, I was once again undertaking responsible tasks. The activities, however, were perfectly strange to me. I had to get used to the process problems, the operation of the carbide plant and the entire field of electrochemistry. Reconstruction had meant a great many makeshift measures from which the works were now suffering. The carbide furnaces were re-built in exactly the same way as before their destruction. It was a considerable disappointment to find that this important Knapsack plant had been allowed to remain in such an antiquated state during the I. G. rule. There were only two covered furnaces that conformed to modern requirements. They had been constructed during the Hitler period under licence from the Union Carbide and Carbon Corporation.

The old tunnel furnace installation for the production of calcium cyanamide that had been Knapsack's first production at the beginning of the century was also started up again. Calcium cyanamide was of tremendous importance for German agriculture and the Knapsack employees owed their jobs to this and to welding carbide required for all the reconstruction work. For this reason, the food situation in Knapsack was much better than in Duisburg, even before the currency reform.

Many plants, however, were still shattered and awaited reconstruction. Fortunately, the British control officer took very little notice of us. We could work undisturbed and largely at our discretion. Because of the continued rationing of raw materials, operation of the reconstructed plants was difficult. We had to fight for lime and coke and particularly for electrical energy which we needed in great amounts. These battles were largely conducted in the allocation office of the Economics Ministry of North Rhine Westphalia in Düsseldorf. During this time, Wolfgang Thies joined us. He was my personal assistant for many years and soon became a member of the board of management of Hoechst. He achieved many successes in the field of petrochemistry and plastics.

To get any allocations at all, the company continually had to prove that it was important to the nation's economy. We therefore speeded up calcium cyanamide production by restoring the badly damaged modern rotary furnace plant. We produced acetic acid for the manufacture of domestic vinegar which was in short supply.

Quite early on, we exported acetic anhydride to Belgium, which provided us with valuable foreign exchange.

At the same time we began to enlarge our production programme. We developed a chloroacetic acid plant of a kind that had existed within the I. G. Farbenindustrie only in Gersthofen. With the aid of a chemist who had fled from the east, where he had his own factory, we took up the production of carbon black. We also engaged in the manufacture of ferrosilicon and other steel refining products which were needed in the Ruhr.

A New Field – Phosphorus

The largest and most important project, however, was the production of elemental phosphorus. Friedbert Ritter, the trustee for Knapsack, had come with some of his colleagues from Bitterfeld, bringing with him a great deal of invaluable experience in this field. The production of elemental phosphorus from calcium phosphate in electric furnaces was similar in many respects to carbide production and could readily be fitted into the Knapsack production programme.

The development of this process went back to the halcyon days of Griesheim when Gustav Pistor had operated it on a small industrial scale. After his move into the lignite area of central Germany, he had effected further improvements to the process and eventually, together with Ritter, erected several large phosphorus furnaces in Piesteritz on the Elbe, on a site belonging to Bayerische Stickstoffwerke.

In the thirties, these were regarded as the most modern in the world. Monsanto of America had taken out a licence for the process. Pure phosphoric acid, which in fact could be obtained economically only by this process, was an ideal raw material for the manufacture of phosphates. These were required in food chemistry, and especially as a component of modern detergents. Elemental phosphorus was manufactured by the I. G. only in its central German works which we lost after the division of Germany. As phosphorus could be used for incendiary bombs, it was on the Allied list of war materials prohibited in the Federal Republic. It could, however, be proved that Germany, in contrast to the Allies, had never dropped phosphorus bombs.

The Economics Ministry in Bonn supported us in talks with the control authorities, who at first created considerable difficulties, so that it was not until 1950–1 that we obtained limited approval. In the meantime, plans for the furnace had progressed to a point where we could have begun reconstruction. It would have been sensible, and certainly economic, to have located this new phosphorus factory directly on the banks of the Rhine. This could not be done though because there were difficulties over current supply and also because the preparation of the intended land would have been too expensive. For this reason, we removed one of the huge slag heaps in Knapsack and thus obtained the necessary space for a phosphorus factory capable of further expansion.

But even then, the realization of these plans met with considerable economic difficulties since the capital requirement was enormous. It was more than Knapsack could cope with by itself. We therefore negotiated with nearby Leverkusen and eventually also with the companies of Henkel and Oetker who were both interested in phosphates. But these companies were themselves burdened by reconstruction problems and could not come to a decision to join us. Phosphorus production, therefore, could be started only after Knapsack had rejoined the Hoechst group. The manufacture of phosphorus chemicals then became a tremendously rewarding new field.

We also made contact with the neighbouring company, UK Wesseling. In these works, a lignite hydrogenation plant had been erected after 1943 under licence from the I. G. Farbenindustrie. It was owned by the Rodder mine and thus formed part of the Rheinisch-Westfälisches Elektrizitätswerk. Wesseling, too, had been confiscated, and was under British control. It had, however, gained permission gradually to convert to peaceful production the installations that had not been dismantled. For example, part of the installations for ammonia manufacture was being operated and supplied the fertilizer plant in Hoechst.

We gave a good deal of thought to the utilization of the large amount of waste gas from the carbide furnaces and whether we could base upon it an ammonia factory or a Fischer-Tropsch synthesis which at that time would still have been of interest. We also had the idea of piping these gases to Wesseling 8 km away. We even succeeded in purifying the gases by a difficult and complicated process to such an extent that they were usable and that they no longer represented a nuisance to the neighbourhood. The purification costs were prohibitive, so we were forced to burn the gases as quickly as possible. Nevertheless, the problem of dust had been solved.

We were also thinking of establishing a joint petrochemical complex with Wesseling which had suitable plants available for the purpose. During the tough and unavoidable negotiations concerning power that we had to conduct with RWE, we thought up an even bolder plan. We proposed that Hoechst and RWE should operate with Wesseling on a fifty-fifty basis. Unfortunately, discussions on this subject with the American and British control officers were unsuccessful because in the meantime a different decision had been taken concerning the future of Wesseling.

Years later, however, we achieved close and cordial collaboration between Wesseling and Hoechst without involving capital participation. It proved extremely fruitful for both parties.

We engaged in these far-reaching technical and economic considerations as though we already had the power to direct our own future. In fact, however, dismemberment of the I. G. was still under discussion and it was not until this had been completed that the final position of Knapsack could be decided. I took part in these discussions only after 1951.

Our primary aim was to secure as large a piece of the I. G. cake as possible to ensure that Knapsack was a large and viable structure. We were successful in acquiring the Griesheim-Autogen works in Frankfurt and a large part of the Vereinigte Sauerstoffwerke. The latter was previously owned equally by Linde and I. G. The acquisition of these companies represented a considerable expansion of business for Knapsack. The association with Friedrich Uhde GmbH in Dortmund was no less important. Thanks to personal relationships with the management, especially with the founder of the company, Friedrich Uhde, who became a great friend, Knapsack was able to obtain the former I. G. interest in this Dortmund engineering company.

As a result of these changes, Knapsack had become a sizeable undertaking, especially in the context of our far-reaching plans. In spite of this, we did not fall victim to the illusion that Knapsack could remain successfully independent in the long run. We knew too much about the structure of the great neighbouring companies of the former I. G. to realize that eventually Knapsack, with its limited product range and low sales volume, would not be able to compete.

Considerable Pharmaceutical Success

We inclined towards a merger with Bayer with whom we had already formed a number of important economic and human relationships in the first years after the war. Our inclinations were reinforced by the fact that both companies belonged to the British zone. On the other hand, important historic and economic reasons made it seem more advisable for Knapsack to look towards Hoechst whose entire solvent and plastics programme relied heavily on the Knapsack acetylene.

Hoechst made intensive efforts to secure collaboration and put out feelers through third parties. In Hoechst, my presence and activities in Knapsack were regarded as a great obstacle. For this reason, the American control officer attempted to persuade his British colleagues to bring about my dismissal. I was much relieved by repeated assurances that I would be able to stay.

What I heard about Hoechst was not very encouraging. Because of disunity among the trustees and the differing views held by many of the new staff who knew little about the economic background, difficulties could be overcome only slowly, as the American control officers displayed little interest in the progress of the company. Nevertheless, the number of people employed in Hoechst had increased from 6,000 in 1946 to 9,400 in 1949.

Considerable successes were recorded by the pharmaceutical division, which had been allowed much freedom by the Americans. Under the management of trustee Michael Erlenbach, great progress was achieved. Fritz Lindner, later a member of the board of management and director of the pharmaceutical division, performed invaluable work in the procurement and preparation of pancreatic glands from animals which were needed for the production of insulin. Diabetics could be kept alive only by the daily insulin injection. Salvarsan also continued to be of considerable importance because during and immediately after a war, the incidence of venereal disease always increases menacingly. Moreover, as early as 1950, the Americans had granted Hoechst a licence for the production of penicillin. This antibiotic had been produced in Farbwerke Hoechst in small amounts during the last years of the war.

During 1949, while we were concerned with our own fate and the dismemberment of the I. G. Farbenindustrie, considerable advances were being made in national politics. The occupation statute had been published in May. In spite of its somewhat unfortunate name, it imposed certain restrictions on the previously unlimited rights of the occupation powers. A few months later, the Ruhr Statute was formulated which gave Germany access to the Ruhr Authority in which seven western nations were represented. They jointly controlled the distribution of coal, coke and iron from the Ruhr.

Most important of all, 1949 saw the birth of the Federal Republic of Germany and the elections for the first Bundestag. The 'ward of court' had become a state with limited sovereignty. Prospects of casting off further Allied fetters increased greatly when the United States appointed John McCloy as High Commissioner for the Federal Republic. He fulfilled his duties in an admirable spirit. I was delighted when many years later I had an opportunity of getting to know him personally in the United States. McCloy certainly was the pioneer of a new German-American friendship.

Three Successors to the I. G.

In the discussions concerning the future of the I. G. Farbenindustrie, widely differing ideas were put forward. In August 1948, the Americans and the British had agreed on final joint dismemberment. Now, for the first time, they also decided to hear the opinion of the Germans themselves. For this reason, a German commission was formed in November 1948, called the I. G. Farben Dispersal Panel. It started its work immediately. Its chairman was Hermann Bücher of the AEG and the commission made a valuable contribution to keeping dismemberment within tolerable limits. The I. G. Farben Dispersal Panel, or FARDIP for short, undertook a close investigation of the situation of the I. G. works in the British and American zones. Chemists and engineers prepared numerous technical and scientific assessments and trustee and auditor companies supplied detailed reports.

Almost two years passed before the final diagnosis had been prepared and the appropriate proposals had been worked out. From the German point of view, this proved a considerable advantage. In the meantime, the Federal Republic had become consolidated, both economically and politically, and was thus able to lend more weight to German views on I. G. dismemberment. If the Allies had come to an earlier agreement about a final solution, it would undoubtedly have been less favourable to us.

In 1950, as the result of recommendations by FARDIP, a commission of the occupation powers arrived at the conclusion that three large companies should be formed from the I. G. inheritance: the Main group, the Bayer group, and BASF.

This was not without serious consequences for Knapsack and its future. We could no longer desist from having reasonable discussions with Hoechst. As a result, I had a very fruitful conversation with Michael Erlenbach, the trustee of the Hoechst works. When the control authorities then decided in the spring that Knapsack should be joined to the Hoechst complex and should be taken into the American control zone with immediate effect, the ice had already been broken.

When the Bunsen Society met in Göttingen in 1951 we met Konrad Weil, trustee of the Griesheim works. Over a glass of beer, we discovered that we shared not only the material conditions needed for profitable collaboration but also a great deal of personal affinity. We met again at breakfast the next day and agreed to meet regularly in future for confidential talks. Our talks were held in Erlenbach's flat in Frankfurt as I did not yet want to go to Hoechst. The participants included all those who were later to occupy management positions in either Hoechst or Knapsack.

The Knapsack board of management was already more or less appointed, but the composition of the future Hoechst board was only just beginning to take shape. The only certain appointments were the trustees of Hoechst, Griesheim and Offenbach.

I regarded myself entirely as a future board member of Knapsack and thought about little else beyond. Partly with borrowed money, partly with money which the British had remitted to us as post-payment of the annual bonus, I was able to fulfil a longstanding desire to build a house in Knapsack on a piece of leased land. My wife and I were tremendously happy when we could move into it in May 1951. My three children too – the elder two went to school in Knapsack and Brühl – were very pleased with their new surroundings.

My professional position and the prospect of membership of the future board, completely satisfied me. I was able to devote a considerable part of what spare time I had to my scientific work on chemical technology.

In Hoechst, preparations for the formation of the new company and its future board were nearing completion. There was fierce competition for the top job in Hoechst. A decision was urgent because in both Leverkusen and Ludwigshafen the boards of management had already crystallized.

I was closely informed about the discussions in Hoechst. But not for one moment did it occur to me that I might be offered the chairmanship of Hoechst. Indeed, there were few prospects of this happening. One obstacle was my earlier membership of the party, and another was that I was relatively unknown. A former I. G. colleague thought that, at forty-eight, I was too young for the post and that I had spent too little time in the nursery of the I. G. I did not mind him saying this as it was only too true.

During August 1951, rumours suddenly thickened that I might, after all, be appointed to the Hoechst board of management. The Federal government and other interested German sources had brought up my name, probably at the suggestion of old colleagues from the I. G. My main protagonist was Ulrich Haberland in Leverkusen.

At the time – it was the end of August 1951 – we were busy in Knapsack preparing our first trip to America. We wanted first-hand information about all that had happened in the U.S.A. during the long period of German seclusion and about the new chemical and technical developments that had taken place during the period when we were not able to travel abroad.

It was extremely difficult to get a visa for the United States. The discussions with the American Consul-General in Bremen were so unsatisfactory that I, for my part, declined to apply for a visa. In the end, therefore, we did not fly to the U.S.A. but to Canada. We had an invitation from the Prime Minister of Newfoundland, Joseph R. Smallwood, whose Economics Minister had previously visited Europe to promote the industrialization of Newfoundland.

In 1951, a flight to Canada was still a somewhat exciting affair. Including intermediate stops in Shannon and Gander, it took nearly twenty hours. We visited a number of Canadian companies in Montreal and then journeyed to the Niagara Falls, close to the American frontier. Here we met some American industrialists whom we had known previously. The conversations were fairly restrained. As yet, there wasn't much to tell.

The visit to Newfoundland was extremely interesting and enjoyable. We soon found, however, that there were hardly any conditions suitable for the development of a chemical industry.

On the return trip from Montreal to Liverpool, which we made by boat, we discussed the results of our journey. One of our companions, Max Edgar Klee, who had argued our case in the British Control Office and who had been selected for the Knapsack board, was to be sent to Canada in order to set up a Hoechst branch there. Later, Klee worked in New York where he was for many years head of our American organization.

Before I left for Canada in September 1951, Randolph H. Newman had asked me to come and see him. A former German solicitor, he was now the American control officer for the I. G. in Frankfurt. Previously, he had been a member of the American prosecutors' office during the Nuremberg trial of the I. G.

I had heard a great deal about Newman but did not know him personally. He received me in a very reserved and almost icy manner and quickly came to the point. He wanted me to move from the Knapsack board to the Hoechst board. I replied that I could join the Hoechst board only as chairman. Newman appeared very surprised at this remark, or at any rate pretended to be. He rejected my demand. I emphasized that my past experience and the earlier decision of the old I.G. management entitled me to the position. We were unable to agree, so I suggested that we should postpone our discussion for twenty-four hours.

On the Back of a Menu

In the afternoon of that day, I visited my former chief, Fritz ter Meer, to ask his advice. Ter Meer told me not to be inflexible. He recommended that I should go to Hoechst whatever the circumstances. Once there, I would be able to reach my goal provided that I had the technical management firmly in my hands. According to his experience in the I. G., this would very soon result in my obtaining overall control of the company.

I went home and drew up a plan as to how I could best secure the technical management for myself. In discussions with my Knapsack colleagues, I drew up the organization of the management on the back of a menu. The plan served as a basis for the resumed negotiations with Newman next day and indeed, its fundamental principles form the basis of the Hoechst organization even today. The plan provided that I would become technical manager of the Maingau group. In this function, I had control over all technical decisions, including research and production, as well as all decisions concerning investments.

In the second, slightly more friendly discussion, Newman eventually agreed to my proposal. The three trustees also concurred. All further negotiations were then based on my organization plan. The future management of Hoechst slowly began to take shape.

It was necessary to find a name for the new company. After many debates, in which a large variety of views were expressed, we agreed with the Allies to the old-fashioned 'Farbwerke Hoechst AG vormals Meister Lucius & Brüning' which we have retained to this day. We adopted this name because it expressed the link with the old Hoechst tradition, of which so many people were still conscious.

Newman had insisted on a provision in the statutes of the company according to which Farbwerke Hoechst was not to have a chairman of the board of management during the first nine months. The members of the board were to share the chairmanship of board meetings in alphabetical rotation.

The board was to have twelve members: Otto Fritz Schulz, manager, dyestuffs division; Michael Erlenbach, manager, pharmaceutical and inorganic division; Kurt Möller, manager, solvent and plastics division; Konrad Weil, manager, intermediate division; Walther Ludwigs, manager, sales. From the control office, Oscar Gierke joined as manager of finance and accounts, and solicitor Heinz Kaufmann as manager of the legal department. Deputy board members were Adolf Sieglitz, research, Ernst Engelbertz, works management, Hoechst, Johannes Moser, accounts, and Josef Wengler, engineer-engineering. I assumed technical direction. Thus, all the preconditions for a reconstitution of Farbwerke Hoechst as one of the successor companies of the I. G. Farbenindustrie had been fulfilled.

On 7 December 1951, we assembled in the presence of a public notary in a conference room of the former Rhine-Main Bank, and founded Farbwerke Hoechst AG. Farbenfabriken Bayer AG performed the same ceremony on 19 December and Badische Anilin & Soda Fabrik AG on 30 January.

The so-called 'one hundred thousand mark companies' were created, the name being derived from the small amount of share capital issued. It was, of course, only a first step to ensure that a holding company was available into which one day part of the former works of the I. G. complex could be incorporated. The shares of the 100,000 Mark AG were held by five founders. The former I.G. shareholders had their rights reinstated only after a long overdue revalidation of securities and final release from occupied control.

The five founders appointed the supervisory board in whose composition the Allies had played a decisive role. Long and complicated discussions had taken place. Fortunately, the Federal government had been able to find men who proved of extreme value for the company.

The first supervisory board consisted of: Hugo Zinsser, chairman, Louis Leisler Kiep, deputy chairman, Max H. Schmid, Hans Sachs, Carl Fr. Müller, Gustav Pistor, Boris Rajewsky, Karl Schirner, Clemens Schöpf, Pierre Vieli. Employee representation in the supervisory board came much later on as the result of special legislation. The formal proceedings closed with the official appointment of the board of management.

In the evening of this memorable 7 December 1951, we met in Newman's flat. An excellent dinner, with even better whisky, loosened our tongues and helped the evening to proceed peacefully even though a good many tensions from the past persisted amongst the guests. Eventually the atmosphere became more and more relaxed and this was undoubtedly highly beneficial for our future collaboration. The British control officer Fowles amused the assembled guests with citations from Wilhelm Busch. The press, which had been kept well informed, reported the event in full.

Coming Home

My family was unenthusiastic about returning to Hoechst. My wife who, like me, had not forgotten the events of the first year after the collapse, could not understand for a long time why I was prepared to go back to Hoechst. Although she came from the Frankfurt suburb of Sossenheim, she would have preferred to remain in Knapsack. She had become very fond of the house which had just been completed, and where we celebrated a happy Christmas in 1951.

To facilitate the transfer from Knapsack to Hoechst, I had asked

Newman for approval for Farbwerke Hoechst to build me a house in the vicinity of Hoechst. I agreed to exchange it for my property in Knapsack, paying for any difference in value. In December 1951, I found a suitable plot of land in Königstein.

When we visited my parents-in-law in the vicarage in Sossenheim that Christmas, I thought I would show my wife and children the land I had acquired. I felt sure that they would all be greatly impressed. The Taunus was clad in white and deep snow covered the plot which offered magnificent views of the ruins of Königstein castle. I fully expected outbursts of enthusiasm. Instead, my nine-year-old son Albrecht, who had seen the ruins in Cologne, simply said in amused resignation: 'If we live here, we shall be watching a heap of rubble all day,' referring most disrespectfully to the old castle.

When the building work began in 1952, the land was still deeply covered in snow. The plans for the house were designed by the same Cologne architect who had just completed the house in Knapsack. Because he had given us complete satisfaction there, we left everything to him on this occasion. In the unanimous opinion of my family, it turned out to be a very pleasant house indeed. We moved in on 1 August 1952.

My years of wandering had come to an end. Farbwerke Hoechst now left us no time for much private life. Back at the starting point of my career, I found a very difficult situation. Hoechst had been truncated and had to rely on other works to a far greater extent than either Bayer or BASF. But it was by no means certain whether the works that Hoechst had once brought into the I. G. would be returned to it.

To turn Hoechst into a company able to compete successfully in international chemistry appeared an almost insoluble task. Moreover, it was to be undertaken by a management that had not evolved through the normal selection process within the company but that had been largely created by the Allies. We knew little of each other, personally or professionally.

It was questionable whether these different people, unknown to one another, could be moulded into a unified management. I wasn't the only one to nurse these anxieties and doubts in the last days of 1951; the press, too, frequently commented on how little people thought of the Hoechst management and its future.

6

A New Start (1952–4)

AT THE beginning of January 1952, the twelve members of the new board appeared in Hoechst to begin their work. We had decided our new offices would be identical. Each of us had the same desk, filing cabinets, the same carpet, the same curtains. Initially, each ordinary member of the board also got the same salary – 60,000 DM.

Although we knew each other only slightly and had many prejudices and reservations, we were completely agreed on one issue: Hoechst had to be made economically viable once more. This demanded from us the highest degree of cooperation and the complete setting aside of any considerations of personal prestige. We knew that if the new management were to allow the formation of cliques and factions, all hopes of a resurgence of Hoechst would be doomed to failure from the beginning.

There was a rather reserved atmosphere to begin with between the members of the management who had come from the American control office and those who had held senior positions in the former I. G. We had been on different sides, after all. Another group in the management were the trustees of the individual works. Only a few of them had come from the former I. G. Farbenindustrie and knew its problems. In the past years, they had largely followed the directions of the American control office. Nevertheless, they were fairly autonomous within their particular works and had been given considerable freedom of decision. The control office was still very much in the background and played an important role in all major decisions. For example, each expenditure of more than 5,000 marks needed the express agreement of the American control officers.

Sharing Responsibility

In this difficult situation, our first functional organization plan and the company statutes were the framework that held the new management together. With the exception of a few changes that appeared necessary after the first few days, the system we then adopted formed the basis of our collaboration until I retired in 1969. All the activities of the company, both in Germany and abroad, covering every plant and all subsidiaries, were divided into five divisions, each one of which was headed by a technical member of the board (see diagram on page 425). Division I included inorganics, nitrogenous fertilizer and plant protection; Division II dyestuffs, their starting products and textile auxiliaries; Division III plastics and solvents; Division IV pharmaceuticals; and Division V fibres and films.

As the responsibility of the divisional heads was so universal, the functions of the trustees, and of the works managers and the board of management of the subsidiaries, were greatly limited. This, of course, gave rise to differences of opinion. Even later, when these early problems had become historic, the divisional system still led to conflicts of responsibility. Usually, however, they could be solved with patience and mutual understanding. Divisional organization proved to be a viable basis for the organization of the company. Today, it is a normal feature of any modern organizational plan.

Naturally, the policy of the different divisions had to be aligned. This was the job of the coordinating members of the board. We were able to convince the American control authorities that coordination was necessary not only in sales, finance and accounting and the legal and patent field, but also in the technical and scientific spheres. Therefore, responsibility for research and engineering was also allocated to board members. Because the Hoechst works, as a result of its size, was a little top heavy inside the Hoechst group, one board member assumed responsibility for the works management of Hoechst. This was later quietly extended to cover the other works of the company. Eventually, it also included the social field and purchasing.

This structure necessarily resulted in corporate responsibility which was a great advantage in such a heterogenous company decentralized even in its manufacturing activities. Every important decision had to be approved by at least two members of the board for it always affected one of the divisions and one of the coordinating departments. For example, the head of the pharmaceutical division had to coordinate sales strategy with central sales, the direction of his research with the head of research, and budget questions with the finance and accounts departments.

The chairman of the board does not have any specific responsibility and does not, therefore, champion any particular causes. According to the company statutes, he has the casting vote if there is deadlock on the board. He is mainly the guardian of proper business procedure and he directs the allocation of responsibilities on the board.

Originally, not all of us were enthusiastic about this system. It was, however, soon found that it represented the only way of achieving the maximum cooperation and efficiency. The organization had the added advantage that it could be readily grasped and that the responsibilities were clearly defined. The lower ranks knew where they were and could readily establish from the obligatory countersignatures whether a company transaction had been brought to the notice of the appropriate officer. This was done with great exactitude, sometimes bordering on pedantry. But it enabled us to point out our mistakes to each other. Naturally, the system did not operate entirely without friction. Sometimes there were differences of opinion that echoed through the board meetings. In time, however, with continued use, the system functioned more and more smoothly.

A Technical General Staff

As technical manager, I had to find a form of coordination in my sphere that would also ensure purposeful and unfettered cooperation. Each technical member of the board was provided with an 'adjutant'. These 'adjutants' formed a joint directorate whose manager was my immediate right-hand man.

In this way, a small technical general staff of about half a dozen young scientists was formed. They represented the fields with which they were specifically concerned, and reconciled the plans of the various divisions – works management and technical scientific research. In this way, a united technical management was soon created. It was not necessary to exercise personal authority for small decisions. This department later had to be enlarged. Today almost twenty people work in it.

We always took great care to fill these positions with outstanding men. No matter how young, they were allowed full access to all important events in the company. They were kept fully informed on all questions and were allowed to join in the discussions, though they were not themselves entitled to give directions. Many leading men of our company and even members of the board of management have risen from the ranks of this department. My successor Rolf Sammet, for example, was chief of the technical directorate from 1 July 1957 to 31 March 1962. In the commercial field, it was far more difficult to create such a coordinating department. The work of the sales management was, of course, closely connected with the technical aspects of the divisions. But the sales people complained, particularly at the beginning, about the undue importance that appeared to be accorded to the technicians. Gradually, however, they recognized that they had been accorded an equal degree of responsibility. The financial and accounts departments and the legal department, who fulfilled special tasks, were the most difficult to incorporate in the overall framework. For this reason, it took a comparatively long time to achieve a coordinating organization – a commercial directorate – in the commercial sphere.

That we managed it at all was due mainly to the efforts of Konrad Weil who, until he was appointed to the board, had been trustee of Griesheim. Weil was a chemist by training and a pupil of the Nobel prizewinner Adolf Windaus of Göttingen. He was also an excellent scientist. In addition, he had exceptional talents combined with fine instincts in the field of finance and accounting and in the commercial sphere generally. He advised me on these questions in a manner that was as unselfish as it was unobtrusive. As I was a complete novice in commercial matters, his support was of extreme value to me. I could trust him completely. In a very short time we became close friends which is, of course, not as easy for older people as it is for young ones.

First Board Meetings

Every two weeks, on a Tuesday, we met at nine o'clock for the board meeting. It was cancelled only rarely and everyone adjusted his timetable so that he could participate. If, for any reason, someone

Crossing by boat to the southern bank of the River Main where the research centre was to be erected (left to right) Emil Thiel, Josef Wengler, Otto Horn, Otto Fritz Schulz, Gustav Ehrhart, Wolfgang Imhoff, Karl Winnacker

The research centre

The canteen after the end of the war. On the right 'Gustel', and below, the 'Russian Hotel'

was unable to do so, he was represented by another member of the board. He then ran the risk, of course, that urgent decisions would be taken without him. Naturally, we were anxious to avoid this unless it was absolutely necessary.

At first, the minutes were taken by a young technician who did not belong to the board. Later, the job was carried out by the head of the technical directorate who found factual and objective minuting easier because he was not actively involved in the negotiations of the board. The confidentiality of the discussions never suffered from the presence of these people. In any case, for young people, taking minutes was a unique educational opportunity.

The minutes had to be extremely factual. After being checked by the legal member on the board, they were distributed amongst those present and discussed and adopted at the next meeting. The minutes only contained the actual decisions of the management. The notes on which they were based were preserved for a few weeks before being destroyed.

The meetings of the board began punctually to the minute. The subjects for discussion were hammered out for four to five hours without interruption and the necessary decisions were then taken. It was an unwritten law that we took lunch together afterwards. During this brief, enjoyable hour, any small differences that might have arisen during the heat of the earlier discussions were usually ironed out. It was also often possible during these lunches to remove any lingering reservations about decisions concerning particularly delicate points.

We had agreed that we would not appeal to the supervisory board or its chairman if there were fundamental differences of opinion before we had told every other member of the board of our intention. We took great care that this agreement was strictly adhered to.

During almost eighteen years as a member of the Hoechst board, I took part in more than 300 board meetings. Many of them produced fundamental differences of view and even violent disputes. But in the end there was always the moment of reconciliation over lunch.

The new organization that we had created had to be imposed throughout the company and had to be given life. To begin with, many of the management functions existed only on paper. Moreover, the management instruments of the individual works and their administrative systems, especially in Hoechst, in no way conformed to the new plans. They had to be adapted gradually to fit into the new organization.

Careful Personnel Policy

Inevitably, the right people were not always available for the leading jobs. There had been much fluctuation in the top management of the various works during the past years. Many of the leading men were not familiar with the tradition of the company. Nevertheless, they had made their contribution and had staked out claims that to some extent had to be taken into account. It was therefore impossible to solve all the personnel problems overnight. We had to proceed very carefully with our new system. Moreover, the supervision and the right of intervention of the American control authorities had also to be taken into account.

Thus, we had to make many concessions during this first period and these were not always easy from the company point of view. We had to accept inadequate forms of organization, at any rate for the time being, and we had to tolerate people who, strictly speaking, were not in the right jobs. Yet it was essential that we should be ready for the industrial competition that was about to begin and that we should keep in step with the rapid technical developments. Although we were forced into many compromises at the beginning, we realized that much would have to be changed as soon as possible. On the other hand, the people who had come to us from outside provided us with many new impulses which proved to be extremely valuable in the long run.

This intense preoccupation with the many personnel problems that are bound to arise during the reconstruction of a company, proved an excellent training in management practice. As more and more companies joined the Hoechst group, so that more qualified people became available, we often had to face the problem of finding jobs which matched their qualifications. During our many later mergers, these problems often gave us more headaches than the technical, legal, or commercial aspects which are usually very similar.

We soon formed study groups and commissions below board-level which had considerable freedom of action. In many cases, examples from the I. G. influenced our ideas. For instance, we introduced the technical directorate meeting in which not only the appropriate members of the board but also the most important technicians of the various works participated. At first, appointments to such commissions were made by the board and later by its chairman. There was a shortage of suitable conference rooms. In the old administrative conference room, where our supervisory board meetings still take place and where the pictures of the three company founders hang above the chimney, the occupation troops had dismantled the large historic conference table. During the initial period, we had therefore to confer on makeshift tables that had been brought from all parts of the building.

As one of our first 'development expenditures', we ordered an imposing new conference table whose cost exceeded 5,000 DM so that it was subject to Allied approval. It was of mahogany and covered in green leather. We didn't have a suitable auditorium for large events either. The original one had been destroyed by a bomb during the first weeks of the war. During the occupation, moreover, valuable furniture and pictures had disappeared from the old administrative building. We therefore had to concern ourselves with these small details.

During 1951 and 1952, our offices looked like a provisional army command post. There was a shortage of rooms and furniture everywhere. Fortunately, the administrative building had been enlarged by the addition of another floor even before the formation of the 100,000 mark company.

Chairman

As a result, at the end of 1952 the board was able to occupy reasonably comfortable offices which it still uses today. In the meantime, I had become chairman of the board of management. Some of my colleagues had realized for quite a time that the board needed a chairman. Two of them approached Hugo Zinsser, the chairman of the supervisory board, with the proposal that I should be appointed to the post.

According to the stipulations of the American control authority, this was not allowed for the first nine months after the reconstitution of the company. Zinsser, the clever and extremely diplomatic head of the Rhein-Main-Bank, later to become the Dresdner Bank, therefore hit upon an ingenious intermediate solution. He persuaded the supervisory board to pass a decision that I should be chairman-designate. Although this did not represent a legal decision, the announcement was sufficient to clear up the situation on the Hoechst board.

The first meeting of the supervisory board was rather unorthodox, like so much else at that time. The board of management had agreed that each member should give a report about his field. As no one wished to be outdone, the allocated times were exceeded and the meeting lasted without interruption from early morning until late afternoon. We could tell from the pained expressions of the supervisory board how trying our first appearance had been. After the general exhaustion had been overcome, a lively evening going on far into the night resulted in many personal contacts, badly needed in those days.

Zinsser, by the way, was an indispensable friend and adviser in all the questions that I was not able to solve by myself. I spent many an evening with him in his Frankfurt office and subsequently in the adjacent 'Kaiserkeller' restaurant to discuss topical questions ranging from dismemberment problems to finance and personnel policy. His wealth of ideas was as astonishing as his knowledge of exquisite wines. In both respects, I have learnt a great deal from him.

When we had guests in Hoechst, we were forced to receive them in the 'Russian Hotel' because our restaurant remained occupied by the Americans until the end of 1953. The 'Russian Hotel' had been erected during the war as barracks for Russian civilians and prisoners of war. Its kitchen was now managed by a down-to-earth caterer whose culinary activities were not distinguished by a great deal of sophistication. On the other hand, his portions were, to say the least, adequate and satisfying, and that we appreciated as much as a good drop of wine.

When I entered the 'Russian Hotel' for the first time at the end of 1951, I encountered almost all the staff of the former restaurant, including 'Gustel'. She had known the former I. G. people for many decades and combined a touching loyalty with profound knowledge of human nature. Gustel judged everyone with an almost uncanny perception and treated him accordingly. It was only after she had retired after more than forty years of employment, first in the pharmaceutical packaging department and then in the restaurant, that I learnt her real name – Fräulein Mäller.

It was often thanks to these simple people that I so quickly felt at home again in Hoechst. They had hardly changed in spite of all the political upheavals and changes. As so often in history, a political hurricane had swept away the top layers and replaced them by others, but the bulk of the people had remained the same, and true to themselves.

Many knew me from earlier days and that it had been the intention to appoint me a director of Hoechst. Many employees had not forgotten that I had spent the difficult war years in the factory and that I had remained loyal to it until the beginning of occupation. My wife had attended college in Hoechst until she took her degree and later worked as an apprentice in the Kaysser pharmacy. This was also a point in my favour in the eyes of the Hoechst people. The fact that I was not from Hesse was therefore compensated for to some extent.

Whenever I could spare the time, I walked alone through the factory. By myself, I visited the plants that I had come to know so well by the end of the war. That had been seven years ago and sometimes the period seemed like eternity. But in spite of all that had happened, I began slowly to feel at home again during these solitary hours. I also began to feel, for the first time, real pleasure in the big task that lay ahead of me. It was a job worthy of all my energies. I don't think that such a feeling can seize a technician sitting behind his desk. It requires live contact with the factory, its people, and its machinery. For this reason alone, the decision, by no means automatic, to place our administrative centre right in the centre of the factory was of considerable advantage.

Inventory at Hoechst

The works had hardly suffered any damage. It looked as though the war had passed us by. But, as in the thirties, the factory gave the impression of being antiquated and delapidated. In fact, it looked as though it had been specially preserved in that condition. In other works which had been destroyed in the war, Knapsack and Leverkusen for example, reconstruction had long since begun. In Hoechst, on the other hand, everything looked dusty and cobwebbed.

The trustee administration, which had had to observe carefully the regulations of the control authority, was, of course, not able to do very much about this. It was somewhat lacking in initiative but even more in financial resources to engage in major investments. Instead, great care had been taken to safeguard existing assets. Even in the first months of 1952, I was warned never to invest more than the depreciation. But in the absence of an up-to-date balance sheet, the exact level of depreciation wasn't even known.

At least the pharmaceutical department could show significant progress. Michael Erlenbach had succeeded, through the agency of the U.S. control office, in acquiring a penicillin licence from Merck in the U.S.A. In 1950, a modern penicillin plant was erected in Hoechst which was inaugurated by the American High Commissioner, John McCloy. It was this event that gave Hoechst, which had once ushered in the era of chemo-therapy with its Salvarsan production, a springboard into the new era of antibiotics.

Weil was able to record a major success in another field. He had established a connection between the electrode factory in Griesheim, which no longer had any graphitization facilities since the loss of the plant in Bitterfeld, and Siemens-Plania in Meitingen. This led to close collaboration between the two companies and eventually to the foundation of a joint company which now enjoys international importance.

In other fields, too, industrial production had been started, however modestly, although all fundamental decisions had been postponed. In the main, though, Hoechst had carefully husbanded its financial resources and had accumulated the sum of 50–60 million DM which in the circumstances was quite a sizeable amount. The aim of this policy was clear and perfectly reasonable. After dismemberment, the plants were to be extended with this money.

But one thing had been forgotten. Since reconstruction of the works in the British and French zones had long since been taken up and was using a great deal of money, the dismemberment authorities had begun to toy with the idea of using the money saved by Hoechst for these other companies. After all, the money was part of the total assets to be distributed. In the final phase of Allied control, therefore, there was a real danger that Hoechst's experience during the I. G. period might be repeated. The money it had earned, but not used for development because of a lack of initiative, was to be made available to the more active companies. Happily, it was in the end possible to prevent such an unfortunate decision.

In Hoechst, too, as the regulations were gradually relaxed, the desire to rebuild grew. Several large buildings, including laboratories, had been started and were later integrated into our expansion programme. Nevertheless, all these initiatives were continually inhibited by the existing regulations to which the works were subjected after confiscation. We could not take decisions on the basis of long-term commercial considerations but only according to trusteeship principles. Each company decision was judged solely in terms of its immediate profitability. For example, capacities were not fully utilized if this meant temporary losses. The finance and accounts department exercised almost absolute powers of control and decision. It must also be remembered that the works of Hoechst, Griesheim and Offenbach had had completely autonomous administrations until 1952. There was hardly any exchange of ideas between them in the first years after the occupation. The reason for this was that the control authorities suspected intrigues behind all joint discussions and attempts to re-merge these complexes. The various works even had independent selling organizations at home and abroad.

Exports were faced with many difficulties. The Americans had separated the Maingau works, at a stroke, from the general sales organization of the I. G. Farbenindustrie. This also seriously affected Bayer and BASF. But in Leverkusen and Ludwigshafen new administrations could be organized without interference while every step that we took at Hoechst was carefully supervised. Great care was taken to ensure that no connections were re-established with the old I. G. offices abroad. This meant that large parts of our efficient foreign organization went to the other two successor companies. We lost many valuable employees with a great deal of foreign experience.

Nonetheless, the sales departments in Hoechst, Griesheim and Offenbach quietly succeeded in creating the framework of a new world-wide selling organization. At first, we could not use the Hoechst symbol of tower and bridge for this. But there were many business contacts in various parts of the world who were willing to act as Hoechst's agents, at their own risk. Hoechst sent abroad many of its sales people and scientists in order to cultivate existing relationships and make new contacts. My own trip to Canada in 1951 served the same purpose.

Unfortunately, 1952 was a bad year economically. This applied to the international situation as much as to the Federal Republic.

Although the Korean crisis had temporarily led to a considerable boom, it was now followed by a serious recession. The Federal Republic, still greatly impeded in its international mobility, was particularly affected by this recession which was further intensified by a world-wide textile crisis.

Farbwerke Hoechst had to record a considerable reduction in exports that was not fully compensated for even by a significant increase in domestic sales. The first year after the re-birth of the company therefore showed a reduction in sales.

The economic situation worried us a great deal. In the first months of 1952, particularly in March and April, some plants were utilized to only 50 per cent of their capacity. This applied particularly to dyestuffs and intermediates. In Offenbach, there was a danger of unemployment. But now, the merger of the various works proved its value. We ferried workers from Offenbach to Hoechst daily and thus convinced even the most hardened critic in Offenbach that it had been wise to join with Hoechst. Before this event, such a view had by no means been universal.

The first months of 1952 therefore put our organizational and creative abilities to a major test. We formed gangs of workers for whom there was temporarily no work and got them to carry out repairs in the factory. We introduced strict stock control and decreed that no more people should be taken on. With these first economy measures, which were relaxed only at the end of 1952, and in part only in 1953, the new board of management proved that it was determined to economize and exercise moderation in its affairs. This was also eventually acknowledged by a critical finance department whose influence we had had to prune a little during reorganization.

In 1952, it needed a great deal of optimism to believe in the future of Hoechst. The public, too – press and radio – dealt frequently with our allegedly fairly limited industrial opportunities. The decisions of the U.S. control authorities in respect of the people on the board of management were also reviewed critically since none of them was known in wider circles. It was, however, precisely these sceptical prognoses that ensured that the human relationships on the board became so close during that time.

Naturally, we seized upon every opportunity of presenting Hoechst in its new, if modest, guise. Achema, the exhibition for chemical apparatus which took place in the summer of 1952 and for the first time received international coverage, again seemed to us an excellent occasion for wooing a wider public.

Hoechst decided to organize a big Achema evening. We hired the opera house in Wiesbaden and the adjacent Kurhaus, both of which had escaped the war practically undamaged. We engaged the Opera di Roma who performed Verdi's 'Masked Ball', and afterwards we invited our 1,200 guests to a ball in the Kurhaus. This event, to which the board of management had agreed unanimously, was regarded by some as a colossal extravaganza in view of the not altogether rosy financial position of the company. But on the other hand, we gained in this way valuable goodwill and made many interesting scientific and commercial contacts.

When we invited the U.S. controller, Randolph Newman and his wife, he gladly accepted although he could not resist telling us that actually we should have asked him for his approval before incurring such a great expenditure. Half seriously and half jokingly, we told him that we intended to use our share capital of 100,000 DM, which was, of course, at our own disposal.

The circle of guests reflected a chapter of both history at large, and of our company. Newman, the prosecutor in the Nuremberg I. G. trials, was flanked by Georg August Zinn, the Minister-President of Hesse, and the former I. G. board members who had just been released from prison. There were also many friends from science and industry. Such a festival, with such an outstanding artistic programme, was a rarity at that time. It is firmly fixed in the memory of the many guests throughout the world. Since then it has become a tradition for Hoechst to have such a function in Wiesbaden every three years on the occasion of Achema. But the enthusiasm and inspiration of 1952 have probably never been matched.

I. G. Share-out

After the Achema festival, the Hoechst board returned to the most pressing question. What would the Hoechst group carved out of the former I. G. look like? This depended, of course, on the funds that would be made available from the I. G. assets and interests.

Of particular importance, for example, was the problem of the share capital of the individual companies. Arrangements for private shareholders could be made only once this had been determined. Also, the claims on the total I. G. assets had to be satisfied. Of these, payments to pensioners appeared the most urgent. Nobody had the faintest idea at the time of the total amount of claims from both Germany and abroad that would have to be met, particularly the restitution claims arising from the war years.

Oscar Gierke and Heinz Kaufmann, Hoechst board members who had come from the control office, gave especially valuable help on these questions. The newly-formed companies, Bayer, BASF and Hoechst, received only assets such as plants or patents, about which there was no dispute. Assets that could not be so clearly defined, including the confiscated foreign assets, remained in the liquidation assets administered by the I. G. Farbenindustrie in Liquidation whose work has not been completed to this day. This arrangement was a happy consequence of the procedure adopted for the re-foundation of Hoechst which we began to appreciate only gradually. It later secured for the newly-founded companies – which the public somewhat unfortunately named I. G. successor companies – the necessary freedom for manoeuvre. Because of this arrangement, no claims in respect of the I. G. could be made upon them.

The division of the I. G. assets was in the hands of three German liquidators appointed in the meantime: Fritz Brinckmann, board member of the Deutsche Treuhandgesellschaft; Franz Reuter, the publisher of the economic weekly, *Der Volkswirt*; and Walter Schmidt, lawyer and expert in share law. They looked after all the assets that had not yet been disposed of and were therefore the negotiating partners of the boards of the successor companies. The liquidators were supported by a committee of eleven, mainly from banking and industrial circles.

The liquidators were not, however, able to act entirely independently. All their decisions required approval by the Allied High Commission, represented by TRIFCOG, or Tripartite I. G. Farben Control Group.

This High Commission resided on the Petersberg near Bonn. Its representatives for the I. G. dismemberment were the three control officers in the American, British and French zones – Randolph H. Newman, E. L. Douglas Fowles and Jean de Fouchier respectively.

The huge and not easily defined total assets of the I. G. Farbenindustrie, in so far as they were located within the territory of the Federal Republic of Germany, had to be distributed item by item among the successor companies. This required a large number of individual decisions which affected not only many fairly large factories but also numerous smaller undertakings and interests. The assets also included a large number of patents and in particular the valuable old trademarks. Everything that once made up the assets in the balance sheet of I. G. Farbenindustrie had to be divided up. Not unnaturally, there were varying opinions among those involved as to what constituted an appropriate share. It was agreed, however, that the three companies to be formed should be approximately the same size and should be internationally competitive and viable. The decision of what was viable remained the prerogative of the three control officers.

Their views differed a great deal. The French and the British judgements were influenced by practical considerations of domestic interests, however different the potential of their chemical industries may have been. It would not be right to criticize the victor powers for this attitude. At least, it was well-defined and allowance could be made for it, at any rate by anyone who had some idea of the situation in European and international chemistry. If the disputes reached a really critical phase, it was possible to negotiate directly with the interested parties in France or Britain. During the last stages of dismemberment, we occasionally did this with varying degrees of success.

These confidential talks and agreements beyond Germany's frontiers were the forerunner of later European cooperation in chemistry. It was by no means a supranational capitalist conspiracy. Quite the contrary: competitor encountered competitor. And when things became really tough, we, as the weaker party, almost always had to yield. But it was by far the simplest way. The attitude of the American control office was far more complicated and far less readily understood. It was dictated primarily by economic theories and political ideologies. The Americans could not rid themselves of their anti-cartel complex which has been a factor in American politics ever since the anti-trust laws and the Sherman Act of 1890. This attitude was, of course, reinforced by the resolve not to allow resurrection of the old I. G. and its competitive power on any account.

Fortunately, economic thinking in the young Federal Republic had not at that time been caught up in the wilderness of political ideology. While today there are again calls for state control of the economy and for constraints on the free interplay of commercial forces, there then existed throughout Germany a spirit of generosity and liberalism.

It will for ever be to the credit of Ludwig Erhard, the German Economics Minister at the time, that his faith in a free market economy provided the decisive dynamic impulses for German recovery.

Not only the Federal government but also public opinion was on the side of industry. Old and young alike were agreed that only courageous enterprise and an active industry could raise the people's standard of living to a tolerable level once more. With commendable unanimity, the Länder governments, local governments, trade unions and the press did their best to create the conditions for successful reconstruction of the German economy.

The Federal government in particular took a personal and positive interest in our problems. This applied to Chancellor Adenauer himself with whom we frequently had to negotiate. Adenauer and his government devoted themselves closely to economic questions although world political problems such as the integration of the Federal Republic in the western defence system commanded much of their attention. The Federal government realized that successful foreign and domestic policies must be based on a solid economic policy.

The Federal government had available the services of outstanding economic experts with whom the Hoechst management had to maintain close contact. I concentrated on the question of what works and assets should be awarded to Farbwerke Hoechst from the total assets of the I. G. It was my job to see that Hoechst got its proper share of the I. G. cake which was about to be cut up. The management of each of the three successor companies took as its starting point the historical development of the individual works and attempted to regain at least those works that it had originally introduced into the I. G. upon its formation in 1925.

Negotiations were conducted by the chairmen of the three companies. Thus there arose the curious situation that a decisive chapter of the dismemberment story was written largely by those men who many years previously had been selected by the management of the old I. G. as directors of the three large I. G. groups – Leverkusen, Ludwigshafen, and Hoechst. Of course, not one of us had any idea then that our first job would be a conflict concerning the inheritance of the I. G. Carl Wurster, the chairman of BASF, had held his job since 1938. Ulrich Haberland, the Bayer chief, had taken over the management of Leverkusen shortly before the war ended. I was three years younger than the others, and had been selected to take over the management of Hoechst some years after the end of the war.

We now met as competitors under totally different circumstances and each tried to wrest the most favourable conditions for his company. We were in an almost unique situation. We knew each other well and we were familiar with the conditions and internal relationships in the other works, because we had all come from the same I. G. Farbenindustrie. The three of us had had the same scientific training, witnessed each other's careers, and had sat together on innumerable occasions on the commissions of I. G. Farbenindustrie.

We all talked the same language. And when we were by ourselves, and this happened quite frequently in the years after 1952, our talks were friendly and open. We could conduct our fights more intensively and more ruthlessly than any other three men in the same position and with the same responsibility would ever have been able to do. But the mutual respect that we had for each other remained unaffected. We never forgot our links but, equally, we never fell victim to sentimentality.

Especially in the first months of 1952, there was a great deal to be discussed and negotiated. I was new to this circle because Haberland and Wurster had been allowed to keep their jobs at the end of the war. We were all still comparatively young and had retained our sense of humour so that we could sit cheerfully through very long meetings. This was an undoubted advantage, both for our negotiations and for our understanding of each other.

One of the meeting points that we frequently chose was the hotel 'Zur Post' in Limburg on the Lahn, which at that time was modest but very homely. Our three cars arrived punctually for each meeting as we had been trained to do in the I. G. We were always driven by the same drivers, who knew each other as well as we did and who were the souls of discretion.

When the 'three professors', as the press afterwards described us, appeared together, for example during receptions abroad, the eldest always acted as spokesman. This fell to Carl Wurster, exactly four days older than Ulrich Haberland who, no doubt, rather regretted this disadvantage because he liked to appear in public. I was the youngest and I did not have to face the limelight on such occasions.

Wurster has probably never found it so difficult to exercise his seniority as when he bade a last farewell to our friend Ulrich Haberland in 1961. After the funeral, Wurster and I drove down the autobahn together to the south and recalled many joint episodes with Haberland.

At the same time, we realized that with the death of Haberland, an important chapter of our life had come to an end. The period of natural agreement, which was very much in evidence in spite of intense competition, had closed. It is difficult to believe that a similar situation among the three heads of the I. G. successor companies, based solely on personal relationships and a common past, could ever happen again.

With the exception of Knapsack, all the companies that Hoechst wanted to take over from the I. G. assets, were located in the U.S. zone. The exaggerated dismemberment aims of the American control authorities had resulted in the appointment of an independent trustee for each works. The size of the works was immaterial to the Americans. Thus it came about that at a trustee meeting under American supervision, the representative of the Hoechst works, numbering some 9,500 employees, would sit, on a basis of equality, next to the trustee of our wine cellar in Eltville where only a few people were employed. No doubt the Americans had originally intended to hive off these units for ever and to conduct them as independent concerns. At one time, there was even a plan for dividing the large Hoechst complex into four separate parts.

The quality of the trustees was necessarily rather varied. Most of them tried their best to conduct the company under their control to the benefit of all, in so far as the control authority allowed them to do so at all. But there were also many mistakes. After all, many trustees were new to the company and did not know its traditions or problems. In addition, and perhaps understandably, personal ambition and attempts to gain personal advantage sometimes played a role, particularly in the case of the smaller units.

By January 1952, the only certainty was that the Hoechst complex would be joined with the Griesheim and Offenbach works as well as Knapsack. The latter would come to Hoechst together with its interests in Sauerstoffwerke Griesheim-Autogen and Uhde. There was also no longer any discussion concerning the takeover of Sperr- und Fassholzfabrik Goldbach near Aschaffenburg. This was a concern that had formerly belonged to BASF and was engaged mainly in the production of wooden drums for chemicals. In the beginning we had a good deal of difficulty with Goldbach. In the last few years, however, the company has developed favourably and has enlarged its manufacturing programme by modern products such as floors and walls for computers and offices.

These assets awarded to Hoechst were clearly too small and in- sufficient to enable us to hold our own against the more powerful competitors. I had no doubt that other companies from the former possessions of Farbwerke Hoechst would have to be joined to Hoechst.

During the ensuing negotiations, we sometimes had to resort to quite devious means. We often had a situation that was not dissimilar to interminable peace talks between delegations from opposing camps who regularly exchange profound proclamations concerning past and future. But no less decisive than the purely factual negoti- ations were the personal relationships. I recall many persuasive discussions in which we tried to win over the leaders of companies that we wanted to incorporate into the Hoechst complex. We knew that we would get their agreement to join us only if we were able to give them confidence in us and in the future of Hoechst. Where it was not possible to create such a personal community of interest, all efforts failed.

This experience probably applies to all industrial mergers. Success can be expected only if, beyond the purely material and economic interests, there is also personal harmony between all those involved. Economic considerations serve little purpose if such a human relationship cannot be established. It will always be an expensive and risky business to buy companies in the stock exchange, as it were, without being sure of the agreement of the people and the management that work there.

The 'grand old men' of the chemical industry helped us at Hoechst immeasurably in our efforts. These people had long retired at the end of the war but knowledge, tradition and sense of history gave them an authority and a power to convince that had proved its value once already during the foundation of the I. G. Farbenindustrie. I am thinking especially of Wilhelm Kalle, Paul Duden, and Gustav Pistor whose help was of inestimable value in those months. These personalities were also beyond reach of the control authority. Their voices could not be ignored.

Hoechst Gains Foothold in Bavaria

The relationship with our Bavarian works in Gersthofen in the vicinity of Augsburg was cleared up quickest and simplest of all. Once the new Hoechst complex in the Maingau had assumed firm outlines, the trustee in Gersthofen, Paul Heisel, as well as the American control authority, quickly realized that this works, founded by Hoechst, was not viable on its own and had to be linked with Hoechst once more.

When the moment appeared opportune, Michael Erlenbach and I drove to Gersthofen and for a whole day discussed with Heisel, who until then had acted independently, the problems that had to be solved at Gersthofen. We parted as good friends. A joint document outlining the arrangement agreed by us was put through the letter box of the American control officer the same evening.

The arguments contained in this letter and the concept proposed by us were so convincing that the Americans gave their agreement without hesitation. At the next meeting of the supervisory board, Heisel was appointed to the board of management of Hoechst.

Shortly afterwards, in the summer of 1952, a big festival took place in Gersthofen to celebrate the fiftieth anniversary of the works. During this event, all the negotiating partners sat together peaceably in the beer tent drinking large steins. Our company included the American control officer whose countenance relaxed more and more as the day wore on. The traditional balloon event was also revived in Gersthofen that day. The balloons were filled with hydrogen obtained from chlorine electrolysis.

It was one of those festivals that helped us overcome the many disagreements and disappointments that were still in store for us. Gersthofen, of course, offered the right atmosphere for such a carefree gathering that conformed to the traditional Bavarian way of life. Actually, the foundation of the Gersthofen works in 1902 did not have an auspicious start. At the time, Hoechst, in competition with BASF, was looking for the most economic process for the

The centenary hall on 11 January 1963. Outside and inside views

Talking to the Minister-President of Hesse, Georg August Zinn (left) and Friedrich Jähne

Amongst the old-age pensioners

synthesis of indigo. One route involved the electrochemical production of chromic acid. Because the required electrical current was
available cheaply in Bavaria, Hoechst decided to construct a works
on the banks of the Lech river. But before production in Gersthofen
could get properly under way, another method proved far more
suitable. For a long period thereafter the factory on the Lech
proved uneconomic.

By 1952, waxes and terpene derivatives had become interesting
products in Gersthofen. Later, Gersthofen became an important
centre for our further plans in Bavaria where today more than a
third of our total industrial activity in the Federal Republic is
concentrated.

Behringwerke Back With Hoechst

Another subsidiary that we were determined to get back into the
fold was Behringwerke. Its foundation had followed the historic
partnership beween Hoechst and Emil von Behring, the first Nobel
prizewinner in medicine. The vaccines and sera produced in
Marburg were used in all parts of the world as effective weapons
in the fight against infectious diseases and epidemics. They formed
an ideal supplementary range for our Hoechst pharmaceutical
products.

At first, however, there appeared to be few avenues for re-
establishing the former connection. Of the many plans for the future
of Behringwerke – drawn up with astonishing facility by qualified
as well as unqualified people, frequently with a total disregard for
the realities of the situation – one was positively harmful to our
interests. It provided that Behringwerke was to be converted into a
state institute on the lines, no doubt, of the Pasteur Institute.

We used all our wiles and arguments to prevent such a development. First of all, we succeeded in winning the government of Hesse
over to our view, and they, in turn, were gradually able to convince
the occupation authorities that such proposals did not accord with
German ideas of a liberal economy independent of the state. This,
however, by no means decided the case. One day I was called to the
Economics Ministry in Bonn where I met Albert Demnitz, manager
of Behringwerke, whom I had not encountered before. It soon
emerged that our views diverged sharply. Eventually, we suspended
negotiations, which had come to a dead end, and agreed to meet

C.Y.—12

again in the evening. Our venue was rather curious for it was a former submarine supply vessel on the Rhine at Bonn which had been converted into a restaurant that was greatly esteemed by gastronomic connoisseurs. During the informal talks over a bottle of fine wine, the ice between Demnitz and myself gradually melted.

I found that the people in Marburg did not have very happy memories of Hoechst. Even during the I. G. time, they tended to look more to Leverkusen than to Hoechst. Demnitz was a veterinary surgeon. He had successfully developed a serum against foot-and-mouth disease and introduced it in Germany and the rest of Europe. This had helped him to get into close contact with Bayer and he was now attempting to re-establish this connection. No doubt one of the decisive factors with him was that the Bayer selling organization with the world-famous Bayer cross was still intact.

After a long discussion, I nevertheless succeeded in getting Demnitz to agree to work with Hoechst, an agreement which offered excellent opportunities to Behringwerke. Later, Demnitz and I became extremely good friends. This honest, rather cumbersome man had many worries when Salk vaccine was introduced into the Federal Republic but he eventually achieved great success together with his colleagues.

After my agreement with Demnitz, I came to an arrangement with Farbenfabriken Bayer who had, of course, also been interested in Behringwerke. The Marburg concern returned to the Hoechst organization and since that date has worked closely with Hoechst's pharmaceutical division. On its own, Behringwerke would not have been able to utilize to the full its outstanding research results. Without belonging to a larger complex with a world-wide sales organization and considerable financial strength, Behringwerke would, no doubt, have become the puppet of various conflicting interests. Behringwerke accounts for a considerable part of Hoechst's pharmaceutical sales of more than 1,500 million DM in 1970. Its contribution to our joint pharmaceutical research is no less significant.

At first, however, a selling company was founded which was shared fifty-fifty by Bayer and Hoechst. As could have been predicted, this did not prove succesful and agreement was therefore reached that Hoechst should take over the sole selling rights for Behringwerke products.

Cassella Stays Single

The reconstitution of Cassella as an independent successor company was a great disappointment to us. This met the wishes of the Cassella management and also those of the U.S. control officer. The fact that Hoechst and Cassella had been closely connected since 1904 was completely ignored. The fusion of Hoechst and Cassella and the merging of their respective capital had initiated the formation of a strong chemical complex in the Maingau which was joined two years later by Kalle in Wiesbaden-Biebrich. Even when the I. G. was set up and coal tar dyestuffs and pharmaceuticals were rationalized, this historical association was taken into account and consolidated through the reciprocal exchange of products.

Arthur von Weinberg, a pupil of Adolf von Baeyer in Munich and a friend of Paul Ehrlich, had worked particularly hard for co-operation with Hoechst. But long before the octogenarian fell victim to the racial ideologies of the Third Reich during the Second World War, there had been little personal contact between the former companies.

All the experts in German industry were of the opinion that Hoechst and Cassella should again merge. It was therefore a serious setback for Hoechst when such a decision could not be implemented. We could expect little support from our new competitors in Leverkusen and Ludwigshafen since Cassella, as a dyestuffs manufacturer, appeared to play a considerable role in the equilibrium of forces within the three I.G. successor companies.

Therefore, it appeared improbable that the independence so surprisingly granted to Cassella would continue for long. Immediately after the foundation of Cassella, secret buying took place on the stock exchange. It was soon found that BASF, Bayer, and Hoechst, the three interested parties, were behind it. Naturally, this situation was not without its human conflicts and animosities.

After three years, the three successor companies between them had acquired some three-quarters of the Cassella shares and eventually they agreed to hold 25 per cent each. The very promising discovery of polyacrylonitrile fibre by Herbert Rein of Cassella was acquired by Leverkusen for a substantial payment. In the succeeding years, Bayer developed its world-famous Dralon on the basis of Rein's invention. Cassella's resources would not have been big enough to realize such an expensive programme.

The tug-of-war concerning Cassella was an outstanding chapter in the stormy and colourful history of the I. G. dismemberment. There appeared at first no reasonable solution and it was a long time before this important company gained its proper place within the German chemical industry. Cassella ultimately joined Hoechst in 1969 as part of the final tidying-up operation in the German chemical industry.

During the fiftieth anniversary celebrations of Cassella in 1920, Arthur von Weinberg was able to say: 'The problem of cooperation between two works, without mutual inhibition, has probably never before been solved so happily as on this occasion.' During the centenary celebrations of Cassella in May 1970, we all felt that this inheritance of an economic and human partnership could now be continued.

Fibres from Bobingen

In 1952 we were rather luckier with the incorporation of Bobingen, near Augsburg, a former artificial silk factory of the I. G. Perlon bristles had been produced there since 1946 and Perlon fibres since 1950. Bobingen therefore offered an important basis upon which to build our further developments in the field of synthetic fibres.

We had quite a fight for Bobingen, particularly as it did not formerly belong to the Hoechst complex. At one time, there was a plan to join all the former fibre plants of the I. G. into an independent company. This would have meant the integration of Dormagen from the Bayer group, Bobingen, Cassella and Rottweil. Fortunately, this idea was buried for all time after a protracted and complicated meeting at the Federal Economics Ministry under the chairmanship of Felix Prentzel, the later chief of Degussa. Its realization would have spelt the death sentence for the entire German fibre industry. Without other fields of production and without the necessary starting products, such a one-sided undertaking would hardly have been able to withstand the violent changes in economic fortunes. To Hoechst, on the other hand, ownership of Bobingen provided a springboard for a successful engagement in the fibre field.

Dismemberment – The Final Act

The final act of the I. G. dismemberment was also the most dramatic. Two unsolved problems, vital for Hoechst, were the fate of Kalle in Wiesbaden and of Wacker-Chemie in Munich. Both companies had been introduced into the I. G. Farbenindustrie by Hoechst. We therefore pleaded that Kalle should be returned to us as a 100 per cent subsidiary which it had been before. We also demanded the return of our 50 per cent interest in Wacker.

Initially, it was very difficult to make clear to the public the thinking behind these demands and their importance. Even the management of Kalle and the Wacker family, the only people with whom we could have serious discussions in the first instance, barely acknowledged our intentions, let alone discussed the resumption of the earlier relationship. They had unhappy memories of Hoechst from the I. G. period.

Kalle, in Wiesbaden-Biebrich, closely connected to Hoechst since 1906, had become a specialized concern as a result of technical developments during the I. G. period. Its products had little to do with classical chemistry. Cellophane manufacture had been introduced by Hoechst after the First World War as a result of a licensing agreement with the French and had been developed by Kalle into a major production field. Cellophane was joined later by interesting cellulose derivatives such as Nalo sausage skin and methyl cellulose. A photocopying process, invented by the monk and photochemist Gustav Kögel and based on the light sensitivity of azo dyestuffs, had become known throughout the world under its trade name 'Ozalid'.

The American control authority very much wanted to take Kalle out of the I. G. successor negotiations altogether. Several attempts had been made to sell the company to outsiders. The management, under a trustee imposed from the outside, fought tenaciously for the existence of the company. Its efforts were by no means without success. Although the plant was fairly antiquated, Kalle succeeded quickly in setting up a modest but profitable production. Kalle products were in great demand. Moreover, there were many relationships in the cellophane field which linked the company closely with French and British industry.

It was therefore all the more difficult to induce the management, which was orientated to a different way of thinking, to rejoin the Hoechst group with which it had lost all technical and administrative connections in the thirties.

We did not come to a fruitful exchange of ideas until the summer of 1952. The senior executive of the company, Wilhelm Kalle and his brother-in-law R. Schreiber-Gastell, played an important mediating role. In many personal discussions, we were eventually able to arouse some sympathy for our view that not only historical factors but also future potentialities rendered cooperation between Hoechst and Kalle desirable.

We pointed out to the Wiesbaden people all the advantages that would arise, for example, from a direct supply of raw materials from Hoechst. We also envisaged that the plastics era was not far away and that it would open up interesting possibilities for plastic films that did not yet form part of the Kalle production range and for which we would be able to supply the starting material. But our biggest concern was that such an attractive company as Kalle would not be able to maintain its independence in the long run. We feared, as happened in the case of Cassella, that the company might quickly fall into outside hands as a result of share transactions.

We did not achieve swift progress in our efforts to persuade the German authorities to support us in accomplishing the return of Kalle because we could not readily prove that the work in Wiesbaden-Biebrich was vital to Hoechst. The other successor companies did not oppose our efforts but urged prompt completion of the I. G. dismemberment measures and were unhappy that Hoechst was still arguing. But our ambitions were not unlimited, as was clearly shown when Hoechst rejected participation in the cellophane factory of Wolff Walsrode, which was also under discussion.

In Leverkusen and Ludwigshafen, consolidation had progressed far more quickly. Hoechst was still in a difficult position. Internal harmony had developed encouragingly and reconstruction was also proceeding speedily, but dismemberment affairs were still unresolved, partly because the American control officer rarely agreed with our ideas. He had little understanding for our continuous efforts to get back Cassella and Kalle. In both cases, he opposed our demands right up to the end. On the other hand, he too was interested in an early conclusion of the dismemberment business.

The presence of an American control authority came to be regarded as an anachronism not only in the Federal Republic but also in the United States. Dwight D. Eisenhower had been elected U.S. President in November 1952. A change of government was imminent and a new era in American politics was about to begin. But since several problems of great importance to us had not yet been satisfactorily resolved, we opposed the termination of dismemberment negotiations and thus invited the displeasure of all the other interested parties.

The question of an interest in Wacker also remained undecided. Indeed, I was not seriously confronted with this question until the early summer of 1952. Wacker-Chemie in Burghausen on the Bavarian-Austrian frontier had been confiscated in 1945 together with the entire I. G. This meant that the interest of the Wacker family was blocked, too, so that it had no income for many years.

The relationship between Wacker and Hoechst had not been particularly good even in the I. G. period. Until he died in 1938, Ludwig Hermann, the Hoechst works manager, who himself came from Bavaria, had an excellent relationship with Johannes Hess of Wacker who died in 1951. Thereafter, however, cooperation between Wacker and Hoechst was minimal and existed only on paper.

Hoechst was no longer represented on the supervisory board of Wacker and the commercial relationships were overshadowed by many competitive problems. A great deal of pettiness further undermined the former relationship. Finally, after the death of the founder, Alexander Wacker, in 1922, the family had little influence on the management of the company. Therefore it now pleaded for greater responsibility and for financial compensation. The American control officer, however, showed little understanding for the family's wishes and needs.

This meant that there was in Munich a fairly intense antipathy to Hoechst and the whole former I. G. Farbenindustrie. Wacker wanted finally to shake off the old fetters. After I had learnt all this for the first time, I began even to understand the attitude of the Wacker family.

Ever since the spring of 1952, a rumour had been circulating that a Bavarian banking consortium was prepared to make an offer to the American control authority for the acquisition of 50 per cent of the capital of Wacker in agreement with the Wacker family. The American control officer took a favourable view of this plan. Little further information could therefore be gained from him. Certainly nobody favoured the sort of solution Hoechst was suggesting.

In the meantime, however, dismemberment had passed largely into German hands. Although the Allied control authority continued to have the last word, we had a little more freedom of movement. Exploratory negotiations that we carried out with the banking consortium were negative. We did not get any information and could not even establish whether, in fact, an offer had been made. This increased our suspicion that the banking consortium was simply acting as a buyer for another, unnamed party. Finally, we succeeded in entering into rather more worthwhile talks with the Wacker family. During careful exploratory discussions and after much diplomatic negotiation, we were at long last able to establish personal contact with the people of the Wacker company and the members of the family.

In order to force a final decision, Economics Minister Ludwig Erhard invited the parties to a discussion in July 1952. In fact he succeeded, and Hoechst has never forgotten this, in bringing about an agreement in a relatively short time. During these negotiations with the Wacker family, we agreed that Hoechst would be given a 49 per cent interest in Wacker-Chemie subject to certain conditions. The shareholding of the family was to be increased by 1 per cent to 51 per cent. We subsequently returned to Hoechst with the representatives of the Wacker family and prepared a seven-point memorandum. This formed the basis for future reorganization. In 1958, we agreed with the Wacker family to revert to the former share ratio of fifty-fifty.

Hoechst had thus achieved a considerable success, particularly since the entire acetylene chemistry of both Wacker and Hoechst was so closely connected. A transfer of the Wacker interest to other hands would have been a serious blow to our plastics chemistry which was still fairly weak at that time.

Although cooperation on a fifty-fifty basis between a family concern and a large-scale company like Hoechst is not a simple affair, we have always managed to achieve a tolerable solution for both parties, whatever the problems. This has, of course, meant that both sides have had to be prepared to show mutual understanding in spite of divergent interests.

Our arguments for a partnership between Wacker and Hoechst have since been proved absolutely right. Wacker-Chemie prospered and the relationship between the family and Hoechst remained satisfactory. As a result of excellent scientific, technical and commercial achievements, the management of Wacker succeeded in raising the company to its present importance. It now employs 7,800 employees and between 1953 and 1970 its annual sales have increased from 114 million to approximately 700 million DM. Both groups of shareholders can justly claim to have kept dividends to the minimum and thus made it possible for the company to finance its investments largely out of its own resources.

Solution for Kalle and Wacker

For the final solution of the two problems, we still needed the agreement of the German and Allied authorities. Before this was eventually obtained, in the second half of 1952, several fairly dramatic disputes occurred. At first the Allied control officers and TRIFCOG completely rejected our proposals in both cases. Incidentally, there were also points of dispute with both Bayer and BASF. Leverkusen was trying to get back Agfa, and Ludwigshafen was after the Auguste-Viktoria mine. In Hoechst, we regarded both these demands as justified.

As the year 1952 drew to a close, there was naturally an increased desire to bring the matter to an end. Adenauer, too, wanted to see a final settlement and took a personal hand in the affair. His friend and adviser, Robert Pferdmenges, the influential banker, was ordered to negotiate a compromise by any means. In the first place, this involved the four outstanding questions: Agfa to Leverkusen, Auguste-Viktoria mine to Ludwigshafen, Kalle and an interest in Wacker to Hoechst. We were the only ones seeking two objectives and, of course, it was not unreasonable for attempts to be made to achieve an arrangement in which each one of the three companies was granted only one of its aims.

I could not agree to such a step even when Pferdmenges pressed me to do so one evening in his home, and Haberland and Wurster also urged me to compromise. It seemed to me unthinkable to forgo assets of such importance simply to achieve agreement. In the interest of Hoechst and its future shareholders, I stuck stubbornly to my guns and to our demand for Kalle and the Wacker shares. We parted rather bad friends. Pferdmenges returned his brief to the Federal government.

Two days before Christmas, Erhard made another attempt to achieve a settlement. He let us know that if we came to an agreement, he would immediately drive to see the Allied control authority on the

Petersberg to conclude this unhappy chapter. According to his suggestion, BASF was to get the Auguste-Viktoria mine, Bayer the Agfa works, and Hoechst the Wacker interest. We would have to forgo Kalle at first but would be free to buy its shares on the stock exchange with the help of the other parties.

This proposal by Erhard faced me with a grave decision. The representatives of Bayer and BASF agreed to the compromise plan of the Federal Economics Minister without any hesitation and attempted to win me over with all the powers at their command. But I felt bound to reject this compromise also. We parted once again without a result.

My stubbornness caused great disappointment, indeed, anger, among the other parties. I travelled home on my own late that night, tortured by doubts as to whether I had acted wisely.

It may seem incomprehensible today that the fate of large companies –at that time Kalle employed some 3,000 people – should be decided so arbitrarily. It can be understood only if we realize the situation of the Federal Republic at that time. Its freedom of action was still fairly limited and it obviously had a considerable interest in arriving at a good understanding with the occupying powers. Subsequently, I celebrated the first Christmas with my family in our new home in Königstein. It could not have been more pleasant. Of course, my thoughts frequently returned to the unsolved problems that would face me again in all their harshness after the holidays. It was one of those moments in life when one feels totally alone in the face of an apparently hopeless situation. Therefore, when my colleagues unanimously approved my attitude at the first board meeting of the new year on 6 January 1953, I was tremendously relieved.

Our Share Capital is being Negotiated

Shortly before Christmas, another important decision had to be made. The experts of the financial and accounts departments had done their homework during the course of the year so successfully that an opening balance sheet of the successor companies appeared a practical possibility. In December 1952, the liquidators, the supervisory board of the I. G. Farbenindustrie in Liquidation and the chairmen of Leverkusen, Ludwigshafen, and Hoechst, joined in a memorable meeting at which the share capital of the three new companies was to be decided.

Of the assets of the I. G. Farbenindustrie confiscated by the Allies, only about 30 per cent were located in the Federal Republic and only about 36 per cent were handed over to the three successor companies. The remainder was in former German territories now under Polish administration, in central Germany and abroad. Naturally, we had to watch that the many former shareholders of the I. G. Farbenindustrie, who came from all levels of society, were adequately compensated. Their claims were to be met, as far as possible without loss, from the modest I. G. assets that had survived in the Federal Republic.

The liquidators had to ensure that after the new companies had been founded, liquidation funds were sufficient to meet any future claims. On the other hand, the successor companies had to have enough capital to enable them to conduct successful operations. To find a just solution to this problem was uncommonly difficult. Everyone was anxious to provide reasonable compensation for the former shareholders but at the same time wanted to see a viable company. During these discussions, the first skirmishes occurred that heralded the subsequent competition between the companies. The amount of the share capital taken over by them, or rather imposed upon them, governed the extent of their obligation towards the later shareholders. The company with fewer shares than its competitors would, of course, enjoy better financing opportunities later on.

It was finally agreed that the three successor companies and Cassella should take over a nominal capital of slightly more than 1,000 million DM. This corresponded to approximately 75 per cent of the former share capital of the I. G. Farbenindustrie which had a value of 1,400 million DM. Bayer, BASF, Hoechst, and Cassella were moreover granted a total claim on the residual capital of something like 135 million DM which had, however, to be assessed very carefully at first because nobody knew the exact value of the residual assets.

In fixing the share capital, everybody had to realize that these funds had become available only as a result of the complete dissolution of the hidden reserves of the old I. G. The transferred assets were revalued sufficiently for appropriate – and necessary – depreciation to be carried out.

The final negotiations, therefore, were preceded by tough internal discussions concerning the valuation of the assets. Again and again, the technicians pointed out that much of the plant was fairly antiquated. Finally, legal and free reserves had to be formed to meet any claims arising under the law concerning the equalization of burdens.

The residual claim of 135 million DM was also a subject for negotiation as was its distribution between the successor companies. Ludwigshafen pointed to the extensive damage that had been caused by an explosion during the occupation and that had not been adequately covered by insurance as the result of negligence on the part of the occupation powers.

The discussions were extremely vociferous and continued until late into the night. Several times, Haberland, Wurster and I retired for separate talks. Eventually, we reached agreement. The capital of Hoechst was fixed at 285·7 million DM, that of Ludwigshafen at 340, and that of Leverkusen at 387·7 million DM. The Cassella capital was determined at 34·1 million DM. These figures alone show the low rank accorded to Hoechst in comparison with BASF and Bayer.

These negotiations were particularly difficult for me because during my I. G. period I had gained practically no experience in questions of finance or accounts. As a scientist, technical tasks had left me little time to occupy myself with commercial and financial problems. My I. G. colleagues, Haberland and Wurster, chiefs of their companies for some years, were clearly superior to me in this field. They had had to occupy themselves with financial problems in the past.

I shall never forget how weighed down I was by the responsibility placed upon me by the events of that 3 December 1952. I had to decide on a most vital question regarding the future of our company and I fully realized that I did not have sufficient experience to make this decision. But no advisers were admitted to these meetings and the situation therefore left me with no other choice. In spite of my comparative ignorance in these matters, I had understood one thing. It was important to keep the share capital as low as possible, and I advanced every possible argument to achieve this.

When I encountered resistance, Hermann Richter, at that time member of the supervisory board of the I. G. Farbenindustrie in

Liquidation, gave me a valuable piece of advice. He told me that if I intended to remain stubborn on this point, I should at least offer some concessions during the distribution of the residual claim. This advice I followed and thus made agreement possible. Later on, Hermann Richter was for many years chairman of the Hoechst supervisory board. The wise counsel he offered me at that time was not the only piece of sound advice that I was to receive from him.

Next morning, my colleagues on the board congratulated me on the solution that had been reached. Ulrich Haberland always complained afterwards that Hoechst had gained a unilateral advantage for itself. It was a fact, of course, that our share capital was 100 million DM less than that of Leverkusen. This provided us with better financing possibilities in the first years. But we urgently needed this advantage because our assets were in fact worth far less and we were lagging considerably behind the others in terms of investments.

On this and later occasions, I recognized that the I. G. had not given its scientists adequate financial and commercial training. We were thoroughly schooled in all questions of works management but commercial decisions remained confined to a small circle. I drew my lessons from this and always took care that the Hoechst management was fully informed about important commercial questions. This is the only way in which the management of a large company can carry the overall responsibility with which it has been charged.

Another difficult question that had to be resolved before the reconstitution of the company could finally take place was the distribution of the pension obligations. Endless conferences by the experts were necessary. First of all, we had to get the Allies to accept that we would have to pay pensions. The Americans especially, who in their country were still at the very beginning of a social insurance system, took a rather negative attitude in this matter. On the other hand, the liquidators had to watch carefully over their residual assets and therefore opposed too great an allocation for pension rights.

Eventually we agreed that the obligations should be taken over by a central pension fund. The payments were charged proportionately to the newly-formed companies. All employees of the I. G. Farbenindustrie who had been employed up to a certain date gained the right to a pension. Hoechst participated in the payments with a fixed percentage. This was a considerable charge on the company finances, especially as there was one pensioner to two employees when the company was reconstituted.

This agreement led to many subsequent discussions and some of these are still occasionally revived today. As time went by, there were calls for re-classifying the number of pensioners and even for changing the classification formula. Since, however, the I. G. dismemberment can be regarded only as a whole, we have always decided not to change this fundamental agreement.

The First Annual General Meeting

At the beginning of 1953, the last decisions were taken. Our firmness had paid off. The control authorities had grown tired of arguing and finally concurred with our stubbornly defended views: Hoechst gained Kalle and a 49 per cent interest in Wacker-Chemie.

But there was excitement right up to the last minute. Suddenly, it was announced that the foundation of Kalle had taken place before that of Hoechst. The Allied control authorities had arranged a meeting of the Kalle supervisory board at which the foundation of the new Kalle AG was decided without any prior notification being sent to Hoechst. Supervisory and management boards were appointed, again without any notification to Hoechst. Federal Chancellor Adenauer protested on behalf of the Federal government against this unilateral action by the control authority. The Hoechst management, too, instead of congratulations, sent a letter of protest which resulted in declarations calculated to calm our nerves. Indeed, the surprising turn of events did not, in the end, result in any fundamental changes in the agreements that had been made.

There was yet a further surprise concerning Kalle. On the evening before the foundation of Hoechst, the French High Commissioner got in touch with me through the Federal Ministry of Economics and asked for my agreement to a plan under which the French group La Cellophane would get a 15 per cent interest in the share capital of Kalle in the form of an increase in capital. This was to compensate the company for claims arising from an old licensing agreement with Kalle which, La Cellophane maintained, had not been fulfilled by the I. G.

By now I had grown tired of arguing, and I agreed and informed the supervisory board next morning. My news was accepted with resignation in spite of some disappointment.

We later persuaded the French to give up their share in Kalle in exchange for Hoechst shares. We also agreed to a continuous exchange of experience in the cellophane field and this was later extended to other fields. In the course of time there even developed a friendly relationship with La Cellophane and particularly with its parent company Rhône-Poulenc, whose former president, Marcel Bô had made a great contribution to the agreement.

In the last days of March 1953, the foundation ceremonies in Leverkusen, Ludwigshafen, and Hoechst at long last took place. Understandably, we were filled with great satisfaction over our renewed freedom of action even if the result did not meet all our wishes and even though some problems remained unsolved.

For example, we had had to abandon all interest in Chemische Werke Hüls. A subsequent attempt was made to solve the ownership problems at Hüls through the foundation of Chemie-Verwaltungs AG. But the problem was not finally settled until the end of 1969, after many intermediate solutions of which the most important was the joint production of Buna by Bayer, Hoechst, and Hüls.

After long and complicated negotiations, the framework for Farbwerke Hoechst AG vormals Meister Lucius & Brüning had been determined. It comprised Chemische Fabrik Griesheim, Napthtol-Chemie Offenbach and Lech-Chemie Gersthofen. The following subsidiaries also belonged to the Hoechst group: Knapsack-Griesheim AG, which in turn brought into the new complex its subsidiaries like Gebrüder Wandesleben GmbH in Stromberg and Friedrich Uhde GmbH in Dortmund, Kalle & Co. AG in Wiesbaden-Biebrich, Bobingen AG für Textil-Faser in Bobingen near Augsburg, Behringwerke AG in Marburg and Sperr- und Fassholzfabrik Goldbach GmbH in Goldbach near Aschaffenburg. Moreover, Farbwerke Hoechst had an interest in Wacker-Chemie in Munich and Duisburger Kupferhütte in Duisburg. On the day of its foundation on 27 March 1953, Farbwerke Hoechst AG employed a total of 26,000 workers and staff.

A general meeting took place in Hoechst on 27 March which passed the annual report for 1952. Subsequently, the agreement concerning incorporation of the various works and subsidiaries was minuted.

The previous capital of 100,000 DM was immediately increased to 285·7 million DM by the general meeting. In a telegram to Federal Chancellor Adenauer, we announced that with this general meeting a new chapter had started in the history of the works comprised in the Farbwerke Hoechst group. At the same time, the supervisory board and the board of management as well as the employees of all the works expressed to the Chancellor their delight and thanks for the help that he had given the company.

Subsequently, a large number of guests and employees assembled in the auditorium which had in the meantime been restored. With pride and satisfaction, but also fully conscious of the responsibility I had accepted, I made my first speech on behalf of the new board of management. On this occasion, I also took the opportunity of delivering an unequivocal vindication of the board of management and the supervisory board of the old I. G. Farbenindustrie (see Appendix).

In our guest house in Eltville, which had been returned to us without argument, we had taken our leave the evening before of Randolph H. Newman and his wife. Our relationship in the last few months had become much more pleasant and friendly. This last encounter was the end of an historic period of Farbwerke Hoechst. A new chapter had begun.

Sales Exceed a Thousand Million DM

The activities of the newly-formed Farbwerke Hoechst were confined to comparatively narrow limits in the first few months. We had taken over only a part of the inheritance of the old I. G. Farbenindustrie. As a result of the war, chemical production in both parts of Germany had fallen greatly behind that of other countries. In 1953, the first year of our full independence, we achieved sales of approximately 1,000 million DM. This represented 9 per cent of the total output of German chemistry. German chemical production, however, was no more than 6 per cent of world output. In 1938, by comparison, 15 per cent of all the chemical products of the world had been manufactured in the area of the present Federal Republic.

In 1953, the situation was similar in most other industries upon whose supplies or orders the chemical industry depended. At home, there was, of course, much leeway to be made up but the demand could be met to only a small extent.

The Federal Republic was still subject to the control council laws of the Allies. Large industries and branches of the economy such as banking and insurance, mining and steel production had been confiscated like the I. G., or at any rate had been placed under control and were able only gradually to return to normal conditions.

Eventually, the banks received permission to found regional institutes. As one of the three successor companies of the Dresdner Bank, the Rhein-Main-Bank was formed on 25 September 1952. Hermann Richter was chairman of the supervisory board and Hugo Zinsser was speaker of the board of management. The three regional banks merged again in 1957 to re-form the Dresdner Bank. I have been a member of the supervisory board of the Dresdner Bank since the foundation of the Rhein-Main-Bank.

The insurance field, so important for industrial life, also took some time to reorganize. My friendly relationships with the Dresdner Bank brought me into contact with the Allianz group. In 1956, I was elected to the supervisory board of the Munich Reinsurance, to which I still belong.

This involvement in banking and insurance, however modest, was a great help to me in my work at Hoechst. I gained an indispensable insight into the workings of the capital market and of finance generally. I also made many valuable acquaintances through holding these offices.

In our first years, finance and the provision of capital were fairly difficult. Investments had to be planned and financed very carefully. It took a great deal of courage to tackle the large tasks that were then facing us.

In the summer of 1954 we held the first ordinary annual general meeting. We met in the recently completed fertilizer silo – the restaurant was still confiscated – and decided upon a bold dividend of 8 per cent. It was our first meeting with the new shareholders who had just exchanged their I. G. shares. In accordance with an Allied decree, registered shares had originally been issued. But as early as the summer of 1955, these were converted into bearer shares because shareholders were clearly not entering their holdings in the share register which was a fairly complicated and expensive process for the company as well.

C.Y.—13

We were very worried, particularly in this first year, that the I. G. shares, and subsequently our own, might be bought up by somebody so that large shareholdings would be formed. In view of our small share capital and the low stock exchange quotation, this would have been easy, particularly for foreigners. Domestically, the danger was not so great because of the weak capital market. Fortunately, the shares of our company remained widely distributed. Even today, there can hardly be anyone who holds more than 1 per cent of our share capital which had increased to 1,482 million DM by 1970.

With the reconstitution and the first general meeting, the first phase of the consolidation of Farbwerke Hoechst had ended. At times, it had led us deeply into the relatively unknown byways of politics and diplomacy and confronted us with many a dramatic situation. This period might well have been a wasteful diversion, especially for our scientists, if it had not also taught us how to understand and utilize the economic potentialities of the company. The aim had been to provide a sufficiently broad basis upon which to build our technical and economic activities, one which would allow us to defend ourselves against the tremendous competition from the major international companies, most of which were many times larger than Hoechst. The purpose of our stubborn demands during the dismemberment negotiations was solely to achieve this competitiveness.

Now the task was to integrate the various parts of the Hoechst complex – so far without proper technical and economic cohesion – into a uniform concern with a common concept.

In the end phase of the dismemberment process, to which we had to devote most of our time, the management and the various production units began to plan for the future. Each factory had its own character and its separate function. It also had its own plans which covered a wide range of industrial chemistry. But these plans had not been correlated and had now to be subordinated to a common target.

First of all, the traditional fields had to be adapted to the new requirements because it was they who had to provide a satisfactory financial return, at any rate for the time being. Dyestuffs and their aromatic starting and intermediate products, as well as pharmaceuticals, were for a long time the centre of production. In the fields of aliphatic chemistry, acetylene chemistry, plastics and man-made fibres, the works that had joined the Hoechst complex offered only limited facilities for successful long-term activities. But now we were able to apply our own initiative and to take our cue from the performance of the international chemical industry, especially in the U.S.A.

Thus, during 1954–5, an investment plan matured, which in its scope and financial requirements far exceeded anything ever undertaken in the I. G. period, or later by Hoechst, or by the other companies in the Hoechst group.

7

Years of Decision

THE STARTING CAPITAL for our first post-war enterprise in the U.S.A. was 20,000 dollars, a meagre amount. Ludwig C. Balling, a business friend who was born in Munich, had lent us the money because at that time we had no foreign exchange available. The location of the company on the other hand fulfilled the highest demands – the eighty-second floor of the Empire State Building. From the window, when the weather was fine, there was a wonderful view of the skyscrapers of Manhattan housing the offices of the American international companies and the major financial institutions. Hoechst occupied only four modest offices and only employed a small number of the staff of over 30,000 that worked in the building. But the name was imposing: Intercontinental Chemical Corporation.

This New York branch was the second on the American continent. At the beginning of 1952, our Knapsack colleague Max E. Klee had founded Trans-Canada Chemicals in Montreal. This decision had been taken on our Canadian trip in 1951. Before the war, Klee had been acting for the I. G. in the U.S.A. for some ten years. He knew American conditions well and he tackled the initial difficulties with considerable élan.

It was clear to us that we would have to pay particular attention to exports. In the last years before the war, the I. G. had exported more than 75 per cent of its dyestuffs production. North America was one of its most important customers. General Aniline, an I. G. foundation in the U.S.A., attained annual sales of approximately 50 million dollars during this period. In the pharmaceutical sector, too, the export share had been considerable, in fact up to 90 per cent.

In the first years after the war, the U.S.A. had become the most important market for mass consumer goods until then relatively unknown in Europe. Intense competition and high quality requirements provided us with valuable lessons, in particular with regard to our plans in the field of man-made fibres and plastics.

On the first day of my U.S. trip, which lasted from 1 to 30 April 1954, we concluded a purchasing contract for a tar factory in Rhode Island. We acquired this small firm from Harry Grimmel, a former chemist at Leverkusen who had settled in the United States at the beginning of the twenties. Immediately after the end of the war, he had formed the Metro-Dyestuff Corporation of West Warwick, Rhode Island. In a former textile factory, a massive old stone building with heavy wooden platforms, he produced a number of dyestuffs with which I was in part familiar from my Hoechst alizarin days. Although the plant looked comparatively small, and although it certainly did not conform to the most modern techniques, Metro-Dyestuffs nevertheless achieved sales of 1·2 million dollars in 1954.

As early as April 1953, we had purchased from Adolf Kuhl the Progressive Color and Chemical Co., New York which had acted as a colour-merchanting house since 1923. A few years later we acquired the far bigger Carbic Color & Chemical Co. so that we had a solid foundation for our dyestuffs and chemicals business in the U.S.A.

The beginnings in the pharmaceutical sector were rather more difficult. The acquisition of a pharmacautical company was out of the question because we did not have the money. We therefore granted a licence to Upjohn in Kalamazoo, with whom we have had a working relationship ever since, for the oral antidiabetic 'Rastinon', our first large post-war success. Upjohn sold Rastinon in the U.S.A. under the name 'Orinase'.

We were not able to acquire the shares of a small pharmaceutical company, namely that of Lloyd Brothers Inc. in Cincinnati, Ohio, until 1960. This company was almost a hundred years old and its sales worth 3·3 million dollars. In the pharmaceutical sector, the problem was the extremely stringent specifications of the American Food and Drug Administration in respect of new pharmaceuticals.

The first preparation released by the F.D.A. and marketed by us in America was 'Lasix', a diuretic brought out in 1966. It made a considerable contribution to the success that we have meanwhile achieved in the American market. When I returned to the U.S.A. in the autumn of 1970 on the occasion of the inauguration of the new headquarters of the American Hoechst Corporation, I had every reason to be satisfied.

Even the external aspects of the new buildings, in the middle of the hills of Somerset in Bridgewater, New Jersey, are very impressive. The buildings occupy 44 hectares of land compared with the four offices in which we started in New York in 1953. The six employees of that time have risen to 500 in Bridgewater. In all, we now employ some 3,500 people in the U.S.A.

In 1970, sales reached 160 million dollars. Between 1965 and 1970, Hoechst invested some 150 million dollars in the U.S.A. which has therefore become by far the most important market for our company outside the European Economic Community.

The Eisenhower Era

But let us go back to 1954. Apart from the early acquisitions, we made every endeavour to inform ourselves as thoroughly as possible about the economic, technical, and political situation in the States. After a pronounced boom in 1951 and 1952, industrial activity there had receded to an astonishing degree by 1953. The gross national product dropped to an all-time low. The steel, car and textile industries were the most seriously affected by this recession.

I was deeply impressed by the comparative lack of concern with which the Americans treated this development. In the Federal Republic, the economic recession following the Korean crisis had created serious anxieties and had resulted in a cut-back in investments. In the U.S.A., on the other hand, increased investments were made in many industries at precisely this point. The American companies could afford to do this even during a crisis so that, when the next boom came round, they had available the necessary capacity to outstrip their competitors.

The fact that they were not greatly worried by the recession was also related to the great confidence that they had in the new Eisenhower administration. The victorious commander of the Second World War, and his Secretary of State, John Foster Dulles, made it clear even during the first months of their government that they regarded Europe, not Asia, as the most important world political arena. The European Defence Community proposed by the French minister René Pleven and the 'German agreement' were intended to secure the integration of the Federal Republic in the western defence system.

Federal Chancellor Adenauer, who pursued this integration of the Federal Republic with single-minded purpose, enjoyed a high reputation in the U.S.A., even at that time. His first visit to the States in April 1953 produced an unusually favourable response. The American press saw in this journey by Konrad Adenauer the beginning of a German-American friendship that was to deepen as the years went by.

German Chemistry – Highly Esteemed

When I travelled to the U.S.A. a year later in 1954, the climate had improved even further. The generosity and hospitality that I encountered during my four weeks' stay in the towns in the east, and in Texas and California, greatly exceeded all my expectations. Perhaps during this visit I was still under the impressions of the first post-war years in Germany, when we could not quite rid ourselves of the feeling that we were being treated as second-class citizens.

At home, however, the Americans behaved quite differently. Perhaps it was also that we met a different type of American from the one who had come to Europe. Wherever there had been former relations with Germany, we found a considerable respect for German chemistry. In discussions, we had often to dispel the illusions of our American partners who, relying on memories of earlier times, greatly overestimated our competitive capability. They pointed to the tremendous increase in sales in the Federal Republic but completely forgot that the rise between 1948 and 1953 looked so enormous only because it had started practically from zero.

Many people I met knew German conditions, especially in the I. G., from the pre-war days. I remember, for instance, my encounter with one of the pioneers of the American oil industry, Frank A. Howard. His book *Buna Rubber* which told of his work with BASF and subsequently with the I. G. Farbenindustrie, provides a vivid picture of the collaboration between American and German chemistry which started as far back as the twenties. I also met George Merck of the famous American pharmaceutical company which had grown out of the former German company of the same name.

Among my very first acquaintances was also Charles Engelhard who died in March 1971 at the age of fifty-three. Apart from his large industrial companies in the U.S.A. and South Africa, he had founded, together with Friedrich Wilhelm von Meister, a small company for reprographic techniques whose products were very similar to the reprographic range of Kalle. We later acquired this company.

Apart from the big industrialists of the older generation, I also got to know on this trip, and increasingly so during my many visits in later years, the leading men of many important chemical companies and these companies themselves. My encounters with their chiefs did not confine themselves only to business. I have developed friendships with many of them that I regard as among the outstanding assets of my life.

I have difficulties with the English language even today. When I was still attending the high school in Barmen, I unfortunately made too little use of the optional English course. But the Americans are very patient, particularly in this respect. They do not themselves like to learn foreign languages but they make every effort to help you along if you are having a discussion with them in very broken English.

I found the same friendliness and informality everywhere. In Europe then it would hardly have been possible to visit the leading men of another company without being asked the reason. In America, on the other hand, this seemed to be the order of the day and one was able to talk from the heart, without hesitation. However, I quickly noticed that I was also expected to say something about ourselves. After lunch or dinner we frequently talked informally, but always absolutely openly. Probably this is an inheritance from the pioneering era.

In Hoechst, I am sure, it would not have been easy to invite three foreign guests to a formal meeting of the board of management for an official welcome as we were in the U.S.A., though, naturally, this American openness has its limits. The same applies to the friendly relations between the staff. The unprejudiced and unvarnished manner in which people in the States talk to one another may well be connected with the fact that the social barriers between the various classes of society have disappeared rather earlier there than in Europe. Of course, in America, too, there are hierarchies and unwritten laws of social standing, the power of money and of individual families. But it is not expressed as ostentatiously in titles and honours as it is in Germany.

Naturally, in America the president of the great industrial company occupies a special place. But this does not prevent a laboratory assistant – as I have seen for myself – from leaving punctually at five o'clock in the afternoon even if at that time you are inspecting his laboratory as a guest of the president. He simply takes his hat, says a friendly goodbye and leaves. For an American, it's the most natural thing in the world.

Finally, of course, the little word 'you' and the widespread use of Christian names greatly facilitates communication between people, without implying friendship for life. Nobody is afraid of losing his authority or respect if addressed by his first name.

I looked forward to my first meeting with German emigrants not entirely without concern. After all, they had every reason to be full of antipathy and bitterness towards a visitor from their homeland from which they had been driven so ingloriously. Such an attitude would have been quite understandable to me, but in fact I seldom encountered any resentment. If it was there, it certainly wasn't shown.

An old friend of mine who had emigrated to the U.S.A. quite early was Albert Frank who around 1900 had discovered the fertilizer action of calcium cyanamide which, in turn, had been found by his father and Heinrich Caro. He was one of the first to visit Knapsack and Hoechst again after the war.

Frank lived close to the Plaza, my favourite hotel in New York in the heart of Manhattan, full of so much European flair and comfort. He used to join me at breakfast at eight in the morning. We talked about the splendid era of German chemistry and the reconstruction of the industrial companies. His interest in this was insatiable. I am glad that on the occasion of his ninetieth birthday we were able to arrange a little party for Albert Frank at the Süddeutsche Kalkstickstoffwerke in Trostberg.

I remember many aspects of this, my first visit to the States, because they were so spontaneous and cordial. For example, on my last evening Adolf Kuhl, who had sold us the Progressive Color and Chemical Co., gave me a large box. It contained an original portrait of Bismarck painted by Lenbach. Kuhl had guarded the picture during the First World War before America sent its troops to Europe in 1917. The picture now adorns a room in the Hoechst restaurant which has long since become known as the Bismarck room because it already contains a Lenbach that recalls the friendship between Bismarck and the founder families of the company.

Americans are Optimists

What I liked so much about the Americans, then as now, was their inexhaustible store of optimism of which, I would like to think, I also have a fair share. Of course, my friends in the American chemical industry had more reason to be optimistic at that time than a German company. One of the essential reasons for this was the sounder economic and financial basis on which they operated. The U.S.A. companies had more company-owned capital and reserves at their disposal and their profits were far higher than ours. Each one of the three largest American companies was able to show a clear profit, after tax, of more than 500 million dollars.

The American companies also have a completely different attitude to competition. For them, hard and sometimes even ruthless competition is one of the most natural things on earth and certainly no reason for falling out with the company that you are in fierce competition with. This sheer enjoyment of an honest and hard competitive situation, and the unconcern with which American companies can throw overboard antiquated views and tackle new problems without reserve, were considerable object-lessons to me.

One of the most topical questions at the time concerned the future of man-made fibres and whether they would really live up to their promises. Not long ago we had acquired a licence for I.C.I.'s polyester fibre and had to decide whether we could risk our modest resources in its development. Although in America man-made fibres were only at the beginning of their development and although the country was experiencing a pronounced textile crisis, almost every forecast was optimistic. This encouraged us a great deal and confirmed us in our conviction that man-made fibres would count among the most successful products of the next decades.

The expectations in the U.S.A. were, of course, based on a domestic market with an annual increase in population of approximately 3·5 million people. Living standards of this market of 160 million people were far ahead of those in Europe.

The consumer market in the U.S.A. aimed at short-life products and a quick replacement cycle. Huge supermarkets with foodstuffs wrapped in foil and films, the first synthetic fibres, suits that could be made in half a day on New York's Fifth Avenue, plastic articles for a few cents, comfortable cars, automatic washing machines – all these achievements of the American way of life greatly impressed me and confirmed me in my view that the notion of new mass-markets based on fibres and plastics was a highly realistic one.

From My Diary . . .

My notes of this American visit contain many other impressions of American industry. Many of these are no longer surprising to Europeans and there have, of course, been many changes in America itself. Here are some extracts from my report:

'American companies were happy to provide information about their organization and their situation. The organization is carefully thought out. I thought it remarkable that the large chemical companies were organized into divisions like ourselves although the management itself is numerically very much stronger. In many large companies, the entire research department forms part of a more or less autonomous subsidiary with its own management. It appears that fiscal reasons are mainly responsible for this arrangement. On the other hand, the Americans believe that the problems of research should be divorced from everyday affairs. This arrangement is contrary to German tradition and we are not convinced by it.

'Because of its high profits, American industry spends a tremendous amount of money on research. We saw research establishments whose dimensions would be simply unimaginable in Germany. The central laboratory of Bell Telephone in Summit, New Jersey, for example, had 9,000 staff and cost 120 million dollars a year to operate. At the time of my visit, the Bell Institute had just developed the revolutionary transistor. By comparison, expenditure on research and development at Hoechst was about 60 million DM. We saw a similarly imposing research establishment at Du Pont in Wilmington, Delaware.

'These research establishments were possible because of the considerable profits that the companies were making. In view of their size, however, they easily gave an impression of over-organization although their equipment could not be regarded as exaggerated. Even the better-equipped laboratories are simpler than our new ones but, on the other hand, physical methods appear to predominate. Mass spectrographs, for example, are standard items of equipment.

'Numerically, too, the physicist plays a more important role than with us. New laboratories are not very tall and are equipped with air conditioning. Surprisingly, the furniture is not of wood but of sheet metal and other materials finished in a high-quality paint. The management of the laboratories is carefully organized, exactly as in the parent company. The number of staff in these laboratories is high because they employ a large number of technical personnel at the middle level. On average, leaving aside auxiliary staff, about half of those employed in the laboratory are laboratory assistants and technicians, a quarter are qualified physicists and the remaining quarter are chemists of Ph.D. and technicians of B.Sc. standard. The fields of activity are strictly defined and one gets the impression that in these laboratories there are only a few people with an overall picture of what's going on.

'America has a grave shortage of chemists and technical staff, in spite of the large number of students. The more powerful companies employ people whose sole job consists of visiting the universities and engaging its best people. Promising chemists are frequently given subsidies even while they are still studying for their degrees. The movement of chemists between the various companies has slowed down considerably because pensions have resulted in increased loyalties. Nevertheless, by our standards, a large number of people change their jobs, including people in leading positions.

'The works managers are not too familiar with the scientific work in their companies. It appears that they are simply administrators of their plants. The production departments have special laboratories that are engaged in the tracking of faults and the development of plant processes. In the selection of staff for these companies, the higher academic grades are always preferred. The starting salaries, in dollars, are comparable to ours in marks. The hourly wages of the workers vary between $1.80 and $2.50 for a 40-hour week. In New York, there is a 35-hour week. Overtime rates are 50 per cent above the standard and Sunday rates are 100 per cent higher.

'Leave is granted only sparingly and there are no legal provisions for it in the States. An ordinary employee is not likely to get more than fourteen days leave. Four weeks leave is a rarity and taken only by top management. The numerous American official holidays are kept but not paid for, apart from Sundays. Company-owned flats or houses are totally unknown and house building is entirely in private hands. Flats can be had in the free market but the rents are extraordinarily high. An employee pays something like 25 per cent of his income for rent.

'All the large American companies have a kind of foreign ministry. Every stranger who has dealings with the company is met by this department. It organizes visits and is fully informed about licence negotiations, sales, etc. Such a central department appears to me to be highly suitable for facilitating good relations with foreign visitors.

'I noticed repeatedly how much value the Americans attach to personal contact. On practically every desk there is a notice with the Christian name and surname of the incumbent. Great importance is attached to people addressing each other by these names.

'The factories are extraordinarily clean, free from all rubbish and with nothing lying about. The chemists do not wear laboratory coats but white shirts. All the protective clothing, including that of the workmen, is provided and maintained by the company.

'After the crisis of the thirties, American industry made great efforts to improve its social services. Non-contributory pension funds are provided by every large company. There is a state social insurance but no sickness benefit. The latter is apparently opposed mainly by the medical profession.

'Particular attention is paid to the prevention of accidents. Discipline in this field is tremendously high. Visitors have to wear protective goggles and usually also metal safety helmets. You can walk for hours through a factory without encountering a single person who has ignored these protective measures. Accident statistics are maintained in every part of the factory. American industry is extremely proud of its low accident rate.

'Manners in the factory are very informal, at any rate measured by pre-war German standards. Workers, staff and management deal with each other in an almost jovial manner but, remarkably, the authority of the management is in no way affected.

'The relationships between black and white differ a great deal in various parts of the country. In the factories of the east, integration has been largely realized. Coloured people work alongside white people and can live in the best hotels. In the south, the differences are more pronounced. However, I got the impression in my many conversations that the Americans are not too far away from a reasonable solution to this problem. Many indeed proudly claim that the States has already reached the ideal of an almost classless society.'

[Looking at this entry in my diary of 1954 now, I am obliged to place a large question mark against it.]

'The openness of the people is particularly pronounced in the west and in Texas. Obviously, people there are doing extremely well. Companies report that it is extremely difficult to move personnel from the west to the east. San Francisco has an influx of 1,500 people a day because it offers a better life. The climate is more favourable, too. There are 60,000 Germans, many Italians and Chinese in this town at the foot of the Golden Gate. During the war, the Japanese who lived in San Francisco were interned in camps and the negroes took over the empty housing estates. This caused a great deal of resentment.

'A busy programme of road construction is evident throughout the country. Although even the existing roads are far broader and more attractive than our own, new ones are being built everywhere, as well as many bridges.'

So much for my diary. Of course, much that appeared new to us in 1954 is now part of the German way of life.

Consequences for the European Market

I was most impressed by American production figures. Compared with the corresponding German figures, they showed just how small our capacities were. Sales per head in Hoechst in 1954 were approximately 30,000 marks, whereas the figure for the United States was almost three times as high. In the case of dyestuffs and pharmaceuticals, the traditional pillars of the company, this was not so important. But in the case of the mass production chemicals that we were now thinking of taking up, it was a decisive factor.

We recognized that in the long run we would have to think in European dimensions and that a European Common Market would be absolutely vital. Apart from strengthening the European business, we would also have to set up branches in overseas countries, including the U.S.A., and thus follow a course that British and particularly Swiss companies had long since adopted.

One tremendous advantage which the Americans had was their apparently unlimited access to sources of energy. There were refineries near every important industrial complex. They satisfied in the first instance the thirst of America's countless cars. The raw materials needed by the chemists were obtained practically as by-products.

There was already in existence a pipeline system for natural gas which led from Houston in Texas to New York. At the time we thought seriously of transporting liquefied methane to Europe by ship. Such plans have in the meantime been realized between Algeria and southern Europe. The enormous horns of a Texas steer, which hung for a long time in the Hoechst board room, were a reminder of the adventurous projects that we discussed with the generous Texans.

For a chemist, the U.S.A. was almost the promised land. Ethylene pipelines traversed the whole of the States. Chemical factories could ask to be connected to these pipelines in the same way that we are connected to water or electricity. Both electricity and coal cost barely half of what we paid in Germany.

In California, we made our first contact with Standard Oil with whom we have since been closely linked. On the Pacific coast, in the bay of San Francisco, is one of the largest refineries in the world which has adopted highly modern methods for the production and isolation of hydrocarbons. This refinery was for a long time the sole supplier of p-xylene, one of the vital raw materials for Trevira fibre.

Getting to Know Computers

At the beginning of my first visit, I met the German Chargé d'Affaires in Washington, Heinz L. Krekeler, whom I knew well from the I. G. days. He later became the first Ambassador of the Federal Republic to the U.S.A. After his return to Europe, he was for a long time the German member of the Euratom commission. He strongly advised me to take an interest in computer and transistor developments. In Germany, practically nothing was known then of these electronic brains.

I saw my first computer at the Research Institute of the Bell Telephone Co. in Summit, New Jersey. Mathematical problems were fed into it in the form of perforated tape. It was on this occasion that I first came round to the view that we would soon have to start in this field at Hoechst too.

In order to apply this progress in electronic data processing in Hoechst as soon as possible, we sent a delegation of experts to I.B.M. in the U.S.A. during the same year. The first computer, equipped with approximately 4,000 valves, was ordered and started to operate at Hoechst in 1956. We were one of the very first companies in Germany therefore to introduce not only a fully mechanized bookkeeping system but also to apply computer techniques to scientific problems and company planning.

During my visit to the research laboratories of Du Pont, I was particularly impressed by their wide range of activities. These included all the scientific disciplines from medicine to biology, from physics to mathematics. Such broadly-based research did not exist even in the I. G. At the same time we recognized that research in Germany proceeded along different lines. The laboratories in the U.S.A. were more modest but they had far more modern apparatus.

During discussions, we learnt that in America more emphasis is placed on physics and chemical engineering. Physical methods of analysis were used in the U.S.A. to a far greater extent than in Germany. In our teaching, preparative and organic chemistry is emphasized much more. I came to the conclusion that in the long term we should aim to retain our preparative training but at the same time include more instruction in physics and chemical engineering.

Because of the many interesting visits, the month in the U.S.A. was over in no time. When we went on board the S.S. *United States* on 30 April 1954 to return to Germany, we were exhausted, but also full of ideas and plans for the future. During the seven-day crossing, I tried to summarize the essential insight that we had gained in the U.S.A. In the main, this covered five fields:

1. If the standard of living in Germany is to increase and approach that of the United States, similar consumer habits will have to be adopted in Germany. Engagement in the great fields of the future such as fibres, plastics, films and detergents is therefore absolutely necessary. At the same time, the expansion of our traditional domain must not be neglected.

2. If we are to operate economically and competitively, our sales per head must be greatly increased. This means that we have to think in far greater capacities. Since the German domestic market will always be too small for this, we shall be successful only through intensified exports and expanded trading within Europe.

3. With regard to power, our situation in Europe, especially in the Federal Republic, is far inferior to that of the United States. Electric power and heat simply cost too much in Germany. The raw materials from petro-chemistry are available to the American chemical industry but not to us and have to be developed first. We can hardly produce at competitive prices on the basis of coal. New sources of energy and raw materials have to be found.

4. We should not simply copy the chemistry of the United States, quite apart from the fact that we would not be able to do so anyway. The special situation of Hoechst and our overall scientific attitude point to forming specific centres and deriving specific advantages from them. A good example of this is the field of synthetic organic chemistry which continues to be of considerable importance for pharmaceuticals, dyestuffs, and starting products of all types.

5. Finally, we shall have to make particular efforts in our publicity and in the establishment of our sales organization. We shall have to prepare ourselves for a tough competitive fight and we will have to adapt ourselves to a market that is entirely free and in no way protected by cartels or other agreements.

After our return from the States, we tried to apply to Hoechst what we had seen. In the foreground of all our efforts stood the power and raw material problems.

The Hoechst 'Coker'

There was one thing that we had already realized during the I. G. period: apart from acetylene, upon which practically our entire plastics and solvent chemistry was based, other hydrocarbons were bound to gain greatly in importance. This applied especially to ethylene and propylene which became important starting materials for a new field of chemistry.

These hydrocarbons had hitherto been obtained in a modest quantity from the hydrogenation plants. Small amounts needed during the war for the production of ethylene oxide and lubricaul polymers were obtained either from ethyl alcohol, by splitting off water, or through hydrogenation of acetylene.

Coke oven gas too had long been a source of small quantities of ethylene.

After the war, we quickly realized the uneconomic nature of these processes by comparison with the U.S.A. The hydrogenation and Fischer-Tropsch synthetic petrol plants had been completely destroyed during the war and their reconstruction prohibited by the Allies. There was no significant production of crude oil in the Federal Republic or the corresponding refinery capacity.

The prospects of a chemical industry based on petroleum hydro-carbons were therefore extremely dim. This was one of the most important facts that we had to accept. When the hydrogenation plant in Wesseling was finally again allowed to take up limited production of fuel oil and petrol, we had already made efforts through Knapsack to cooperate with Wesseling. These attempts, however, had failed because in 1952, when the first approaches were made, no such steps could be taken without Allied approval and this was not available.

In the autumn of 1952, we were able to acquire a process for the production of hydrocarbons by the thermal splitting of crude oil developed by the American engineering company of Lummus in New York, whom we knew.

The process had by no means passed all its technical tests. It was simply described in detail in a comprehensive study. We were given this study during a discussion in Paris which set the seal on a rather interesting agreement: we were given an opportunity of perfecting the process to technical maturity. If we achieved this, we had to provide the Americans with the know-how free of charge. We gratefully accepted this generous offer and maintained our excellent friendship with Lummus.

At home in Hoechst, the experts examined the American study

with great enthusiasm. According to the process, crude oil was to be sprayed on to hot coke balls circulating in a current of gas. The crude oil would then be cracked at temperatures of approximately 800°C. Gaseous hydrocarbons were formed, particularly ethylene and propylene. Liquid products were obtained too. The carbon formed separated on the coke balls which thus increased their diameter. Once this had reached 6 to 8 mm, the balls were withdrawn from the gas stream. The carbon was very useful because the need for electrode coke for the production of graphite was all the time increasing.

We built a fairly large experimental plant in a very short period of time so that we could try out the basic principles of the process. The plant went on stream at the end of 1955. It was located inside a tower, 100 metres high, which we named the 'coker'. It was a symbol of Hoechst for almost fifteen years.

The 'coker' was pulled down in 1970, long after it had served its purpose, because of the danger of corrosion. Many young chemists and engineers earned their laurels in this crude oil cracking plant, the first big development by Hoechst after the war. By an outstanding joint effort, teething troubles were quickly overcome and all those involved were able to feel once again that they had been involved in developing something that was largely new.

The need for ethylene continued to increase. Soon there came the day when the 'coker' output was no longer adequate. In the meantime, we had acquired processes in which naphtha could be cracked through indirect heating. We built a new plant in which we were able to distill the naphtha from the crude oil. The residue oil was passed into the 'coker' or burnt in the boiler house. The naphtha was pumped into the new medium temperature pyrolysis furnaces. In this way, a small, specialized refinery developed in Hoechst which used crude oil as a starting product and eventually produced some 20,000 tons of ethylene per year.

We also needed increasing amounts of acetylene. Our entire solvent and polyvinyl acetate programme, our only plastic at that time, was based on the carbide production of Knapsack and the acetylene obtained from it. Coke and electric power needed for this operation were rationed and expensive so we were not able to obtain adequate amounts. Great progress had been made with the construction and operation of the carbide furnaces but the situation remained unsatisfactory especially as Hoechst had also to pay enormous transport costs for the carbide. We therefore had to tackle the problem of obtaining acetylene through the cracking of hydrocarbon.

Once more, we entered technical no-man's land. In a comparatively short period of time, we succeeded in developing the so-called high temperature pyrolysis. In this process, light naphtha fractions as obtained during crude oil distillation, are injected into a flame of hydrogen, methane and oxygen at temperatures of more than 2,000°C. A fifty-fifty mixture of acetylene and ethylene is formed. This can be removed from the gas stream by suitable methods and separated into its individual components.

When we reported with some pride about our coker at the Achema 1955, this high temperature pyrolysis was still in its infancy. We were able to start up a large-scale plant towards the end of 1959. It still covers Hoechst's acetylene requirements.

Through these developments, Hoechst attracted increasing international attention. The large oil companies became interested in these new processes and many organizations tried to establish contacts with us. Petrochemistry became a world-wide topic.

Nevertheless, the press speculated whether German chemistry would be able to master the new technology. Our work was topical. We reported these first steps in detail and with much satisfaction.

Polyethylene from the Jam-jar

Almost simultaneous with this petrochemical development, which served only for the production of starting materials, our work on plastics also received unexpected impulses. Until then, Hoechst had been involved in the development of plastics only in respect of polyvinyl acetate and its derivative, polyvinyl alcohol.

Fritz Klatte, the Griesheim chemist, had been granted a patent in 1913 for the synthetic resin 'Mowilith' developed on this basis. This development had been taken up by Hoechst both in competition and cooperation with Wacker-Chemie. After the reconstitution of Hoechst, Mowilith became a world-wide business and gained an important place in the field of paint raw materials. For a very long time there was no competitor abroad, not even the U.S.A.

Now the plastics field urgently needed to be expanded. Farbwerke Hoechst had always maintained close contacts with the Coal Research institute at Mülheim. After the war, when the institute was able to resume its work, even if only under great difficulties, these contacts were renewed. We closely followed the work carried out at Mülheim which for a long time, however, resulted only in the polymerization of ethylene to give liquid products.

At the end of 1952, Karl Ziegler, the manager of the institute, which had in the meantime been taken over by the Max Planck Society, surprised the world with news of tremendous importance. He had succeeded in obtaining a solid polyethylene by the reaction of olefines with the aid of metallorganic compounds. It was a sensational achievement for which Ziegler received the Nobel prize in 1963. Until then, ethylene could be polymerized only under a pressure of approximately 2,000 atmospheres. The production of this high-pressure polyethylene had been accomplished for the first time in the early thirties in the laboratories of I.C.I. According to Ziegler's method, the reaction now took place without the application of pressure and at almost normal temperature. When we were shown this process for the first time, an ordinary jam-jar served as the reaction vessel.

We acquired from Ziegler the right to be the first to exploit his invention. However, the licence was not granted to us alone. We soon had to compete with many other licensees abroad. It was therefore important to perfect the discovery technically as soon as possible.

Hoechst was particularly well equipped to do this. Our organic chemists had been intensively engaged on work with metalorganic compounds, especially with aluminium organic compounds of the kind used as catalyst in the Ziegler process. It was precisely the preparation of these catalysts that caused our competitors so much difficulty and cost them so much time. We were able to submit concrete projects to the supervisory board as early as November 1954. A year later, the first large-scale plant with an output of 2,000 tons per month went on stream.

First applications of the new plastic were shown by Hoechst at the Hanover Fair in 1955. We had on our stand an injection mould-ing machine that produced small liqueur glasses in large numbers causing a great deal of excitement amongst visitors. We called the new plastic Hostalen and attached considerable importance to it right from the start. Like so many of our trade marks, the name was again derived from Hostato, a squire allegedly knighted by Charlemagne at Hoechst. In 1957, polyethylene was joined by polypropylene.

When we started the first polymerization experiments in Hoechst, the 'coker' was not yet ready. We had to get the ethylene from Gendorf where it was being produced through the hydrogenation of acetylene. From Union Carbide in the U.S.A., we had acquired the know-how for the construction of liquid gas trucks suitable for the transport of hydrocarbons. The ethylene obtained in this way served as the starting material for polymerization until the first cracking plant in Hoechst went on stream. Incidentally, this particular ethylene was probably the most expensive ever to be used as a raw material.

Nylon and Perlon Start their Career

The other major field to which we turned was man-made fibres. As a result of the I. G. dismemberment, we had acquired the Bobingen works with its viscose production. A few chemists from the fibre industry in Central Germany had found a refuge and a new field of activity there. They included Paul Schlack who, together with Wallace Hume Carothers, was one of the founders of man-made fibres.

Young Carothers started his work on the production of a fully synthetic textile fibre in 1928 at Du Pont. In 1932, he succeeded in developing the famous nylon from hexamethylenediamine and adipic acid. Du Pont had to spend vast sums of money before the process was ready for production. Indeed, it was not until 1938, shortly before the war, that the fibre was produced on a large scale. It was a triumph that Carothers sadly did not live to witness.

Work on a synthetic fibre of similar structure was being carried on in Germany at the same time. Fibres from polyvinyl chloride had already been produced but they did not even approximate the outstanding properties of the polyamides such as nylon.

Paul Schlack was scientific manager of the Berlin-Lichtenberg works of the I. G. when he discovered Perlon in 1938. According to its chemical structure, it was also a polyamide fibre. It was, however, made from a different raw material, namely caprolactam. Carothers, too, had experimented with this and had come to the conclusion that it could not be polymerized. Schlack on the other hand succeeded in polymerizing caprolactam through intensive, repeated purification. During the Second World War, Perlon factories with a modest output were set up in Germany. It was soon found that the fibre was in no way inferior to Du Pont's nylon.

After the war, Schlack and his colleagues ended up in Bobingen where they built a Perlon factory with modest means. When Hoechst took over Bobingen, we immediately became interested in this work. First of all, we erected a large plant for the production of continuous Perlon filaments alongside the existing Perlon staple plant. Bristles and monofilaments were also produced. This provided Bobingen with an entirely new production basis for it was soon found that viscose output could not be maintained.

We recognized quickly that Perlon, being the only fibre, did not offer an adequate basis either for Bobingen or for a future fibre division of Hoechst. Bobingen had come too late to the market place with its products and moreover was greatly dependent on suppliers as a result of inadequate raw material contracts. A satisfactory profit could not be expected under these circumstances. Hoechst had been working on its own methods for the production of caprolactam but it could not come to a decision to set up its own production.

It was therefore important to include another synthetic fibre in the Bobingen range. We had followed with great interest the development of polyacrylonitrile fibre and had, in fact, worked on the production of the acrylic nitrile monomer. During the I. G. period, the chemist Herbert Rein had succeeded in developing a fairly interesting process for the spinning of polyacrylonitrile which, after 1945, was acquired by Cassella. Since we had been unsuccessful in our efforts to incorporate Cassella in the Hoechst group, we had to abandon our efforts in this direction. When later on we took over the share capital of Cassella together with the other I. G. successors, work on polyacrylonitrile fibres was taken up by Bayer.

The Dawn of 'Trevira'

We urgently needed to find another fibre. Success came quickly. As early as 1954, we obtained from I.C.I. a licence for its polyester fibre. This fibre, whose starting materials are terephthalic acid and ethylene glycol, was discovered by two English chemists, John R. Whinfield and James T. Dickson, working for Calico Printers. Actually, they were engaged on something quite different and pursued man-made fibres almost as a spare-time occupation. Their discovery was quickly snapped up by I.C.I.

Our licence from I.C.I. for the production of fibres and filaments was confined to the Federal Republic and even there we had to share it with Glanzstoff. Hoechst also obtained a licence from I.C.I. for the production of polyester film which became of tremendous interest to our subsidiary Kalle who sold it most successfully under the trade name 'Hostaphan'. As we were only one of many polyester producers, we had to expect fierce competition especially as we were unable for many years to export Trevira, as we named our new fibre, in contrast to low pressure polyethylene, our other major product. These limitations were removed only after the I.C.I. patents expired in 1968. Then we were able at long last to think in terms of erecting plants outside Germany.

Polyester production was of particular interest to us because we were able to combine within the group all the processing stages from the crude oil to the finished fibre. A large number of chemists was working simultaneously on the various phases of this process. In contrast to the low pressure polyethylene development, we acquired extensive know-how in this case. A group of chemists visited Britain and for an outright payment and a continuous royalty brought back the experience of I.C.I. in the production of the fibre, from the starting product right up to the finished, spun material.

These fundamentally new tasks were augmented by the installation of a new phosphorus furnace in Knapsack. The realization of all these large projects required extraordinary efforts. Where suitable conditions, either scientific or technical, were not available, they were created as quickly as possible. The acquisition of the licences enabled us to make an early start. But only qualified staff and modern production plants could ensure that the knowledge acquired would be properly utilized and then become economically successful.

Incentive to Research

Research required vigorous incentives. The most favourable situation prevailed in the pharmaceutical division. Here, the great traditions of the past were still alive and under the guidance of Gustav Ehrhart and Fritz Lindner, both of whom later became members of the board of management, the organization and teams had remained more or less intact after the war.

The centenaries of Emil von Behring and Paul Ehrlich in 1954 provided a good opportunity for re-establishing contact with international pharmaceutical research. Impressive celebrations took place for four successive days in Marburg, Frankfurt, and Hoechst where the two scientists had worked. Nothing of the kind had happened in Germany since the end of the war. At the same time, the new laboratory for microbiology and pharmacology was inaugurated in Hoechst. It was named the Paul Ehrlich laboratory. Michael Erlenbach had started it during his trusteeship. It was located in the middle of the old factory, near the coal depot and in the vicinity of the old pharmaceutical laboratory in which Robert Koch had worked on tuberculin in the nineties.

These celebrations were significant to us in Hoechst in a number of respects. They recalled, not only the great period of the Hoechst pharmaceutical department and the cooperation with Koch, Behring and Ehrlich, but also marked the end of an isolation that had had serious effects on German medicine particularly biochemistry and immunology. The greatest progress in this field of science was achieved by the U.S.A. and Great Britain after 1933. These countries had offered asylum to the outstanding Jewish biochemists who had had to flee from the racial intolerance of the National Socialist regime.

German science has still not fully recovered from this bloodletting which at that time it suffered in many fields. A large number of internationally known scientists in medicine and biochemistry, from both Germany and abroad, met in Hoechst under the chairmanship of Otto Hahn, the president of the Max Planck Society. It included Nobel prizewinners like Ernst Boris Chain, who played an essential role in the production and development of penicillin, Otto Heinrich Warburg, the discoverer of the respiratory ferments, Adolf Butenandt who confirmed the steroid nature of the hormones, Richard Kuhn, who was engaged in enzyme and vitamin research, and many others. The families of Ehrlich and Behring were also there. Over a glass of good Rhine wine, old relationships were re-established in the Hoechst restaurant which had in the meantime been released by the occupational forces.

These days also offered a welcome opportunity to consolidate our relationship with Behringwerke in Marburg and the world-famous Paul Ehrlich Institute in Frankfurt; we now overcame the separation of decades and joined in a new beginning.

In biochemistry, medicine, and immuno-biology, it wasn't only the scientific basis that was lacking in Germany. There was also the absence of a proper health policy to deal with epidemics. This was a result of our Federal constitution. Under these circumstances, we made many mistakes in our first steps into increasingly important virology, for example during the production of polio vaccine. We suffered many setbacks as a result of the scepticism of the authorities and the inadequate cooperation of the testing institutes.

The scientific laboratories in Hoechst were widely scattered, antiquated and badly equipped. Above all, there was not the right organization or proper intellectual concept without which a large group of scientists cannot work together successfully. This had been one of the drawbacks during the I. G. period. We had, therefore, to start afresh even in research which was so vital to us.

Fortunately, after the depressing years that were now behind us, everyone was resolved to give of his best in the new start that had to be made. Very many young people went into industrial laboratories, many of them former soldiers who had only just finished their studies. They wanted to make up for lost time as quickly as possible and they all suffered from the material shortcomings that still existed. In most cases, they even had difficulties in obtaining the essentials of life for their young families.

It simply was not possible to establish a new research potential with these young and often inexperienced people alone. Fortunately for us, many former colleagues from the I. G. and other companies became available. We welcomed them with open arms. This blood transfusion was also good for Hoechst as far as research was concerned.

During my university days and my first years at I. G., I had gained a fairly good idea of the requirements needed for scientific work and its organization. I was thus able to help create a climate in which there was enjoyment in research although the essential prerequisites were completely lacking. Laboratory conditions were inadequate and the living standards of our scientists were not very high.

Relationships between employees and among the works management were furthermore not conducive to creating an atmosphere of open-mindedness and pleasure in discovery. Anger, frustration and economic need are not favourable conditions for scientific work which demands much patience and optimism. Scientists who may be on the wrong track for years and who have to accept disappointment in their experiments, require external and internal harmony to a greater extent than anybody else. Only then will they show the persistence that may, perhaps, lead to success at the end of the day.

Therefore in those first years we spent a great deal of time discussing and making plans with our scientists. It didn't take that much to be successful at this time, eager and thirsting for a lead. You had only to choose the right moment and to realize how favourable conditions were after the many years of inactivity. It was a rewarding experience to see the great optimism that suddenly seized everybody. In those days I learnt that nothing makes people happier than to be given important jobs with a great deal of responsibility.

The reorganization of research and the erection of new laboratories was absolutely essential. We had to find a concept for a research potential that could achieve very large dimensions in the shortest possible time. In 1955, research expenditure since re-foundation had almost doubled to 60 million DM. Fifteen years later, in 1970, it was more than 400 million DM.

In the first years, when profits and dividends were still low, we were often criticized for the high level of our research expenditure. It took some time before shareholders and employees realized that we had to ask them to make sacrifices to secure the future of the company through our research effort. Of course, money was not the only factor. The most beautiful laboratories and equipment are useless if the right people are not available. It was only gradually realized in Germany that research must have first priority and that the necessary conditions for this had to be created in the German universities.

We suffered greatly from the fact that certain fields of science were no longer represented in Hoechst. During the I. G. era, they had been pursued in other works. It was therefore important for us to complement the existing disciplines as quickly as possible. The old research fields such as pharmaceuticals and dyestuffs, which had been rationalized during the I. G. period and distributed over various works, had to be reorganized before a homogenous research programme could again be evolved.

Engineering Technology

The post-war interregnum and Allied control did not help to promote the existing incomplete research facilities at Hoechst. The process engineering department that I had founded in 1936 had been practically forgotten. Yet it would have been so essential for reconstruction.

There were also great gaps in the engineering field. My Darmstadt student friend, Josef Wengler, who had returned from Silesia and later became a member of the board of management of Hoechst, successfully built up a modern process engineering department, since the increase in investment volume urgently called for strengthening of the engineering organization. The major shortcomings were in measuring techniques, physics, material testing, engineering offices and much else besides.

In those years, many buildings were erected in a form and on sites which we well knew were far from ideal and would probably not fit into our final concept. But we often had to compromise because we could wait no longer. Provisional measures were adopted until a really satisfactory solution could be reached. In the first years, there was neither the time nor the money for fundamental long-term replanning.

We also had to deal with the problem of research in the other works of Hoechst and in the subsidiary companies. Here, too, we encountered considerable difficulties that were related to the history of Hoechst and the decentralization during the I. G. period. We were determined not to imitate the U.S.A. where small and specialized branch works often do not have their own research departments. Our subsidiaries and the various works were to accept the fullest responsibility in this field.

We thus set up a small main laboratory in every works for the purpose of developing production processes on site. They were also to undertake parts of the overall scientific research programme in close collaboration with the central research laboratories. This decision led to the construction of expensive laboratories on many sites but in the long run it proved a highly satisfactory solution for Hoechst.

These 'local' laboratories, which developed into intellectual and scientific centres for the people that worked in the plants, were later linked administratively to the central laboratory in Hoechst. But even then, it remained our principle that the local management should have a decisive say in the work of these laboratories.

First Programme

In September 1955, slightly more than two years after re-constitution, technical and economic considerations had progressed to such an extent that we were able to submit a bold and far-reaching three-year investment programme to the supervisory board. It amounted to approximately 750 million DM and covered the years from 1954 to 1956. The first steps in the realization of this programme had actually been taken in 1954. We had not been able to await the result of all the calculations and discussions before making a start. Since the other I. G. successor companies had started much earlier with their expansion plans, we were frequently asked when we intended to set up our programme. At long last the moment had arrived.

These first fundamental decisions regarding future developments were not easy. The investment capital of Hoechst in 1955 was only 575 million DM. It was to be more than doubled within three years. To achieve this, the annual investments, which were only 100 million DM in 1953, had to be increased to approximately 250 million DM a year.

The money available from depreciation for financing these projects was increasing but for the last three years it amounted to little more than 300 million DM altogether. Provision of the necessary funds therefore faced us with great problems. In attempting to solve such financial questions, we always proceeded very cautiously, however enterprising we might be in other respects. In any case, the risk in all these steps was so great that we had to make sure that we always had sufficient liquid funds available. This is the reason why we often secured the money in good time but at high interest rates.

We received much support for this policy from our chairman of the supervisory board, Hugo Zinsser. On his advice, we decided to increase the company's capital in March 1955 and this was approved at an extraordinary general meeting. Both these steps – the capital increase and the extraordinary general meeting – gave rise to a great deal of public comment since such measures were new and unknown in the Federal Republic.

Between 1955 and 1969, we held four extraordinary meetings, all concerned with increases in capital. Our shareholders showed a great deal of understanding for these steps, and we were always able to convince them of the need for more money. The rapid, sometimes almost breathtaking growth of the company, and the investments at home and abroad, required a continuous supply of capital. As our profits were still limited, we were not able to meet these requirements from our own proceeds.

Jähne becomes Chairman of the Supervisory Board

Immediately after the ordinary general meeting in June 1955, Hugo Zinsser, the chairman of the supervisory board and valuable adviser to the company, died. He had been suffering for some time from a cardiac complaint. Hermann Richter succeeded Zinsser on the supervisory board. Together with Hanns Deuss of the Commerzbank, he looked after the financial policy of the company for many years.

In the meantime, the final liquidation law had been decreed and had liberated us from all the discriminating provisions of the dismemberment period. We were therefore able to propose to the annual general meeting that Friedrich Jähne, the former chief engineer of the old I. G., should join the supervisory board of which he was, in fact, chairman until 1963. Neither of us would have thought in 1945 that we would once again work together in this way at the head of our company.

The launching of an extensive investment programme such as we had decided upon in 1955 represented a considerable risk for Farbwerke Hoechst. The profits of the company still accrued exclusively from the traditional fields of activity in which we were now facing keen international competition. We had to reckon with high starting costs for the new projects that we were planning. Design and erection of plants and the marketing of new products required time. It was clear to us that in a field like fibres, for example, it would take five to six years before the new products could make a contribution to our profits.

Such far-reaching plans, which required precise formulation, were not nearly as commonplace then as they are today. As scientists, we knew how long it takes for new projects and new plants to offer a return. But global calculations concerning operating efficiency, of the type and extent that had now to be prepared, were entirely new to us.

In this respect we encountered a variety of philosophies within our management. The risk that we were quite clearly running was not approved of by all my colleagues. There were many, and sometimes heated, discussions on the board. Some of us felt that we must enter scientific no-man's land. Others were concerned to ensure that the pace of development did not endanger the stability of the young company still susceptible to crises.

But it was probably precisely this heterogenous composition of the board and the different philosophies that were expressed which forced us to prepare very careful and comprehensive budgets and investment programmes much earlier than many other German companies.

Such investment programmes were initially conceived for one year and submitted to the supervisory board almost as a complete budget. Principles were established to keep the ratio between productive and non-productive expenditure in some kind of balance. Because of our many antiquated works, the amount of unproductive expenditure was at first fairly high. The sales and profit likely to accrue from the investments were calculated.

The 'Green Folder'

We tried to find out how long it would be before we achieved our sales target once the investments had been made. Together with the economists, technicians, and commercial people, we calculated a 'programme end figure' for these sales. In general, it was to be achieved approximately three years after approval of the programme. Price reductions and profits were estimated so that in the end such an investment programme demanded fairly extensive calculations. These calculations are still known in Hoechst as the 'green folder' because all the statistics, when they were first produced, were placed in a green folder.

As a result of our subsequent experience, the present-day 'green folder' is far more complete than in 1955 when we submitted it for the first time to the supervisory board. At that time, we forecast that with the investment programme begun in 1954, amounting to 770 million DM, sales of 1,720 million DM would be achieved. In actual fact, they were around 1,760 million in 1957, which was fairly close to our estimates at the time. In the years to come, variations from the target were never more than two to three per cent.

All the preparations and discussions involved in such an invest-ment programme did a great deal to promote mutual confidence. Many people in the company took part in them. Whoever wanted to build something, and needed money for it from the programme, had to present us with concrete ideas of his project.

We did not meet all the targets. In particular, our profit estimates were not always realized. Frequently, programmes had to be changed because the economic and technical conditions changed. At such moments of disappointment or mistake, it was important not to discourage those involved but to give them an opportunity of learning from their experience.

The programme unanimously approved by the supervisory board in 1955 has played a decisive role in the future of Hoechst. From then on, we had a clear aim in front of us that aroused the en-thusiasm of everyone involved. This meant that Hoechst could now think in the proper dimensions and respond to the competitive challenge of the major international chemical companies both with its traditional and its new products. I do not believe that during the twenty years of Hoechst's post-war history, there has been a more significant interval than these two years of 1954 and 1955.

Back in the U.S.A.

A few days after this decision, in September 1955, I travelled to the United States for the second time. On this occasion, my stay lasted six weeks. Once again there was much to see in this large country which offers so many different impressions to the visitor. This time we had far more concrete ideas of what was to be done at Hoechst and what we should look out for in the U.S.A. In addition, we had to negotiate on several occasions over the realization of the decisions taken in Hoechst because with some of the projects it was advisable to seek collaboration with American companies.

One of our most important negotiations in the U.S.A. was con-cerned with the erection of our first large foreign production unit in Brazil. Together with the American Peter Grace and his quickly growing company, we started manufacturing D.D.T. and other much-needed chemicals near São Paulo. We had many difficulties with this first foreign plant because the political and economic conditions in Brazil were extremely unstable. The factory itself, and the capital invested in it, were probably also too big for the prevailing market situation.

A few years later, Peter Grace and Hoechst parted company on friendly terms. It was a long time before the factory finally overcame its difficulties. Today it is a vital pillar of our Brazil organization.

This was not the only occasion when we found that it is fairly difficult in a fifty-fifty partnership with another chemical company to arrive at a satisfactory working relationship whatever the advantages might be. However much the interests of the two companies may coincide, sooner or later they will tend to go their separate ways. In the case of our first plant in Brazil, it simply proved impossible to operate this distant factory, located in a foreign country, from two headquarters – New York and Frankfurt – thousands of miles apart. We have had to separate from American partners on several subsequent occasions after difficult but always fair disputes. Not only in chemistry but throughout their entire commercial life, the Americans have a different attitude from ours. The question is not whether theirs is better or worse than ours. The Americans are more sober and they calculate more. Our way of doing business is a little more sensitive and not quite so wedded to figures.

Time has shown that it is possible to progress by either method and that the one can compete with the other in a friendly manner. The personal contacts that I gradually made in America have never suffered even after the toughest business disputes.

A Cheque for 11 Million DM

In 1954, I signed a cheque for 11 million DM. That was a sum I did not deal with every day, even as chairman of Hoechst. The money was intended for the purchase of a new works in Bavaria. Friedrich Jähne, my old chief from the I. G. days, finally discharged from Landsberg prison and now living in Bavaria, and another former I. G. chief, Carl Krauch, who had also been released from Landsberg, had drawn my attention to the works hidden in the woods in Gendorf near the Bavarian-Austrian frontier.

One Saturday evening, therefore, I took an unofficial look at the complex known to everyone in east Bavaria as 'Anorgana'. I was quite impressed by the activities of the Gendorf works. The centre-piece was a war plant set up during the Third Reich. It had belonged to the state and had been administered by the I. G. Farbenindustrie.

The I. G. had also transferred several other plants to Gendorf in order to protect them from air attack. At the end of the war, the works, with a few exceptions, had been completely dismantled. Afterwards, a large number of refugees from the central German works had come to Gendorf and set up small factories there. Although there were a number of outstanding chemists and engineers among these refugees, it was clear that the very small plants that they had established would not be able to survive in the face of the intense competition of the ensuing years. Gendorf threatened to become a real liability for Bavaria.

Hanns Seidel, the Economics Minister of Bavaria and later its Minister-President, to whom the economy of Bavaria owes its timely adjustment to the modern industrial conditions of the post-war period, was anxious to solve the problem. He was very interested in cooperating with us, although the Hoechst people from Social Democratic Hesse were not at first exactly the most welcome of visitors to this Christian Socialist politician. The Bavarian government eventually succeeded, with a great deal of ingenuity, in bringing order into the somewhat complicated ownership conditions of Gendorf.

The only permanent solution was for the Bavarian state to take over the remainder of the works from the Federal government and then to sell it to Hoechst. In addition, the plants which still formed part of the I. G. assets had to be returned. This complicated transaction arose because of the somewhat confused ownership situation of that time and our political dependence on the Allies. The deal required much discretion and mutual confidence.

Funds from the Bavarian state were not available. The matter could not be revealed to either Parliament or the public as Allied approval could not be obtained. It was for this reason that one day I signed the cheque for 11 million DM and handed it to a Bavarian official who was not able to give me a proper receipt for it, let alone a written agreement for the future transfer of the property to Hoechst. With this money, Bavaria discreetly bought all the plants in order to transfer them to Hoechst in 1955.

Prior to that, however, there was a change of government in Bavaria. The government under Christian Socialist Hans Ehard was replaced by a coalition consisting of the four main parties. Now the situation threatened to become really complicated. The new

Minister-President, Wilhelm Hoegner of the SPD, whom I visited because of my concern over Gendorf, assured me that his government would honour any earlier agreements about which, of course, he knew very little.

In the end, however, this is precisely what happened and the acquisition of Gendorf was publicly announced. In the summer of 1955, the supervisory board of Hoechst gave its final approval to the deal. At first, the situation of the Gendorf works caused us considerable concern in spite of the important fields in which the company was engaged.

Gendorf operated an ethylene oxide and glycol plant, based on an intact chlorine-alkali electrolysis, which, in turn, supported the production of interesting textile auxiliaries. Gendorf got its carbide, which it needed as starting material, from the adjacent Süddeutsche Kalkstickstoffwerke in which, as successor to the I. G. Farbenindustrie, we were able to acquire a 15 per cent interest on 1 January 1955.

Other Gendorf manufacturing activities were of an improvised nature that hardly offered any real prospects. For example, a method had been developed for the production of carbide in a bell-bottom generator.

Like Hoechst, Gendorf had also started to develop a crude oil cracking plant which, in fact, eventually ran for several years. P.V.C. film was produced on antiquated calenders and was used for the manufacture of handbags, wallets and similar articles. All these items were much in demand in the hard times immediately after the war, but they were no longer of any interest now.

The most valuable asset in Gendorf, however, was its 2,000 employees, all interested in a secure future. I still remember the day in August 1955 when I presided over the first employee meeting in Gendorf. Above the speaker's desk there was a flag which showed the Hoechst emblem against the white and blue colours of Bavaria. I have seldom seen such happy faces as those that looked up at me when I announced the future programme for Gendorf.

With Gersthofen and Bobingen, where the production of Trevira polyester fibre was soon to begin, with Gendorf, and eventually with our interest in Wacker and Süddeutsche Kalkstickstoffwerke, we were now strongly entrenched in Bavaria which even then was still dominated by an agrarian economy and the tourist trade.

The road to industrialization was a long one. But the Bavarians value good work and they are, moreover, a solid and completely open-minded people. The many refugees integrated happily with the locals and this mixture had a very beneficial effect on our Bavarian works.

As I had so much to do in Bavaria, this beautiful country and its people became very dear to me. I nearly became a naturalized Bavarian. Since 1953, I have regularly taken my family to the banks of Lake Staffel for my summer leave and I eventually had a holiday retreat built in Seehausen.

The Federal Republic Gains its Sovereignty

We would not have been able to acquire Gendorf in 1955 if the last fetters of the occupation statutes and other Allied restrictions had not been removed. In May 1955, a complex set of agreements was enacted which allowed the Federal Republic, almost ten years after capitulation, to proclaim its freedom and independence.

The centrepiece were the Paris Agreements which had been concluded in October 1954. The purpose of these agreements was also to free the Federal Republic of Germany from all restrictions placed upon the economy which hampered its flexibility and initiative. But previous to that, separate decisions and exemptions from the many prohibitions had become necessary in the chemical industry. For example, it had become absolutely essential to approve the production of ammonia. Similarly, phosphorus production in Knapsack was authorized.

The Paris Agreements created the conditions for the free development of the Federal Republic of Germany and were of inestimable value for its progress. What was later described, somewhat euphemistically, as the German economic miracle had not been possible until that moment. It was only now that the Federal Republic gained its freedom of action with regard to both internal and external politics.

This offered many opportunities and presented numerous challenges. For example, the large banks, the Commerzbank, the Deutsche Bank, and the Dresdner Bank, were again allowed to merge to form central institutes, a step of decisive importance. The same applied to the insurance companies and similar institutions whose proper functioning is essential to a healthy national economy.

The agreements were also intended to pave the way for the integration of the Federal Republic into the western world and thus of Europe, something which almost everybody longed for at that time. In view of the increasing tension between east and west, the U.S.A. and other western powers were greatly interested in re-arming the Federal Republic and creating a German army as part of a system of alliances.

The serious public debate which ensued over the question of German rearmament went on for almost five years. As early as October 1950, the French Prime Minister, René Pleven, had sub-mitted a bold plan which had been inspired by the general European enthusiasm. According to this plan, a completely integrated European army was to be created and was to be under the control of a European Defence Minister appointed by the European Council at Strasbourg.

This European Defence Community was greatly welcomed by the governments and the ruling parties of both France and Germany but it also encountered much opposition. Although the Bonn govern-ment signed the E.D.C. agreement in 1952, its ratification was delayed for a long time as a result of a constitutional appeal signed by 144 opposition members of the Bundestag.

By the time the legal obstacles were finally cleared away, the climate in France had changed decisively. The French had suddenly lost their enthusiasm for such a profound European solution. General de Gaulle, at that time out of the government and retired in Colombey-les-Deux-Églises, had in any case opposed the defence community from the day it was first mooted. In August 1954 it was also rejected by the French national assembly. Like de Gaulle later in the case of the European Economic Community, France was no longer interested in such a truly supranational European community.

Under pressure from John Foster Dulles, the American Secretary of State, and Winston Churchill's government, both of whom were very anxious to secure a German defence contribution, a conference was arranged in London in October 1954. As a result of this confer-ence, the enlargement of the Western European Union and the accession to it of the Federal Republic were agreed as a substitute for the failed European Defence Community. This agreement was ratified by the European members on 5 May 1955. Four days later, the Federal Republic became a member of NATO and the official rearmament of Germany began.

However great satisfaction may have been in Germany over the western agreements and restored sovereignty, the Paris Agreements signified the end for a long time to come of a European policy aimed at political, military and economic integration. Moreover, German reunification now became increasingly unlikely as closer military and economic cooperation in eastern Europe was also being established under the leadership of the Soviet Union. The cold war was moving inexorably to its climax.

No Interest in Rearmament

To the complete surprise of the outside world, the rearmament measures now taking effect in the Federal Republic were by no means enthusiastically welcomed by the German people. Soldiers and uniforms no longer rated very highly. In view of all the suspicions and the grave charges that had been levelled at the end of the war at German industry as a whole, and the large chemical companies in particular, especially in their Nuremberg trials, nobody was really interested in production for military purposes.

It may interest the reader to know what I told the supervisory board at its meeting on 25 January 1955 on this subject: 'In this connection, we are, of course, concerned with the question of the influence of rearmament. First of all, we are afraid that our investments may be slowed down as a result of delays in supplies. There are already such delays even if they have not been the result of rearmament. Over and above this, our manufacturing programme in all fields forms part and parcel of an army's supplies. Dyestuffs, nitric acid, plastics, pharmaceuticals, light metals are commodities required by any army. We do not, fortunately, supply any products for actual weapons so that we need not assume that requirements will be made upon us in this sector which might interfere with our dispositions arising from normal requirements. It was an advantage for Hoechst even during the Third Reich that we did not take part in the direct production of weapons. We hope therefore that in this case also we shall not be involved in developments that will interfere with further peaceful development.'

After the enactment of the Paris Agreements in 1955, the problem of Buna production, until then prohibited in the Federal Republic, could be tackled once more. This was closely linked to the fate of Chemische Werke Hüls. No satisfactory solution had been found for Hüls during the dismemberment negotiations. In order to ensure the continued existence of this company, a reorganization of the ownership situation became essential.

Chemische Werke Hüls had been constructed before the war as a Buna rubber works. After 1945, its complete dismantlement was fortunately prevented. Hüls produced acetylene by cracking natural gas, supplied from the Dutch frontier, by means of an electric light arc. On this basis, the present works manager, physicist Paul Baumann who came from BASF, had launched a number of new manufacturing activities and thus provided jobs for his people. The original Buna works were owned 74 per cent by I. G. Farbenindustrie and 26 per cent by Bergwerksgesellschaft Hibernia, a company owned by Prussia. The dismemberment measures after the war had not ended very happily for Hüls and could not possibly become permanent. The Allies tried to prevent Hüls from falling into the hands of one of the three successor companies of the I. G. They feared that this would unduly unbalance the equilibrium between them. The Hibernia share was therefore reduced to 25 per cent and another 25 per cent made over to a group of mining companies under the leadership of Gelsenkirchener Bergwerksgesellschaft (GBAG). At the direction of the Allies, the remaining 50 per cent of Hüls were transferred to a newly-founded Chemie-Verwaltungs AG, whose shares were to be offered to former I. G. shareholders.

When these shares were about to be issued in 1955, a great deal of speculation was anticipated, as had been the case when the Cassella shares were offered. BASF, Bayer and Hoechst, who had learnt a bitter lesson in the Cassella case, tried to find a joint solution with the two mining companies that would ensure a healthy existence for Hüls. One possibility was a joint Buna factory for which Hüls was the ideal site.

The three chemical companies agreed to acquire the shares of Chemie-Verwaltungs AG in equal parts and then to operate Hüls together with the mining companies. Unfortunately, it did not prove possible to get hold of the shares that were issued in 1955. They were quickly bought up by outside sources and thus became subject to a great deal of speculation on the stock exchange.

Later, when the new Buna factory was already operating, the shares had risen so high that it was not possible to buy them at an economic price. It soon became doubtful whether the ownership situation in Hüls could be normalized at all in the proposed manner.

The sudden Cuba crisis in 1962 unsettled the situation even further. As share prices faltered, a considerable number of Chemie-Verwaltungs AG shares suddenly became available and looked as though they might be bought by a foreign purchaser.

Fortunately, the Dresdner Bank, with the help of Hoechst, was quicker off the mark. But even on the basis of this share acquisition, of which the partners were notified, no generally acceptable solution could be found. Moreover, in the course of time, the interests of the three companies in Hüls had also changed. It is simply not possible to leave a problem of such tremendous economic importance in abeyance for so many years.

In 1967, GBAG suddenly sold its 25 per cent holding in Hüls to Farbenfabriken Bayer. This completely changed the original ideas about the distribution of the Hüls shares. Since Chemische Werke Hüls had in the meantime become the fourth largest German chemical company, with sales of more than 1,000 million DM, we could not possibly remain indifferent as to who was to have the final control. A race began for the shares of Chemie-Verwaltungs AG which caused us a great deal of expenditure and, until the matter was finally resolved, a great deal of annoyance.

A solution was not found until 1969. Farbenfabriken Bayer and Veba, which had in the meantime acquired Bergwerksgesellschaft Hibernia, took over the entire shares of Chemie-Verwaltungs AG available to the contractual partners. Since each of these companies already held 25 per cent of the share capital of Hüls, they were now joint owners. Hoechst acquired 75 per cent of the shares of Cassella and was also given a sum in compensation. BASF had already lost interest in this whole question some years ago and sold its interest in Cassella also to Hoechst.

Some twenty-five years had passed since the end of the war before this last chapter of the I. G. dismemberment had finally been concluded.

It was not, as the reader might assume today, a running fight for power or a succession of stock exchange transactions. It was the largest and most expensive conflict in the German chemical industry after the war. A random dismemberment measure had created an unhealthy situation that had to be put right.

Buna in Joint Production

At that time, in 1955, the production of synthetic rubber was a vital requirement for the motorization of the Federal Republic. The Americans had set up a Buna production during the war on the basis of an I. G. Farbenindustrie licence. After the war, they had decided never to return to natural rubber. This was very much easier for them because they had available both natural gas and petrochemicals, especially butane and butylene cracking gases, from their refineries. In Germany, on the other hand, the route was via acetylene and it was a much longer route. During the war, Germany had achieved a Buna capacity of 120,000 tons. When the question of rubber supplies again became acute in the changed post-war conditions, our situation proved to be completely different from that of America. Our modest tyre production was converted to natural rubber and only small amounts of synthetic rubber were imported. To build up a new Buna production was therefore not entirely without risk. The Federal Ministry of Economics was instrumental in obtaining a compensation agreement from the German tyre industry which recognized in good time that it was not possible to obtain this important raw material through imports alone.

Buna production in the Federal Republic could not be taken up in the old form because the route via acetylene was simply no longer economic. A licence for the production of butadiene from butane and butylene, the Houdry process, was therefore acquired from the Americans and used in Hüls. Incidentally, it was by no means easy to find the required amounts of hydrocarbons because German refinery capacity was still extremely limited.

Under Baumann's guidance, Hüls had thoroughly familiarized itself with the latest progress in the Buna field. It was, therefore, able to achieve an output of approximately 80,000 tons per year fairly quickly. This was gradually increased to 150,000 tons. Neither Chemische Werke Hüls nor the mining companies nor one of the 'big three' would have been able to bear the investment costs and resultant risks on its own. The joint undertaking, in which the three I. G. successor companies and Hüls had a share of 50 per cent each, started operations in 1958.

Increasing motorization throughout the world caused the production of synthetic rubber to rise steeply. The consumption of synthetic rubber has exceeded that of natural rubber for many years now, especially since at one time the suppliers of the natural product, particularly Indonesia and Malaysia, could only partly meet the world requirements because of their political instability.

Other processes for polymerization of butadiene were also found. The original synthetic rubber, consisting of 70 per cent butadiene and 30 per cent styrene and polymerized by the cold rubber process, was replaced by the discoveries of Karl Ziegler from Mülheim and his isotactic polybutadiene. This is also produced in direct collaboration between Hüls and Bayer.

German Oil Industry

The development of the German economy has been influenced until this very day by the problems of energy. In 1955, there was a shortage of coal in Germany. In 1952, the mining companies had entered the Coal and Steel Community which then controlled coal production. Large amounts had to be exported, which meant that German industry was suffering from a continuous shortage of coal. Hoechst had to import large amounts from America in order to fulfil its plans.

The supply of electric power was also inadequate in those first years because the electricity works had been destroyed and fuel was in short supply. It was, therefore, vital to establish a petrochemical industry in Germany. Since motorization was progressing only slowly, the strongest impetus for the construction of refineries in Western Germany emanated from the increasing need for light and heavy fuel oils. The hydrogenation plants that had survived the war on the Rhine and in the Ruhr looked suitable as starting points. The cancellation in 1955 of the ban on the manufacture of synthetic petrol was no longer of any significance. There were now no prospects of profitably operating these processes developed during the era of self-sufficiency. Even today, when in view of the serious situation in the coal industry new uses are being explored, it must remain doubtful whether under European mining conditions coal hydrogenation, valuable as it may be in itself, is likely to be revived. Conditions may be different one day in America where coal can be produced at far lower cost.

In the Federal Republic the hydrogenation plants provided the skeletons for the first refinery capacities when the threat of dismantlement ceased to hang over them.

After Hoechst had taken the first steps into petrochemistry, exploring its own ideas, and had accumulated a certain amount of valuable experience, it felt qualified to seek contact with the new refineries. In the Federal Republic, interest focused on the production of fuel oil, petrol for cars playing a far less important role. German refineries were therefore designed for the distillation of crude oil in which large amounts of light naphtha are obtained. This light naphtha is decomposed in cracking plants and forms a suitable raw material for the production of olefines, especially ethylene and propylene. It was important for the chemical industry to secure access to these starting materials.

It was strict Hoechst policy right from the start not to enter into any financial partnerships with the oil companies or, unlike other chemical companies, to build its own refineries. This was a fundamental question of business policy for which there are probably no generally valid rules. From the present standpoint, it was the right decision for Hoechst. It saved us a great deal of investment capital which was thus released for other uses, and it secured for us the ready cooperation of many suppliers both in Germany and abroad.

This, in turn, resulted in business connections that were useful in other fields as well. The contacts with the oil companies, secured by long-term contracts, guaranteed our supplies of all required petroleum hydrocarbons. Such contracts were eventually concluded for all the various Hoechst works in Germany.

In addition to UK Wesseling, originally inhibited by other contracts, Standard Oil of California became our first petrochemical partner. After I had visited this company in San Francisco in 1954, we concluded supply contracts for a variety of petroleum hydrocarbons. In 1961, a contract for the erection of the Caltex refinery near Hoechst was signed. This ensured the supply of the petrochemical plants at Hoechst for many years to come.

The supply of methane was another one of our worries. We needed this gas for the methane chlorination process at Hoechst which, until the end of the war, had been based on coke oven gas. Adequate amounts of this gas were now no longer available. Moreover, the price of the methane produced by this method was far too high. Karl Schirner, one of the first members of the Hoechst supervisory board and formerly director-general of Deutsche Erdölgesellschaft (DEA) put us in touch with his former company, with whose manager, Günther Schlicht, we collaborated closely for many years.

DEA was looking for natural gas in the area of Darmstadt. We participated financially in these drillings and were anxiously awaiting results because each drilling cost some 250,000 DM. We had little experience in such matters, and hesitated for a long time before we finally signed. I remember that Schlicht rang me up one day and told me that gas would probably be found within the next few days. If we didn't sign soon, we might have to forget all about the cheap gas. Indeed, Schlicht's prediction came true the next day. The gas field near Pfungstadt in the vicinity of Darmstadt was connected to Hoechst by a 25-kilometre pipeline. It was one of the first gas pipelines in Germany. The gas had the advantage of great purity and could be used directly for chlorination. The deposits proved to be far greater than had originally been assumed and sufficed to supply Hoechst, at any rate until methane from the Caltex refinery became available.

In this and similar ways, a complex supply system for petro-chemicals developed in the Federal Republic within a few years. It was based on refineries and cracking plants which were soon connected to international ports in the north by means of an extensive pipeline system. In part, they were also interconnected through end product lines. Following the American example, these developments proceeded with incredible speed in Central Europe and especially in the Federal Republic.

Progress in the construction of large tankers and in pipeline technology played a large role in this. It meant that the chemical plants could remain on their traditional sites well inland. It now became possible to transport raw materials to the point where they were really needed. This gradually enabled us to market our products at prices that rendered them competitive throughout the world.

Supplying Our Bavarian Works

Particularly critical for us was the supply problem in Bavaria. Our companies there were far removed from energy sources and had, moreover, to cope with long transport routes not only for the raw materials but also for the finished products. The resulting competitive disadvantage has remained a problem.

The development of petrochemistry in Bavaria started for us with a visit in 1959 by Hjalmar Schacht, the former president of the German Reichsbank. Schacht, who died in 1970, had come to see me at the request of Enrico Mattei, the president of the Italian petroleum company ENI. He told me about negotiations with the Bavarian Economics Ministry concerning the construction of petrochemical plants near Ingolstadt. Later, I met Mattei and gained some insight into the dynamic policy of ENI. We quickly received the vigorous support of the Bavarian Economics Minister, Otto Schedl, for this project. We owe a great deal of gratitude to Schedl for the establishment of petrochemistry in Bavaria.

As early as 1955, Süd-Petrol AG für Erdölwirtschaft was founded in Munich together with ENI. The refinery is now operated by Erdöl-Raffinerie Ingolstadt AG, a subsidiary of ENI. Before this plant went on stream, Esso and Shell decided to go to Bavaria. Their refineries were erected, too, in the area of Ingolstadt and went on stream in 1963.

Giant pipelines from Marseilles, Genoa and Trieste connected the new Bavarian refineries to the Mediterranean ports. Later, further refineries were built at Ingolstadt. Eventually, we were able to induce the American Marathon Company to build at Burghausen.

Ingolstadt was not the ideal location for either Hoechst or the Bavarian chemical industry. The distance from Gersthofen and Bobingen, the chemical factories of Farbwerke Hoechst in the vicinity of Augsburg, was too great. Nevertheless, the development of the refinery centre at Ingolstadt heralded industrial penetration of Bavaria. It now offered cheap fuel oil and naphtha urgently needed for our plants.

In 1968, our Bavarian possessions were increased by the Süddeutsche Chemiefaser AG in Kelheim with its polyacrylonitrile and rayon staple range. This company also needed raw materials which are now obtained from the refinery of Gelsenberg AG in Neustadt. They are converted to acrylonitrile monomer in a new factory of Süddeutsche Kalkstickstoffwerke.

In this roundabout way, a competitive chemical complex based on petrochemistry has developed in Bavaria. This is all the more remarkable because it happened in a comparatively short time in an area which at the end of the war was filled with barracks housing hundreds of thousands of refugees, and making its living exclusively from agriculture and tourism.

The development of this new raw material basis throughout the Federal Republic extended over a number of years so that naturally we were not able to abandon our old one completely. For example, in Knapsack we had actually to expand the production of calcium carbide. Constructive innovations and favourable electricity contracts made it possible to market carbide competitively for many years as a raw material. In Bavaria too, Süddeutsche Kalkstickstoff-werke and Wacker-Chemie had erected new carbide capacities. Unfortunately, as a result of the recent increases in the price of coke resulting from the reorganization of the coal industry on the Ruhr, carbide manufacture, as a basis for chemistry, has probably for ever lost all chances of remaining competitive. In future, acetylene will have to be produced, if at all, on the basis of the new petrochemical processes.

Oxo Chemistry

During the discussions of the board and in the technical commissions, we soon recognized the need to find new fields of activity. This led to new interests and partnerships on the Ruhr. In the fifties, we started a fruitful exchange of ideas with Mannesmann and HOAG with whom we then jointly took over Ruhrchemie AG in Oberhausen-Holten. The basic idea was that the partners from the Ruhr should supply us with coke-oven gas and other carbon materials from their coke-oven works. Later, products of petro-chemistry had to take over the part of coal also in this field.

One of the most interesting fields that we found in Oberhausen was oxo chemistry which had started there with discoveries by the chemist Otto Roelen in 1938. Ruhrchemie, originally a joint under-taking of the mining companies on the Ruhr, had developed oxo synthesis together with the I. G. The I. G. interest in these inventions and patents had been given to BASF. Our participation in Ruhr-chemie provided us with a welcome opportunity to take up the chemistry of oxo alcohols and to develop it into an industry that has become tremendously important throughout the world.

In this process, synthesis gas – carbon monoxide and hydrogen – is reacted with olefines, i.e. unsaturated hydrocarbons, in the presence of suitable catalysts and under high pressure. Aldehydes are formed and from these, as a result of reduction, alcohols. The alcohols play an important part in the paint industry and the production of plasticizers.

Together with the aldehyde syntheses, which resulted from co-operation with Wacker-Chemie, Hoechst acquired processes and syntheses for alcohols, aldehydes and ketones based upon ethylene, propylene and the higher hydrocarbons. Today, they form a separate field in chemistry and are of great importance for plastics, lacquer raw materials and lacquer manufacture itself. In the last few years, oxo chemistry has provided a rewarding field of activity for Hoechst and also Uhde.

Was It Really An Economic Miracle?

Between 1954 and 1959, sales had more than doubled because of continuous investments and the great research effort in both new and traditional fields. This development ran parallel with the phenomenal and unexpected upsurge of the German economy. It was during this period that the phrase 'the German economic miracle' was coined, an expression that I have always regarded as a little unfortunate and which in the long run did not prove a blessing to our economy. It simply gave rise to an attitude of smugness and self-assurance and created concern and increased counter-efforts abroad.

There was a great deal of theorizing about the laws governing boom developments, the alleged need for control, the question of exchange rates and many other issues. In view of the near-arrogance of many economists and politicians, people abroad were prone to forget the weak foundations on which the German economy was really based and how much it still had to make up for.

For example, few took into account the fact that the German share of the chemical business had formerly been very much larger. If allowance was made for the reduced area of the Federal Republic, our share of world chemical production in 1958 was only 7 per cent or about half of the pre-war figure. In the chemical field, intense competition soon arose and the recessions in the U.S. did not remain without effect upon conditions in Germany.

Apart from investments for technical development and research, special efforts had to be made to consolidate business abroad. There were not enough people and there was a lack of experience and particularly a shortage of capital.

With a company name difficult for foreigners to pronounce and with our tower and bridge as the new company emblem, we had to set up a completely new sales organization throughout the world based on our small domestic platform. This involved new people who had to rely entirely upon themselves abroad and who had to try to make friends and create goodwill as a firm basis for more ambitious operations.

There were no new products available at first. The old trademarks were still partly confiscated or had been acquired by other companies. Other trade marks, like Indanthren, were no longer of significance or had to be bought back, as in the case of the famous pharmaceutical products.

During these first years, it needed a great deal of ingenuity on the part of our sales people to gain a foothold in the world with this product range which was not exactly modern. New products like the antibiotic Reverin, a derivative of tetracycline, which quickly gained a large market, or the oral antidiabetics like Rastinon, came along only slowly. Rastinon was developed jointly with Boehringer in Mannheim and represented the first really new product of the German pharmaceutical industry after the war.

In the dyestuffs field, we shared product ranges with other German chemical companies and in many places of the world had to sell them jointly with these companies. With regard both to production and selling, it would have been too expensive immediately to change this organization which had been created during the I. G. period. New products that each company was able to sell independently came on to the market only gradually.

The Remazol dyestuffs are a famous example. This was a new type of dyestuff which entered into a true chemical reaction with the fibre. It possessed valuable new properties and allowed new dyeing methods to be employed. Organic pigments were developed for the printing of textiles, the paint industry and the colouring of plastics. Currently, the majority of our dyestuffs range is sold outside the textile sector. The dyestuffs business is therefore rather less dependent upon the textile industry and its repeated crises than it used to be.

It was a great advantage that we had devised an appropriate structure for the sales organization from the start. It differed considerably from that of the old I. G. Farbenindustrie. Immediately after reconstitution, a joint sales directorate had been created, first under Walther Ludwigs and, after he retired in 1954, under Kurt

Inauguration of the Carl-Bosch House in Frankfurt-on-Main 1957
Above (left to right): *Georg Schreiber, Richard Kuhn, Karl Winnacker, Otto Hahn, Else Bosch*

Below (left to right): *Carl Wurster, Ulrich Haberland, Karl Winnacker, Werner Bockelmann, Mayor of Frankfurt, Else Bosch, Burchkardt Helferich, Theo Goldschmidt, Burgomaster Walter Leiske*

Press conference (left to right): *Hans Reintges, Rolf Sammet, Karl Winnacker, Kurt Lanz*

Lanz. It was responsible for every product of the company in every field and region of the world. Naturally, to fulfil its task it needed the support of a strongly-staffed headquarters, the Verkaufsleitung.

During 1954, a new sales building was erected in an extremely short period and it was therefore subject to a number of shortcomings. Nevertheless, intense activity soon radiated from the new building. With only a few experienced people from former days but a great deal of youthful élan, the new sales organization set about conquering the new world market. This often meant overcoming strong resistance.

In Hoechst itself, not everybody – either at board level or below – was convinced that it was right to invest so much money in exports and in countries whose political stability frequently appeared doubtful. These hesitations and doubts were to some extent nurtured by the fact that we had been shut off from the world for so many years. I personally shared this concern which was the main reason for many of the extended journeys that I undertook together with Kurt Lanz.

The organization of the application and technical service departments which tested the new products of chemical research for their potential applications and then communicated the results to customers throughout the world, also proved extremely difficult.

It had been these very application and technical service departments that had contributed so much to the fame of the coal tar dyestuffs industry with its coloristic tradition. This principle of providing customers with technical service had now to be extended from the dyestuffs sphere to all the other fields. It was absolutely essential to provide this technical service for the new plastics and fibres as well because processors and users were suddenly faced with the choice of using an unknown plastic material instead of the familiar wood or metal, and of using Trevira instead of the traditional silk. Such a service organization is now generally accepted as a most important selling tool and its need is no longer disputed.

These technical service departments always gave rise to animated internal discussions, for they cost a great deal of money. The issue as to whether these laboratories, staffed with scientists and technicians, were closer to sales or technology, and to which side they should therefore be subordinated, was a subject for continous dispute.

At first, we solved this problem purely geographically and

erected the new laboratories in the immediate vicinity of the central sales building. The number of chemists, physicists, engineers and technical personnel working in them grew steadily. We had to take great care that our technical service remained linked to science but was also familiar with the commercial sphere.

The importance and weight of this organization is reflected by the number of people it employs. In 1970, 17,500 people worked in the sales organization at home and abroad and 3,600 people in the application and technical service departments. The total number of Hoechst employees throughout the world was 139,000.

Centre for a Thousand Research Workers

Gradually, conditions in Hoechst had consolidated to the point where the erection of a large research centre could begin. With the help of the government of Hesse, we had succeeded in acquiring on the southern side of the Main an area of more than two square kilometres which was integrated with the main works on the other side of the river.

As a first decisive step in the reorganization of our scientific activities, we re-established a central laboratory of a kind that ought to form part of every scientific complex. Its forerunner had been decentralized in 1931. It was located in the middle of the factory in the 'lion pharmacy', known to the old chemists by this name because of the two stern lions that kept guard in front of the building.

In 1957, Werner Schultheis tackled the problem of merging four large research departments into one central scientific laboratory. In autumn 1958, the plans for the new research centre were submitted to the supervisory board. The proposals included a company-owned bridge across the Main to link the old Hoechst complex in the north with the new research centre.

In the planning of the new research centre, we borrowed many ideas from abroad. In the U.S.A. we had realized the need for concentrating large laboratories covering various faculties – medicine, biology, chemistry, physics, engineering – as far as possible in one place. On the other hand, it seemed essential to us that the research centre should not be too far removed from the production plants and the administrative headquarters. The location on the south side of the Main therefore offered an ideal solution.

Walter Henn of Brunswick University provided the design for the large number of buildings that were eventually to house a thousand scientists together with the appropriate laboratory personnel. We expected the new centre would cost some 250 million DM before it was completed.

The Next Ten Years

As chemical industry throughout the world was taking immense strides forward, its growth potential and profitability were at times regarded as unlimited and thus greatly overestimated, even by international experts. In such an atmosphere, recessions occur much more readily and sometimes they can assume dangerous proportions. For example, this excessive optimism resulted in over-capacities which, whenever there was a downturn in business, were not fully utilized, resulting, in turn, in a collapse of prices. This succession of events is still happening in chemistry today and, I suppose, one has to learn to live with it. In any case, sooner or later reduced prices result in increased sales so that the enlarged capacity opens up new prospects of profits after all.

In an industry with as much future potential as the chemical industry with its constantly increasing range of products, such a cycle, which up to now has always produced an economic equilibrium between prices and costs is, in the end, probably inevitable. The general rules of economics have only a limited application to the chemical industry. They cannot take into account the extent to which existing products and markets may change, and the extent to which new products and sales opportunities create entirely new conditions for commerce.

During the first ten years after our reconstitution in particular, we found ourselves in just such a special and unusual situation, where general rules did not apply. Almost half of the products that we were now selling had been developed during these last ten years. Moreover, there were large parts of the world in which we were not yet active or in which the market for chemical products had not yet been opened up. We had therefore to go our own way, in line with the particular requirements of our company.

On the other hand, German industry was still fairly sensitive to economic fluctuations. Small recessions such as those which occurred in the U.S.A. in 1956 and which had only little influence on the investment policy of the large and capital-intensive companies there, had a far greater effect upon us and quickly generated a general air of pessimism.

This is quite understandable if it is remembered that the American companies at that time distributed only about 20 per cent of their profits among shareholders and used the remaining 80 per cent to finance their activities. Also, the interest rate in Germany for long-term money was almost twice as high as in America and Switzerland.

The E.E.C., established in 1958, was welcomed in Germany by all far-sighted people. But in those first years it also caused us a great deal of concern. There was the threat of serious differences with the west European countries that had not joined the E.E.C. These included Great Britain, Denmark, Norway, Sweden, Switzerland, Austria and Portugal, which now organized themselves in EFTA. It was precisely with these countries that Germany, and particularly Hoechst, had so much commercial contact. In addition, the tariffs of the Federal Republic were originally only about half those of the other E.E.C. countries. This handicap, probably necessary to enable us to make the first step towards European integration, resulted in many disadvantages for us during the first years.

In 1958, industrial production in Germany dropped. Many companies lowered their dividends. In Hoechst, the increase in sales, contrary to our expectation, was only 6 per cent. Other chemical companies even recorded a reduction in sales. Our investment policy was criticized both by shareholders and trade unions. We felt the time had come, therefore, to form our own view of the future which would be more reliable than the counsels and theories offered to us by other people of varying degrees of sympathy.

The new data-processing department and the staff available to the management for such work, engaged in the first attempts to prepare a long-term forecast. Since then, Farbwerke Hoechst has regularly produced such forecasts which include the current year and extend over a period of ten years. The forecasts are linked to an investment programme for five years and these investments should be fully reflected, in both sales and profit, at the end of the ten-year period. The ten-year plan is revised every year and extended by a further year.

The experience and the knowledge that we have gained through the operation of this plan have been extremely valuable, even if initially the preparation of the forecasts met with a great deal of opposition amongst a large number of the staff involved.

The thinking called for by this plan occupied many people throughout the company; it gave rise to serious reflection on the meaning of one's job and also promoted the exchange of ideas. The foremen in the factory were asked by their superiors about the potential of their workshops. In the plants there were discussions about capacities and how these might most usefully be extended. The sales people had to intensify market research and had to prepare concrete sales forecasts, although in this field especially, long-term planning is the most difficult of all.

Such estimates are especially unreliable so far as research is concerned. Even today, research forecasts face considerable obstacles. In the past, 30 to 40 per cent of all products sold were developed during the preceeding ten years. A similar situation therefore may also be expected for the future. Research will continue to contribute significantly to the growth of chemistry.

It is necessary to examine very carefully, in every branch of science, whether there are any growth opportunities and where new developments are likely during such a long time. Research, too, needs forecasts for its fields although the results are most difficult to estimate. Nevertheless such forecasts impel research to undertake continuous, critical, self-examination of its work. Research has to accept part of the overall responsibility for the company and it must provide convincing arguments for its financial requirements.

The considerable investments that derive from such a comprehensive plan require many years of preparation. It is necessary to determine a suitable location, the necessary land has to be bought, the raw material and power supply have to be organized and traffic problems have to be solved. Will there be enough labour and will the necessary accommodation be available for them? What is the social and political situation? These and many other questions have to be cleared up before any progress can be made. Staff departments for research, sales, and production are continuously working on this planning system which is then rendered into a comprehensive study with the aid of the accounts and finance department.

Such long-term planning, is not, of course, without risks. Success depends upon a large number of external factors over which the company has no control. Annual budgets provide an opportunity for intermediate revision, since not all decisions are made at the same time. In fact, it is not so important that the target is really achieved after ten years. Even if it takes eleven or twelve years, the thinking and the calculations that have gone into the project will not have been in vain.

On the occasion of our first forecast in 1958, when the economic situation was by no means calculated to give rise to excessive optimism, we came to the conclusion that the existing sales programme of Hoechst would enable us to increase sales by 7 to 8 per cent per annum. The successes achieved by our new divisions gave us a great deal of hope. On the other hand, it was absolutely clear that increases in wages and salaries and considerable pressure on prices made such a volume growth essential if we were not to stand still or even suffer a recession. This, in turn, meant that the investment volume of Hoechst, which in the last few years had remained at approximately 270 million DM, had to be increased to 450 or 500 million DM per annum.

By September 1958, the recession which had caused so much pessimism, had been mastered. The inauguration of the central laboratory and of the bridge across the Main coincided with far-reaching decisions of our supervisory board. South of the Main, in the area of Kelsterbach and Raunheim, we bought an area of approximately 400 hectares – approximately the size of Hoechst on both sides of the Main – on which the Caltex refinery was later erected. It was to supply Hoechst with all petrochemical raw materials on the basis of a long-term contract and was connected through an oil pipeline with the North Sea ports.

The splendid support of the government of Hesse, which sold us a large part of the required land from state possessions, finally made it possible for us to remain in Hesse with the modern field of petrochemistry and its derivatives. We were able to turn Hoechst into a modern factory with room for expansion for many years to come.

In September 1958, we informed the supervisory board of a long-term contract with UK-Wesseling which had erected a cracker for the supply of Knapsack where the acquisition of more land had also become inevitable. An ethylene pipeline, 180 kilometres long, was constructed between Knapsack and Hoechst.

A month later, I presented the supervisory board with a comprehensive account of the economic situation of the Federal Republic. Among other things, I stated at the time:

'Thirteen years after the end of the war, the principles that Germany adopted for its economic policy are beginning to bear fruit. Basically, we see the first consequences of liberalization only at a moment when the economic progress of the peoples in the western world is no longer proceeding at exactly the same rate or in the same sense.

'It is when we suffer economic crises, as in the U.S.A., or political crises, as in France, that we feel the consequences of liberalization which we ourselves wanted, and which we also have widely practised, but which the majority of our commercial partners are only just beginning to adopt. The unhealthy mixture of free trade on the one hand and out-of-date barriers on the other, is a situation that presents us with great difficulties at the present time. The European Economic Community, we hope, will help to reduce these difficulties. In the long run, we will derive advantages from the E.E.C. once we have overcome the intermediate phases.

'If peace continues in the world, our commercial prospects will go on increasing. In spite of all the threatening clouds, and in spite of the Iron Curtain, we have, I feel, good reason to remain optimistic. During the last few months we have for the first time established personal contact with China and Russia. This beginning, however modest, seems to me one of the most significant achievements of the past year. I am convinced that slowly but surely there will be an exchange of both commodities and experience with these countries even if of a different nature than formerly. We have not known such wide horizons, and such completely free trade, at any rate as far as we are concerned, for many decades, in fact not since 1914.

'There are only few of us here who remember such freedom of trade backed by an internationally respected currency. Although domestic sales are rising steeply because of the increasing living standards of the people, we are nevertheless facing many anxieties in the Federal Republic. For example, the long expected food and drug legislation will have a great impact on our affairs. Laws concerning pollution of air and water will also affect us greatly. These measures show that the nation is increasingly facing up to the problems posed by modern technology. However desirable such controls may be in the interests of individuals, there is a great danger that we may have to incur great expense and general difficulties as a result of ill-advised regulations and demands.'

The meeting of the supervisory board of September 1960, resolved to erect a large centre for employees, shareholders' meetings, and the cultural activities of the Rhine-Main area in general to commemorate the centenary of Farbwerke Hoechst. We were in any case faced by the need for a new canteen and a restaurant for the company's many guests from home and abroad. An international jury selected a design by Friedrich Wilhelm Kraemer of Brunswick from a large number that had been submitted. During the next few years a large complex was erected whose main feature was a vast domed hall holding 4,000 people and equipped with all modern stage facilities.

While we were taking these far-reaching and optimistic decisions about the expansion of our company, the political horizon had darkened alarmingly. When we acquired Spinnstofffabrik Zehlendorf in Berlin in 1960 to strengthen our fibres division, the divided city was once more hitting the headlines of the international press. Khrushchev, the Soviet leader, began his dangerous policy of brinkmanship over Berlin. For a long period, there was a real danger of world war until eventually the strict attitude of the west convinced the choleric Soviet premier that his plans of turning Berlin into a 'free city' were bound to fail.

In March 1961, contrary to all expectations and warnings, the Federal government decided to revalue the Deutschmark by 5 per cent. The financial experts who wanted to ban the spectre of an allegedly overheated economy had won the day.

The measure appeared to us all the more incomprehensible because only a few weeks previously German industry had been asked to lend its support to an investment loan precisely in order to avoid such a fundamental change in the rate of exchange. For the first time since the currency reform in 1948, the Deutschmark lost its hard-won and greatly envied stability. We entered a phase of instability which has impaired German economy ever since and which in November 1969 gave rise to renewed unrest.

As we had introduced a programme of vast expansion in 1961, revaluation landed us in very great difficulties. Profits from our vastly increased exports were affected by almost 5 per cent because international competition did not allow us to pass on price increases to our customers abroad and our relatively small foreign companies were not in a position to compensate us for the losses with which we were faced.

The totally unexpected revaluation had cast great doubts on our careful long-term planning. Press conferences and annual general meetings provoked searching questions about the profit situation of Hoechst. True, we always managed to distribute an adequate and increasing dividend to our shareholders, but we had hardly any money left for our own finance.

The anxious times during which we had to overcome the consequences of DM revaluation, lasted for almost five years. It was a hard trial for us. All that we had created after re-formation and during the years of decision was being severely tested.

8

Science and Industry, Two Good Partners

IT HAD to happen one day. As president of Dechema, I was standing in front of the speaker's rostrum during the final event of 1970. I intended to present a review of our progress in chemical technology, as demonstrated in the exhibition, followed by some fundamental comments on scientific education and the position of chemists and engineers in technology generally. The usual polite applause had ebbed away. I started my introductory sentences and then picked up my manuscript. Although I have given many speeches in my life without a manuscript, I never did so in lectures which had a precisely formulated content.

Almost immediately I noticed that I had brought along the wrong manuscript. What I held in my hands was a lecture on chemistry and nuclear technology which I had given a few days previously in Frankfurt.

For a few seconds I was completely stunned. My wife, who was sitting in the front row, gave me a worried look. She had obviously realized what had happened. But in the meantime I had overcome my first shock and decided that I had no choice but to reconstruct my speech from memory. That I succeeded in this reasonably well and that what I said roughly corresponded to the English and French translations being projected on to the screen, was probably due to the fact that my subject dealt with fundamental questions that had fascinated me since my student days: the close connection between science and industry within the framework of chemical technology.

This symbiosis has been effectively demonstrated for many years at Achema, the exhibition for chemical apparatus. After an interval of three years, Achema 1970 once again provided an illuminating documentation of all the forces and faculties that were interacting in chemical technology. Achema also held a great attraction for allied associations such as the Society of German Chemists and the Society of German Engineers, with its Society for Process Engineering, which had arranged a programme of lectures during Achema, as had the German Atomic Forum which had, in addition, provided a special exhibition.

The centre point of Achema was once again the exhibition of chemical apparatus. More than 2,000 companies had participated, a third of them from abroad. The range of apparatus displayed, and the exhibition space required to show it, had increased from year to year. The Frankfurt exhibition site had to be enlarged. More than 20,000 people visited the exhibition and attended the lectures. Achema 1970 received some 150,000 visitors.

During the final ceremonial session, I vacated the chairmanship of Dechema, which I had held since 1955, in favour of Hellmut Ley, the chairman of Metallgesellschaft. I knew Ley from our student days in Darmstadt and had long shared his beliefs concerning the development of chemical technology.

On the occasion of the sixteenth Achema, we recalled that some fifty years had passed since this event had taken place for the first time two years after the end of the First World War. The idea had originated with Max Buchner, a manufacturer from Hanover. His idea was to provide an opportunity for exhibitors and designers to discuss the exhibits of chemical apparatus with scientists and engineers on the stand itself – a unique opportunity for an exchange of experience between the manufacturers and users of such apparatus.

His idea had proved extraordinarily useful. After initial difficulties and interruptions due to economic crises and war, Achema became a regular international event at which scientists from all fields of chemical technology throughout the world gathered together.

Chemistry and chemical technology, in so far as they were based on the results of the exact sciences, had developed during the middle of the last century in a relatively short period of time and had created the basis of a flourishing industry. Scientific progress continuously gave rise to new developments in the chemical industry which as a result grew into an important branch of the economy. In a way each Achema was a barometer of the progress of technology. More and more people participated in these encounters between technicians concerned with the construction of chemical apparatus, and chemists and engineers from industry, in order to discuss the opportunities and needs of research and education with the teachers from the universities and polytechnics wherever possible. An essential subject of these meetings therefore was vocational training which had, of course, to be brought into line with the rapid technological development.

Liebig's Example

Even as a student in Darmstadt, I was greatly interested in the history of science and its economic consequences. Our teacher Berl attached a great deal of importance to the history of chemistry and its beginnings under Justus von Liebig and August Kekulé and interwove the historical development of chemistry with his excellent technology lectures. The history of chemistry teaches that science and industry have always shared the same fate, especially in the field of chemistry. Unforgettable for me in this connection are the excursions to the Liebig Museum in Giessen which Berl frequently undertook with his students. The museum, which is open to the public, was originally the guard-room of a barracks which was made available to Giessen University by Ludwig I, Grand Duke of Hesse, after the soldiers had been transferred elsewhere. In 1824, at the age of twenty-one and just appointed professor extraordinary, Liebig fitted out his chemical laboratory in this guard-room. It was the first of its kind in Germany. It was enlarged later on and finally comprised twelve rooms, as well as Liebig's flat on the first floor.

With its historic laboratory equipment and apparatus, Liebig's old furniture and the numerous pictures, documents, letters and books, the museum provides a vivid impression of this first school of preparative chemistry established during the middle of the last century. Its instructions and its methods continue to be the prototype for the teaching of chemistry at German universities even today. Such famous scientists as August Wilhelm von Hofmann and Adolf von Baeyer, as well as many of the founders of the German coal tar dyestuffs industry all graduated from Giessen, for example Gustav von Brüning of Farbwerke Hoechst and Heinrich Caro of BASF, Ludwigshafen.

As twentieth-century students, we stood almost reverently in these old rooms with their brick kilns, retorts, crucible and tongs. In the 'pharmaceutical laboratory' we discussed the liquefaction apparatus with its iron hand-wheel, or the distillation apparatus with Liebig's condenser, and in the study we saw the simple desk at which Liebig had written many of his scientific works.

Liebig himself is an example of the need for close symbiosis between science and industry in the field of chemistry. Although he had always warned against the danger of allowing materialism or utilitarian principles to gain ground in a teaching institute, he fought tirelessly for the practical application of the knowledge he had gained. Liebig was a bitter enemy of natural philosophy which offered much resistance to scientific progress in Germany.

As the founder of agricultural chemistry, Liebig recorded achievements that have been of tremendous benefit for agriculture as a whole. In the Giessen Museum there is still the original site plan of the so-called 'Liebig Heights' where he carried out his first experiments with mineral fertilizers. He was not too proud to work out specifications for many practical things, for example for the manufacture of silver mirrors or baking powders. We should not forget either his instructions for the preparation of Liebig's meat extract which even in my childhood was still a major item in my mother's kitchen.

Since Liebig's days and the succeeding founder years of the German chemical industry, the economic success of the chemical companies would have been unthinkable without the continuous contact with science.

During the reconstruction of the German chemical industry after 1945, neither the laudable efforts of all those involved nor the considerable investments made would, by themselves, have led to the desired result. The nutrient ground for new scientific knowledge could not have been provided if the growing economy, in addition to its preoccupation with reconstruction, had not taken an interest in those institutions that had to provide the prerequisites for competitive industrial activity. Anyone who had the opportunity of going to university between the two world wars and who had then entered the chemical industry, had been taught both by his teachers at university and the leaders of industry the value of close collaboration between science and industry, and the importance to both sides of an intellectual and organizational community.

After the First World War, such close collaboration had become even more vital because the situation then, just as twenty-five years later, was characterized by shortages and poverty. As a result of the initiative of the Prussian Minister of Culture, an Emergency Society of German Science was founded in Berlin in 1920, the year of the first Achema. It was devoted above all to the encouragement of scientific recruits, collaboration between research workers, and the support of individual research projects. It was the forerunner of the present German Research Association. It also presented the Liebig scholarships which were in very great demand during the economic and currency crises of the twenties and thirties.

The heydays of the Kaiser Wilhelm Society also fell between the wars. Its foundation had been proposed by Kaiser Wilhelm II on the occasion of the centenary jubilee of Berlin University in the autumn of 1910. The idea had emanated from the protestant theologian Adolf von Harnack, the first president of the society, Friedrich Althoff the director of the university department in the Prussian Ministry of Culture who had died in 1908, and Friedrich Schmidt-Ott, the Prussian Minister of Culture during 1917–18 and the first president of the emergency association.

The interest of German industry was quickly aroused; the Kaiser Wilhelm Society was founded as early as January 1911. It was equipped with sizeable financial funds by industry and other donors. Twenty million gold marks of initial capital and the promise of an annual payment of six million gold marks were huge sums for that period and provided a firm basis upon which to conduct further scientific development.

The aim of the society was the cultivation of scientific research. For this purpose, independent research institutes were founded which belonged neither to the state nor industry, although they were financed largely by industry. Many famous scientists and Nobel prizewinners were members of the society. Amongst the early directors of the institutes were Otto Hahn, Lise Meitner and Fritz Haber. The Kaiser Wilhelm Society became the example for many foundations in the U.S.A. Today, its material and intellectual inheritance has been taken over by the Max Planck Society. The foundation of the German Museum in Munich by Oskar von Miller fell into the same period. It was developed by science and industry between the wars and turned into a fascinating record of technological history. The museum was extensively damaged during the war but it has been rebuilt and is now ideally suited to arouse the interest of youth in technology. I will never forget my first visit to the German Museum in 1921.

It was in institutions of this kind that we chemists first witnessed the community of science and industry. During our student excursions, at exhibitions and seminars and during the annual meetings of the scientific societies, we saw our academic teachers joining with leading men of the chemical industry, such as Carl Duisberg of Leverkusen, Carl Bosch of Ludwigshafen, or Paul Duden, who had created acetylene chemistry in Hoechst.

Probably in no other industrial branch was the intellectual affinity between research and university teaching on the one hand, and the leaders of industry on the other, so pronounced as in chemistry. This was reflected in the fact that all the rapidly growing companies of large-scale chemistry were headed almost exclusively by natural scientists. Hundreds of chemists and physicists worked in the increasing number of laboratories in chemical industry. These scientists, particularly where they were encouraged to do this by their company, continued to maintain close links with their teachers and the universities whence they had come and to which they sometimes returned. One of the fundamental reasons for the excellent progress of the chemical industry in Germany is probably its deep conviction of the need for research and its close contact with the universities, scientific associations, and other scientific societies formed in particular fields.

During the period of the I. G., we young scientists were greatly encouraged to attend scientific conferences. Numerous lectures by important scientists from Germany and abroad were held in our works. Anyone in the least receptive to such ideas was provided with plenty of examples of the close relationship between science and economy, and their constant need for reciprocal assistance and mutual inspiration.

Naturally, over the years, the emphasis changed from time to time. The fundamental theories of Walther Nernst and Fritz Haber found their technical realization in the Haber-Bosch synthesis – producing ammonia from air. The pharmaceutical industry was the source of great developments in the fields of drugs and modern medicine. Ideas and inventions were readily exchanged between both sides. The material side – donations, invention awards and advisory fees – was accepted without ethical reservations and in no way interfered with the freedom of research.

In those days, the state adopted a very reticent attitude. It controlled the life of the universities with great circumspection and accepted the patronage of the large foundations like the Kaiser Wilhelm Society which was administered jointly by science and industry. The result of this generous liberal attitude was the golden age of science during the Weimar Republic. The results of research, particularly at the institutes of the Kaiser Wilhelm Society, were internationally recognized through the award of many Nobel prizes to German scientists. Many of the new discoveries and inventions were of particularly great value to the chemical industry which had to fight hard in those years. At the end of the First World War, German industry had lost its entire patent possessions to the victorious powers and was now compelled to fill this gap as quickly as possible.

With the arrival of the National Socialists in 1933, the community of science and industry, which had stood so many tests, was subjected to the severest test of all. With unforeseen haste, the new rulers interfered fundamentally with university life. They were not concerned with practical reforms but with the realization of purely National Socialist aims.

These had, of course, been laid down in the party programme but their radical consequences had not been foreseen, even by the majority of party members. Even those students who were sympathetic to National Socialism were aghast when they found that respected university professors were brutally removed from their posts purely on the grounds of race.

Research and teaching suffered a severe blood-letting that has not been made good even today. Many irreplaceable and world-famous scientists emigrated. Others broke down under the strain of degradation and bitter disillusionment. Industry, which was closely linked with them and their life's work, could help in only a few cases. It was threatened by the same action. In many cases it was possible to mitigate undue hardship and to contain the interference of the state. In the chemical industry, and this is often forgotten today, there was considerable resistance.

Carl Bosch, too, was a bitter enemy of the National Socialist regime. The audience with Hitler during which Bosch warned

Inauguration of the plastics factory in Bombay (on the right) : *Arvind N. Mafatlal*

Below: *View of the factory*

Reception during the Foratom congress 1965 (left to right) *Heinz Göschel, Gertrud Winnacker, Karl Winnacker, Otto Hahn*

against the consequences of the rigorous dismissal of Jewish scientists is on record as is Hitler's reply: 'Then we work for a century without physics or chemistry.' Mention should also be made in this connection of the memorial service for the racially persecuted Fritz Haber which took place on 21 January 1935. It was arranged by Carl Bosch. Against the express order of Bernhard Rust, the Minister of Science and Education, Otto Hahn gave the memorial address.

The community of science and industry once more played its part when, after unconditional surrender, reconstruction had to be faced. The havoc wrought by the war and the division of Germany into four zones had paralysed all scientific life. The institutes were closed, their buildings demolished. Following the loss of racially persecuted scientists during the National Socialist era, detention and emigration now caused a second blood-letting.

When the young soldiers returned to resume their studies, the remaining professors took up teaching and research once more with great enthusiasm, albeit under modest conditions. They trained the generation of chemists that is now controlling our industry. They maintained the unity of research and teaching even in those difficult years and they achieved many important research results.

During all the present discussions regarding university and high school reforms, it should never be forgotten that during the critical period after the war the universities passed the greatest test to which they have ever been subjected.

They had to rely on help from all sides and this was readily forthcoming. The Königstein agreement concluded in 1949 between the Cultural and Finance Ministries of the Länder, created the conditions for the financing and reconstruction of the universities. The donations from industry had lost their value as the result of the currency reform, as they did during the inflation of the twenties. The state had to help therefore until industry, which was still greatly restricted in its freedom of action, could again play an active part. The Kaiser Wilhelm Society was re-established in February 1948 taking the name of the white-haired Max Planck who survived till the end of the war. Fortunately, the old generation contained many people who were not suspected of National Socialist sympathies and who could not therefore be attacked. It was a great event for me to meet these people who were a whole generation older than I and whose experience and recollections went back to the last century.

C.Y.—17

My activities in the senate of the Max Planck Society as well as on several trustee boards of the institutes that were being re-established were of great personal value. Although I could not, of course, take part in the actual work of the institutes, I did make the acquaintance of the many personalities that were now recreating the society.

I remember, for example, an evening in the Hoechst restaurant. The Max Planck Society had again become an esteemed and active institution. On the morning of 27 November 1959, a meeting of the senate had taken place in Hoechst at which Adolf Butenandt was elected successor to the eighty-year-old president, Otto Hahn. There was a small party afterwards to which Otto Hahn, Otto Warburg, Max von Laue and the Catholic theologian Georg Schreiber, and many others, were invited. Our over-anxious canteen chef served wine of what he thought was a particularly good vintage. After the theologian Schreiber had tasted it, he said with a smile, 'Well, my young man, this should make a good wine soup for your staff one day.'

The reconstruction of old institutions and societies required the official approval of the Allied occupation authorities. This was granted most quickly and generously of all in the British zone. After the British and American zones were joined into the Bi-zone, larger associations were formed which we eventually extended to the French zone of occupation.

When the various chemical companies were allowed to form the Association of German Chemical Industry in December 1950, more money was available for science to be backed substantially. In February 1950, a chemical industry fund was created under the auspices of the association's co-founder and long-term first president, Wilhelm Alexander Menne, who later also became a member of the Hoechst board for some considerable time. The patronage was accepted by Theodor Heuss, then Federal President of Germany.

The companies of the chemical industry undertook to donate a fixed monthly sum per employee and per hour worked. This was increased from year to year. In the twenty years since this fund was established some 200 million DM have been collected in this way and used for the promotion of research.

In September 1949, the Society of German Chemists was reborn. It represented chemists in science and industry. As on other occasions, the society quickly succeeded in enlisting the active cooperation of leading men of the chemical industry. Scientists and industrialists are represented in the management of the society and share the presidency on a two-year basis.

Since the society had lost its assets and its buildings in Berlin, to say nothing of the ability to do its work, it had to be provided with entirely new facilities. When I became treasurer of the society, we succeeded, with the grateful help and generosity of the town of Frankfurt, in erecting the Carl Bosch House. Apart from the offices of the Society of German Chemists and the German Bunsen Society, this building now also houses the editorial offices of the two chemical handbooks of Gmelin and Beilstein – household names for every chemist. The Carl Bosch House also contains a replacement for the August Wilhelm von Hofmann library, which is no longer available to the west, in the form of a comprehensive chemical central library which we named after Adolf von Baeyer, Liebig's famous pupil.

As soon as I was able to be active in the field of chemistry once more, I naturally also assumed the obligation of participating in the organization and work of such associations and societies. The industrial reconstruction in Hoechst would not have been possible if we had not personally played our part in this reawakening of scientific life.

Hobby Horse: Chemical Technology

My personal inclinations remained fixed on my original field – chemical technology. Whenever I was asked whether I had a hobby, I was always able to answer in all honesty that it was my chemical technology. I came back to it whenever I had any spare time.

It was a fortunate turn of events that I had chosen a branch of science during my student years in Darmstadt which fitted in well with my career in industry and also enabled me to remain faithful to my favourite subject in my senior responsibilities. In this way, I was able to participate personally in the technical developments required in Hoechst in the fields of petrochemistry, plastics, and technical electro-chemistry.

Articles and lectures that could easily and conveniently be related to this subject happily complemented my industrial activities at home and abroad and enabled me to make many interesting and important contacts throughout the world.

After my dismissal from Hoechst in 1945, it was essentially the handbook of chemical technology, which I published jointly with Ernst Weingärtner, that heralded my return to chemistry. My stay at the Duisburger Kupferhütte and the electro-chemical work at Knapsack provided new and interesting aspects and enlarged my technical knowledge.

During the Knapsack period, I was also offered an opportunity of a university chair in technology and thus of returning to academic life. But I was then so closely linked with the reconstruction work in Knapsack that I did not feel I could abandon the work that had been started.

In 1953, however, I gladly accepted an appointment as honorary professor at the University of Frankfurt. Since that time, with only a few exceptions, I have regularly presented papers on special aspects of chemical technology. Excursions frequently extending over several days were essential complements to these lectures. This activity has given me extraordinary satisfaction although naturally I had to enlist the help of my young colleagues at Hoechst for many of the details.

I devoted myself to my academic obligations with much enthusiasm. I remembered from my own university days how important it is for young students to meet representatives of those companies for whom many of them may one day work.

It was with particular delight that I accepted the chairmanship of Dechema, the German Society for Chemical Apparatus, in 1955. The society's main task, the organization of Achema, had been taken up again after the Second World War. In 1950 and 1952, exhibitions supplemented by lectures had again taken place even if only on a modest scale. On the whole, however, many facilities were still lacking. For example, the offices in Frankfurt which were destroyed during the war, had not yet been restored. Even more difficult was the problem of adopting the scientific life of the society to the changed conditions of the post-war period. During the first years after its refoundation, Dechema had simply not been able to pay sufficient attention to this. Now it ran the risk of giving too much prominence to the exhibition aspect and of neglecting the essential functions of a scientific society.

Chemists and engineers, as well as the manufacturers of chemical apparatus and chemical industry, fully expected that Dechema would again provide a point of reference for their work. For various reasons, they were, however, dissatisfied with the affairs of the society and discussed among themselves how best to promote their interests within Dechema. On the board, too, there had been profound arguments over personnel questions and the selection of new fields of activity.

In the chemical industry, the nature of cooperation between chemists and engineers has always been a problem. Even after the turn of the century, preparative chemistry dominated the activities in the factory. Its great success paved the way for the later achievements.

It was not until 1900 that the engineer began to enjoy the same importance as the chemist. At this time, manufacturing techniques became rather more sophisticated than the processes employed until then which, in many cases, closely resembled the classic organic laboratory procedures. High pressure processes and catalytic reactions made new demands on measuring and control technology, on design instruction and on material knowledge. During the period between the two wars, these adjustments were still being effected. Within the I. G., too, there were large differences in the quality of technical thinking. On the one hand, there were classic plants devoted to dyestuff and pharmaceutical production and on the other hand the new processes of high pressure technology, ammonia synthesis and acetylene chemistry, in fact all of inorganic industry which had always been exposed to a major engineering influence. Dechema had not been able to reconcile these different interests for some time.

In 1936, as the result of an initiative by Friedrich Jähne, at that time chief engineer at Hoechst and chairman of the engineering commission of the I. G., and by Rudolf Plank and Arnold Eucken, and in particular at the instance of Siegfried Kiesskalt, the Society for Consumer-Goods Technology was founded. Its aim was to familiarize engineers with chemistry, its thermodynamics, reaction kinetics and many other aspects. This new branch of science was eventually described as process engineering.

With the help of a number of people, Arnold Eucken, who was one of the outstanding personalities in physical chemistry, wrote a handbook of physical methods in the chemical and allied industries. In fact, this work defined the functions of process engineering and its declared purpose was to enlarge the horizons of the engineers whose thinking and training in Germany had been too closely confined to classic engineering technology such as the construction of tools, turbines, pumps and compressors. Process engineering in this sense could not be confined to chemical technology and its manufacturing processes but had to be extended to all branches of industry that required new processes. This involved transport, mining and ore dressing, packaging and many other industries.

When the scientific functions of Dechema were re-defined in the early fifties, chemists and process engineers expressed different views and apparently unsurmountable rivalries at times developed. These differences did not, of course, affect day to day professional life. In practice, there had long been sensible cooperation and a realistic evaluation of the potential contribution by each side. The problem now was to define the respective functions of chemist and engineer in chemical industry.

Oil technology in the U.S.A. and Britain, which was then playing such an important role and which was becoming a major factor in Continental Europe, had launched the concept of chemical engineering. This involved a mixture of chemical and engineering knowledge that did not quite fit the German situation. Germany adhered to a division between chemical technology and engineering. The former extended from the mere description of processes to applied physical chemistry. It trained chemists who could work in the factory and who also understood the work of the engineer and the physicist. Engineering, on the other hand, included the teaching and research aspects of process engineering, which is based on conventional engineering and which, in practice, shares with the chemist a knowledge of physical and chemical processes.

The outsider may regard these discussions, which are still going on, as hair splitting. But for the chemical industry it is important to find the proper delineation because the nature of its technical development will be decisively influenced by it.

In Germany, the chemical industry does not greatly value mixed educational systems such as that represented by the chemical engineer. At any rate, they are not so highly regarded as in the United States or Britain. We in Germany prefer to have the fully trained chemist working together with the fully trained engineer.

The remarkable successes of chemical technology in Germany would appear to indicate that it is not a bad system. Of course, its usefulness and necessity will have to be evaluated continuously especially since many other disciplines are now exerting an increasing influence on chemical technology. When the problems of biology, physics and, as a result of the computer, mathematics, entered the orbit of the chemist, it was recognized that the interaction of different disciplines had become indispensable to progress. But, of course, nobody could be equally at home in all these scientific fields.

The majority of us continue to believe that it is not possible to study the various scientific disciplines only in their marginal aspects and in the areas they have in common. We are convinced that young scientists must first of all complete a fundamental study of one of the disciplines with which they are involved before they venture into threshold areas.

Of course, to meet the multitude of large and small problems in chemical companies, there will always be a need for people who are at home in more than one field of science.

Discussions about the integration of the various specialized professions have greatly stimulated the scientific life of Dechema. In many expert committees and study groups of the society, topical problems of chemical technology were subjected to searching enquiry involving all points of view. Specialists in a variety of fields jointly worked out vital data which they published in important papers and on which they reported during comprehensive conferences.

Once the financial conditions had been met, the Dechema Institute was constructed in 1961. Apart from an auditorium, it included laboratories which serve the investigation of specific scientific problems within the orbit of Dechema and its interested parties.

As a result, Dechema has meanwhile become the focus of all the forces responsible for the reorganization of chemical technology. All the industries represented in Dechema – chemical, chemical engineering, apparatus, measuring techniques and electrical engineering – have played an important part in this and have made their contribution to universal progress.

With the foundation of the European Federation for Chemical Engineering in 1953, and later with the foundation of a European

Federation for Corrosion, we achieved international cooperation in chemical technology much earlier than in either the political or the economic field where even now it has not been attained on the same scale.

In western Europe, the major scientific events, including Achema, assumed supranational significance and were held under the auspices of the joint European Federation. This provided them with additional impact and attracted more visitors and exhibitors. Industrial countries from east and west are regular participants. The events became the accepted rendezvous for world chemistry. They offered an opportunity of establishing personal and business contacts beyond the national frontiers.

The activity of Dechema is symbolic of the new scientific approach of the present generation. The times when individual disciplines worked for themselves and achieved great successes as a result of their own efforts alone, have finally passed. Our technology has become so complicated that all those involved must cooperate closely. Joint research has become the order of the day throughout the world.

A striking example of this new form of interdisciplinary effort known earlier only in exceptional cases is the peaceful use of atomic energy. We had to occupy ourselves intensively with this problem, in Germany, too, if we were not to be left hopelessly behind.

German Atomic Technology

The Federal Republic of Germany could turn to nuclear energy only after it had finally been released in May 1955 from the occupation statute and had become a sovereign state as a consequence of the Paris Agreements signed the year before.

Seventeen years previously, the chemists Otto Hahn and Fritz Strassmann had discovered nuclear fission at the Kaiser Wilhelm Institute in Berlin-Dahlem. They had reported about it on 6 January 1939 in the magazine *Die Naturwissenschaften*. The innocuous title of this fundamental article was 'Detection and Behavior of the Earth. Alkali Metals formed during the Radiation of Uranium with Neutrons'

Otto Hahn communicated his results by letter to his former colleague Lise Meitner who had had to emigrate to Sweden in 1938. Lise Meitner discussed Hahn's experiment with her nephew, Otto Robert Frisch, and arrived at a proper explanation of the phenomenon that Hahn had discovered. In a joint report in the British magazine *Nature*, Meitner and Frisch coined the phrase 'nuclear fission' and at the same time drew attention to the large amount of energy liberated during this process.

In Germany, Siegfried Flügge, a colleague of Hahn, published an article three months before the outbreak of war in which he asked whether atomic energy could be rendered technically useful in future. Strangely enough, this important article hardly caused a stir. During the succeeding period, little reference was made in Germany to atomic energy. The leadership of that time did not appreciate the possibilities inherent in these scientific advances. Fortunately, the physicists around Hahn had no ambition to construct an atomic weapon. They concentrated instead on the technical exploitation of the new atomic energy: on the construction of an atomic reactor. This work, however, was only on a modest scale. The U.S.A. on the other hand quickly recognized the strategic possibilities of an atomic bomb and drew up a huge programme for its development. Immense reserves were mobilized in order to create such an atomic bomb. The dreadful results of these efforts, the dropping of atomic bombs on Hiroshima and Nagasaki in August 1945, are among the greatest tragedies in world history.

It was understandable that after the war the Allies should prevent Germany from engaging in any kind of activity in the field of atomic energy. In any case, this prohibition probably corresponded to the wishes of most Germans. The shock produced by the events in Hiroshima and Nagasaki was so great that the whole field of nuclear physics and its exploitation for the production of energy had become suspect.

In the end, after the terrible shock of the atomic bomb, it had to be recognized that nuclear fission was offering a source of energy that would ensure the future of mankind. No country that wanted to keep abreast of world-wide technical developments and share in the increasing living standards could afford to dissociate itself from this work. In the end, therefore, the western Allies were forced to acknowledge that the Federal Republic had to have an opportunity of developing its own nuclear industry, especially since it had expressly undertaken – in the Paris Agreements of 1954 – to forego the manufacture, development and possession of atomic weapons in whatever form.

Until 1954, Hoechst had not concerned itself with questions of nuclear technology. The many tasks that we had to face after the war, and the vast new technical fields that had been opened up, had claimed all our attention until then. Even I did not know about the modest German development work on an atomic reactor during the war, let alone what had been done in the immediate post-war period.

Rendezvous Geneva

I came into contact with the problems of nuclear energy only when the United Nations, at the suggestion of President Eisenhower, issued a world-wide invitation for an international scientific conference on the peaceful uses of atomic energy. It was to take place in Geneva in August 1955. Eisenhower, in a sensational speech before the United Nations in New York in December 1953, had announced his 'atoms for peace' plan. According to this, the atomic powers were to make available fissionable material to a proposed international atomic energy commission which would supply the material for research purposes and as a nuclear fuel to states that did not produce it themselves. When the invitations for the Geneva atomic conference were issued, the German public did not fully appreciate the significance of the subject. It transpired, however, that Germany had also undertaken preliminary work although only to a modest extent. Following the signing of the Paris Agreements, I learnt of an initiative by the Federal Ministry of Economics which after much discussion eventually led to the foundation of a physical study group in November 1954.

Sixteen companies, including Farbwerke Hoechst, participated in this, each contributing 100,000 DM to promote work that was being conducted under the aegis of the Max Planck Society.

The project was closely linked to the person of Werner Heisenberg who was one of the founders of quantum mechanics and who was awarded the Nobel prize for physics in 1932. Since 1941, Heisenberg had been director of the Kaiser Wilhelm Institute in Berlin-Dahlem, and during the last years of the war he had played a leading part in efforts to construct a small reactor. However, the project, sited in the south German village of Haigerloch, never got under way.

After the war, Heisenberg moved his Berlin Institute, which had become part of the Max Planck Society, to Göttingen. There he tried to reconstruct the modest experience gained in Haigerloch and to undertake theoretical preparation for the construction of a larger reactor. Initially, the occupation powers permitted an output of only $1\frac{1}{2}$ kilowatts for this project. This was later increased to 5 kilowatts. After the conclusion of the Paris Agreements of 1955, these limitations were lifted altogether.

The physics study group that was to realize Heisenberg's plans constituted itself under the chairmanship of the Düsseldorf banker Wilhelm Bötzkes, who was at the same time vice-president of the Max Planck Society. In the constituent meeting of 8 November 1954, I learnt of these plans for the first time. Committees had calculated that the reactor would cost approximately 40 million DM. The supervisory board and a technical scientific sub-committee were engaged in the acquisition of the necessary means and the selection of a suitable location. A decision was reached only slowly as to whether this courageous step to build a reactor should be risked at all or whether a finished reactor should be purchased from the United States or Great Britain instead. Those directly concerned proposed Munich as the site for the reactor. The main protagonist for this proposal was Heisenberg who wanted to move his Göttingen Institute to Munich as well. Industry was quite prepared to comply with his wishes because Heisenberg and his collaborators were essential for the realization of the project. Considerable competition arose over the site, new arguments being continuously advanced by various sections.

In the end, Federal Chancellor Adenauer himself came down in favour of Karlsruhe. To our surprise, Adenauer defended his decision with the argument that Munich was out of the question for strategic reasons because it was too close to the Czechoslovak border. With the greatest respect to the Chancellor, we accepted this explanation with some amusement because to us a difference of twenty flying minutes between Munich and Karlsruhe did not appear exactly convincing. But then with Adenauer there was always some subtle point of policy involved when he was conducting his Federal orchestra.

We were, in fact, quite happy to establish our project in Karlsruhe where with the help of the authorities we found a suitable site in Leopoldshafen in the neighbourhood of the universities of Karlsruhe, Heidelberg and Stuttgart.

While this skirmish was going on, the date of the Geneva conference was fast approaching. The German delegation included Otto Hahn, the Heidelberg physicist Wolfgang Gentner, Ambassador Carl-Friedrich Ophüls, Economics Ministry official Walter Hinsch, and myself. It was my first visit to Geneva, where delegations from seventy-three nations assembled on 8 August 1955 for the solemn opening session in the large chamber of the former Palace of the League of Nations. Each delegation was seated separately in the manner of a church congregation. Immediately behind the German representatives were the four giant delegates from Ghana whom I have always remembered for their extreme friendliness. I doubt whether they understood any more than I of the very complicated conference subjects and the numerous scientific lectures that very soon degenerated into tiresome detail. The conference languages were English, French, Russian, and Spanish.

There was a large number of visitors to Geneva who did not form part of the official delegations. From the Federal Republic, too, hundreds of representatives from public life, press, science and industry turned up. In the beautiful summer weather of Geneva, the conference developed into an unforgettable event.

As a newcomer to the international scene, Germany played a modest role. The U.S.A. had most to offer. On their stand at the comprehensive technical exhibition that formed part of the conference, were the pictures of famous atomic physicians. Unfortunately, there was a major omission: There was no picture of Otto Hahn who had discovered nuclear fission as such. The young American physicists and scientists who were in attendance on the stand, didn't even know who Otto Hahn was. After a long, friendly chat with the Americans, his picture was hung up. I have no doubt that the American physicists did not find it easy to display the portrait of a German chemist in Geneva at that particular time.

With his humour and tremendous self-confidence, Otto Hahn soon became popular at the Geneva conference and the other members of the German delegation greatly profited from this. We were even invited to the official Soviet reception where we were once more able to bask in the sunshine of Hahn's scientific fame. Our visit incidentally was against the wishes of the representative of the German Foreign Office, for at that time the Federal Republic did not have any diplomatic relations with Moscow. The twelve days of the conference were filled from early morning until late at night. Lectures, whose content was sometimes truly sensational, were followed by receptions and individual talks. The representatives of the atomic powers competed with one another in the revelation of what was until then secret information. The United States alone contributed to the conference 512 scientific and technical papers, or 48 per cent of all the material submitted. Out of all the contributions submitted, the United Nations had selected 450 papers for verbal delivery and discussion at the conference itself. Of these, 176 originated in the U.S.A.

We regarded it as a sensation when we saw the first swimming pool reactor in Geneva. In this type of reactor, which is particularly suitable for instructional and research purposes, water also serves as a coolant, radiation screen and moderator for the enriched uranium which is used as fuel element. The reactor had been flown from the U.S.A. in two American air force planes and had been re-assembled in a special building in the grounds of the League of Nations palace.

When it wasn't in operation, the swimming pool was illuminated by underwater lighting. Every fifteen minutes, however, it was started up to its full performance of 100 kw. It was then possible to see what the Soviet physicist and Nobel prizewinner Pavel Tscherenkov had discovered in 1934: if electrons move in a given medium, in this case water, at a speed exceeding that of light in this medium, electromagnetic radiation occurs. The blue luminescence of the Tscherenkov radiation seemed to us in Geneva like the radiation from Aladdin's magic lamp. After the conference, during which 60,000 people viewed the reactor, the latter was presented by the Americans to the Swiss government and found its final resting-place in the Swiss nuclear research centre at Meyrin near Geneva.

Deeply impressed by the first few hours in Geneva, I telephoned Hoechst and thus caused an additional stream of visitors from our company. We were at times almost bewildered by the plentitude of information that was showered upon us. The prospects of achieving something in this field did not appear very bright at first. The other participants in the conference and the press did not give Germany much of a chance.

Through the good offices of my board colleague Menne, I was given an opportunity of meeting the chairman of the American Atomic Energy Commission, Admiral Lewis Strauss, in his headquarters in the Hotel Monopole where he resided with the 327 official members and staff of the American delegation. The reception was courteous but fairly cool. There was a great gulf between us, partly, no doubt, because of political considerations and partly because of the realization of the oppressive economic and technical superiority of the U.S.A. Politically, economically and scientifically, the Federal Republic was still fairly unimportant.

In his reminiscences, which cover the period up to 1961, Strauss doesn't even mention Germany in connection with nuclear problems. Closer cooperation between the Federal Republic and the U.S.A. in the field of atomic research developed slowly although, so far as individual American scientists were concerned, some had felt keenly disposed to help right from the beginning.

What I saw and experienced in Geneva moved me more than many another event in my life. It wasn't only the scientific perspectives that we perceived for the first time. We also learned of the beneficial results that the utilization of nuclear energy could have for mankind.

Equally moving was the experience of a conference that for the first time discussed on an international basis the peaceful use of forces which previously had caused destruction to an extent never before recorded in the history of mankind. But behind all the generosity and open-mindedness of the atomic powers, one could not fail to detect the political explosiveness of the subjects that had been discussed. Germany was given a great chance of active cooperation at a time when even the atomic powers had not yet progressed very far in the peaceful exploitation of nuclear energy.

The deeper significance of this first Geneva conference was probably that for the first time after the war, a world-wide exchange of ideas between scientists had taken place. In spite of the cold war, and in spite of many later upsets in world affairs, this contact has never ceased and has in fact extended to other fields. The International Geophysical Year from 1 July 1957 to 31 December 1958 is perhaps the most outstanding example. It would seem that scientific and technical problems are more suitable than anything else for bringing people together for a peaceful exchange of ideas.

When Germany became involved in nuclear technology, it benefited from the fact that the bureaucratic apparatus of the Federal Republic, which had only just achieved its sovereignty, was still imperfect, so that quick and flexible action could be taken. Against the background of the atmosphere in Geneva, it was possible rapidly to establish a suitable organization for nuclear technology in the Federal Republic.

The German Atomic Commission

Above all, it was clear that a German Atomic Commission would have to be formed as a partner to the existing commissions in other industrial countries. In contrast to the foreign institutions, however, the German commission was not to be subject to state direction because, in view of the renunciation by the Federal Republic of the production of atomic weapons, it did not have to exercise military functions. It was to be a commission whose members enjoyed a certain personal respect so that their voice, even if the commission was only advisory, could not be ignored.

In order to safeguard this committee and its work against the general suspicions that many people had about the utilization of atomic energy, the Atomic Commission had to gain the confidence of the German public. It was therefore essential that apart from the representatives of science and industry, who naturally had to carry out the main work, representatives from politics and the public at large should also belong to it. It was also essential that within these groups, no party should secure predominance. Finally, it was necessary that the commission should have access to a negotiating partner of cabinet rank who would be able to represent and realize any proposals and suggestions with the appropriate authority. The Federal government gladly met this request and appointed Franz Josef Strauss as Federal Minister for atomic questions in October 1955. Strauss familiarized himself with the new office and the rather difficult subject matter in a very short period of time.

When Strauss took over the Federal Ministry of Defence in 1956, he was followed in October that year as Atomic Minister by Siegfried Balke, who, being a chemist, could claim a considerable knowledge of the subject and who held the post until 1962. As president of the Federal Association of German Employers Federations and as one of the oldest presidial members of the Association of German Chemical Industry, he has earned the everlasting gratitude of the chemistry industry for his work on behalf of the development of chemistry in Germany.

As its responsibilities grew, the Atomic Ministry was converted into the present Federal Ministry for Education and Science. This development, which provided the government with some say over research and training policy, was without doubt an important by-product of its involvement in the field of atomic energy. On the other hand, it took a long time before it was recognized in Germany that in this field federalism needed to be curtailed.

On 26 January 1956, the German Atomic Commission, under the presidency of Strauss, met for the first time in the Palais Schaumburg in Bonn, the official residence of the Federal Chancellor who received us afterwards. As always when Otto Hahn was around, there were some amusing episodes, especially during the election of the three deputy chairmen. At the suggestion that he become a deputy chairman, Hahn firmly declared that he was much too old to hold such an office. Strauss replied that in the Palais Schaumburg entirely different notions about age prevailed. After some argument, Hahn gave in, yielding, as he put it, to the obstinacy of the minister. To which Strauss replied: 'We also have different notions about obstinacy in this building.'

Apart from Strauss, the presidium of the commission consisted of Hahn, State Secretary Leo Brandt from Düsseldorf, who died in April 1971, and myself. The commission agreed upon statutes and founded special committees which, in turn, appointed specialized study groups. The officers from the Ministry, of which there were only a few to start with, participated in all these various bodies. Their composition had the added advantage that several hundred honorary officers were available at any time.

The system proved highly successful. It permitted open and truly democratic cooperation between many experts. Appointments to the working committees were made officially by the Minister after they had been agreed upon by the presidium. This provided these bodies with a certain authority although they did not possess any executive powers. Generally, we always tried to appoint people representing a variety of opinions so as to be able to take into account as many views as possible.

The German Atomic Commission has survived in its original form until this day although its problems have altered somewhat. Plenary sessions were rare and did not take place more than once a year. The actual work was done by the expert committees and study groups in continuous cooperation with the officers of the Ministry. By 1971, more than 600 meetings had taken place in which special committees and study groups comprising more than 400 experts from various walks of life participated. If Bonn is now considering a complete reorganization of the advisory system, thus also changing the system of the Atomic Commission itself, care will have to be taken that this independent advisory body is not replaced by a bureaucratic organization that can easily escape public criticism.

During the first discussions, divergent interests emerged. Moreover, the problems of atomic energy and its application contained political dynamite. The scientists, who alone were able to provide the conditions for the activities that were envisaged, were concerned about the freedom of their research if this was to be integrated into the operation and approval system of a commission appointed by the state. Independent scientific organizations, especially the Max Planck Society, felt that an enormous research potential, over which they could not exert any influence, would be controlled by the Atomic Commission. In the event, however, even the Max Planck institutes derived considerable benefit from the awakening state interest.

After considerable initial scepticism, it was quickly realized that the peaceful use of atomic energy not only involved scientific questions but also gave rise to a vast techno-commercial problem whose solution was beyond the limited resources and methods of purely scientific institutes. In the end, all the scientists who worked on the atomic programme did so with enthusiasm. New means had to be found for performing the practical work, for example, nuclear research centres like the one in Karlsruhe. Once again, collaboration of science and commerce was of decisive importance.

At the end of the day, the atomic programme yielded a great many benefits to German science. Several research reactors were bought quite quickly from the U.S.A. and Great Britain. Without the general financial support of the new organization, it would hardly have been possible to acquire them. High energy physics, like general nuclear physics, derived a great many stimuli from the broadly based programme.

Without doubt, many scientists were concerned that industry might take over the atomic energy field if it succeeded in gaining control of the nuclear research centres to be set up. I recall many such conversations with leading research workers. Slowly we succeeded in convincing them of our sincere intention to confine ourselves strictly to promoting the peaceful uses of atomic energy in general. Naturally, in the end we also hoped to derive some economic benefit from all these activities.

The initial scepticism only slowly disappeared. On the other hand, there was increasing recognition that for the practical utilization of atomic energy, a great deal of technical experience would have to be accumulated before there was any chance of its practical exploitation. As things stood, this experience could only be provided by industry. What finally convinced all those involved was the frankness with which all these problems were discussed. There was no secrecy either in the activities of the Atomic Commission or its special committees.

In 1957, a considerable hiatus arose in the Federal Republic. Eighteen physicists, including such world famous personalities as Otto Hahn, Werner Heisenberg, Max von Laue, Fritz Strassmann, and Carl Friedrich von Weizsäcker, addressed a joint appeal to the German public protesting against atomic weapons for the Bundeswehr. The appeal stated that none of the signatories would be prepared to take any part in the production, trial, or use of atomic weapons of any kind or form. The reason for this massive intervention was the news that the German government was in favour, not of producing, but of storing atomic weapons on German soil. This appeared to these scientists as a violation of the undertaking in the Paris Agreements that the Federal Republic would not acquire atomic weapons.

The activities of the German Atomic Commission were in no way affected by this declaration of the physicists which was directed exclusively against the policy of the Federal government. Indeed, the appeal had expressly stated: '. . .we emphasize that it is extremely important to promote the peaceful use of atomic energy by all the means available and we intend to continue to collaborate to this end.' It was, of course, precisely this peaceful use of atomic energy to which the work of the commission was devoted, as indeed it still is today.

Industry was resolved to make available considerable funds for this development. It expected above all that nuclear energy would introduce some movement into the then almost static energy policy of the Federal Republic. In 1955, there was a serious coal crisis simply because – and this has long since been forgotten – not enough coal was available. Large quantities had to be imported from America. In any event, energy costs in the Federal Republic were far too high compared with those of our industrial neighbours and this, too, had produced an emergency situation.

Naturally, industry expected to have a future opportunity of exporting atomic power stations just as it had sold conventional power stations in the past. For this reason it argued for the most liberal atomic energy legislation. At the same time, however, it expected the state to provide considerable funds for the promotion of nuclear research and subsidies for the erection of large research installations with their comprehensive technical equipment. It was unavoidable that this should result in a conflict of views.

In view of the money demanded from them, the Federal government and Parliament insisted on their rights. Moreover, the Federal Republic and the Länder were not entirely in agreement about the direction to be taken. The financial and budget responsibility of the state, therefore, has proved a double-edged weapon in our research and educational policy. It is perhaps one of the reasons why there are so many difficulties in these fields in the Federal Republic.

Within the governmental offices and Parliament, discussions were at first concerned with political questions. Many people thought that involvement with dangerous atomic energy should in any case be the preserve of the state or, at least, that it should have exclusive control over nuclear fuel, as was the case in many other countries.

In these comparisons with conditions abroad, it was, however, overlooked that the nuclear research problems of most countries in the world were closely linked to military aspects. Moreover, there was surely a great deal to be said for the argument that private institutions were more accessible to control and supervision by the public, and thus by official authorities, than the state itself.

Finally, the Federal government had to face the task of reconciling this highly explosive issue of German atomic energy policy with the European policy that it was pursuing so vigorously at the time.

It was a delicate situation and successful work was possible only if all the issues and decisions were frankly debated in public. This applied equally to the many members of the Atomic Commission, to industry, and to the authorities, to say nothing of the press, which devoted itself to this interesting subject with a great deal of enthusiasm. Many newspapers and journals strongly supported our efforts even if not all the reports and commentaries conformed fully to the opinion of the scientists and technicians.

One of the first tasks of the Atomic Commission was close co-operation over the concept and formulation of a German atomic law. It was surprising that this important law, which in many respects departed considerably from the examples of other countries, was passed by the Bundestag as early as December 1959, especially since it required a large majority to change the constitution.

The law interfered considerably with the responsibilities of the Länder as laid down in the German constitution. We may look upon this law today as the beginning of a gradual development which has provided the Federal Republic with a degree of authority in the field of research and the universities. In this respect too, therefore, atomic energy has performed a pioneering service. The atomic legislation also conferred on the Atomic Minister the power to issue decrees concerning radiation protection which was indispensable for all further work.

Construction of the Karlsruhe Reactor

The physical study society concentrated in 1955 on the con-struction of the reactor in Karlsruhe which was no longer a subject of dispute. Several people from industry have earned our particular gratitude in the realization of this project. I recall vividly the many preliminary discussions in which Hermann Winkhaus of Mannes-mann, Hans Reuter of Demag, Hermann Reusch of Gutehoffnungs-hütte, Hans-Constantin Boden of AEG, Carl Knott of Siemens, Alfred Petersen of Metallgesellschaft, Hermann Schlosser of Degussa, and finally Ulrich Haberland of Bayer and myself regularly partici-pated. It was an unofficial circle that met fairly frequently and provided the decisive initiative for the development of nuclear power. In return for industry having a voice in the planning and design of the reactor, the German government demanded a 50 per cent financial participation in the project.

As a result, a nuclear reactor finance company was founded in Hoechst in 1956. No fewer than fifty-six German concerns par-ticipated. The initial capital of the new company was 15 million DM, the Federal government contributing an equal amount. A fortnight later, the Kernreaktor-Bau-Betriebsgesellschaft was founded with a total capital of 30 million DM. It undertook the construction of the Karlsruhe reactor. Its capital had to be increased later on to 40 million DM because the installation turned out to be much more expensive than had originally been estimated.

Even though the project turned out to be a complete scientific and technical success, formal cooperation with the Federal and the Länder governments proved fairly difficult on this basis of parity. The price of a liberal atomic policy was frequently a rather mean budget policy. The representatives of the government, especially those from the Finance Ministry, were simply bound by their regulations, however much goodwill they may personally have had.

We, therefore, experienced an example of those bureaucratic difficulties that can always endanger effective state initiative. When in the end more and more money was needed to expand the Karlsruhe reactor, industry had to give up its interests in the project. In 1963 therefore, it presented its share of the capital, amounting to 20 million DM, to the Federal and the Länder governments. This was a fairly generous private gift which had been made on only rare occasions after the last war. The gratitude we received hardly matched our gesture. From then on, industry had little influence over what happened in Karlsruhe. In the end, the only right that we retained was to appoint two representatives to the supervisory board of the now limited company operated by the Federal and Länder governments.

Still, in spite of the many irritations provoked by bureaucratic procedures, construction of the reactor proceeded fairly briskly. Industry played its full part, irrespective of the company statutes, or whether or not it had a vote. The cost of the reactor, including the first nuclear fuel, was 75 million DM. It became critical for the first time early in March 1961 and achieved its full output of 12,000 kw in December 1962 after several technical difficulties had been overcome. It was precisely these difficulties that increased the cooperation of industry in the project and provided us with an opportunity of learning from Karlsruhe and for training our staff.

The project had been given the name Research Reactor FR2. The FR2 was the first such plant in the nuclear research centre in Karlsruhe which has in the meantime been enlarged by three further reactors as well as a cyclotron and several other installations. There are institutes at Karlsruhe for neutron physics and reactor technology, applied reactor physics, reactor construction elements, 'hot' chemistry, radiochemistry and radiation biology as well as many other disciplines. The centre also includes a school for nuclear technology and the European Institute for Transuranium. Independently of Karlsruhe, and as a result of the efforts of Leo Brandt, a second nuclear research centre was established in North-Rhine Westphalia which was based on two reactors purchased from England.

Hoechst's Activities in Nuclear Technology

German industry developed a number of activities in the field of nuclear technology, independently of Karlsruhe. Hoechst especially became very much involved in this field and considerable funds were needed for the work. An experimental plant for the production of heavy water through the distillation of liquid hydrogen was established in our ammonia factory. It was designed by Messrs Linde and operated very satisfactorily. Its annual capacity was four tons. Compared with the relatively low price for heavy water from the United States, however, which had not been calculated on an economic basis but had been fixed more or less at random, our product proved far too expensive.

Altogether, Hoechst produced no more than five or six tons of heavy water. The plant was then stopped and eventually dismantled. The Federal Republic and the Länder were not in a position to buy heavy water from us at this fairly high price. We, on the other hand, did not want to sell it for less than cost price. The Hoechst plant later served as a prototype for a similar plant in India. Uhde, our engineering subsidiary, continued to work for some time on the production of heavy water through exchange with normal water. In Germany, interest in the subject then waned because technology moved away from the reactors that operated with natural uranium as fuel and therefore required heavy water.

Farbwerke Hoechst provided the Institute of Nuclear Physics at the University of Frankfurt with a small research reactor with an output of 50 kw. It was acquired from an American company and went on stream in 1958. Finally, we also began with the construction of a radiochemical laboratory in our Griesheim works which has been enlarged annually. It serves for the preparation of nuclear medicines and is also involved in a number of important research projects. The laboratory, which belongs organizationally to the applied physics department at Hoechst, also concerned itself with the processing of fuel elements and worked out the fundamental principles for the Karlsruhe reprocessing plant which had been erected in the meantime. Sigri Elektrographit GmbH is engaged in the production of high-purity graphite for nuclear energy purposes.

In addition to Karlsruhe and Jülich, several other nuclear research plants have been erected in the Federal Republic so that a wide variety of working and training opportunities now exist for nuclear technicians and physicists. During the first years, these activities may well have appeared rather unplanned and, indeed, they were subject to a lot of criticism on this score. But at that time, the urgent need was to generate initiative at various levels wherever the opportunity arose. This was the only way in which we could hope to make up the considerable lead that other countries had gained over us in the field of nuclear technology.

During the second international conference in Geneva in 1958 on the peaceful uses of atomic energy, I inspected the site of the nuclear research centre of the European organization for nuclear research – CERN – which comprises thirteen western European countries including the Federal Republic of Germany. A huge Proton-Synchrotron with a diameter of approximately 200 metres has been constructed here at a cost of approximately 120 million DM. CERN is the most important example of international cooperation in the field of nuclear physics. It is only as a result of such joint efforts by several nations that the research tasks that loom ahead will be mastered. CERN is an outstanding example for many other scientific fields in which no attempt has so far been made to form international partnerships of such dimensions.

In the autumn of 1957, committee III of the German Atomic Commission met in the guest house of Farbwerke Hoechst in Eltville. On that occasion, a first German atomic programme, the 'Eltville programme', was drawn up and formed the framework for all further German efforts. It was a generous plan which attracted a great deal of attention even outside Germany, because it departed considerably from the existing programmes of other countries.

The German programme was concerned most of all with the development of capacity reactors. The construction of a gas-cooled, high temperature reactor in Jülich, a multi-purpose research reactor in Karlsruhe, and a nuclear power station at Lingen all flowed from the Eltville programme. At the twenty-fifth session of the relevant expert committee, which also took place in Eltville in April 1970, we recalled the fairly wide-ranging proposals of the earlier occasion. Ministerial director Joachim Pretsch, one of the founders of German atomic policy, who unfortunately died soon afterwards, also took part in this meeting.

In these early years of German nuclear technology, it was important for us to know in what way we could cooperate in international fields. We needed such cooperation urgently but had to risk limiting our freedom of action because our situation was completely different from that of other industrial nations.

But as early as 1956 and 1957, generous bilateral agreements were concluded with Great Britain, Canada, and the U.S.A. as a result of which these powers made available to us much of their experience. The Federal Republic also joined the International Atomic Energy Organization, I.A.E.O., founded by the United Nations in autumn 1956 at the suggestion of the Americans. It held its first meeting in Vienna in October 1957 and has since then resided in the Austrian capital.

The Federal government was energetically pursuing its plans for the integration of Europe. This included the conclusion of the Euratom agreements of 1957. This European atomic community is not only concerned with common research projects but also seeks to ensure, through a strict supervisory system, that materials destined for peaceful uses are not misused. Surprisingly, and contrary to our original expectations, these agreements left us sufficient room for our own developments.

Official cooperation in Euratom was, however, fairly difficult, particularly because France, in contrast to the other five member countries, aimed at the establishment of its own atomic military capability and thus pursued independent interests. I was appointed to the advisory commission of Euratom in Brussels but had to resign from it soon afterwards. Its complicated method of operation demanded more time than I had available in view of the many other problems that I had to take on in so many other fields.

In any case, it appeared to me more important to cooperate in the consolidation of the German developments. Without this, effective participation in the work of Euratom would not have been possible. In the Federal Republic, a number of societies and associations had sprung up in the meantime, in addition to the Atomic Commission, who devoted themselves, from a variety of motives, to the promotion of nuclear technology. At the beginning, all these individual initiatives were highly welcome because as many people as possible had to be converted to the nuclear view. In the meantime, however, this phase had been concluded and closer coordination of the various efforts had become necessary. The various bodies engaged in nuclear technology had to be associated.

In May 1959, the German Atomic Forum was founded which based not only its name but also its aims on examples in other countries. Parliamentarians of all the parties represented in the Bundestag, members of many public bodies, industrial companies and scientific societies joined in this atomic forum. I was appointed president of this body, which aimed at preparing the ground for the peaceful uses of nuclear energy. This work gave us a great deal of satisfaction in succeeding years and also provided us with interesting pointers for the propagation of other scientific issues in the Federal Republic.

The Atomic Forum, which soon joined the international Foratom organization, became an important factor in public opinion. As in the Atomic Commission, there was no secrecy. All questions were reported and publicly discussed. Everyone involved, whether he had any scientific training or not, made his contribution to promoting the common aim and to acting as a kind of public conscience. The German Atomic Forum has been in existence now for more than ten years and has fully justified its existence.

Naturally, we also suffered setbacks, and, in the course of further development, the tempo slowed down. This was shown clearly in 1958 at the second Geneva conference. The exhibition that formed part of the conference was highly topical and the enormous amount of equipment for electronic and high vacuum technology was truly impressive. For a time, it even appeared as though the solution of the problem of nuclear fusion was imminent. In contrast to the nuclear fission reactions used hitherto on a technical scale where fission of the nucleus into two or more parts is involved, nuclear fusion, as its name indicates, is the fusion of two atomic nuclei to form a heavier nucleus.

The advantage of nuclear fusion, compared to nuclear fission, is that, among other things, only heavy water is needed. This can be made available in large amounts. Moreover, enormous amounts of energy can be released in this way, and the process does not yield radioactive waste products. Nuclear fusion has long since been employed for hydrogen bombs. In peaceful use, however, the big problem is how to convert the uncontrolled reaction into a technically useful and controlled reaction.

The exhibits in Geneva in 1958, however, were largely wishful thinking. Far more intensive research into these problems started after this conference also in the Federal Republic. Important contributions to plasma physics, as it is called, were provided by Heisenberg's Munich Institute. In 1970, it was thought that the basic ideas for a fusion reactor had been sufficiently developed for first plans to be made.

The third Geneva atomic conference in 1964 again did not provide anything fundamentally new, even though companies from the Federal Republic were for the first time able to present developments that were internationally competitive. The public, however, and this was clearly reflected in the press reports, was basically disappointed. After the great initial enthusiasm, there had been little inclination for continued complicated development work. It was essential to get used to the idea that scientific and technical progress often requires long periods of time, that obstacles have to be overcome and that mistakes have to be accepted.

There was also the additional factor that differences of opinion are unavoidable in research establishments of the dimensions required by nuclear physics and its related disciplines. In a democracy, however, they must be publicly discussed. This is yet another example of how a democratic system, however great its advantages, has drawbacks which have to be taken into account.

German post-war developments in nuclear technology provide a good example of how the synthesis of exact scientific research, planned and realistic economic thinking and an open-minded attitude on the part of the state can ensure success that is generally recognized. The fourth atomic conference in Geneva in 1971 shows that the road to more intensive utilization of nuclear energy has now become more clearly defined. I am convinced that it will lead to a satisfactory solution of the world-wide energy problem.

The Marburg University Federation

Since its foundation in 1920, the Marburg University Federation had been linked closely to the Behringwerke in Marburg and to Hoechst. In the beginning, it saw as its task the maintenance and promotion of the university, then in some danger, in all the fields of research and teaching with which it was concerned. I was not altogether surprised when in 1957 I was asked to become chairman of this federation though I had not studied in Marburg and did not have any other personal relationships with the town or its university, except perhaps for the fact that my father had studied mathematics and physics there in the eighties.

Participation in university life, the friendships and animated discussions with the professors and friends of the Marburg Alma Mater, and the encounters with its students, greatly enriched my life and the time I spent on this has certainly been well rewarded.

In 1957, the university and thus the Federation were still operating on conventional lines. There was as yet no sign of the clouds that were later to threaten the academic scene. We of the older generation greatly enjoyed the traditions of an academic life because they represented to us a piece of our own history. We therefore made our contribution to ensure their survival during the post-war period of reconstruction.

Nevertheless, the University Federation was, in principle, a happy and progressive body that did not regard itself simply as the guardian of tradition. Suggestions were invited, and taken up, from the many people outside the university interested in its promotion. Under the direction of Friedrich A. Pinkerneil, its former enthusiastic treasurer who later became an honorary member, the association, with the help of long-standing donations, had been able to accumulate considerable assets that could now be usefully employed.

But even these sizeable assets together with the accruing interest and many new donations would have been of little effect if we had applied them to traditional promotion of the university and its training and research functions. Requirements had become so comprehensive that only the state could meet them satisfactorily. The University Federation had to confine itself to occasional support of research expeditions and student excursions as well as to subsidies for scientific work.

We, therefore, looked for other ways of using this money and came to the conclusion that the most rewarding fields would be improvements in student life and the creation of a better image for the university. From the funds of the University Federation, therefore, and with loans and subsidies from the public authorities, the Christian Wolff House, a beautiful student home, was constructed in Marburg. The idea behind it was to enable students to complete their studies in more comfortable surroundings, with better furniture than was usual at that time in student homes, and in a more friendly atmosphere.

Following this, the University Federation, again out of its own funds, public subsidies, and generous donations from industry, erected a skiing and sport centre in the Walser valley. It provides ski-training courses and excursions in which professors, assistants, and students can participate. To this day, we have never found in either of these places any of the unhappiness that is making life in the other institutions of the German universities so difficult.

To improve the public image of the university it was necessary to go beyond the academic confines and to promote understanding of university problems among wide circles of the public. We were able to make numerous contributions in this direction even if they were only modest in scope. We founded a University Federation newspaper, the *Alma Mater Philippina*, which was not intended to fulfil any major scientific ambitions but to describe life in Marburg and at the university. There can be no doubt that this newspaper was partly responsible for the increase in University Federation members, including students, from only a few hundred at the beginning to more than 3,000.

With the ready support of university colleagues, we organized lectures in the surrounding towns of Hesse and founded branches of the Federation that became very active.

The most successful innovation was the 'forum philippinum'. It drew its inspiration from the historic religious Marburg discussion of 1529 in which the reformers Luther and Zwingli disputed their concepts of the holy communion without reaching any agreement.

It was our intention to present at the forum important present-day problems that were engaging the interest of the public. We wanted to ensure that the university, with its wide-ranging knowledge, should have an opportunity of contributing its views on the topical problems of the day. Collectively, we felt the people of the university, at all levels, were best fitted to discuss such essential technical, social and economic problems which, in contrast to the views of many present-day students, concern not only academic youth but the public as a whole. The events of the 'forum philippinum', which took place annually or bi-annually and which always lasted two days, usually started with a public lecture and were tremendously successful. Pharmaceutical legislation, share law reform, co-determination in industry, and the problem of leisure are some of the subjects with which the forum has concerned itself.

The most recent forum dealt with problems of 'genetics and society.' The Federation has also resolved to retain controversial subjects of interest to the public at large in its future programme.

As far as possible, the Federation has kept away from the hotly disputed issue of university reform because it felt it had neither the necessary factual nor topical knowledge of local conditions and problems to be able to make a useful contribution. On the other hand, the members of the Federation have learnt a great deal about the problems of university reform as a result of their work.

For example, in 1966 we organized in Marburg a meeting of all university federations to discuss the areas in which we could make a useful contribution to the progress of the universities. We came to the conclusion that in the future it would have to be one of the tasks of these societies to arouse understanding for the universities. If we can succeed in awakening the interest of the public at large, then it may be possible to help the universities in their search for the right road into the future which, apparently, they are no longer able to find by themselves.

Anyone who looks at the present situation in the universities on the basis of experience gained in the Federation, will not find it easy to come to a decision about the direction that ought to be followed. Many of the present problems could be solved, however, if, for a start, the universities were equipped with an effective administrative apparatus. This, of course, would cost money.

Comprehensive institutions like a modern university, with their great number of students, large staff and numerous technical personnel, can no longer be administered by a handful of people operating in accordance with antiquated official regulations. Reform in this field would, I am sure, avoid a great deal of friction. I am firmly of the opinion that an essential cause of the lack of harmonious cooperation is the out-of-date administration and the inadequate arrangements for the social intercourse of so many people of different origin and outlook.

It is, of course, difficult to decide to what extent the ferment in the academic institutions is due solely to the natural and indeed welcome impetuosity of youth exceeding its aims, or to what extent it is really a fundamental attack on our democratic system of society.

There can be no doubt that a contemporary form will have to be found for teaching and research in the universities. An early solution to these problems is of vital importance for our whole social order.

9

Hoechst has a Birthday

THE ORCHESTRA was playing Beethoven's fifth symphony. I had specially requested it for the centenary celebrations of our company. It was 11 January 1963, a bright winter's day. The factory had closed and a festive gathering had assembled under the huge dome of our new centenary hall. Delegations representing all our foreign companies joined with friends of the company and representatives from science, industry, and public life. Nobody present could fail to catch the significance of the hour, or fail to be impressed by the history of Hoechst which had comprised so many generations and which was so rich in successes and disappointments.

We had given careful thought to the choice of speakers. As far as possible, we wanted to confine them to people from our own ranks. The only spokesman for the public was the Minister-President of Hesse, Georg August Zinn, with whom we had had such friendly relations ever since the reconstruction of the company had begun. Eighty-three-year-old Friedrich Jähne spoke on behalf of the supervisory board. He embodied a chapter in Hoechst's history, and he was obviously deeply moved as he stood in front of the speaker's rostrum. He had spent more than sixty years of his life in the chemical industry and more than half of this period at Hoechst.

The chairman of the works council, Hans Bassing, spoke on behalf of the employees. He came from an old Hoechst workers' family which had been linked to the company through many generations. He possessed undisputed authority and was one of those invaluable men from the trade union movement without whom the years of reconstruction would not have been possible. My own speech is reproduced in the appendix to this book.

It was not surprising that on this occasion our thoughts should

centre on the future of the company. After the stormy years following reconstitution, the approaching centenary of Farbwerke Hoechst
had given rise to a great deal of critical self-examination. Although
we were fully occupied in solving our large international tasks,
it was worth looking back to the history of the chemical
industry which, like that of Hoechst, virtually covered the last
century.

In the 1860s, during a period of two to three years, enterprising
industrialists and scientists founded all those companies that today
account for the major part of Germany's chemical industry. The
first of these was Hoechst. Wilhelm Meister, August Müller, Eugen
Lucius, and Adolf Brüning – the latter a pupil of Justus von Liebig –
had established their small dyestuffs factory on the banks of the
Main at Hoechst in 1863. Soon afterwards, similar factories were
established in Elberfeld and Ludwigshafen.

There was therefore every reason to seize upon the occasion of
our centenary as a suitable event for writing down the history of
this period. The book was entitled *A Century of Chemistry* and its
author was Ernst Bäumler, then a journalist and now head of our
public relations. Drawing freely on the Hoechst archives and
following many conversations with the Hoechst administration, he
produced a fascinating volume of which we presented a copy to
each of our employees and to the many friends of the company.
The book describes not only the discoveries and developments that
spread the name of German chemical science throughout the world,
such as the preparation of the first synthetic indigo and of many
famous drugs, but also recounts the numerous setbacks and difficulties that Hoechst had to face during its continuous expeditions
into virgin scientific and industrial fields.

Festivities in a New Style

The jubilee celebrations were intended to express the renewed
optimism that had been generated during the period of reconstruction. They were also characterized by the advances in science
and technology, in international economic policy, and above all,
in the social life of our industrial society. Many people from our
company participated enthusiastically in these preparations. The
event that we celebrated and the manner in which we presented it
was deliberately designed to form a sharp contrast to the picture

that had been drawn twenty-five years previously on the occasion of our seventy-fifth jubilee in 1938.

At that time, Hoechst was part of the I. G. Farbenindustrie, a modest member of a concern constrained by recession and illusions of self-sufficiency in which Hoechst's fortunes had not, in any case, prospered. German chemistry had been closed off from the world outside. The country was dominated by a regime that was to lead us into a new war. In these events, chemistry played only a minor part but their consequences had a profound, almost traumatic, effect on the industry.

Few of the employees and guests who had taken part in the austere festivities of 1938 were present in 1963. This time the festive framework was rather more generous than in 1938. Then, apart from the very modest presents to the employees, the I. G. board had donated a community centre for which, as for so many similar projects, the foundation stone was ceremoniously laid, though the centre itself was never built.

The Centenary Hall

Our hall had been completed towards the end of 1962. It was called Centenary Hall by the man in the street before this became its official designation. It was used for the first time at Christmas 1962, almost by way of a dress rehearsal, for the festivities of our old-age pensioners. We greatly appreciated the size and the harmonious proportions of the well-designed hall in the company of our employees.

We had decided to build this hall in 1960 and had arranged an international competition for its design. An international jury of architects had awarded prizes for several plans. The first prize went to the French architect Bernard H. Zehrfuss. However, we chose the design submitted by Friedrich Wilhelm Kraemer from Brunswick, which won second prize. It seemed more suitable for us, particularly because its costs were rather more in line with what we had intended.

It was probably unique in the history of German industry that a company should build such an edifice out of the money from its pension fund. The building, including the restaurant for guests and a canteen for some 2,000 staff daily, cost 30 million marks. With its seating capacity for almost 4,000, comparable to the largest halls in the Federal Republic, the centenary hall soon became the social and cultural centre for the population living in the vicinity of Hoechst. Staff and shareholder meetings, scientific conferences, operas, concerts, plays, ballets, exhibitions, and even sports events have developed the centenary hall into a cultural centre that has achieved fame throughout the Rhine/Main area for the high level of its entertainment.

A centenary imposes obligations in many respects. Several million marks were donated to scientific societies and universities. In addition, we produced gold coins of comparable weight to the former twenty mark coin. Every member of Hoechst received one of these coins which were also given to our guests and friends. Finally, every one of our employees, irrespective of his position in Hoechst, was given a Hoechst share to the nominal value of 100 DM. At that time this corresponded to a quoted value of approximately 450 marks. Anyone who had served us for more than twenty-five years was awarded two shares.

We had devised something special for the presentation of these shares. We proposed to give the recipient the original share because we wanted our people to hold an actual Hoechst share in their hands – a rare event. This caused a few problems at the Hoechst post office when several thousand registered letters were posted in a single day. The recipients were advised to handle this valuable document carefully and to deposit it as soon as possible at a suitable financial institution. At first this, too, caused confusion at the counters of the banks and savings banks. When we met for a reception in the old casino building after the official jubilee celebrations, some of our guests were informed by the banks that queues were forming in front of their counters. Fortunately, these were not queues of people who had suddenly decided to withdraw their money but simply the new Hoechst shareholders anxious to deposit their shares in a safe place as soon as possible.

Amongst the other honours awarded on this day were medals to several employees. At a smaller gathering, Minister-President Zinn had, on the previous day, awarded me the Grand Federal Cross of Merit with Star and Sash. I received it gladly and I mention it here only because I feel that this honour was meant for the company rather than for me personally. The town of Frankfurt presented us with the valuable sculpture 'Spring' by Gerhard Marcks which has been placed in the inner courtyard of the centenary hall.

Worries After the Jubilee

When the festivities were over, we returned to the everyday problems. They were not nearly as enjoyable as the festivities we had just celebrated. The year 1962, for which the balance sheet had now to be prepared, had been disappointing. The revaluation of the Deutschmark in spring 1961, and considerable increases in wages, which were not justified by company progress, had seriously affected the profits.

The situation at that time has many parallels with 1970 after the second revaluation of the Deutschmark. In 1961, sales had increased by only 6·4 per cent and in 1962 by only 7·1 per cent. In view of the large investments at that time, this was not nearly enough. In addition we had to suffer considerable price reductions. The final balance sheet showed that the profits of 1962 barely enabled us to maintain the dividend at 18 per cent. We were, however, able to take advantage of all the depreciation that was fiscally permitted. No allocations to reserves were possible because of the poor result. As we had increased our capital in 1962, the distributed dividend was, in fact, considerably above that of the year before.

The shareholders reacted fairly negatively to this balance sheet. At the annual general meeting in the new centenary hall in June 1963, there was an explosive rather than a jubilee atmosphere amongst the almost 3,000 people present. The shareholders did not receive a jubilee bonus as the profits would not have been sufficient for this. In any case, in our view, the shareholders had changed so frequently that the majority of them hardly had a close connection with the company and its hundred-year-old history.

Having received nothing, some shareholders did not hesitate to voice their criticism. In particular, they complained about the expense of the centenary hall and the donations to the employees. There were violent discussions. Although the construction of the hall had not affected the annual results, these remained disappointing, even if the jubilee costs of approximately 15 million DM were taken into account.

There was therefore a vigorous clash of opinion between some of the shareholders and the administration and, as far as I recall, both sides made their points strongly.

Next year, the atmosphere was far more optimistic. We had

achieved a far better result and had sales of 3,742 million DM. It was still modest but it allowed us to pay an unchanged dividend of 18 per cent and, for the first time after the reconstitution of the company, also to form a small reserve over and above this. The shareholders were more content because on the same day we submitted an increase in capital at extraordinarily attractive terms.

However, in the summer of 1963, both employees and shareholders were dissatisfied. In view of the considerable increase in wages and salaries, it had been agreed with the trade unions that 4 per cent of the increase should form part of the supplements paid over and above the agreed rates. Just as today, agreements of this kind can be concluded readily enough with the trade unions, but they produce a great deal of ill-will and a sense of injustice within the company and are almost impossible to carry out strictly.

Sniping from Three Fronts

The centenary therefore highlighted the critical situation of the German economy in general, and of Farbwerke Hoechst in particular. As living standards improved, it became clear that industry was facing attacks from three fronts, each aimed at a different target.

First, industrial concerns had to come to terms with the economic and fiscal policy of the state; secondly, with the clamour of the shareholders for more direct participation, a new departure in Germany; and thirdly, with the increased demands of the employees. The latter's aims and interests were energetically represented by the trade unions, even if at times they did not accord at all with trade union ideas.

The State

The extraordinarily complex German fiscal laws required the almost permanent presence of tax inspectors who became familiar with all the measures and decisions of the administration. We were engaged in many years of litigation because the German treasury even wanted to see the minutes of our board meetings. Because the tax inspectors' reports are then years out of date as a result of the complicated procedure, the company is subject to continuous control and the results can at no time be predicted with any degree of certainty.

This is an extremely unhealthy situation and it can only be hoped that the fiscal reforms, so long promised, will improve it.

The Shareholders

After the German economy had passed through the first phase of reconstruction and consolidation, and when the population had again achieved a somewhat improved standard of living, a remarkable savings fervour and an encouraging interest in the capital market developed. German public companies tried to awaken an interest in shares. Until then, in complete contrast to the United States, this had been comparatively rare and confined to the wealthier sections of the population. In addition, German shareholders, particularly those of the former I. G. Farbenindustrie, had suffered considerable losses during the previous years. Although they had been compensated for the best part of the value of their shares after dismemberment, no dividend had been paid for many years. As a result, dividend policy was a recurring and often acrimonious subject at our annual general meetings.

The state promoted the acquisition of shares and facilitated dividend payment. In the Federal Republic, a split corporation tax was introduced. According to this, the profit distributed as dividend attracts less tax than the part of the profit that is returned to the reserves.

Public interest in the capital market increased when the newly-formed companies required large funds for investments that they were not able to finance from their own capital resources. As far as capital increases were concerned, the chemical industry easily led the rest of the field.

The formalities of such capital increases, and the value of the preferential rights or concessions that a shareholder gained, or did not gain, were largely unknown in Germany where there had been practically no experience in share dealings for almost thirty years. Understandably, shareholders now wanted to get some idea of the profitability of a company that was growing so quickly and so extensively. The shareholders were no longer satisfied with approving decisions that in earlier annual general meetings had taken no more than a few minutes.

This new type of cooperation between the company and critical shareholders, who numbered 210,000 in the jubilee year increasing to 370,000 by 1970, had yet to be learnt. This applied to the share-holders and their representatives at the annual general meetings; it certainly applied to the management of the company.

After many years of preparation and discussion, a new share law came into force in 1965. It demanded increased disclosure of in-formation from the public companies and thus fulfilled many of the investors' wishes. But a large number of important questions remained unanswered even by the new legislation. One of the most difficult problems is always how to enable a large number of shareholders to express opinions and take decisions in a truly democratic manner. This subject is discussed at every annual general meeting.

In the Federal Republic, as in many other countries, voting by proxy was eventually adopted. The shareholder can instruct the banks or other institutions that administer his shares to represent him at the annual general meeting. Nevertheless, the number of shareholders who take the trouble personally to attend annual general meetings of their company, or to give instructions to their banks on the exercise of their voting rights, has increased con-siderably in recent years.

Today between 3,000 and 4,000 shareholders participate in a Hoechst annual general meeting, which has to be carefully prepared by the administration of the company. It is the most important day of the year for the management, and everyone tries to answer all the questions, including the provocative ones, in as much detail as possible. Unfortunately, business considerations sometimes make it necessary to refuse an answer. This results in protests and, in the worst case, may lead to litigation though, fortunately, that has never yet happened in Hoechst.

Both sides have learnt much in the course of the years. With a few rare exceptions, the discussions have become factual and pro-ductive. The management has tried to make its policy more under-standable with the aid of press conferences, shareholders' letters, intermediate reports and films. I don't think it has done any harm to have been forced to have long and frank discussions about the complex finances and numerous decisions that arise during the year. These discussions and the gradual increase in mutual confidence between shareholders or their spokesmen and the company have, in the long run, been highly beneficial.

But all this welcome publicity has its disadvantages as well. It provides the experts from the public, and thus the trade unions, with a completely unvarnished picture of the conditions within the company. If the conditions are good, then the demands are made by both shareholders and trade unions. These demands cannot always be fulfilled by the company because it also has to make provision for the future. If, on the other hand, the conditions are less favourable, at any rate temporarily, then there is quick and vociferous criticism. This, in turn, may further harm the company because the stock exchange, always sensitive to such situations, may react irrationally.

The supervisory board plays an important role in the company's relationship with the public and with shareholders. Its election, so far as the shareholder representatives are concerned, takes place at the annual general meeting. Nominations for election are submitted jointly by the supervisory board and the board of management. After the reconstitution of Hoechst, the supervisory board originally consisted of ten members. When the industrial partnership law came into force in October 1952, five representatives of the employees and the trade unions were added. The first supervisory board was formed in 1951 as a result of negotiations between the American control authorities, the Federal government, and leading figures from public life. It was appointed by the five founders of the new Farbwerke Hoechst. The board of management, which was then only being formed, had very little say in the matter.

On the supervisory board, too, a method peculiar to Hoechst was developed which was carefully considered right from the very beginning. A number of committees were formed. There was a finance committee, a technical/scientific committee and a committee for social questions. Every member of the supervisory board was involved in one of these committees at some point. In this way, an advisory system evolved that probably far exceeded the normal obligations laid down in the company laws. In the committee meetings, talks were given by members of the board of management and leading employees to provide detailed information on certain aspects of the company's activities.

The composition of this supervisory board reflected the varied requirements of the company. It was proposed by the management and approved by the shareholders. The supervisory board consists primarily of experts who can be of real use to the board of management. It includes representatives of financial institutes and banks, science and public life. There are also foreign members who are important in relation to the world-wide connections of the company. In addition, there are always one or two representatives of companies with which Hoechst has close relations. The fact that one or two former members of the board of management also belong to the supervisory board has done a great deal to promote co-operation between the two bodies.

At annual general meetings, there are frequently vigorous discussions concerning the composition of the supervisory board. Groups of shareholders often demand specific representation. Frequently attention is also drawn to an area of potential conflict. Outsiders sometimes have a false idea of the work and function of such a supervisory board. Its most important and undisputed task is the appointment of the board of management. By selecting the most effective leaders, it carries the responsibility for the future of the company.

The supervisory board helps to decide and shares responsibility in the overall development policy. On the other hand, it will never be in a position – and ought never to be – to examine every action of the board of management. Far more important than control is advice, provided always that there is a true relationship of confidence between board of management and supervisory board. In view of the great responsibility carried by the board of management of a company, this must have the backing provided by the supervisory board. It is one of the most important factors in arriving at major decisions.

This means, however, that the supervisory board must be given continuous and detailed information. It is the only way in which it can act as the true guardian of the shareholders. In addition, it forms a bridge between management and the various branches of industry, as well as with personalities from industrial and political life. It thus widens the horizons against which decisions are taken. In Hoechst, the supervisory board plays an important role. In the course of time, and in spite of – or probably because of – the changes in its composition, it has become a valuable instrument of Hoechst's administration. Smooth functioning between supervisory board and board of management is a vital requirement for every company.

Certainly the success of Hoechst would not have been possible without this cooperation.

It was inevitable that I should be appointed to a number of supervisory boards of other companies. Usually, business connections made such cooperation advisable. These boards, whether of banks, insurance or industrial companies, always had to deal with interesting problems in whose solution I was allowed to participate.

Moreover, personal acquaintanceships established in this way are of tremendous value for the prosperity of the German economy and thus for each company within that economy. The employees' representatives play an important role, too. Their advice cannot be ignored even if their rights and duties can be realized more effectively in the daily work of the works council for it is here that the law provides them with far greater opportunities than are open to the supervisory board.

Employees

It is a welcome sign that the general public, because of the increase in publicity, is becoming better informed about the activities in the various companies and is showing growing understanding of the factors involved in an international economic policy. It is, however, essential that employees should be especially informed about affairs in their company so that they become more familiar with its policy. This is a vital factor in the new social climate that is forming in our society.

During the years of reconstruction, German industry had to find new forms for its social and labour relations. Neither the legislation surviving from the Third Reich nor the older institutions of the Weimar Republic provided suitable models. The legal foundation for the reorganization of conditions within the company and the relationships between employees and management were created in 1952 as a result of the industrial partnership law.

The coal and steel industry was subject to special regulations. A British initiative in the British zone of occupation introduced the concept of co-determination based on parity. According to this, shareholders and employees each elect an equal number of representatives to the supervisory board which then, in turn, appoints a further, neutral, member. Outside the coal industry, including Hoechst, shareholders elect two-thirds and employees one-third of the supervisory board.

The basis of our social initiative was the feeling of human solidarity which we probably first acquired under the unusual circumstances of the post-war period, and then more particularly during the memorable events of the reconstitution period. Each of us had by then learnt how important such links with the company were. The majority of us were happy to be employed once more by a company whose future now appeared far more hopeful. This sense of partnership was, without question, of considerable help to the company during its first difficult years.

Pay structures and rates of pay as well as general working conditions were agreed with the newly-formed trade unions and employers associations. A decisive factor, of course, was Hoechst's additional specific contribution over and above this general framework in order to establish a harmonious relationship with the continually growing number of employees.

According to the new law, our discussion partner for all these internal problems is the works council. In our rapidly growing company, the organization of this council and cooperation with it was a problem in itself. First of all, a central works council of the parent company, i.e. of Farbwerke Hoechst AG, was constituted which, in turn, had to agree on a common policy with the corresponding councils of the subsidiary companies. Then, a social commission was formed which consisted of six representatives of the works council and six members of the board of management.

We had established this system, for which the law had not provided, during the first months of our renewed existence. It has since formed the basis of our cooperation in matters of social policy until this day. In the field of our social policy, no fundamental decision has been taken that was not first worked out and approved by this social policy committee. Comparable committees were formed in the individual works although their specific function was to deal continuously with the local questions rather than general, central decisions which are the preserve of the central committee.

In this way, a system was evolved in the social field that allowed us to deal quickly and decisively with all major and minor complaints. The system was soon accepted by the employees and strengthened their feeling of being members of a balanced partnership, able to ventilate their own individual problems and not simply tools of industry to be directed at will.

Since every decision in the social field usually costs money, economic questions were also dealt with in these committees. The fortunes of the company were discussed frankly and in detail. In this way, an information system was established that greatly exceeded the provisions of the industrial partnership law and the participation of the employees in the supervisory board and the economic committee specified there. The system has led to excellent relations between the two sides even if only because of the frequency with which they met.

The meetings were often followed by social get-togethers. On days like jubilees and birthdays, I have always been grateful to experience how much at home one feels in such an organization and how close relationships can be.

All those involved – the members of the social department and of the works council as well as the employees – have always found ways of improving this collaboration. For example, because mass meetings are hardly possible in such a large company as Hoechst, we introduced a system of delegates which has been sanctioned by factory agreement. The employees in the individual factories or departments elect several hundred such delegates to represent them, and this group is small enough to assemble in one room.

Under this system, all problems directly affecting the employees and concerning, as it were, their everyday life, are dealt with as a matter of joint responsibility. For example, committees for plant safety, protective clothing, bonus and supplement schemes, housing and many other matters were set up under this system.

Problems of Everyday Life

In the forefront of the actual practical social work, there were always the very simple, but therefore all the more important, problems of everyday life. Many people did not have a flat or lived separately from their families. In the plants, there were no up-to-date washing and changing rooms, kitchens or other facilities. In so far as our economic conditions allowed it, it was important to remedy this situation at once. When Hoechst began to expand, we also replaced many hundreds of flats in our popular, but completely antiquated, estates. Earmarking the funds required for such projects has always been an essential part of our investment plans.

We had to build some 500 to 1,000 flats a year. For this purpose, only some public money was available. Moreover, the related questions of planning, purchasing suitable land, road building, and many other details were a new field for a chemical company. Also, within the immediate vicinity of the works, we had to contribute to the erection of hospitals, schools, churches, swimming pools, sports facilities, kindergartens, and similar institutions.

Fortunately, in administration, the works council, and the employees, there was many a hidden talent in this field which ensured that justice, reason, and economy prevailed in the fulfilment of everyone's wishes. It was only rarely that these questions caused me aggravation or annoyance. On the contrary, I derived a great deal of enjoyment from watching the matter-of-factness and the resourcefulness with which solutions were found whose benefits are not always fully appreciated today. Perhaps people then were rather less demanding than they are today in our affluent society. People took pleasure in even the smallest achievement.

After the worst had been put right, we had to think of ways of forging even stronger links between employees and the company. At the same time, the basis of a secure existence for each individual had to be found. This included the opportunity to acquire personal assets. Security in old age was one of the most important factors even though later the state relieved us of a great deal of responsibility in this field. We had to take into account that our employees included a large number of senior staff and scientists for whom the state provided a differential pension system so that the company continues to be saddled with a considerable responsibility for them.

Foreign Workers Arrive

Concern over losing one's job, which had haunted us for so long, soon became a subject of the past, and we hope it will never become acute again. Dismissals, because of the lack of employment, have never been necessary since the re-constitution of Farbwerke Hoechst. Indeed, from 1958, there was a distinct shortage of labour so that very soon workers from abroad had to be engaged. The first of them arrived in 1960, mainly from Italy. Since then, Hoechst has engaged workers from many other European nations, including Spain, Yugoslavia, Greece, and Turkey.

The transplantation of people into entirely new surroundings calls for a fundamental readjustment on their part. There are, first of all, language problems which, if they give rise to misunderstandings in the plant, may have dangerous consequences. Then there are the ordinary, everyday problems that are bound to arise when a person has to adapt himself to the way of life of another country. In this situation, it is essential to ease the transitional period through the provision of many auxiliary services and in this we were fairly successful. In 1971, the German works of Farbwerke Hoechst employed some 8,400 people from other European countries. They work together with their German colleagues in almost perfect harmony.

When the standard of living began to rise in the Federal Republic, there was soon a justified desire for more holidays and leisure time. In the autumn of 1955, we were one of the first German companies to stop Saturday work. This had nothing at all to do with the systematic efforts of the trade unions for shorter working hours. During my American trips I had learnt the value of having Saturday free. We needed about a year, however, to convince everybody of its advantages. Finally, the employees indicated their readiness to accept 40 per cent of the resultant loss of wages themselves, the other 60 per cent being borne by the company. This was a fine example of a reasonable agreement. The problem was finally solved through an arrangement within the pay structure, allowing for full wage compensation.

Owner-occupied Homes and Employee Shares

From an early date we thought carefully as to how we could interest our employees in the economic success of the company. Once again, the past offered few worthwhile examples. The old Marxist notions of the class war with the unbridgeable contrast between capital and work were as much out of date as the slogans of the regime regarding 'liberation from usury'. Everyone in the Federal Republic was convinced that a completely new beginning had to be made.

Soon after its foundation, the I. G. Farbenindustrie had introduced, even if only to an inadequate extent, a dividend-controlled bonus. Ernst Kuss, of whom I have already written, re-introduced the scheme during my time with the Duisburger Kupferhütte after the war and caused quite a sensation in the Ruhr. Unfortunately, his well-meant system, however progressive the basic idea, could not be maintained. It was found that for the calculation of such a bonus under the conditions existing at the Kupferhütte, no generally valid standards could be established that would be understood and could be checked by all concerned. The profits of the Kupferhütte were reflected not only in dividends but also in the fluctuating price of sulphur. It is, however, one of the most important criteria of all social benefits that their basis and standards of calculation can be readily understood by all concerned.

Together with the works council, we came to an agreement, improved continuously in succeeding years, whereby each employee received an annual bonus or a share in the profit as from 1953. Its level depended on the rate of dividend, the length of service (in the case of the annual bonus) and the annual income.

The basic idea then, as now, was to move away from the out-of-date and patriarchal forms of Christmas bonuses and similar provisions which, like all personal benefits, have to be re-negotiated year after year. Instead, we intended to link the interests of the employees with those of the shareholders.

These bonuses paid out every year after the annual general meeting increased considerably as the rate of dividend increased. They now amount to more than a month's salary. Shareholders have frequently discussed this system and initially were sceptical about it. In the meantime, however, they have shown an increasing amount of understanding.

This new system meant that all emoluments, including those of the supervisory board and the board of management, depend to a considerable, even if differential, degree on the rate of dividend that the shareholders decide upon at the annual general meeting on the basis of the annual report. As a result, in the course of time, employees developed a growing understanding of dividends and a remarkable degree of solidarity developed between shareholders and employees. It even happened that employees or members of the works council pleaded for an increase in the rate of dividend. Formerly, this would of course have been unthinkable.

The most important factor, however, was that from then on also those workers and staff whose income was regulated by agreed rates could expect each year a substantial payment that would allow them to fulfil a particular wish. For example, an employee with twenty years service and a monthly income of 1,000 marks, receives, on the day after the annual general meeting – assuming a 20 per cent dividend has been agreed upon – 1,676 DM, of which 520 DM are paid in the December of the preceding year.

When the Bundestag passed a law under which everyone was entitled to use 312 marks, later increased to 624 marks, free of income tax, for long-term investment every year, recipients of the annual bonus additionally enjoyed a considerable tax saving if they invested part of their money in this way.

The company was anxious from the beginning to give the best advice to employees in this respect and to provide them with suitable opportunities. This included a campaign for the erection or acquisition of owner-occupied houses which we began in 1953. Anyone able to put down 20 per cent of the cost of the house and completing an agreement with the company for a long-term repayment plan, could become the owner of such a house. They were offered in a variety of price ranges.

We formed a housing commission from among the employees which ensured that fair decisions were taken. We also took care to ensure that nobody undertook commitments that he could not meet. The pension fund very often helped with loans.

Some 5,600 owner-occupied homes have been erected in this way. There is hardly a better recipe for the happiness and well-being of a family than to be able to live within its own four walls, even if it means that it has to tighten its belt in the first few years. I for my part never missed an opportunity of encouraging my colleagues to sponsor the construction of owner-occupied houses.

When the economic recovery in the Federal Republic and the general standard of living had further improved, we devoted our attention to the problem of employee shares. We wanted to encourage employees to acquire shares themselves. For most people, however, shares were a fairly nebulous concept although understanding had increased a little as a result of the dividend-controlled bonus.

We wanted nothing better for our new industrial and social order than that we should succeed in encouraging our employees to participate in the company to which they gave their services. Owning a home and some shares in the company guaranteed a far closer identification with it and the job than in a nationalized and centrally-controlled economy. It really was a great step forward when our employees began to study more closely the shareholders' letter, the economic sections of the papers, and, in some cases, even the stock exchange bulletins.

Of course, we could recommend such investments only to people who had met their most urgent needs and who had managed to accumulate some savings. Also, the issue price of such shares had to be fixed at a level which ensured as far as humanly possible that there was no risk for example when a sudden family emergency made it necessary to sell the shares.

In 1958, the state decided to grant tax concessions for the acquisition of such shares and allowed the companies to buy shares on the stock exchange for this purpose. Subsequently, Hoechst offered employee shares at certain intervals, always at the nominal value of 100 DM per employee. The price generally corresponded to that offered to the shareholders in the relevant period. It was always emphasized that this issue of employee shares had nothing to do with any decision to increase the capital of the company.

This kind of share issue originally encountered a certain amount of scepticism among employees' unions and employers. In the meantime, people have changed their minds and are even thinking of other ways of promoting the acquisition of personal assets.

Today, more than 40 per cent of the employees participate in such schemes and are anxious for their continuation. They enjoy a financial advantage of approximately 250 DM compared with the stock exchange purchase price per share of 100 DM nominal value. Any Hoechst employee who has taken advantage of all the opportunities offered since 1960, today possesses sixteen shares to the nominal value of 50 DM each, including the shares donated on the occasion of the centenary. Shareholders had to get used to this new measure and gradually they showed sympathy and understanding.

All these internal social policy measures could be successful only once we had come to an agreement with the trade unions concerning wages and salaries. Employers' associations and trade unions had agreed early on to an arbitration system that helped to avoid serious labour disputes. Naturally, there were soon disputes concerning wage increases on which the two sides will probably never quite see eye to eye.

Common memories of the tough period of reconstruction have forged close personal relationships in this field which have stood the test of even the most critical times. More serious difficulties were overcome solely on the basis of these excellent personal relationships. In spite of the bad experience of the Weimar Republic, when as a young student one was forced to become a union member if one wanted to work during holidays, and in spite of the misuse of trade unionism during the National Socialist period when such solidarity was simply imposed upon one, I have always remained a firm supporter of the trade union concept.

It is absolutely essential for industrialists to have in the trade unions a discussion partner independent of the life of the factory itself. On the other hand, one must remember that the interests of the trade union and of the employees are not always identical. The employees are concerned with wages and salaries and reasonable working conditions, while the trade unions, as superior organizations, also pursue power politics. Such a strong partner is not always easy to get along with. Sometimes he wrests concessions from industry that are virtually impossible to meet. At Hoechst, too, we have sometimes been forced to make concessions under pressure which greatly affected the cost structure of the company. It then took us years to restore the economic equilibrium through business expansion and rationalization. Nevertheless, in our economic system we have so far always been able to achieve an acceptable compromise between the interests of the company, the shareholders, and the employees.

The industrial partnership law has given workers in the Federal Republic an opportunity to participate in all social and labour questions. The rights of the works councils are in many respects more important and more effective for the employees than the results achieved through cooperation in the supervisory board. This law has always been more progressive than similar laws throughout the world, to say nothing of the communist states which deny workers such primitive rights as the right to strike.

In the Federal Republic incidentally, the general pay structure negotiated with the trade unions, always left sufficient latitude for individual social services within the company. These special social efforts not only contribute to peace in the works but also to the well-being of each employee in his relationship with the company in which he spends a large part of his life. If a new generation of trade union management is now trying to incorporate these in-

C.Y.—20

dividual supplements and benefits into the general structure, then, from the point of view of the social atmosphere in the factories, this can only be regretted.

The Dispute About Co-determination

In the last few years, the dispute over increased union co-determination has been pushed by the unions into the foreground using every means available so that now it has also become a subject for discussion in the Bundestag. Some of the ideas put forward in this connection are of such a basic nature that if they were realized they would probably cause a fundamental change in our economic system.

The prototype for most of the proposals received so far is fifty-fifty co-determination as introduced in the Ruhr in 1952. According to this, supervisory board members are appointed on behalf of the employees not only by the works council but independently, and in larger numbers, also by the trade unions. In the management, there is a labour director who can be appointed and dismissed only if the majority of the employee representatives on the supervisory board agree.

The supervisory board has an equal number of representatives of shareholders and trade unions and employees. If voting results in deadlock, an additional member of the supervisory board, agreed to by both parties, has to make the final decision.

Anybody familiar with conditions in the coal and steel industry cannot possibly claim that this form of co-determination has brought any economic advantages to the companies concerned or, indeed, that the people in the industry are any better off than their colleagues in other branches of the economy.

During 1968 and 1969, the Biedenkopf Commission, which took its name from the chairman, acting on behalf of the Federal government, prepared an evaluation of the problems of increased co-determination. On this occasion, it arranged for a number of hearings of representatives from industry. From the companies not subject to this form of co-determination, Farbwerke Hoechst was selected to represent the chemical industry. Hermann Richter, chairman of the supervisory board, Erhard Klein, chairman of the works council, and myself as chairman of the board of management, were invited independently of one another to testify in front of this body.

The three of us did not discuss our respective statements either before or after we had made them. I was given ample opportunity to describe what we were doing at Hoechst in this field and to what extent we allowed our employees to participate in company policy. My remarks and the following lively discussion made it clear to what extent powers of decision are disseminated at Hoechst among almost 4,000 senior employees and to what extent the employees and the works council share in the responsibility. That this cooperation is still capable of further development, and that our system can also be further improved, is beyond doubt.

We should always strive for such improvement in the cooperation within the factories and the company. Without doubt, we shall always be able to make progress in this respect. On the other hand, we should never forget that every company has a concrete economic target. It has to ensure for the shareholders a proper return on their capital and through its large number of suppliers and customers, it has a tremendous economic responsibility to the public at large. Finally, it is responsible for ensuring that the employees can keep their jobs and that each member of the company earns an adequate income.

Such an economic obligation, however, must be taken on by a body that can make clear decisions and whose responsibility is clearly defined. What I told the Biedenkopf Commission about this in May 1969 is basically what I said at the annual general meeting in 1968:

'Before we subject our entire economy to such fundamental changes for the sake of ideological and theoretical ideas, we should examine honestly and factually whether the system of a fifty-fifty co-determination, which arose from a special situation, has really proved effective. It is a dangerous mistake to expect from this form of extended co-determination positive results for the social conditions of our employees. We are concerned about the dangers that this system harbours for the free economic development of the company and its freedom of action at home and abroad, and we have reason to fear that our hard-won international confidence and credibility in the world may once again be lost.

'Our company has always been conscious of its social obligations within the framework of the legal opportunities open to us and far beyond this. Through many new measures, for example, the

dividend-controlled profit-sharing and annual bonuses, the issue
of employee shares, and a liberally-designed system of administration within our internal organization, we have greatly developed
the social tradition of our company.

'We should also regard this as our task in the future and we
should try to achieve it in reasonable and practical collaboration
with the employees, their representatives, and the trade union
partners. We should not, however, expose our economy to outside
influences and to controls alien to the company. Such a development, however much good will there might be amongst all concerned, would lead to paralysis of company decisions and thus
endanger the further development of our international business
which is facing such difficult challenges.

'Cooperation in society and industry, and this also applies to
our company, will have to be based in the future, too, on practical
understanding resting on ability, training and experience, and on
clear undivided responsibility in the management of the company
with which we have been charged by its owners.'

Private Matters in the Centenary Year

My sixtieth birthday also fell in the centenary year of 1963. Such
a day, whether one likes it or not, is a turning point in the life of
us all. Amongst the good wishes for such an event are those from
the younger generation which indicate, sincerely and friendly, that
as of now one has joined the 'old ones'. Those that have long since
passed this dividing line, welcome you in their midst with relief, if
nothing else.

On the day of my sixtieth birthday, I was able to receive many
good wishes from both camps. As a result of my position, I was
overwhelmed with presents and congratulations. Naturally, I was
very pleased by this and by the fact that so many people from all
the fields with which I had come into contact since my youth
had remembered me. My colleagues and friends convinced me that
I could not forgo a birthday celebration within the company. They
had, however, ensured that this celebration remained on a scale
that was in line with my wishes. Hermann Richter, who had become
the chairman of the supervisory board in the summer of 1963 in
succession to Friedrich Jähne, and Erich Bauer, the senior member of
the board of management and also my deputy, planned the evening

with much care and found very kind words for me. The company donated a substantial amount of money and thus strengthened a fund which had been made available to me on the occasion of my twenty-fifth year of service in 1958 and which was used to promote young graduates in their scientific career. I was advised in this work by a scientific committee.

We celebrated my birthday around a large table in the old restaurant. The organizers had taken my likes into account and had invited many of the people that belonged to my present and earlier life. From the company there were the members of the administration, the directorate, the workers' representatives and the closer circle of my young colleagues. Next to Friedrich Jähne, at the top of the table, there was the almost ninety-year-old Else von Meister, the widow of the son of the founder, who had died in 1919.

There were also many management members of the old I. G. as well as the chairman of the board of management of Bayer and BASF. On their behalf, Carl Wurster expressed friendly freetings and recalled many common experiences.

From the scientific sphere, there were the representatives of the Max Planck Society, the Society of German Chemists, the universities, especially from Frankfurt and Marburg, and many others. The oldest among them was Otto Hahn. Richard Kuhn, who has since died, conveyed the best wishes of everyone. In place of the Minister-President of Hesse, Georg August Zinn, who was prevented from being present, Finance Minister Albert Osswald, who later succeeded Zinn, brought greetings from the Land government, with which I have always had close contact. Lord Mayor Werner Bockelmann congratulated me on behalf of the city of Frankfurt.

My collaborator on the *Chemical Technology*, Leopold Küchler, had produced a book, helped by my colleagues, entitled *Chemistry Through the Ages*. It contained many publications concerning work carried out during my period in Hoechst. During the festivities, I was flanked by my wife and one of my sons who had also been invited to the party. The day itself I spent with my wife and three children on a trip to the Black Forest.

On such a day, the congratulations, the speeches, and the newspaper portraits confront the subject with a mirror into which he simply has to look, whether he likes it or not, and which reflects his image in the outside world. Such an occasion leads to introspection;

the sixty-year-old looks at the years ahead of him and is bound to realize that the last chapter of his life is opening.

On these occasions the public asks what the everyday life of such a man is like. No doubt the reader of this book is also interested in this. Anybody who is professionally exposed to such publicity tries, of course, very hard to retain as much privacy as possible. In practice, however, the profession and family life cannot completely be separated unless you want to lead a double life. Also, contact with colleagues becomes rather more human if there is a slight private note in your dealings. You have to know a little of the private life of the people with whom you are together daily. This works both ways in the relationship between staff and management. In our house in Königstein, we have not had too many official guests. In any case, the living-room would not have held more than a dozen.

Unless I was travelling, my normal working day began at 6.45 when I had breakfast with the family. Regularly, just after seven o'clock, my driver, Anton Hausmann, arrived. He sat with us at the table for a few minutes and discussed the daily timetable. He has driven me since 1949, and still does so today. During this time we have covered more than 1·3 million kilometres. This is more than 15,000 hours or almost seven whole years if you regard a working year as having 2,000 hours. Of course, in a life like mine it's rather more than that, for my working day often extended to twelve hours.

It frequently takes a great deal of mutual consideration to spend so long a time in such a small space. I have not driven myself for many years now. Hausmann has always had absolute control over departure time, route, and speed. He comes from Cologne and has the humour and the repartée of the Rhineland people. If now and again we did not agree, he used to complain at the right moment: 'Always the underdog!'

Office hours started at 7.30 a.m. The close circle of the secretariat consisted, apart from myself, of a man and woman secretary who divided the work between them. Amongst my immediate collaborators there was also the manager of the technical directorate, always a young scientist, and his secretary. These few people were fully informed about everything concerning me. They had access to all the mail, even if it was private or related to family matters.

They looked after all telephone calls and kept my diary. Naturally, there was never any breach of the required confidence.

When I entered my office, there were usually people waiting who needed to see me urgently. These were mainly members of the board of management and both young and old members of staff departments of various ranks. I have no doubt that in the background these discussions were discreetly controlled by my secretary, Tilly Dörr, and my long-serving secretary, Adam Blum, who was later replaced by Herbert Spahn.

During such a brief and informal gathering, a great deal can be settled. This early hour was the most fruitful part of our working day. Later, usually around nine o'clock, – only the technical directorate meeting started traditionally at eight o'clock – the internal meetings began on fixed days of the week. At midday I almost always had visitors with whom I took lunch. Work then continued in the office until about seven in the evening. That was a typical day when I was in Hoechst. But often, of course, I was travelling either in Germany, or Europe, or even overseas.

During the week there was little time for any private life. After dinner I had to read the mail so that I would be able to discuss certain subjects next morning. I expected everyone who participated in these early discussions to be fully informed about all the latest developments.

However, I did my best to keep Saturday and Sunday free. My wife and I expressly declined almost all weekend social engagements. Except when I was travelling, I almost always spent the weekend at home and was only seldom telephoned by the company. In Hoechst, all current matters were distributed amongst my board members, as appropriate, before I became involved with them.

Nevertheless, there was still a great deal for me to do at home with the mail, speeches, lectures, and publications. I always left the door to my room open while I was working, and had no difficulty in concentrating when the record player was going, since the whole family loved gramophone music. Neither my wife nor I play any kind of instrument, and this probably accounts for our delight in listening to our children playing the piano, violin, violin-cello or flute. But these weekends also provided a fair amount of time for meals together, for walks, and for a game of cards after lunch. The weekends and the holidays were adequate to maintain a close family life. But they were not sufficient for me to develop a hobby.

There were many colleagues who had arranged their life similarly. In those cases where the style of life and the daily routine was different, we nevertheless tried to come to a workable arrangement. It was a great help to me that my office was always fully informed and that I had appointed in the management a fully authorized representative for every question arising in all the fields over which I was responsible. When I was abroad for several months or when I was on leave, I received each week a short general report from Hoechst. Only very rarely did I have a query and even more rarely did I have to telephone my office.

This was fully in conformity with the principle that you can 'rule' only if you are present at your desk and have the possibility of personal discussions with your colleague. If you are away, you must have an authorized representative who enjoys your full confidence. This was the reason why even after an absence of many weeks, no issue was decided upon at Hoechst that ran counter to my ideas, even though I had not been able to participate personally in the decisions.

New Men on the Board

1963, quite apart from the centenary celebrations, was an important year for Hoechst. After many years of preparation, the trend was steeply upwards. Between 1963 and 1970 sales rose from 3,000 million to 12,000 million DM. The technical decisions of the preceding years began to take effect. Now that the political conditions were favourable, a great period of international planning began.

But it was precisely at this moment that many personnel problems arose. In 1962 and 1963 there were numerous changes in our management, mainly because the people concerned had reached pensionable age. Konrad Weil, who unfortunately died soon afterwards, and Emil Thiel, the manager of the dyestuffs division, retired as did chief engineer Josef Wengler. Michael Erlenbach died at the age of sixty-two and the finance chief Berthold Gamer took up another important position elsewhere.

These losses put a great strain on the company. Now it had to be seen whether, so shortly after our re-establishment, we would

Above: Inauguration at Flushing in 1968 with Prince Bernhard of the Netherlands
Overleaf: The Hoechst site in 1969

Inauguration of the Trevira factory in Spartanburg, South Carolina (right to left) *Max E. Klee, Hermann Rossow, Robert Zoller*

View of the factory

be able to move from the stage of improvisation to a consolidated personnel policy. An additional complication was that two of our older colleagues in the management were taken seriously ill. Management and supervisory boards were therefore faced with the need to take courageous decisions.

So far as the normal retirements were concerned, we had already made our plans. The place of Emil Thiel was taken by Rudolf Frank who had grown up in our technical directorate. Hans Ohliger, who had earned our gratitude in the establishment of the Trevira business, entered the sales management. Fritz Lindner, who had already helped Erlenbach in the management of the pharmaceutical division, took over Michael Erlenbach's job. Helmut Wagner had long been intended as successor to Josef Wengler as chief engineer, and when Berthold Gamer left us, we asked Robert Hegels to come from Knapsack to look after financial matters. Since his retirement in 1966, the finance department has been managed by Hans Reintges.

When in addition, some of our colleagues fell ill, we appointed Rolf Sammet, then forty-two, and Jürgen Schaafhausen, then thirty-nine, to the board in 1962. We did not have any specific duties for them at that time, but we simply needed two energetic young persons to lend a hand whenever needed. Later, Sammet took on the management of the Hoechst works and of the films division. Schaafhausen became chief of the inorganic division and, as a special task, took on the organization of a department for environment protection. We thought this so important that we felt we ought to give the job to a member of the board. By 1971, this department had a staff of more than a hundred.

In this way, all the gaps in the management were filled by the end of 1963. The company had overcome this period of strain and we were all rather proud that we had not had to fall back on outside help. The reason for this was that we had had a good organization in Hoechst from the beginning. But it also required a far-sighted and unprejudiced personnel policy. Six years later, when I retired, there was another generation change in the management. But this time it was caused not by fate, or illness or death.

10

Becoming a Multi-National Company

ON 14 JANUARY 1963, Charles de Gaulle, the grand old man
of France, announced his merciless 'Non' to the entry of Great
Britain into the European Common Market. On 29 January, the
negotiations in Brussels were called off. I happened to be in London
at that time and thus felt more acutely than I would have done
anywhere else the significance and fatefulness of a decision that
tried to keep a country of the political, civilizing, and economic
significance of Great Britain out of the badly-needed European
economic integration.

Initially, of course, it was the British, with their insular independence, who found difficulty in getting used to the idea of linking their
economy closely to that of the Continent. As a result of this attitude,
and as a counter to the European Common Market, EFTA had
been formed which was a far looser structure, comprising Great
Britain, Denmark, Norway, Sweden, Austria, Switzerland and
Portugal. An economic division of Europe threatened and this was
of considerable concern to everyone involved. But now, when reason
seemed at long last to prevail and London was prepared, at any
rate in the economic field, to start on the road to Europe, the
General's veto was like a cold shower.

On that 14 January, the occasion of the centenary, we had
arranged a world sales conference in Hoechst. Almost 250 managers
from our foreign organizations participated. The gay jubilee mood
soon gave way to serious discussions concerning the progress of our
world business. When all the representatives had joined in the Festival Hall and reported on progress since the new beginning, under

the special conditions of their country, we all felt some of the self-consciousness of a company that was again achieving world renown.

In spite of the very difficult starting conditions, foreign business in 1962 had achieved a 38 per cent share of our total sales of 3,460 million DM. In 1954, when our foreign organization hardly existed, world sales were 1,140 million DM, foreign business accounting for 32 per cent. Our efforts to intensify sales beyond the German frontiers through the erection of additional manufacturing facilities abroad had achieved certain initial successes. Other large chemical companies, including our most important German competitors, had, however, in the meantime achieved a far greater percentage share of foreign business.

It was also clear in 1963 that further possibilities of expansion within the German domestic market were at least limited, and that we could not expect miracles. We therefore had to seek means of expanding our foreign business. This meant primarily that we had to open up other business areas in which we had not until then been seriously engaged.

On the other hand, our salesmen now were offered new opportunities because the manufacturing range was continuously increasing and new products that represented the successes of research and development in the fields of man-made fibres, plastics and many chemicals, gradually became available for export. Nevertheless, in January 1963 sales management forecasts for our foreign business were not excessively optimistic in view of the difficult situation of the time. Exports to the value of 1,400 million DM were planned as a target for 1970. This forecast was the first real piece of long-term planning for our world business. As it turned out, exports in 1970 reached the far higher sum of 3,900 million DM. This success was the result of our earlier decision to intensify the work abroad and to initiate fundamental steps for the improvement of our foreign business.

In 1963, however, nobody expected the chemical industry to achieve such growth. We could not foresee what opportunities would arise or what demands we would have to satisfy to penetrate the international market. The mood of resignation that prevailed throughout the entire chemical industry at the beginning of the sixties was completely overcome by the later events.

It was clear that foreign manufacture had to play an important role in these plans. But it was precisely in this field that forecasts were impossible to make. All we knew was that we had to undertake radical changes and that we had to increase our efforts significantly. We had to find new starting points. And therefore at this world sales conference in 1963, we were faced by a strange mixture of disappointment and hopes.

My own remarks concerning Hoechst ended with the following resumé:

'Our export share is too small and structurally too dominated by the past. We know that there are many fields in which exports are limited. We have also opened up new fields that are not yet ripe for exports. We must therefore intensify our export organization. We must take into account the consolidation of Europe. We have to grow together with the countries of Europe without imagining that the Europe of tomorrow will become a uniform area. In ten and even twenty years there will still be a French, Italian, and an English economic area that we must regard as separate from the point of view of our company. The economic procedures in Germany will not become identical in the foreseeable future with those of the British or the Italians or any other European people. We shall have to relate our entire European policy to each country individually.

'The sales figure of 374 million DM achieved by our plants abroad is far too small, and perhaps this is one of the weaknesses of our company. Such production facilities abroad, which give efficient support to our exports, are available on only a small scale because we arrived on the scene far too late. In the foreign market we encounter the capital-intensive Americans and the British who were there long before us.'

At the end of my speech I appealed to the participants of this world sales conference to concentrate on the question of how we could find our way into the countries outside Germany more strongly, more intensively, and, if necessary, with a greater monetary investment.

Before me, Walter Hallstein, the president of the E.E.C. Commission, had given a fascinating speech entitled 'The Common Market in a Decisive Phase'. Hallstein, who resigned from the E.E.C. office after being its president for ten years and who then became a member of our supervisory board, at that time gave a fairly optimistic picture of the position in Brussels. As an enthusiastic European, customs and economic union were to him by no means the final target. He visualized an even larger aim: the political union of Europe.

After de Gaulle's veto, it appeared as though the hopes for an economically and politically integrated Europe would have to be buried for a very long time.

Dramatic Hours During the Cuba Crisis

On the other hand, the Kennedy era had provided the whole western world with considerable impetus. The refreshing, open policy of the young president, who embodied a completely new type of statesman, seemed all of a sudden to solve many of the problems that had beset the world since the end of the war. Even the possibility of a better understanding with the Soviet Union seemed to be on the horizon. At the same time, Khrushchev was left in no doubt about the limits that Kennedy had set to world communism. In the autumn of 1962, the world was suddenly threatened with the danger of an atomic conflict as a result of the Cuba crisis. I was in California during these hours of possible confrontation between the Soviet rocket freighters for Cuba and the American fleet. Far away from home, where our families lived hardly 100 kilometres from the Russian zone, we experienced the tremendous tension of the situation perhaps even more closely and dramatically than the Americans.

When my colleagues and I – after discussing for some hours whether or not to return immediately to Germany – continued our trip as planned to Japan, where we were no further from home than in California, the immediate crisis had passed. The Soviet freighters had changed course at the last minute. The world had escaped disaster once more. We were able to continue our trip via Hong Kong, Manila, to Australia and New Zealand and finally home via Singapore and Malaysia.

After this trial of strength between the super-powers, a little of the political ice that had formed during the years of the cold war began to melt. Kennedy's trade expansion act appeared to open the commercial channels for world trade. In Latin America, a common market was established in 1960 which comprised the Argentine,

Brazil and Chile, as well as Columbia, Mexico, Paraguay, Peru and Uruguay.

The world was in a state of flux. Step by step, old groupings were being abolished. Germany could only profit from such turbulence. Unfortunately, counter forces soon began to stir. It was found that the efforts for a more liberal trade, however well meant and cleverly conceived, were losing their momentum. Neither Europe nor the overseas countries were ready for such generous ideas of far-reaching liberalization.

After the assassination of President Kennedy, I read the book *Kennedy's Thousand Days*, and once more relived the drama of those days. The murdered President probably had more friends in Germany than in his native country. His speech in the Frankfurt Paulskirche during his trip to Germany in 1963 caught our imagination as much by its burning confession of freedom as by his youthful, radiating personality that one could not escape even in personal contact. I met Kennedy after his speech at a small reception given in Wiesbaden by the Minister-President of Hesse.

There could hardly have been a greater contrast between Kennedy and General de Gaulle whose jealousy he quickly aroused. De Gaulle's admirer, André Malraux, the former French Minister of Culture, characterized him excellently when he described him as 'a man of the day before yesterday and of the day after tomorrow'.

The General never forgave his western allies for what was, in his view, the humiliating treatment of France during the negotiations in Yalta and Potsdam. When after years of retirement, he again became active in politics in 1958 and was elected head of state, he fired his countrymen with a magic formula of the historic role and grandeur of his nation. De Gaulle said: 'During the whole of my life, I have had a certain idea about France. So far as I am concerned, France was the fairy tale princess, the madonna on the frescoes, elected to fulfil a noble and unusual fate. In short, in my view, France cannot be France without grandeur.'

The authority which he quickly acquired after the continuous changes of government in France grew even more because he did succeed in finishing the Algerian conflict. It was a statesmanlike performance for even his own followers threatened him with mutiny at that time. Now he felt himself strong enough to question the role of the U.S.A. as the leading power in the west. He did not even shrink from taking France out of NATO and from successfully demanding the withdrawal of the headquarters and of all the bases of the Western Defence Community.

The relationship between the U.S.A. and France deteriorated rapidly. De Gaulle dreamt his dream of Europe as a third force and – overestimating the potentiality – of a French-led Europe as mediator between east and west.

Conflict

An important role in the increasing conflict was the inadequate economic equilibrium, the intensive activity of the U.S. companies in Europe, in other words, the dollar invasion. Because of their capital resources, the Americans were able to establish extensive economic bases in the old world. Their own, huge, domestic market on the other hand was protected by tariffs that were as high as they were antiquated.

Europe became seriously concerned in the face of such an aggressive economic policy. France, yesterday still a largely agricultural country, was about to give itself a new industrial profile. Its economic development was moving steeply upwards. But its industry was suffering from fragmentation; there were far too many small companies usually with very complicated ownership conditions. Planned economy notions constricted freedom of action. The state had secured considerable influence over coal, oil and power. It was from this quarter that the opposition against the advance of American capital crystallized.

The situation in Great Britain was comparable in many respects, although, in principle, different conditions existed there. Although Churchill had made his moving European confession as early as 1946, London continued to look primarily towards the Commonwealth. For a long time, many Britons could not reconcile themselves to the idea of European integration. The country kept a cool distance to continental Europe. Only slowly did it become clear, not least because of many nationalization failures, that political and social developments in Great Britain did not conform to the requirements of a modern industrial society.

These conditions in France, Great Britain, and other countries produced considerable inferiority complexes and resignation in relation to the politically, economically and militarily far stronger partner overseas. The prevailing sense of hopelessness swept away the frothy European enthusiasm of the previous years.

The fact that the European economy had been revived only by the American Marshall Plan and European Recovery Programme credits was overlooked almost everywhere. The benefactor of yesterday was suddenly no longer the friend of today. This was manifested in the irrational anti-Americanism expressed by many groups in western Europe. The advance of American economic power was often too robust and did not sufficiently take into account European sensitivities.

The countries of the old continent were simply over-exerted and therefore on the point of relapsing into out-of-date political prejudices. Moreover, it was not only the economic challenge of the U.S.A. that threatened to lead to misunderstandings. Amongst themselves, too, European countries drifted apart from each other again. Old national antipathies reared their head once more.

The U.S.A. also felt exploited by the extent and intensity of its world political engagements, and by its military involvement in many theatres throughout the world. These commitments did not leave enough time for a solution of internal political problems. The climate in the country had changed. Every visit showed this in an almost embarrassing fashion. The unsolved racial problem suddenly produced almost unbearable tensions which discharged themselves in the long hot summers of 1967 and 1968 in demonstrations and bloody confrontations.

Even today there is no truly satisfactory solution between black and white. A visit to Harlem has become extremely dangerous for white people. Every friend of the U.S.A., however, wishes this basically so generous and free country an early solution to the problem.

The German Position

Because of its unconsolidated and susceptible position, the German economy had to move carefully in an international field so full of tension. In the Federal Republic, several branches of the economy were still suffering from the consequences of the war and the immediate post-war period. For example, the German coal and steel industry was beset by considerable structural problems. As in France so in the Federal Republic there were many small and medium-sized, family-owned companies. Under the most difficult conditions, they had succeeded in rising again after the war, but they were now unable to meet the new and expensive demands of technical development. Also, the generation changes that would have been necessary at the head of many of these companies after construction were, in many cases, carried out inadequately or postponed altogether.

Mergers

The German chemical industry was on the whole better prepared for this situation in the sixties than its competitors in neighbouring industrial countries. It had overcome the damage and obstacles of the immediate post-war period fairly well. Like the three chemical giants, BASF, Bayer, Hoechst, which formed a kind of protective shield in international competition, the chemical industry of Germany had a fairly healthy structure with strong medium-sized and small companies. But even the most successful medium-sized companies could not grow beyond a certain size through their own resources because they simply had not the means available for the required investment and for the establishment of an international sales organization. They were therefore all the more concerned with foreign influence and control, particularly because some avaricious companies announced their take-over intentions fairly vociferously.

However, most of these companies in the German chemical industry preferred to merge with a German company. On the whole, these concentrations remained within modest limits, at any rate so far as Hoechst was concerned.

Such take-overs have in the meantime become the subject of public discussion. There are voices that repeatedly plead for state control. But even its proponents cannot ignore the fact that within a liberal economic order, small companies feel the need for fusion or collaboration with larger partners. Large economic areas such as the E.E.C., structural changes in production, and particularly changes in the conditions of ownership, will always lead to mergers. The alternative would be a state-controlled organization of the entire economy which is not desirable and which could only damage the German position in international competition.

An outsider may well believe that a large company is always

tempted to extend its field of operation and its influence. The possibility of buying up other companies is bigger today than ever before.

In Hoechst, however, we have always applied a very strict yardstick for such plans and have carefully weighed the positive and negative aspects. In principle, we were governed in our decisions by the following guidelines:

1. Acquisitions and mergers make sense only if they open up to the company a field that represents a valuable and desirable extension to the existing programme. We have always taken care that we do not buy up our customers or that we enter into fields that have hitherto been the prerogative of our suppliers.
2. Plans and actions by the competition can, of course, force one to take aggressive action. Very often the behaviour of foreign, particularly of American companies, has required us to take measures that we would never have envisaged on our own initiative.
3. Complete agreement with the previous owner, his possible partners, and above all, the management and employees of the company concerned, are absolute prerequisites. It is in any case difficult enough to achieve unprejudiced cooperation after a merger.

I believe that Hoechst has always exercised moderation in such mergers within the Federal Republic, however valuable they may have been to us. Larger take-overs became necessary abroad at a later date when we were intent upon becoming a European undertaking. But even in these cases, the above principles always operated.

Albert Joins Us

One of the first acquisitions at the beginning of the sixties was the highly respected Chemische Werke Albert, with its long tradition. The grandson of the founder, Alexander Albert, had collaborated with us in a friendly manner for many years. We had also talked from time to time about the acquisition of his company, whose management he took on in 1959. We did not, however, come to any concrete decision. Then suddenly, in the spring of 1964, a large American company, whose name we learnt only later, made a massive offer to Albert. The quiet, reticent but very self-confident and energetic Alexander Albert visited me unannounced in my office. He declared that it was now his intention to sell Chemische Werke Albert to Hoechst. He insisted that we should act quickly and that we should make him a concrete offer as soon as possible. Indeed, we succeeded within a few weeks in getting some idea of the various complex questions connected with such an acquisition.

When Rolf Sammet, who conducted the negotiations, reported the result to the management, there was no unanimous opinion at first. Some of us were not fully convinced of the significance of this old established company nor its value to Hoechst. At the end of the day, however, we decided in principle to buy and informed Alexander Albert to this effect. His reaction was as noble as it was remarkable. When we wanted to start negotiations with him concerning the price, he simply asked me over the telephone for an offer by about five o'clock the next day.

I called my board together once more. We examined the calculations we had made. Next afternoon my driver took a sealed personal letter containing our offer to Alexander Albert. Over the telephone, he announced that he would visit me the same evening in my home. When I offered to visit him, he declined the offer and said that he would prefer to come and see me together with the chairman of his supervisory board, Gerd Stieler von Heydekampf.

He arrived, in fact, the same evening, sat down, and after a short greeting declared without further ado that he accepted our offer. And with that the matter was closed, as far as he was concerned. The final decision to sell had obviously taken its toll of him. We drank a whisky and then I asked him whether we should discuss tax problems, because my colleague Heinz Kaufmann had drawn my attention to this. But this only seemed to annoy him. He said he had made his decision and had said his last word and the rest was his own affair.

This important transaction, therefore, took place in a fairly strange and unusual manner. So far as I can remember, I do not think that in the whole of my active life I have ever concluded a business deal all on my own and in such a direct way. The independent entrepreneur from the rich family, however, insisted on such strict personal negotiations and quick decisions.

Once the company belonged to us and we worked closely together with Alexander Albert, it transpired that he was much relieved to

have discharged his responsibilities. He had many strange characteristics for the owner of such an undertaking. For example, he had
never taken a salary. This made the situation rather unpleasant for
me because Albert, after we had taken over his company, remained
active as chairman of the board of management and I had to ask
him to accept a salary. At the beginning he again reacted, as so
often, negatively. Eventually, he said he would be prepared to
accept a salary provided that the money could be used for a
social purpose on behalf of the employees. Previous to that,
he had privately financed many social measures throughout the
factory.

In the end, Albert liked participating in the meetings of our
technical directorate, to which I invited him. Although he was not
himself a technician, he was greatly interested in these problems.
He was also greatly pleased with the stormy discussions and the lively
atmosphere that prevailed during these meetings.

When he had convinced himself that the take-over of his company
had passed off satisfactorily, he told us surprisingly that he now
intended to retire completely. He said he felt no longer up to the
physical and mental stress of industrial life. This was, of course,
much earlier than we had agreed. As a very sensitive personality,
he intended to devote himself to intellectual pursuits. Indeed, he
read Greek at the University of Mainz and intended to study
philosophy there and take his doctorate.

But death intervened – at far too early a date. Alexander Albert
died in 1968 in a Bavarian monastery, where he was a frequent and
welcome visitor, from the effects of phlebitis.

Synthetic Resins and the Consequences

When we took over Chemische Werke Albert in 1964, the company
had a sales volume of 124 million DM. This was not a large amount
in comparison to Hoechst, whose sales at that time were something
like 4,500 million DM, but the fields that we had gained as a
result of this acquisition were all the more important. The founder
of the company, the apothecary Heinrich Albert, had begun manufacturing in 1858 by grinding Thomas slag in a mill that he had
invented himself and selling the product as a phosphate fertilizer.
This had eventually developed into a superphosphate factory, and
finally the production of highly developed phosphates for various

purposes. These plants, particularly their modern part, were of considerable interest to us.

Later, we joined this plant administratively to Knapsack and in addition started a very fruitful collaboration with the Ludwigshafen company of Joh. A. Benckiser which was engaged in a similar field. This led eventually to the foundation of Benckiser-Knapsack GmbH, which for many years now has been producing and selling high-grade phosphates for special purposes.

Another Albert field was pharmaceuticals. The company had a small pharmaceutical department with a very modern laboratory. One of the first preparations produced by this department was Recresal which was based on phosphate. Recresal was followed by other interesting pharmaceuticals. Fusion with Hoechst offered this small but very highly regarded pharmaceutical department with a welcome opportunity in the fields of research and marketing.

When some years later, in 1968, collaboration with Roussel-Uclaf in Paris was agreed upon, we founded Albert-Roussel Pharma GmbH. This company sells preparations from Albert and Roussel as well as a few products of Behringwerke.

The field of synthetic resins which Kurt Albert, the father of Alexander Albert, had opened up, was entirely new for us. Kurt Albert had laid the foundation for the first industrially produced synthetic resins in 1910 with his 'Albertols'.

It is interesting to note that Chemische Werke Albert is located in the immediate vicinity of Kalle AG in Wiesbaden-Biebrich, which, in turn, had insufficient possibilities of expansion. The two factories are in fact separated only by a road. There was, therefore, much scope here for rationalizing power supply, stock-keeping, workshops and other auxiliary services of the two subsidiaries.

The take-over of the synthetic resins resulted in consequences that we had not originally foreseen. As a first step we joined this field with that of the aqueous synthetic resin emulsions which we were already selling world-wide under the name Mowilith.

As a result of our link with Albert, Reichhold Chemie AG in Hamburg became of interest to us. This company had a sales volume then of approximately 67 million DM. Curiously enough, Reichhold had close historical connections with Albert, but hardly anybody was aware of them. The brothers Otto and Henry Reichhold, who had founded a lacquer resin factory in Vienna after the

First World War, engaged the Austrian chemist Herbert Hönel. He had once worked for Albert at Wiesbaden but had then returned to his native country. Hönel now opened a further production field at Reichhold in Vienna with the development and preparation of synthetic resins for lacquers.

Henry Reichhold had in the meantime emigrated to America where he imported synthetic resins, first from Albert and then from his own Viennese production. In 1927 he formed his own company in the U.S.A. for the production of these resins. When the business in Vienna and the U.S.A. developed successfully, the brothers Reichhold built manufacturing plants for synthetic resins in England, France, and Germany. The German plant was sited in Hamburg. It was acquired by Hoechst in 1965 after Henry Reichhold had withdrawn completely from the company.

As a result of the collaboration between Albert and Reichhold, our potential in the field of synthetic resins grew enormously. It also brought us additional international contacts. These led in 1968 to the acquisition of Vianova Kunstharz AG near Graz in Austria. This company, too, owed its existence and success to the Reichhold chemist Hönel. He had seen the end of the Second World War in Hamburg but in view of the catastrophic economic situation after 1945, he could not see any possibility of continuing his work there. He therefore moved to Graz where he founded the Vianova with other partners. It was there that water soluble synthetic resins were invented. They now formed part of the new Reichhold-Albert Chemie AG.

After we had considerably strengthened our interests in paint raw materials in this way, we were faced unequivocally by the question as to whether we should also become engaged in the field of the paint industry itself. Until then we had always decided against such an extension of our activities for it would have meant that we had to enter into competition with our own customers.

When, however, other large European chemical manufacturers acquired shares in important paint companies, we were no longer able to maintain our attitude. Indeed, we had been asked at press conferences whether we intended to witness this development without acting. In due course we took appropriate steps. Through Vianova, we established collaboration with Stolllack AG in Vienna which had developed water soluble paints and important lacquering processes. In addition, we acquired the lacquer factory of Flamuco GmbH in Munich which has established a wide network of branches and retail outlets in many important towns of the Federal Republic.

The most comprehensive step in this programme, however, was taken towards the end of 1969 with the take-over of the British paint manufacturer Berger, Jenson & Nicholson. The nucleus of this company had been formed in 1760 by the German immigrant Ludwig Steigenberger, who had begun with the production of prussian blue. He later changed his name to Lewis Berger, which was more readily pronounced by British tongues.

Today Berger, Jenson & Nicholson is, after I.C.I., the second largest paint manufacturer in Great Britain with many plants abroad, especially in Commonwealth countries. As during the acquisition of Reichhold, when there had been a public counter-offer by an American consortium, we had to compete for BJN on the British stock exchange against an American competitor. It was only after we had increased our offer considerably that this competitor withdrew.

Starting with the acquisition of Albert, therefore, a new field had been opened up for us on an international scale. It comprised all the aspects of raw materials for lacquer and finished paints. It was a logical chain of developments which, as so often happens in industrial life, had started more or less accidentally but then engendered many further developments.

Through Messer to Low Temperature Technology

A different development was set in train through our merger with the Frankfurt company of Messer. This well-respected family undertaking had been founded in 1898 by Adolf Messer. It was concerned initially with the production of acetylene burners for illumination purposes. Later Messer turned to welding and cutting techniques and took up the further field of low temperature technology and the decomposition of air.

Even during the I. G. period, there had been close contact with the Messer family. After the war points of contact arose with Knapsack-Griesheim AG which, amongst other things, was active in welding technology.

In this field too, because of increasing international pressure, competitiveness had to be secured. It was especially the activities of the

French company, Air Liquide, and the second largest American chemical company, Union Carbide, that dictated a merger of Messer and Hoechst.

The Messer company, under the guidance of its young chairman Hans Messer, the son of the founder, had pursued a vigorous and expansive policy in many industrialized countries, which it was, however, unable to sustain because of its relatively limited financial basis. When we became interested in Messer, its sales amounted to approximately 85 million DM.

During our autumn press conference on 1 October 1964, I was able to announce the planned collaboration with Messer. We had decided to found a new company, Messer Griesheim GmbH. This company, apart from the former Adolf Messer GmbH, was also to comprise Griesheim-Autogen at Frankfurt and the oxygen division of Knapsack-Griesheim AG at Düsseldorf.

In this way, a fairly comprehensive undertaking was formed on I January 1965 which engaged in the construction of oxygen plants, the production and selling of technical gases, and the manufacture of welding and cutting equipment.

Hoechst thus entered the new field of low and minimum temperature technology. The decomposition of air at low temperatures occupies a particularly important position in modern technology. The oxygen obtained is increasingly needed by the chemical industry, but especially in steel production. The nitrogen obtained at the same time serves, amongst other things, for the machining of highly oxygen-sensitive metals and plastics. Moreover, the low temperatures needed in refrigerated vehicles and plants for the storage of meat and other foodstuffs are obtained by the evaporation of liquid nitrogen. Food can be frozen quickly in this way in appropriate deep freeze plants.

The rare gases such as argon, which is used for the welding and soldering of sensitive metals, neon, which is used in fluorescent tubes, and crypton, all have a variety of technical applications.

Helium introduced us to the field of minimum temperatures, almost down to absolute zero point. With its aid, for example, it is possible to achieve those very low temperatures at which some metals no longer offer any resistance to electric current. This effect is known as supraconduction. It was particularly valuable for us to acquire a staff of specialized people who were able to fill a gap in our own organization. Georg Janning, the manager of Knapsack, deserves much of the credit for bringing about this merger. He joined the Hoechst board of management in 1965, and looked after a new division which comprised the engineering company of Uhde in Dortmund and the new Messer Griesheim GmbH.

Sales of Messer Griesheim GmbH in 1970 were about 532 million DM and the company had some 6,000 employees.

A New Fibre from Kelheim

As a result of the acquisition of the Berliner Spinnstofffabrik Zehlendorf in 1960, we had entered the field of spun rayon. During the period of self-sufficiency, the production of this viscose rayon staple had been greatly promoted because of the shortage of cotton. But even in peacetime, spun rayon became a useful fibre which was of particular interest especially in combination with the new fully synthetic fibres.

In the thirties, spun rayon factories had been established in Germany and Austria and these had joined in the so-called German spun rayon ring. The owners were a variety of companies in the textile industry and the chemical industry. The National Socialist economic bureaucracy had exerted gentle pressure to get everyone to work together. After the war, these factories suffered a variety of fates. The spun rayon factory in Lenzing, Austria, for example, was acquired by the state. In conjunction with this company – Chemiefaser Lenzing AG – we founded the Austria-Faserwerke GmbH and erected a Trevira plant on the same site in 1966.

The Süddeutsche Chemiefaser AG in Kelheim also belonged to the old spun rayon ring. The works were situated on the Danube near Regensburg. The management of this company, whom our fibre specialists knew well, had been particularly effective in rationalizing the factory and increasing the quality of the goods to such an extent that they were regarded as one of the best. The Kelheim people had also successfully developed a polyacrylonitrile fibre which achieved considerable success under the name Dolan. Kelheim could thus boast of a fairly healthy base.

The Bavarian banks and the textile industrialists, to whom the works belonged, nevertheless became concerned about the competitiveness of the undertaking because the fibre producers were engaged in a bitter price war. When finally, in 1968, an American company made an offer for Kelheim, a take-over by Hoechst was quickly arranged with the benevolent support of the Bavarian state government. Thus we now had available a broad and balanced programme in the field of man-made fibres. In 1970, our total capacity was 300,000 tons per year and world turnover amounted to 1,400 million DM.

Into Cosmetics

Even at the time of reconstitution, we had made attempts to get into cosmetics. Our efforts, however, to get the company of Curta as part of the I. G. dismemberment were completely unsuccessful. We acquired this company only much later and then by way of Cassella who got it in the early days.

We realized at an early date that the commercial problems in the field of body care products and cosmetics could readily be solved through our activities in the pharmaceutical field. Experience from pharmacology and toxicology can be usefully employed in the development of products for cosmetic applications. Also, filling and packaging, as well as sales, have many points of contact with pharmaceuticals, although, of course, the customers and the market conditions call for a particular kind of experience. This is the reason why we needed such a long time before we could make a suitable start.

As a first step, we acquired the cosmetic firm of Marbert in Düsseldorf in 1969. The company employed some 450 people and achieved sales of almost 29 million marks in 1970.

The second step was an agreement with the Hamburg company of Hans Schwarzkopf GmbH as a result of which we took over the sales of their hair and body care products in a number of countries overseas. In the meantime, we have managed to obtain a holding of almost 49 per cent in Hans Schwarzkopf GmbH.

Finally, in 1970, we took over 'Prue Acton' Cosmetics in Australia. This company produces cosmetics, particularly for teenagers, in a very modern plant in Melbourne.

From these small beginnings, we hope that in the future a business will develop that will be appropriate to the vast role that cosmetics play in our life.

Hoechst as a European Undertaking

Consolidation of the domestic position and the successful warding off of take-over bids by competitors, were only partial answers to the challenge of international competition which now became increasingly fierce in the chemical markets of the world.

Our European neighbours were basically in the same situation. They were all reaching the limits of their domestic market and had to face world-wide competition. On the one hand, they were threatened by the powerful U.S.A. and on the other hand they were faced by the unified and not readily accessible economic bloc of the east. At the same time, the Japanese were getting ready for a commercial offensive in Europe.

It was important that the countries of western Europe should not shut themselves off from each other as they did between the wars and that they should not organize their markets and exports through cartels and conventions. The Second World War had finally destroyed Europe's position of power and superiority.

Victors, neutrals, and particularly the defeated recognized remarkably quickly that they were all in the same boat and that they had to rely upon each other. It is to the credit of the Americans that during the first five to ten years after the war, they not only helped Europe with large funds, but also used their political influence in order to prevent intolerable restitution demands.

With a remarkable lack of self-interest, they promoted every effort towards European cooperation. Resistance and differences of opinion arose only when Europe had again got stronger and was once more becoming a considerable economic power. Before this cooperation could be reached, however, many difficulties had to be overcome, difficulties that we tend to forget these days.

The European people had moved away from each other in the past as a result of many conflicts. World war and economic upsets were to a large extent responsible for the mutual mistrust. Europeans had become strangers to one another.

I, too, suffered from inadequate knowledge of neighbouring nations. The modest family situation, the worrying university period, and the isolation of the Third Reich, which made journeys abroad almost impossible for average citizens, had resulted in my hardly ever being out of Germany. As a young I. G. chemist I once spent a few hours in London and Paris and on another occasion, during the war, I had to make a short business trip to a chemical factory in Italy. But that was all that I knew about the world

outside the German frontiers when I took on the office of chairman
at the age of forty-eight.

Valuable Experience: Trips Abroad

What I now came to see, with each journey that I made, was both
a professional as well as an intense personal experience. Naturally,
responsibility for our business abroad lay with the commercial
management of the company. But it was nevertheless invaluable
that I, too, should travel a great deal. Our foreign business partners,
as well as our staff abroad, got to know me much better through the
visits that I paid to them, than from brief discussions in Hoechst.
During all my trips, which initially led mainly to the neighbouring
European countries, I always made certain that we had a few hours
of sightseeing under expert guidance. These leisure contacts very
often brought us closer to our foreign business partners than many
commercial negotiations.

As soon as it became possible, I also took my family abroad, to the
capitals of Europe; to Italy, Spain and Portugal. In the meantime,
my wife had made short trips to Belgium and Holland together
with the children.

Everyone at that time was concerned to resume relationships
with a world that had been closed to us Germans for many years.
Moreover, we at home had lost many monuments of our culture.
Our cities had been destroyed and it was not likely that they would
ever be re-erected in their former historical splendour. Also, the
continuity of our historical consciousness had been broken abruptly.
We had to gain a firm point of reference once more. Proper
evaluation of positive and negative factors in the past and present
was, however, a problem that each of us had to solve personally.
This led to an increasing desire to orientate ourselves abroad.
Every trip to a foreign country, even to our immediate European
neighbours, was like entering a wonderland. True, we had caused
a great deal of destruction and unhappiness in these countries but,
by the time I crossed the frontiers, the external damage had mostly
been made good. I was therefore able to enjoy the beauty and
traditions of Europe as reflected in its famous cities with their
numerous cultural monuments. With most of our neighbours,
national consciousness had not been affected. Others had quickly
regained it. Therefore, I encountered very different attitudes to the

plans for a new Europe. Enthusiasm depended very much on how the individual peoples judged their own situation. There can be no doubt that in Germany the urge for a European Community was greatest of all.

When I took up negotiations with business partners from the other European states, comprehensive preliminary discussions at a variety of levels had usually already taken place so that we did not meet entirely without preparation. Nevertheless, it took me a long time before I overcame my embarrassment in such encounters and no longer experienced inhibitions, especially in front of people whose families I knew had suffered a great deal under the Hitler regime. I had to overcome the same sentiments when I visited countries that had suffered at the hands of Germany.

Looking back on all this today, it is remarkable that interest in collaboration in the end proved stronger than all the memories of the dark era of the Third Reich. During those years, many Europeans probably felt for the first time the sensation of a community of fate. Also, the younger generation made it much easier for us older ones to meet our European colleagues because it was not burdened with the past and could approach the idea of a new Europe with fewer prejudices.

Marginal Areas Look for Industry

The conditions for a future partnership differed, of course, from country to country. For this reason, our activities in the various European countries depended at the beginning upon many co-incidences, upon personal relationships and economic factors.

Today, our engagement in Europe is so extensive that it would be difficult to say which country is closest to us. Whether we achieved an extensive commercial agreement, whether we acquired interests, whether there were agreements concerning joint research or the construction of our own factory, depended upon the local situation and the point in time at which we could start our activities. In addition, there were, and still are, areas in Europe that have their particular development difficulties.

Structural problems are very similar in the marginal European areas that are unfavourably situated from the point of view of communication. This applies to Ireland, Scotland, Spain, Southern Italy and also to those areas of the Federal Republic that have been cut off from their natural economic spheres of influence as a result of the Iron Curtain. The Saar is another similar area. The governments and authorities of these countries were greatly interested in attracting industry to their territory. They tried to promote this through particularly favourable conditions. For industry, on the other hand, it was often difficult to find the right sites for new plants at the appropriate time, and to make the proper decision.

But in spite of all the difficulties that beset the European ideal, there was a great deal of progress. One should never forget the very unfavourable conditions in which we began.

Friendship with France

The most impressive examples of this are the relations between France and Germany. That an understanding should have developed between these two countries, whose history is highlighted by so many bloody conflicts and who at one time appeared to live in perpetual enmity, so soon after the last war, was something of a miracle, particularly to those of us who belong to the older generation.

In 1953, when I had just been appointed chairman of the board of management, I travelled for the first time to Paris for discussions. I also visited the battlefields of Verdun where my brother had fought for two years at Fort Douaumont before he fell in Flanders in 1918. It was here that I experienced most deeply the fundamental change that had taken place.

Hoechst was exceptionally fortunate in France. But then it had available a very good mediator. Paul Neumann, former member of the board of management of the Schering group, had emigrated from Berlin during the Hitler period and had had to live in Paris under dishonourable and dangerous circumstances during the period of occupation. He did not, however, lose his love for his native country. Together with French friends he founded Peralta in 1950, a latinization reminiscent of our name Hoechst, which became the centre point of our activities in France for many years. At that time, we hardly took a step in France without first asking Neumann for his advice. He died in 1970 at the age of eighty-six.

Following the beginnings with Peralta we later established direct relationships with large French companies. Raoul de Vitry, for many years president of the French chemical company Péchiney, had engaged after the war the two Dorrer brothers, sons of an old

Ludwigshafen chemist. One of them, Eugen Dorrer, remained in France until the end of his days. The other, Otto Dorrer, came to Hoechst quite early on and became one of my closest collaborators. He was particularly valuable to me as travel companion because of his outstanding knowledge of French, English and Italian. The two brothers – we nicknamed them the organization Dorrer frères – were instrumental in establishing our longstanding friendship with de Vitry.

It was in his company that I got to know a large part of France. Our companies continuously exchanged ideas in the techno-commercial field, on energy questions and on social problems. As a result of our relationship, bilateral discussions took place between the French and the German chemical industry which could not have been more friendly or more fruitful with any other country. There were also close contacts between Dechema in Frankfurt and the Société de Chimie Industrielle.

We had particularly close links with the former French Ambassador in Bonn, François Seydoux. For example, Seydoux came to Hoechst on the occasion of a Franco-German cultural week and gave a lecture on his positive ideas on European integration.

In autumn 1969 I travelled to Lyon where the recent graduates had appointed me patron of the local École Supérieure de Commerce et d'Administration des Enterprises. I was particularly delighted at the friendliness shown to Germany and the enthusiasm of French youth for Europe. It was really impressive to watch some hundred young people, in ceremonial dress, kneeling as though they were about to be knighted and solemnly undertaking – not to the rector but to the chairman of their own student association – to play their part for France and Europe. In the evening I participated in a lively student festival that had been staged with all the bubbling charm so typical of the French.

In this atmosphere of Franco-German friendship our commercial management, especially Kurt Lanz who has a special love for France, succeeded in developing a versatile and close cooperation which included both traditional and new fields. As in many other countries, the beginning was a small pharmaceutical plant. This was followed by two joint ventures with French chemical companies in the field of plastics and solvents. The most important connection was established in the summer of 1968 with the French pharmaceutical company, Roussel-Uclaf. This related to joint activities in research, production and selling. The basis was a minority interest of Hoechst in the family company of Chimio, which has a majority holding in Roussel-Uclaf.

The negotiations and the signing of the agreement with Jean Claude Roussel which took place during the period of the serious May disturbances in France in 1968, were attended by difficult circumstances. As can be imagined, other companies, too, were interested in collaboration with this large pharmaceutical undertaking which at that time had annual sales of approximately 1,500 million francs. Initially there were American competitors but in the last phase we also encountered competition from a European company.

When we had reached final agreement with Roussel we needed the consent of the French government. In the case of such a large project, this meant that de Gaulle himself would have to make the final decision. At that time the General had opposed a partnership between Fiat and Citroën. The German Economics Minister, Karl Schiller, for his part had prevented the acquisition of shares in the Gelsenkirchener Bergwerks-AG by the French company Compagnie Française des Pétroles. The situation was critical.

The Press as Important Partner

In this connection, there is a small incident that I like to recall when thinking about the press. Shortly after we had agreed with the Roussel family about our participation, one of our big press conferences was to take place in Hoechst. As normally happened in the autumn, we wanted to present a review of business developments during the year that was coming to a close, and we also wanted to give the latest information about our investments. Naturally the journalists had already heard something about our agreement with the second largest French pharmaceutical company. I was prepared to give them a full report.

A few hours before our press conference began, however, we got the news that President de Gaulle was going to Bonn. We wondered how the General, whose permission for our acquisition we had not yet obtained, would react if he were to read about the planned collaboration for the first time in German papers and in the capital of the Federal Republic at that.

Under the circumstances, neither we nor our French friends wanted to make any public announcement. On the other hand, if a journalist asked me about the Roussel-Uclaf project, I could not escape the question or tell a lie. It was, therefore, essential that this subject should not be raised at all during the conference. To prevent this was one of the greatest tests of our relations with the press. There were eighty journalists present but not one raised the question of Roussel with me. Two weeks later, after the General had returned to France and had given his assent, we of course immediately published our agreement with Roussel-Uclaf.

I do not believe that the silence and understanding of the German press would have been possible if during the course of the years we had not ensured a very close contact with both trade and financial press. We have learnt that one can ask a great deal of journalists and can always expect objective and sympathetic reporting if the press is openly informed in good time. It must be informed about company policy, it must be able to understand the motives and the decisions behind that policy, and it must know that we do not turn to the press only when we need it. Very often industry makes the mistake of turning to the press only when the fire has already started.

Dealing with reporters and the question and answer sessions during press conferences was something that I had to learn from scratch. Before the war, such encounters did not happen in Germany. In the meantime, things have changed completely. No large company today can get along without its public relations department which is in constant contact with the trade and financial press, and with radio and television. But this department can fulfil its task only if it is fully informed right from the beginning about all that is happening within the company. I have always derived a great deal of satisfaction from my dealings with the press, both in Germany and abroad. And I have rarely experienced a journalist who has written anything negative or derogatory about me. During my innumerable encounters with journalists, I have always found conditions very similar everywhere in the world. German, English, French or Italian journalists are all primarily interested in factual, unvarnished information. If this is presented with a little humour and quick repartee as well, it greatly helps to foster mutual understanding and respect.

C.Y.—22

But back to France. Apart from Roussel-Uclaf, whose pharmaceutical range is today sold in the Federal Republic together with that of Albert through the Albert-Roussel Pharma GmbH founded in 1969, we have many old partnerships in France with companies in the fibre and film industry. I like to think that Hoechst has made a significant contribution to European consolidation through promoting close Franco-German friendship.

I would not, however, wish to give the impression that we oriented ourselves unilaterally towards France. We soon resumed harmonious personal and economic relations with the chemical industry of Switzerland and its rich traditions. This has been nursed and strengthened as a result of continuous mutual visits. This contact has solid historical roots for even at the beginnings of the chemical industry, Basle chemistry enjoyed both friendly relations and a fair competition with German chemical industry.

Quite apart from this, I also have family connections in Switzerland. In fond memory of my teacher Berl who, before he came to Darmstadt, had been active at the Eidgenössische Technische Hochschule in Zurich, I allowed my son to study there. Perhaps not surprisingly, he eventually married a young woman from Zurich.

One of our first foreign connections was in Spain. At the end of the last century, the Chemische Fabrik Griesheim Elektron had built an electrolysis plant at Flix near Tarragona on a dam on the Ebro river which went back to the Moorish period. This plant was taken over during the Second World War by the Spanish company of Cros. Soon after the re-constitution of Hoechst, however, we were able to gain a renewed interest in it. The president of Cros, Francisco A. Ripoll, was a gentleman of the old Spanish school who, throughout his long life, had a great deal of sympathy for us. More recently, however, the interests of the two partners diverged so that Hoechst has now left the partnership with Cros by mutual agreement.

In Austria and Italy, too, efficient chemical industries developed and we established interesting contacts with them. Shortly after the conclusion of the Austrian state treaty in 1955, the Austrian Federal Chancellor Julius Raab paid a call on Hoechst during his visit to the Federal Republic. This resulted in good relations with Austria which were rapidly intensified.

Pivot Vienna

Shortly after the departure of the Russian troops in 1955, I spent a few days on the Semmering in return for the visit by Raab. Everywhere I saw traces and results of the disastrous times which had actually begun for Austria with the collapse of the Danube monarchy at the end of the First World War. But after a few years of recovery, Vienna again became a city of worldwide importance with a marvellous opera house and the famous Burgtheater. It was now the capital of a small country. But, thanks to its rich cultural treasures and its lovely people, it continues to exert a great attraction. Its geographical position and its historical affinity to eastern Europe also make it an important starting point and a pivot for commercial relations with the east.

After the conclusion of the Austrian State Treaty, there had been much discussion as to whether it was really necessary to accept so many harsh regulations and discriminating provisions. But if we look at the continuing precarious situation of Berlin, we ought to realize how beneficial it was that Julius Raab and his Foreign Minister Leopold Figl, in a fortunate hour, took this road for Austria, a road that unfortunately was never open to us in Berlin. I also got to know Figl when he received me in the palace on the Ballhausplatz where in former days Count Metternich had so cleverly manipulated the threads of European politics.

As Hoechst became more active in European countries, so the complexity of the organizational problems grew. It was necessary to establish a uniform commercial policy within the companies abroad which were based on so many different traditions and in which, apart from the few German employees, a large number of local people were employed. Also, the individual companies had to get to know each other and gain each other's confidence. For this reason, we started to hold European conferences. It was found that mutual contact became closer if these meetings did not take place in Hoechst. As a result, we met for the first time in the autumn of 1960 in Switzerland where the company of Plüss-Staufer, our first and oldest agency, has its headquarters.

The second European conference was held in Vienna in 1966. At this conference, we were able to report on two decisive steps which had resulted in important projects on the Dutch North Sea coast. In the efforts toward European integration, the Benelux countries had from the beginning occupied a central position. Luxembourg is the seat of the European court, offices of the European Community commission, and also the headquarters of an increasing number of holding and finance companies. The commission of the European Community itself settled in Brussels as did the Euratom authority. It was therefore necessary to make many trips to this European centre. From the beginning, our Belgian partners did successful business and profited from the traditional Belgian relationships with Africa.

The North Sea coast was, and remains, however, of particular economic importance as a catchment area, so to speak, and port of western Europe. Unfortunately, the German ports of Hamburg and Bremen do not have the best connections with the sites of the Hoechst factories in Germany. The Dutch North Sea coast offers a far more advantageous system of communications, particularly since the Dutch, with their tenacity of purpose, had understood in good time how to open their country to the whole world. The reconstruction of Rotterdam, which had been destroyed in the war, made this town an even more important port than before and probably the largest in the world today.

In Hoechst we recognized from the start that in the long term our site on the Main, however successfully we had expanded it, would be subject to limitations. We were therefore forced to look for an additional site that offered favourable international communications, fulfilled vital manufacturing conditions, was easily accessible from Frankfurt, and offered a simplified transport route to the world at large.

Communications via the Main and the Rhine are subject to much interference. For many weeks throughout the year, therefore, we have to transport our goods by rail. The distance to the coast is great and thus results in high freight costs. Moreover, because of the increasing amount of effluent, the problems created by additional production become more and more difficult to solve.

We therefore took an early interest in the opportunities offered by the North Sea coast and particularly in Holland. Due to extensive finds of natural gas, the energy situation there was also very favourable. In Germany, on the other hand, the energy policy had entered a very difficult phase in the sixties. When, at that time, we tried to secure the supply of additional large amounts of electric power by means of long-term contracts, there was simply no adequate opportunity for doing this throughout the Federal Republic.

Hoechst at the Mouth of the Scheldt

During the autumn of 1966, therefore, I travelled with a number of my colleagues to the North Sea coast for several days in order to study the geographical and economic situation in detail. We ranged throughout the area by helicopter, car and small charter plane, our commercial friends in Amsterdam and Brussels having carried out the preliminary arrangements. We inspected the new harbour of Rotterdam and discussed the possibility of settling in Europoort. We also visited the port of Antwerp and the sites where other European companies had already erected their factories.

Eventually, we chose Flushing at the mouth of the Scheldt as the site for our new works. We gratefully accepted the considerable help of the Dutch government who received us most cordially and gave us a great deal of assistance. Energy supplies in particular had to be arranged satisfactorily. Moreover, we needed enough land to allow us to carry out phased construction extending over several decades. Having got this, we worked out a long-term plan for the Flushing works which provides for considerable annual investments.

Initially, we constructed a phosphorus plant with two large furnaces and a salt plant. Prince Bernhard of the Netherlands attended the inauguration in August 1968. In the meantime, a further phosphorus furnace has been constructed as has a plant for dimethyl-terephthalate, the primary product for our Trevira fibre. Further production facilities are to be constructed gradually in Flushing. Energy supplies are now no longer based purely on the rich natural gas deposits but there is also an atomic power station. Other industries have in the meantime followed the Hoechst example and also built in Flushing.

The other important event also concerned the Netherlands. The American company of Foster Grant had a small polystyrene factory in Breda in which we originally acquired a 50 per cent interest. Later, in full agreement with the Americans, we took over this company completely. In the meantime, this, too, has developed into an extensive production plant. Previous to this, we had acquired a film factory in Weert in the province of Limburg.

The Atomium in Brussels

In autumn 1969, we held our third European conference, this time in Brussels. The commercial management of the company had hired the Atomium in Brussels which had, of course, originally been built for the Brussels World Fair. Presumably, the venue was to remind me of my link with atomic energy.

A few months before this, I had exchanged the chairmanship of the board of management with that of the supervisory board. The conference was, therefore, of particular importance for me. Apart from these personal aspects, however, it also marked an important development stage for Hoechst.

When we met in 1963 to celebrate our centenary with our foreign partners, we had only made a modest beginning in our international and European organization. We were saddled with many problems and we only knew roughly the road that we proposed to follow. No one was able then to tell where it would lead.

Subsequently we had become a European company that not only was represented in all the countries of free Europe but also had production plants in many of them. Seventy-five per cent of our world business of more than 9,000 million DM were accounted for by Europe. It was necessary therefore that in Brussels we should devote most of our time to the complex organizational questions which had given rise to so many complicated problems.

Problems of European Integration

After the foundation of the Coal and Steel Community and of the E.E.C., integration had initially made tremendous progress. The reduction of tariffs allowed the volume of goods exchanged between the member states to increase to an extraordinary extent.

By 1969, however, the situation had become rather disappointing. Objections from all sides, and particularly from France, had prevented any decisive progress. Neither Brussels nor the European Council at Strasbourg was ready for fundamental solutions. There was endless dispute over questions that only the experts could understand. There was total disarray over such issues as the quotas of butter, eggs or wine. The picture in Brussels in no way conformed to the expectations and hopes of the European peoples and certainly not to those of the young people.

The situation with respect to common and commercial law and economic policy generally was still inadequate for a truly European company like Hoechst. The old objections to an enlargement of the European Economic Community to include other countries continued to be raised. But even within the E.E.C., the limitations of differential company legislation continued to exist.

At the time of our Brussels conference, the currency issue in the Community had once more reached boiling point. We had to think again as to how, under such conditions, it was possible to lead a European company with any chance of success. Year after year, we had founded an increasing number of companies in a variety of European countries. But even where several of these subsidiaries existed within the same state, they were frequently subject to different ownership legislation, and could not be joined because of fiscal reasons. It was questions like these that formed the centrepoint of our conference.

In the summer of 1969, I was asked to prepare, together with the British industrialist and former president of the United Kingdom Atomic Energy Authority, Lord Plowden, a report on both the technical parallels and requirements of an integrated Europe. We both agreed that the fusion of the industrial forces of western Europe would create an economic potential that would also be competitive in relation to the U.S.A. We were not only thinking of uniform taxes and tariffs but even more of a common system for the exchange of goods, a generally valid pharmaceutical and food legislation, uniform safety regulations or purchasing conditions, and many other things. In our view, these were essential conditions for a truly common domestic market.

This report was submitted in July 1969 to the Monnet Committee. On this occasion, I had the opportunity of visiting Jean Monnet, the enthusiastic European – a contemporary of Robert Schuman and Konrad Adenauer – in his home in a suburb of Paris. In 1952, Monnet had become the first president of the Coal and Steel Community and he was full of memories of the excitement of this early period of a new Europe.

Since then, however, we have grown no closer to realizing our aim. But a common Europe with uniform economic conditions is an absolute necessity, not only for Hoechst but for the entire chemical industry and for all the other industrial branches of our continent.

Resistance to such a market is anachronistic. It is no longer understood by European youth.

The absence of European integration also makes our relationships with the rest of the world more difficult, particularly with the eastern bloc and the economically powerful America. The negotiations of the Kennedy Round finished in 1967. When I presided over a congress of the Association of German Chemical Industry in Kronberg in the Taunus, the representatives of the E.E.C. countries agreed, for the first time, to adopt a common attitude during the forthcoming GATT negotiations.

The American representative, who participated at this Kronberg meeting, together with the political and economic representatives of the western European countries, found it heavy going in spite of the friendly atmosphere that governed the discussion. We were arguing about the 'American selling price', a protective concept dating back to the period after the First World War. Organic dyestuffs and all their primary products, as well as aromatic compounds generally, are subject to a tariff system – not practised anywhere else in the world – which is not based on the actual value of the goods in the manufacturing country. Instead, duty is calculated from case to case on the basis of the usually higher price at which the corresponding products are sold in the U.S.A. by American competitors. This means that duty of 100 per cent or more may be, and often is, levied.

The subsequent GATT negotiations in Geneva resulted in only a modest success for Europe. Nevertheless, on this occasion the E.E.C. countries, for the first time, acted jointly as negotiating partners. The removal by the Americans of this prehistoric duty system had, however, still not been accomplished even in 1971.

Latin America: Wealth and Poverty

Latin America has always been a traditional market for German products. This applied also to the output of the German chemical industry. It was therefore not surprising that one of my first extensive journeys, other than to the United States, also took me to Latin-America in 1957.

The Hoechst delegation, which was usually the same on later extended trips, consisted of Kurt Lanz, the sales director, Otto Horn, one of our scientific departmental heads who in the course of time has earned our gratitude for his work to promote international cooperation, and myself. In spite of our widely differing interests, we quickly agreed on a joint style of travelling and programme which enabled us, with the minimum amount of time, to gain a general impression of the cultural life of the countries we visited, their economic conditions, their educational and university life, as well as their political conditions. This required exact preparation through detailed correspondence with our initially still modest foreign agencies and also very careful studies by our economics department in Hoechst.

When we finally left, we had a very full and extensive programme ahead of us. These trips were no holiday. We came back usually filled with a wealth of ideas and experiences which we could put to good use in arriving at further decisions. Of course, the group was usually joined by two or three other people from Hoechst, depending on the destination and purpose of the visit. In this way, we have visited gradually all parts of the world, repeating some journeys in order to continue projects that we had started.

The long interruption in trade communications as a result of the war and the subsequent downturn in economic life, had resulted in emanicipation trends in Latin America. The countries there attempted to free themselves from foreign influences in their political and economic life. National pride had been awakened everywhere and this did not allow them any longer to remain in their previous state of dependence. Latin America hoped that increased economic autonomy would also result in an improvement of the social situation which was still characterized by a great gulf between rich and poor.

During the war and post-war periods the American influence had become all powerful, especially in the north, in Mexico and Venezuela. As a reaction to this, the Latin American states resorted to confiscation, and occasionally there was also a nationalistic movement, for example, the dictatorship of Juan Perón in the Argentine, which at that time had just come to an end. Later, starting in Cuba, the pendulum swung towards communism. Poverty, huge social contrasts, the increase in the population, and the almost unstoppable drift from the rural areas into the towns worsened the situation and caused revolutions to break out in these countries.

Nevertheless, our first impression was overpowering. We recognized the great economic potential and the readiness of the governments to work together with German partners. Everywhere we encountered people with vivid memories of earlier commercial dealings with Germany. In the meantime, we had established agencies in almost all the countries that we visited. It was a happy surprise for us to find that German business people continued to play a certain role in these countries and that they had been able to maintain a firm position for themselves in commercial life.

For the successors of the I. G. Farbenindustrie, the starting point of the re-establishment of former business connections was probably always the import of dyestuffs. During the war there was a pronounced lack of these materials wherever the Swiss had been unable to fill the gap. This was one of the reasons why we were able to regain a foothold in this field so very quickly. In order to consolidate this success, it was necessary to send colorists and technical advisers to our customers and eventually to set up application laboratories in the various countries.

The other large field that offered good prospects for Hoechst was pharmaceuticals. In Latin America, as elsewhere in the world, Hoechst was faced with the task of building up an independent organization. During the I. G. period, the pharmaceuticals developed and produced in Hoechst had been sold under the joint Bayer cross. In view of the friendly relationships that Hoechst had always had with Leverkusen, and the great cost that an independent sales network would entail, there was at first considerable temptation to consider a joint selling organization, at any rate in those countries where the market opportunities were initially limited. In the end, however, both sides recognized that each company, in this field too, would have to walk the long and difficult road into the future on its own. This was perhaps one of the most important and significant decisions of the trip.

We were able to get into the pharmacautical market in Latin America only after the governments there had agreed, with varying degrees of enthusiasm, to return our trademarks to us. In any case, their temporary loss was to prove one of the greatest setbacks of the war. Names like Aspirin by Bayer, Pyramidon or Novalgin from Hoechst, had an inestimable value particularly as new drugs were not at that time available. The old Bayer organization had possessed finishing and packaging plants for pharmaceuticals in many of these countries. They had to be bought back as well, even if they were in part considerably antiquated. In this field, too, Hoechst decided to go its own way and to build up an appropriate medical and pharmaceutical staff. We were fortunate on this occasion that many people from the former Bayer organization decided to join us. Another positive gain for Hoechst were the Behring Institutes that had been set up in several countries between the two wars and many of which we were able to get back to use as a basis for our agencies.

On the whole, however, it was difficult to sell general chemicals, fertilizers, for example, in view of the competition from neighbouring countries and of the beginning of domestic production. We had to confine ourselves to specialities.

The industrialization trends were a continuous subject of discussion during these first trips. It was clear to us how much the governments in these countries were hoping for positive cooperation with the Germans. The Latin Americans think highly of German engineers and were happy if we designed plants for them so that they could quickly familiarize themselves with the most recent technological progress.

It was in this way that our subsidiary, Friedrich Uhde of Dortmund, quickly achieved great importance. The construction of ammonia and fertilizer plants was one of the traditional fields of this company. It was therefore able to submit offers very quickly and thus rapidly clinch the business. Not only in Latin America but throughout the world, there arose at that time a considerable demand for chemical plants. A new branch of industry grew up: the trading in chemical plants and the appropriate know-how.

The international chemical companies had previously taken great care not to divulge their patent wealth or their operating experience, let alone sell it. Where this was done in exceptional cases, it was in exchange for equivalent knowledge or at an extraordinarily high price. But now, starting in the crude oil industry, an almost unlimited plant business developed in the immediate post-war years. The leaders in this field, who had been in this market for some time, were mainly American engineering companies. These were now joined by the chemical concerns from Europe. This open-minded exchange greatly promoted the expansion of the chemical industry in the world even if many companies at first rejected the idea of publishing experience that had usually cost them large sums of money to acquire.

In Hoechst, too, there was initial opposition to the efforts by Uhde to make available to them our know-how for such plants. People were simply against releasing too early what had just been developed. Eventually, we created a special organization in Hoechst which took joint decisions with Uhde, as each case arose, on what processes should be released. As our research continued to gain ground in the new fields of petrochemistry and its derivatives, Hostalen and polyester fibres, a considerable and profitable field opened up for Uhde.

Our connections with Uhde, and in particular with its founder, Friedrich Uhde, go back to the years following the I. G. dismemberment. At that time, it was a small engineering office with approximately 550 employees which had previously been closely linked to the Leuna works near Halle and which was now seeking links with a chemical company. The tremendous development in chemical plant business, unforeseen at that time, has provided Uhde, which apart from its headquarters in Dortmund now also has a big branch in Bad Soden near Hoechst, with considerable significance. More than 2,300 people now work for the company. In 1970, its world-wide plant business achieved a value of approximately 345 million DM.

Our views concerning the suitability of issuing patent and process licences changed decisively during this period. The ratio between licence expenditure and income is not only of financial importance. It is also regarded by outsiders as one of the yardsticks of the research potential of a company. We have often been asked at our annual general meetings and by the public for these licence balance sheets.

When we acquired the important licences for Hostalen and Trevira and exploited them on a large scale, the balance sheet for Hoechst was negative. Later this changed fundamentally after we achieved greater success with our own research.

I would like to emphasize, however, that in contrast to a widely held belief, no unequivocal conclusions can be drawn from a licence balance sheet in respect of the scientific performance of a company. If the favourable purchase of a valuable licence leads to the development of large new fields, as was the case in Hoechst with plastics and synthetic fibres, then such expenditures are of great benefit to the company.

In the footsteps of the Incas

In this way, our foreign agencies gained concrete support and contact with the industry of the country concerned. The new chemical producers were in any case always potential customers. We learnt in these years of international expansion that chemical business thrives if it can be transacted more and more in countries where there is already a chemical industry. On the other hand, we found in Latin America just how long it takes to set up a chemical industry if one has to start practically from scratch.

Our journey in 1957 took us from Mexico via Panama to Venezuela with short stops in the Central American coffee and banana countries like Guatemala, El Salvador, Honduras, Nicaragua and Costa Rica, where we did not yet have any agencies. In Venezuela we inspected the oil drilling operations and got to know something of the life in the drilling camps which offered many interesting sales opportunities. We also visited the ore mines on the Orinoco. Then we went to Chile, via Columbia and Peru. Here we inspected the nitrate plants and also undertook the famous obligatory diversion to Cuzco and Machúpichú, the refuge of the Incas and home of the potato and the lamas. Messrs Uhde later erected a fertilizer factory right in the centre of the Peruvian Andes.

We crossed the Andes in the far south, near Puerto Montt, and reached Bariloche in southern Argentina. We eventually got to Rio by way of Buenos Aires and Montevideo. Here, as everywhere, we were welcomed by the many Germans as well as by the locals, business people, and governments. Near São Paulo, a chemical factory had gone on stream which we had built jointly with Grace, the American company. In this first foreign production plant of Hoechst, agro-chemicals, chlorine and caustic soda, detergents, solvents and Frigen are produced.

Six weeks later we returned home, loaded with photos and films, with presents and rarities of all kinds, including scorpions and bird spiders from the snake farm in the Brazilian Instituto Butantan, which had former relations to the Behringwerke. We were welcomed with warmth and curiosity. We were full of ideas which, of course, would cost a great deal of money to realize. Many of these ideas were initially rejected as being premature and hasty but in every case these trips formed a starting point for long-term business decisions.

Naturally, I returned to Latin America many times. Progress

there was rather slower than we had originally hoped and expected, but we were able to record greater progress each year. In 1959 we inaugurated our office building in Mexico and at the same time held our first Latin American conference there. In 1966, at a similar conference, we decided to found a Hoechst organization in the central American countries including the Caribbean. As the centre we chose Guatemala.

In 1969, when I had already left active service, we inaugurated a pharmaceutical factory and a polyvinylacetate plant in Guatemala, whose beautiful scenery and Indian culture had made a deep impression upon us. We had a happy evening at the home of the German Ambassador, Count Spreti, who was taken hostage by rebels and murdered shortly afterwards.

Change in Japan

The World Fair in 1970 showed that Japan was a country of growth and progress. The thousands of Europeans and Americans who walked daily through the exhibition were hardly noticed among the millions of Japanese who looked upon this vision of the future almost as if it were a place of pilgrimage. The simple peasants, solemnly walking around with their wives and children, were as fascinated as the enthusiastic pupils in their uniform.

Japan has abandoned its former reticence and its attitude as the knowledge seeking pupil of the western industrial nations. It is set on a victorious road into the future, not with weapons and soldiers but with an industrial potential whose growth far exceeds anything that we ever experienced in the years of the so-called German economic miracle.

But during my first visit to Japan, things had not yet reached this pitch. In the late autumn of 1958, a five-week trip led us to the Far East. The flight from Copenhagen via Anchorage in Alaska to the country of the Tenno took some thirty-five hours. It was the first time that we experienced a world outside European culture, with entirely different customs, based upon a completely different mental approach.

In Tokyo, as in the Japanese textile centre of Osaka, Hoechst had erected an organization, albeit a modest one, which could nevertheless point to considerable export successes in this highly industrialized country, even if in other respects it had to submit to a controlled economy. To give some idea of how modest this first organization was, I should like to relate the story of the last evening that we were together, when we asked our people what we could give them as a present. The answer was that they would like to have two scooters for the medical representatives. The success of the Hoechst agency was no doubt also partly based on old connections and sympathies that survived in Japan for a long time. Before the First World War, Paul Ehrlich and his Japanese co-worker, Sahachiro Hata, had developed Salvarsan in conjunction with Farbwerke Hoechst. Emil von Behring's closest collaborator was Shibasaburo Kitasato. These old memories provided a sound foundation for further collaboration with Japanese scientists.

It was surprising to find how conscious Japan was of this distant past. The Medical Society of Japan received us with great hospitality. Choei Ishibashi, who was then its director and is now the honorary president, has since tried hard to consolidate this friendship. He visits Hoechst almost every year. His Japanese joy in giving presents is evidenced by the Japanese garden at the entrance to the restaurant of our centenary hall in Hoechst, for which he brings a new item every time he comes.

Landscaping is a symbol of the Japanese mentality. Away from the sober bee-like preoccupation with the working day, the Japanese cultivate the emotional and mystic side of their nature in their gardens. Much of the symbolism is not readily understood by Europeans but it does give some indication of the values that lie behind.

Such traditions similarly permeated public life in the large towns of Japan in 1958. The defeat in war had obviously resulted in a great deal of self-examination. On the other hand, the American influence from the period of occupation was quickly overcome. In the giant city of Tokyo, for example, the American innovation of providing street names, an accepted custom in every western town, was quickly abolished when the Americans left. If a European was accorded the rare honour of being invited privately into a Japanese home, it was very difficult for him to find the given address without the aid of these street names.

At that time the predominant dress of the women was still the kimono. Small children were carried on their mother's back, and as far as I know, even today prams are hardly ever seen in Japan.

The scenes in the large temple cities of Nikko, Nara, and Kyoto were also full of contrasts. In addition to the religious adoration of the few old people who visited the holy places and made their donations, there were many young people, usually classes of school-children in uniform. We Europeans had the impression that they regarded these temples less with religious feelings than with national sentiments, visibly proud of the testimonial of their national tradition.

External contrasts between age-old tradition and modern civiliza-tion were, and are, characteristic of Japan. For example, the Hotel Imperial in which we stayed, but which has now been pulled down, consisted of an old and a new part. In the old part, much had been preserved in the original style of the country, with genuine Japanese equipment and hospitality.

The tea ceremony and the geisha parties could be experienced in their conventional, unspoilt manner, totally unaffected by the emancipation that was proceeding apace elsewhere. These geisha parties were at that time a standard honour for highly respected guests. They began very solemnly and respectfully, accompanied by music and songs. But then they ended in childish gaiety and playful-ness in which there was a curious mixture of naïveté and reverence towards the honoured guest. We were also impressed by the exquisite art of offering presents, which is peculiar to the Japanese, and which we Europeans have yet to learn.

For such events, one didn't mind sitting for hours on the floor. The body of a European is not trained for such procedures, but the host usually has certain ways of facilitating the ordeal.

At such geisha parties, there is a great deal of singing. I still recall with pleasure how our representative in Japan, kneeling on the floor, sang folk songs from a German song book. German folk songs and music are very popular in Japan, while on the other hand Japanese music is strange to our ears. During this trip, I visited Hiroshima. A sober exhibition commemorates the terrible event of the atomic bomb of 1945 in all its detail. It is a permanent warning to all future generations.

A Young Industrial Nation

Apart from the traditional aspects of everyday life in Japan, we also saw the other aspect of the country, the face of an industrial

Karl Winnacker at London airport on his way to visit the Hoechst UK headquarters. On the right is
Gustav Bunge, managing director of Hoechst UK

Left: *Lord Kings Norton, chairman of B.J.N.*, and right: *A. J. Hughes, managing director*

Inauguration of Hoechst Fibre Industries, UK Ltd, Limavady, Northern Ireland, in May 1970. Second from left, E. Daase, managing director H.F.I.; fourth from left, K. Lanz, sales director Farbwerke Hoechst; next to him, Lord Naunton of Grey, then Governor of Northern Ireland, talking to R. Sammet, chairman Farbwerke Hoechst AG

nation and the hard, energetic ceaseless application to the requirements of daily life. Industrialization had already made great
progress. But the Japanese still believed that they had to study
indefatigably in order to catch up with western technology. In
spite of almost exaggerated politeness, one was thoroughly questioned about technical developments. Japanese experts were
interested in every detail. They could conduct interminable discussions and were always ready to negotiate on every point.

During my first days in Tokyo, I gave a lecture to the Japanese
Chemical Society. The audience was large and the lecture took
some three to four hours because an interpreter had to translate the
whole lecture sentence by sentence. This was followed by a detailed
discussion which was possible only because of the infinite patience
and tenacity of the audience.

On the same day, I also gave a press conference. It was extremely
lively and the Japanese journalists asked me innumerable topical
questions. Many of these questions resulted from the visit of the
Federal Economics Minister Ludwig Erhard, who happened to be
in Japan at the same time. Erhard's free market economy, which
had made possible the rise of the Federal Republic in the post-war
period, has found surprisingly little sympathy in Japan, even
now.

The 1951 peace treaty had imposed hard conditions upon the
Japanese. In contrast to the treatment of the Federal Republic, however, the Americans had left the vanquished a closely limited but
nevertheless clear field of activity. The Japanese understood how to
seize upon this opportunity energetically but not ostentatiously. A
new economic order, conforming to the new conditions, was built up
in a short period. As much of the original structure as possible was
retained. Large companies remained a characteristic of the Japanese
economy. The Americans had enthusiastically attempted to dis-
member them but with little success. The large Japanese companies
are different in character and organization from those of the United
States or Europe. They resemble far more the conglomerates that
had been formed after the First World War, for example the Stinnes
concern in Germany, and that are now becoming popular again in
the States.

A wide variety of interests are contained within such large
Japanese concerns as Mitsui or Mitsubishi which are managed by

a bank holding company. The activities may range from chemical products and textiles to steel and shipbuilding. The type of sales organization in Japan also varies from that of the west. There are powerful traders without whom it is difficult to get into the market.

State supervision of the economy, including foreign currency and the conclusion of international contracts and participations, is still very pronounced even today. This state control is apparently tolerated by industry because it can itself participate in it, and because it also provides for close contact between industry and the ministries. As Japanese competition advances in the world markets, however, this type of economic direction is opposed abroad.

We found that among the Japanese there was a sympathetic attitude, in particular to plans for industrial cooperation with German companies. Even during this first contact, we established connections that soon resulted in suitable projects. For example, during the succeeding years Uhde was able to execute numerous orders for the construction of production plants for aldehyde and acetone using the Wacker-Hoechst process. Close links were also forged in the field of plastics and synthetic fibres in which Japanese industry was already very active. In any case, the Japanese had an uncanny ability of taking over everything that was new and developing it with considerable ingenuity. An exchange in experience resulted, therefore, that was mutually beneficial for all involved.

In 1962, I again visited Japan during a trip to Australia. We had already realized a joint project with the Japanese chemical company of Nippon Gosei which concerned a polyvinylacetate plant. We later also founded a joint company for the manufacture of dyestuffs, which had formed the start of Hoechst's Japanese business, with Mitsubishi Chemicals, the largest Japanese chemical concern. This company is called Kasei Hoechst, and it now operates a factory in Ohamamachi between Tokyo and Osaka.

In the four years since our first visit, Japanese emancipation had progressed far more quickly than in most other parts of the world. In the streets there were already far fewer kimonos, and geisha parties had become much rarer. The European style of life was becoming more and more prominent. Cinemas and theatres were ruled by western, and in particular American, sensationalism, even if, in part, Japanese customs and habits were maintained.

As far as the economy is concerned, foreign companies are still not allowed to erect production facilities entirely under their own steam. There must always be a fifty-fifty participation with Japanese companies. However, once a company has gained a foothold in the country and been approved as reliable, then it is not difficult to cement firm and reliable friendships. In this way, our business in Japan developed slowly but steadily and successfully.

In 1967, I visited Japan for the third time. By then, our partnership with the domestic chemical industry had been consolidated further. This applied particularly to pharmaceuticals where we had in the meantime founded a joint undertaking with Mitsui Petrochemicals Company. Pharmaceuticals in Japan have experienced an uninterrupted rise. In terms of Hoechst sales in a country, Japan for some years past has been the third largest foreign pharmaceutical market after Italy and the U.S.A. We began in 1955 in an office of fourteen square metres and with a staff of two. In 1970, more than 700 people were engaged in producing and selling Hoechst pharmaceuticals in Japan.

In view of this mixture of tradition and emancipation, we experienced more and more clearly the great powers of assimilation of the Japanese people, whose energy has shown itself in indefatigable activity in almost all parts of the world. Even in Europe, the slogan of the Japanese challenge has been heard.

Gateway to China

The next port of call on our Far East trip in 1958 was Hong Kong where the political tensions had just reached a climax. We had forgone a visit to Formosa. The German newspapers were giving detailed reports of the bombardments of the island of Quemoy off the Chinese mainland. As a result, we believed that National China was involved in a serious crisis. It was only when we arrived in Hong Kong that the huge distances involved here became clear to us. We saw what a subordinate role such events played at a distance of several thousand kilometres.

A huge flood of refugees from Red China was at that time entering Hong Kong. They usually came through Portuguese Macao into the British Crown Colony. The town was marked by a Chinese atmosphere and the reminders of the peak period of British imperialism. At the same time, however, modern skyscrapers and luxury hotels were shooting up, and right in the middle of it all there stood, as a solid power block, the Red China Bank.

From Hong Kong – and this appeared to make this location particularly interesting – our business friends were still able to travel to Canton and report their impressions of life there which were full of foreboding but did not in any way indicate later developments. Even as late as 1964, after careful arrangements with the Chinese embassy in Berne, a Hoechst delegation of seven technicians and commercial people were allowed to make a most illuminating trip through Maoist China. Immediately after the cultural revolution in 1966, such a project became completely impossible. More recently, however, opportunities have again opened up for talks between China and the western world.

Hong Kong, on the other hand, has remained at all times an important base from which to maintain unusual connections. No doubt it is as interesting and valuable as a contact post for Red China as it is for the rest of the world and therefore of great importance for trade with the Far East.

From Hong Kong, we flew to the Philippines which still reflected the immediate post-war situation. The American influence was noticeable everywhere. Life was still very much dominated by the events of the war, the Japanese occupation and finally the arrival of the Americans. Business opportunities only opened up slowly but then appeared to be full of prospects.

In Burma, too, our next stop, the political conditions were still tense and unclear. The beauty and opulence of the golden roof of the central Buddhist holy shrine in Rangoon were in deep contrast to the endless poverty of the country ravaged by war.

In the Land of the White Elephant

A subsequent stay in Bangkok provided totally different impressions. Thailand, the former Siam, is probably the only area in the Far East that has been spared colonization and revolution for centuries. It appeared as an island of peace and freedom. There we were to see some new aspects of the complex kaleidoscope of Asia: the temple cities, the Buddhist monks walking through the streets early in the morning, the people meditating in the temple courtyards where all those beginning a new chapter of life, changing their job, or just recovering from an illness, retire for some weeks.

I will never forget an excursion from Thailand to Angkor Wat in Cambodia. This site of the old Khmeric culture, overwhelmed by the jungle, was a favourite excursion at that time. There you stayed in a relatively well-kept hotel, operated by a Swiss, and located on the edge of the primeval forest, where large numbers of monkeys and exotic birds kept you company. Today, this gem is probably in the middle of the fighting zone between the Vietcong and the Cambodian troops.

In the bazaars of Bangkok, we found Hoechst dyestuffs and also our pharmaceuticals. The tablets were being sold singly. Only when one has experienced this personally, can one judge just how difficult it is to sell the highly developed products of our civilization in a country so far removed in distance and culture.

Eight years later, during my second visit to Bangkok, when I was accompanied by my wife, the situation had changed completely. Hoechst had in the meantime erected a modern, fair-sized pharmaceutical factory in Thailand. King Bhumibol and his beautiful wife Sirikit granted us an audience in their fairytale palace in which our native companions moved on their knees in front of the royal couple. But in the background one sensed the Vietnam conflict, although it was still far away.

In the meantime, much money had been poured into Bangkok. We were still able to see the old temples and to watch the Klongs with their picturesque huts, standing very close to the water, but life in the city had changed fundamentally. Large hotels and impressive skyscrapers were shooting out of the ground. The centre of Bangkok gave the impression of a prosperous war supply town.

Danger Zone: Middle East

After our first visit to the capital of Thailand in 1958, we returned to Europe via Cairo. The Suez crisis had just passed. The British and the French, as a result of their indecisive behaviour, had thrown away a great deal of prestige and under combined pressure from the Americans and the Russians had had to accept a painful retreat from their militarily and psychologically ill-prepared adventure. Eden's cabinet had resigned and the career of one of the most famous British diplomats had come to a sudden end. Discussions over western aid for the construction of the Aswan Dam had been broken off by the atmosphere of the Cold War. Later, Aswan, thanks to Soviet support, became a communist symbol throughout the Arab world.

Nasser, the then Egyptian President, was still trying to maintain good relations with both east and west through a clever game of setting one against the other. The distinct pro-Soviet course of the later years was hardly noticeable in 1958. In the beginning, purely national aspirations were involved. Egypt was also still prepared to accept American and western support where it was needed. But there was ferment among the Arab nationalists and minorities. Our Egyptian partners, who belonged to the Christian minority in the country, had to leave their homes.

In spite of increasing political and economic uncertainty, we decided to spend 6 to 7 million DM on the construction of a pharmaceutical factory. It became a showpiece. Nasser's government granted us a majority interest even before the construction work had begun. During the official inauguration, which took place in 1960 in the presence of many official guests, Nasser's deputy promised that our majority interest and the resulting rights would never be interfered with. This promise has been kept to the present day. The operation of the plant on the other hand is extraordinarily difficult because there simply isn't enough foreign currency to import the required starting products.

Egypt has always been an interesting partner for Hoechst. Our exports to this country were, however, quickly reduced in succeeding years. The trade in fertilizers, in particular, shrank because Egypt erected more and more factories of its own. Messrs Uhde, however, played a considerable part in the erection of these plants. Many negotiations took place for further projects of cooperation, but up to now, no larger projects have been realized. In 1966, when we undertook a journey from Cairo through the Arab states of the eastern Mediterranean, diplomatic relations between these countries and the Federal Republic had already been broken off. Nevertheless, there was still a great deal of goodwill for the Germans in Egypt, Jordan, Kuwait, the Lebanon and Syria. We noticed, however, that the approaching Middle East conflict, with all its tensions, made fruitful cooperation increasingly difficult.

From this Middle East trip, I shall always remember with some sadness the imposing sight of the Aswan Dam and the cultural monuments of the past from both the Egyptian and the Roman world which at the same time encompass the history of Christianity and its beginnings in Jerusalem.

Focus on the Third World

As the international exchange of ideas developed again after the consequences of the war had been overcome, and as the contacts became closer thanks to modern means of communication and transport, the existing differences in the standard of living and industrial development between the various countries became more pronounced. Two world wars and their consequences had meant that the nations involved had had to concentrate their entire resources on their own requirements, an effort that greatly sapped their energies. Wide areas of the world such as Latin America, a large part of Africa, India and even Far Eastern countries were, it is true, spared the actual war but they did suffer by being cut off from the industrial supply sources, by no longer having any adequate markets for their raw materials.

The division between a western and an eastern power bloc left a third world which was exposed to this dangerous field of tension and which, after the disappearance of the colonial empires, was faced above all by the problem of how to cope with the independence that they had so greatly desired. The young nations that had just achieved their freedom first had to create their state organization and administration and then build up a viable economy. It was difficult for them to meet these tasks from their own resources. It should have come as no surprise that, as a result of their lack of experience, they should have suffered failure in so many projects.

This third world, with its needs and claims, presented a more or less common front on the international scene and became a politically important factor, not through military might, but because of its enormous population. It was clear that if the justifiable desire of these masses of people to share in a tolerable standard of living was not fulfilled, world peace would be threatened sooner or later. The western countries, under the leadership of the U.S.A., recognized this quickly. Partly from political considerations, partly for economic expectations, but also from idealistic motives, they began to help these nations.

Fortunately, the concept of 'underdeveloped countries', then used to describe these nations in need of help, was soon replaced by the more appropriate term 'development countries'. But even this summary classification of all the peoples that lagged behind in their industrial development implied a certain degree of arrogance and somewhat of an over-simplification. A variety of regions were subjected to the same considerations without regard to their different history or, indeed, the different potential of their peoples.

For example, Latin America, which is culturally so close to Europe, had quite different requirements from the peoples of Africa and Asia who were striving for their independence.

We Germans were not inhibited by the odium of colonial arrogance. But we, too, had to understand that it was necessary to gather completely unprejudiced experience in relations with development countries. Of course, our basis for this was far smaller than that of the large powers or even that of many of our European neighbours.

An industrial company like Hoechst had to assess its interests soberly and evaluate its opportunities critically. Of course, as a chemical company we had much to offer, particularly because in these developing countries demand for our products was very great. Everywhere there was a shortage of pharmaceuticals, fertilizers, and many other chemical products.

But the development countries only had a limited amount of foreign currency available, and usually a negative balance of payments. This also limited the supply of industrial plants through Uhde even though the government of the Federal Republic granted a great deal of aid in the form of credit facilities, E.R.P. credits and economic guarantees. This state support was small, however, in comparison to that of other countries, for example the U.S.A. There, industry was supported through favourable depreciation allowances and state-backed guarantees for the political risks involved in business with development countries. A classic example of this is the system of 'American aid'. According to this, the American government makes public money available to nations that need help on condition that they undertake to buy with this money machinery and plant exclusively from the U.S.A.

The Federal Republic was not able to come to a similar decision probably because it feared that it would be accused of ulterior material ambitions. We Germans are always anxious to be regarded as idealists. As a result, the German economy missed a great many opportunities. It had to forgo participation in projects that had been financed with the money of the German taxpayer.

It was therefore both courageous and expensive for the young Hoechst company to become gradually active in all parts of the world. Large funds had to be spent in order to create the necessary sales organizations in the various countries. Often, many years passed before the costs that arose as a result had been balanced by the profits made. Also, we had to undertake repeated depreciations particularly in respect of the production plants.

We examined these costs each year to decide whether they were economically tolerable. So far, we have not suffered total loss in a single case, either through political or economic intervention. On the whole, it can be said that the organization of such an international business was absolutely necessary from the beginning. This was the only way in which the great central research departments, the commercial department, the applications department, and the engineering department, could remain financially viable propositions.

Of course, we could not avoid mistakes. After all we had to start afresh in each country, taking into account the characteristics of that country and paying regard to the historical peculiarities and also to the particular mentality of the people. Also, the chemical industry requires rather more requisites for its establishment than other industries. One of these, for example, is a high degree of technical development in the country concerned, and the existence of processing industries. In the European industrial countries, too, chemistry could expand only when this fundamental condition, for example a highly developed machinery industry, had been fulfilled. Moreover, the chemical industry requires highly qualified craftsmen. These were simply not available in some countries and had to be trained in an extensive programme. However similar the problems in many countries may be, they are never exactly identical and they always require individual answers. I saw this during my many trips as chairman of the board. I gained my strongest impressions perhaps in the Indian sub-continent which, with its 500 million inhabitants, represents one of the most important factors in world politics.

Sacred Cows and Modern Factories

Even as part of the British Empire, India was a valuable market for the German chemical industry and its dyestuffs and pharmaceuticals. Therefore, many people from the sales organization of the former I. G. had worked in India. After the war, sometimes after prolonged internment in British camps, they had started once more to look after the German business interests in the country.

Nevertheless, we had no detailed knowledge of India. In 1960, therefore, we decided to get a comprehensive first-hand impression of the economic opportunities of India and of its political situation. We landed in Bombay in late autumn on a scheduled flight. From there we hired a small charter plane with which we travelled up and down the country. Our journey went from Bombay to Delhi, from Calcutta to Chittagong in East Pakistan. From Calcutta we made a detour to Darjeeling and Benares. Then we flew south via Rourkela, visited Madras and from there the Malabar coast by car. Finally we returned to Bombay via Cochin and Calicut where Vasco da Gama had first discovered the western coast of India in 1498. On the journey back we also stopped in Karachi, in West Pakistan.

We were facing great problems in India. Together with our domestic partners we had erected the first pharmaceutical agency in the vicinity of Bombay. We had also succeeded in establishing a modest sales organization for dyestuffs and chemicals and in acquiring an interest in a dyestuffs factory. This had been built by Farbenfabriken Bayer together with Indian partners in the vicinity of Bombay.

When India became independent in 1947, and when the last Viceroy, Lord Mountbatten, had left the country at the famous gate in Bombay, there was already a viable government, supported by a democratic parliamentary system. The legal system, universities and education had developed greatly under British influence and a new and self-confident upper class had become established. The birth of the Indian union had been accompanied by bloody internal conflicts. The Moslem part of the north Indian population had founded its own state, Pakistan, whose eastern and western parts were more than 2,000 kilometres apart, with no land connection. This resulted not only in tension between Pakistan with its 100 million inhabitants and India, but also in continuous sharp conflicts between West and East Pakistan which grew into a homogenous state only slowly. This situation was highlighted in 1971 by the unsuccessful attempt of East Pakistan to gain its freedom from West Pakistan, though it was to succeed a year later.

Question Time with Nehru

When we visited the country in 1960, Jawaharlal Nehru was firmly in control of India. His Congress Party had a large and stable majority in parliament. Its leaders were men who, with the aid of Gandhi's policy of non-violent opposition, had gained freedom for the country and thus possessed great authority.

We were able to participate in one of the question sessions in the wonderful Congress building in Delhi. Leaving aside external aspects, this question time differed little from similar institutions in European parliaments. Nehru spoke several times, either in elegant English or in Hindi which is to become the official language of the country, although it is understood as yet only by a small number of Indians.

Nehru was possessed by great political ambition. He saw himself as an international mediator, sometimes even a referee, between the great power blocs. No doubt he achieved much in this self-appointed role but it also meant that at times he had to neglect the incredibly difficult internal political situation of his own country.

I also met Nehru during his visit to Germany in 1960. At that time, he presented himself as the self-confident representative of the non-aligned world. He looked at Germany through British rather than continental European eyes. He was not a friend of the E.E.C. because he feared that with the aid of the E.E.C., French colonial rule in Africa, at least in part, might be perpetuated.

Nehru's policy of peace and non-violence frequently suffered from almost tragic contradiction. In 1961, shortly after our stay in India, armed Indian units, without warning, simply occupied the small Portuguese colony of Goa. The bloody events that accompanied the separation of West and East Pakistan from India had not yet been forgotten. India, too, had to learn that it was not immune from frontier conflicts and violence.

At the Foot of the Himalayas

When we travelled from Darjeeling, the former holiday resort of the British administration, to the Tiger Hills early in the morning, we met many Tibetan refugees. They stood motionless in the lonely landscape and looked quietly and longingly towards the giant mountains of the Himalayas through which a pass led into their lost homeland. The frontier problem with China has not really been solved by the barrier of the almost insuperable mountain range. We saw a similar picture later on when we met Tibetans in Katmandu in Nepal, again refugees from their home.

The ruling class in India is British by training, sympathetic and educated. Conservative, orthodox Indians exist side by side with open-minded, well-informed, lively and modern people. Many of them demonstrate a kind of self-confidence that does not always facilitate collaboration with European and western peoples. The administrative apparatus is extensive and bureaucratic. India, which has yet to collect its experience in this field, will not be able to manage for the time being without a controlled economy and an appropriate administrative apparatus.

We were received cordially by the Indians who were very interested in cooperation with us. The support of the Indian government was highly satisfactory. At their invitation, a young German professor took us on a guided tour of the university and the temple of Benares, the important holy place. None of us were able to escape the deep impression made by the profound religiousness and philosophy of the Indians.

Indian attitudes to the Germans differ a great deal. They have a high regard for our scientific and industrial successes. They are particularly impressed by the fact that it was German scientists who revealed Sanskrit to them and thus re-created the foundation of an Indian historical consciousness.

When we were in Benares, we were able to see the places where the Indians burn their dead early in the morning and throw their ashes into the River Ganges. The mysticism of the Indian character, which had enthralled us as young people after the First World War in the poems of the Nobel prizewinner Rabindranath Tagore, is something that most people cannot escape. Nowhere else in the world does one begin to experience so acutely the original beginnings of history and culture.

Europeans have to re-think their ideas about India. They are faced by a culture that is only hesitantly opening out. The outsider has to learn to understand the breadth, and the difference in

character, of a country of 500 million people. The Indians themselves vary a great deal in respect of religion, custom, language and
mode of life. For example, the inhabitants of Madras may no longer
understand those on the western coast. And yet, in comparison to
the Europeans, they appear as an entity. We must learn to understand the patience and the tolerance of this people, its adherence to
holy traditions, from the still strongly pronounced caste systems to
the sacred cows. The Indian government and the reformers have to
guide their land very carefully into modern times if it is not to be
engulfed by anarchy before the goal is reached.

There is infinite poverty next door to great wealth. Religious
fatalism and rigid habits often mitigate against modern hygiene.
That this does not lead regularly to vast epidemics is a phenomenon
that merely confirms many Indians in their religiousness. On the
other hand, government and provincial authorities pay great
attention to medicine and hygiene. Medical science is actively
promoted and highly respected.

A visit to a large hospital in Madras made a deep impression
upon us. The hospital had some 1,700 beds but was greatly overcrowded. Some 300 patients had been placed on the stone floor,
though under perfectly clean conditions. Apparently this did not
affect the patients, most of whom appeared to have been used to
sleeping on the floor at home. The chief surgeon, an Indian of
course, and British trained, was an excellent medical man. We spent
more than two hours walking with him through the corridors and
wards. The patients, some of them seriously ill, looked upon him
not only as a helper but almost as a holy man.

Every morning, some 4,000 people arrived for out-patient treatment. From amongst this mass of people, those most seriously ill and
urgently needing hospitalization had to be selected. Civilized treatment of 4,000 patients in a single room is extraordinarily difficult.
For people with an income of approximately 100 rupees a year,
corresponding to approximately 70 marks, treatment has to be free
of charge. Nevertheless, the most modern pharmaceutical preparations are used. Even in a primitive chemist shop in the north
high up in the foothills of the Himalayas we discovered the most
recent Hoechst preparations.

In India, where the contrast between yesterday and today is still
very strong, it was not possible ten years ago to operate industrial

undertakings on European principles. This is something we learned very quickly. On the initiative of Farbenfabriken Bayer, a bold project had been worked out. Its purpose was to create a universal plant for the production of the most important organic aromatic hydrocarbons in order to provide the entire Indian chemical industry with a broad basis.

Ulrich Haberland, who had visited the country two years before me, had developed this idea in Leverkusen. He hoped that with the erection of such a central plant for basic chemicals, most problems of the chemical industry in India could be solved at a stroke. When he told us about his plan at Hoechst, we were very enthusiastic. We, too, saw in this project the possibility of providing the country with a basis for the production of dyestuffs, pharmaceuticals and agro-chemicals. Bayer, Hoechst and BASF were also prepared to make available, free of charge, the entire technical know-how and planning required. Naturally, we expected that this, to be financed from public funds, and its products would also benefit our plans in India.

Unfortunately, the plan was never realized. It failed not because of finance, but because of timing: it was simply premature for the India of that time. Such a plant, with its complicated chemical processes and the interlinking of by- and end-products, was a copy of the factories that had been erected in Germany during the reconstruction phase after the war. The project represented the result of experience extending over many decades which had not yet been gained by the young chemical industry of India. We therefore became involved in tiresome discussions with Indian technicians who did not want to accept this knowledge without criticism. Perhaps the gradually awakening desire for independent initiative also played a part in this.

After some years, and with the agreement of the Indian government, we shelved the plan without too much upset or disappointment. It had been well meant but it did not conform to the local situation.

An example of the difficulties of engaging in industrial activity in India during the fifties occurred during my inspection of the Rourkela steelworks. As a member of the supervisory board of Demag, I was familiar with this project and had therefore expressed the wish to visit Rourkela. Erected by a consortium of German companies under the sponsorship of Demag, it was the most modern works of its kind in the whole world. It had been handed over to the Indian government only a year previously. An important phase in India's quest to become a modern industrial country appeared to have begun.

But the plant had to be stopped after only a short period of operation. It was said that technical mistakes had been made during construction, and that the plant did not function properly. There was a great deal of anger and vigorous and unjust criticisms were levelled, even in the German papers. I was therefore very anxious to learn something about this failure at Rourkela.

When we arrived, the crisis was practically over. The fault by no means lay in the technical failure of the German engineers. The consortium of German companies had not taken sufficient measures to ensure that it would have adequate control over starting up the works and selecting suitably trained personnel. Instead, the fully automatic and highly modern steel works had been given to the Indians too soon, and before an adequately trained crew was available.

The Indians accepted the new works with pride, but also with understandable over-estimation of their technical resources. The unavoidable technical difficulties resulted in political controversies which appeared to jeopardize much of the industrial prestige that Germany enjoyed in India. Fortunately, these controversies could be resolved. Gradually, the Rourkela steel works began to operate, and they were even enlarged. When Federal President Heinrich Lübke visited India, he also went to Rourkela. Today the steel plant there is a showpiece of German engineering skill in Asia.

At the Edge of Bombay

Quite independent of this joint project with Bayer and BASF, we also thought in Hoechst about setting up an Indian plant of our own in the field of plastics. We were in close contact with the industrial family of Mafatlal. This is one of the large Indian industrial families who until that time had been engaged mainly in the textile field. We were received by the Mafatlal family in Bombay in an almost royal palace. Four branches of the family lived there, three brothers and a nephew under the patronage, or, more accurately, the matriarchy, of the mother. The father had died some years previously. The family, with its many children and large number of personnel lived in a style that, in Europe, would be thinkable only in royal courts.

We arrived at an acceptable form of cooperation with this family although it required a great deal of understanding on both sides. An important project was involved. It was our intention to build up an ethylene industry, on the basis of ethylene, or even ethyl alcohol, of the type that we were operating in Hoechst. We proposed to make a whole range of products right down to polyethylene. Because the project was going to cost several 100 million marks, we required powerful partners in India, particularly in the field of finance. In any case, foreign companies in India are not allowed to have more than a comparatively small holding in a new company.

The project also soon proved to be too comprehensive. It took a long time to reduce it to its proper scale and resolve it into several individual projects. It was, therefore, not until 1968, eight years later, that we were able to inaugurate a Hostalen factory in the vicinity of Bombay with an initial capacity of almost 24,000 tons of polyethylene a year. For this event, we had invited more than a hundred journalists from most of the European countries. The purpose of this was to ensure broad reportage about Hoechst in newspapers and journals throughout the world, but also to inform the German public about India through first-hand observation. At the same time, we intended to encourage German industrial initiatives.

A modern factory had been erected in the suburbs of Bombay. The inauguration took place according to Indian ritual and at a time determined by astrologers, using all the festive paraphernalia and colour that India offers on such occasions. The factory has developed well in spite of the fact that in the absence of suitable processing facilities and appropriate consumer habits, the introduction of a new plastic takes a certain amount of time.

I had not seen the Hoechst companies in India for some eight years, but in the meantime, our greatly extended pharmaceutical factory in Mulund near Bombay had become a real showpiece. It produces a large part of the pharmaceutical range of Farbwerke Hoechst, based on imported raw materials. The requirements on the quality and reliability of our pharmaceuticals are controlled as strictly as in Germany. Since 1971, the company also has its own

Trevira High Tenacity Tri-Sail, based on a Frei Otto design, in the grounds of the Bishop's Palace at Wells, Somerset, on the occasion of the R.I.B.A. congress in the autumn of 1971

Hoechst House at Hounslow, the headquarters of Hoechst UK Ltd

research laboratory which is intended to devote itself particularly to the testing of plant alkaloids and the study of indigenous diseases.

The training workshop in Mulund was particularly impressive. The manager of the factory had recognized at an early date that he would always need many dexterous craftsmen. Fortunately, the Indians are in any case gifted manually and technically. As a result, a large trainee and engineering workshop was set up. This is capable of producing all the complicated pharmaceutical packaging machinery. The workshop is also most important for the further technical development of the Mulund plant.

From Bombay we continued our flight to Delhi in order to conduct talks with the government. Together with Mr Mafatlal, we were able to visit the revered State President, Zakir Husain. In the precious palace of the former Viceroy, I met the distinguished old gentleman who had studied philosophy in Heidelberg and Berlin and who talked with enthusiasm of Germany whose problems interested him greatly. Unfortunately, Husain was already very ill at that time, and he died six months after our conversation. Germany lost a true friend in him.

India, a sub-continent of contrasts, thirteen times as large as the Federal Republic of Germany, will have to wrestle for a long time with its problems, particularly poverty and the population explosion. There has been no decisive change in the situation since 1968. The once strong Congress Party, led with authority, seemed temporarily to fall apart. Nobody is yet able to foretell whether the internal and external threats will be competently mastered. For Hoechst, India with its vast requirements for goods of all types, has in the meantime become a most important business partner.

African Exploration

Commercial opportunities in Africa only opened up late, after the end of the Second World War. The continent, consisting of many former colonial areas, suffered a series of crises, which have not yet passed, when the colonial powers, at varying times and under different conditions, abandoned their rule.

Many of these crises arose because in Africa the frontiers of the now autonomous states had originally been determined at random by the colonizing Europeans. The continent does not have a common anthropological or ethnological history. The frontiers drawn from

C.Y.—24

the coast to the deep interior of the country as though by a ruler resulted in artificially created administrative areas encompassing great tribal and language differences. It is these differences that today present so many problems in the now independent African countries and that are probably the main reasons for the continuous unrest.

The various colonial powers had ruled their territories in different ways and their withdrawal was similarly different. It looks to me as though the French were the best at preparing their colonies for self-administration. During his historical African trip of 1958, General de Gaulle left these countries to decide whether they wanted to continue to collaborate with France after independence, or not.

The French then acted decisively and with severity. Where the answer to the question was 'No', as for example in Guinea, France rejected any kind of aid and retired from the administration so suddenly that its action had serious consequences for the country. The former French colonies that decided to collaborate within the framework of the 'Communauté', later also joined the E.E.C. through an associate membership agreement.

The training of the natives and the evolution of a managerial class also progressed differently in the various countries. In the French colonies there was already an elite of African officials, doctors, and judges, who had mainly visited French universities and who could now take over the government.

In the former Belgian Congo, however, and in the former British colonies, the conditions were, and still are, less clear. It will, therefore, be a long time yet before Africa is at peace. Moreover, the internal tensions are continuously being influenced by outside factors. This is especially true in the case of the Soviet Union and Red China, although the west also intervenes from time to time.

When we undertook our first journey to Africa in 1964, our branches in the various countries were still fairly weak. In many places, we were represented simply by independent African businessmen or by Europeans domiciled in Africa. The purpose of the trip was to find out whether there was a case for more intensive involvement.

The sole exception was South Africa, where we had been active for some time and which I visited only at a later date. In this country, as a result of British initiative, economic life had been greatly developed during the period of South Africa's membership of the Commonwealth. With its various rich ore deposits, particularly platinum, silver, gold, chromium and uranium, South Africa has long since been a centre of international interest. The economic boom is continuing, though the South African policy of racial segregation has opened up a deep schism.

The destination of our extensive charter flight of 1964 was Black Africa. With the exception of Libya, we did not visit the African Mediterranean coast embracing Morocco, Algeria, Tunisia and Egypt. On this trip, I visited almost all the important places on this continent, beginning in Dakar and West Africa and making a number of excursions into the interior of the continent. The climax of the Congo crisis appeared to have passed at that time. Léopoldville, however, still presented a very sad picture in spite of much European building and equipment. The Hoechst business was transacted through our agency in Brussels and for a long time not very much was happening. In the meantime, however, the situation has improved significantly.

We were able to visit many rulers of the young African states including Léopold Sédar Senghor in Senegal, who in 1968 was awarded the Peace prize of the German Book Trade in the Frankfurt Paulskirche. I talked with Sekou Touré in Guinea who had been to Hoechst once and also with President Félix Houphouet-Boigny of the Ivory Coast. They were all proud, highly active intellectual personalities, who had been educated in European schools and who remembered colonial rule with mixed feelings. Attitudes to Europe and the white people as such ranged from pronounced gratitude to deep hatred. So far as Germany was concerned, the mood was generally friendly. Memories of German colonial rule, going back to before the First World War, were too remote to be significant. In any case, what was remembered was usually favourable because Prussian thoroughness promoted agriculture so successfully that the well-equipped and well-organized plantations are in part still flourishing today.

For Hoechst, the commercial opportunities in Africa were slight. There were modest dyestuffs sales. The bright naphthol dyestuffs, which I still knew from my time in the dyestuffs division, were particularly popular. Other opportunities were offered by pharmaceuticals, preparations for veterinary medicine and finally agro-chemicals. We realized that we would have to establish an experimental farm as the only way of testing our fertilizers, plant protection agents, pesticides, and feed additives under the different vegetation conditions of Africa. The experimental farm, however, could not be realized until 1969.

In 1964, central Africa offered few opportunities for large-scale production. There were small manufacturing plants only in the ports and along the coast. The population grew phenomenally but the gross national product increased only slowly.

I still remember the visit of the very friendly President of Togo, Sylvanus Olympio, who was assassinated in 1963. He had been educated in a German missionary school and thought highly of Germany. He greatly admired an injection moulding machine in our applications department at Hoechst which produced innumerable plastic beakers in seconds. We presented him with this machine. The Minister-President of Hesse, Georg August Zinn, who was present during Olympio's visit, donated a diesel engine to drive the machine. It needed a great deal of effort to get the small, but first production of plastic articles going in Togo. In the end, it was regarded as a small miracle of modern technology.

Serious and visible contrasts between black and white actually exist only in South Africa. In the other countries of the African continent, with only a few exceptions, the reservations against the whites seem to be disappearing. There are very few Americans and the natives like working with Europeans. There is a great antipathy to the immigrant Chinese and Indians on the eastern coast of Africa.

The most southern point of our journey was Madagascar. Its population, and its flora and fauna are actually not African at all. From across the Indian Ocean, a strong Malayan influence has swept the country. Madagascar is wealthy, agriculturally fertile, and very much concerned with progressive economic development. A visit to the botanical gardens in the capital Tananarivo is as worthwhile as a visit to the botanical gardens in Melbourne, Australia. Both exhibit a plant world that cannot be seen anywhere else in the world.

The return flight passed along the African eastern coast. We stopped at Kenya where we had an opportunity of visiting a few animal reserves. Then we went on to Addis Ababa and via Khartoum to Libya, the final stop of our trip.

Many years have passed since this visit, and Hoechst has been able to consolidate its position in most of these countries. Numerous pharmaceutical filling, finishing and packaging plants have been erected. The chemical business, too, has achieved certain initial successes. In 1970, Africa accounted for 3 per cent of Hoechst's world sales. Although development is proceeding slowly, no one doubts the great opportunities for future industrialization in Africa. In particular, there is a great opportunity for helping in the production of mineral raw materials.

Hostalen in Four Continents

When in 1963, during our centenary festival, we drew up the balance sheet of our foreign manufacturing plants, we had reached a turning point. To support the greatly expanding sales organization, a number of production units had been set up. By 1970, we had built some thirty-three plants for Hoechst pharmaceuticals in twenty-eight countries. These plants and our exports accounted for 70 per cent of our pharmaceutical world sales in 1970.

At the same time, we started to establish a world-wide network of polymerization plants for Mowilith. These plastic dispersions were one of the preconditions for our later activities in the field of paint raw materials and paints. By 1970, we had twenty-four plants for Mowilith with a total capacity of 150,000 tons a year. A number of larger and smaller plants for the production of coal tar dyestuffs and textile auxiliaries were also either in operation or under construction. Finally, our subsidiary Kalle had become most active in its traditional Ozalid field, extending its operation to many foreign countries. All these production plants, however, were originally no more than processing plants. They did not represent a chemical industry in our sense.

This only happened when new developments at Hoechst progressed to such an extent that we could also present them abroad. Our salesmen had started as early as possible to offer these new products outside the German frontiers. An outstanding example was Hoechst's high density polyethylene 'Hostalen' which was marketed at a very early stage. In this way, we acquired important markets which we could only retain if we began to manufacture in the country itself. That was one of the most important tasks during the sixties.

A prerequisite for Hostalen manufacture was an adequate petro-chemical industry near the manufacturing site from which the required ethylene could be obtained. We ourselves were not able to undertake the erection of refinery or cracking plants because our investment funds were inadequate for this purpose.

One of the first sites that appeared suitable for a Hostalen plant was Australia. In the face of strong competition from the Japanese and, of course, the British, we had been able to establish a market there at a very early date. The large, sparsely populated continent offered innumerable applications for pipelines from plastics. Imported material soon proved inadequate. We had to manu-facture in the country itself but this was not without risk in view of the superior influence of the British industry. I had visited Australia and New Zealand in 1962 in order to get an idea of the opportunities available there for Hoechst products. In Australia, there is a great contrast between the sparsely populated interior, where large tracts of land are uninhabitable, and the modern, highly developed cities on the coast like Sydney and Melbourne. We were greatly interested also in sheep breeding and the market it offered for our veterinary products. During a visit to a sheep farm in the Snowy Mountains near Canberra, I calculated that the highly rationalized sheep farming system there achieved the same sales per head of employee as our Trevira plant in Bobingen. This came as a very great surprise to me.

A similar impression of the competitiveness of the natural raw materials was gained during a subsequent visit to Malaysia and its capital Kuala Lumpur. In the vicinity of the capital, we were able to make comparisons between the rubber plantations and our new Buna production. In New Zealand, we looked towards Antarctica, the only continent I have not visited, standing on the site from which the American, Admiral Richard Evelyn Byrd, started on his flight across the South Pole in 1929.

As a result of our flight to Australia, we selected a piece of land in Melbourne on which we intended to build a universal chemical factory. First of all, we constructed a dyestuffs plant, then a Mowilith plant, and finally a pharmaceutical finishing and packaging plant. In 1967, a Hostalen plant was added which, by the middle of 1972, will have a capacity of 46,000 tons a year. In 1964, we had a joint agency in Australia with the other successor companies of the I. G.

Farbenindustrie and at that time this was sufficient for the conditions in Australia. Today, however, we have our own organization with approximately 500 commercial, scientific and technically qualified people.

The next opportunity for a Hostalen factory arose in India as soon as an ethylene supplier became available near Bombay. A third plant has been erected recently in South Africa, near Sasolburg and it will go on stream in 1972.

In all these countries, we had to take great care that the plants had the right capacities. At the beginning, the markets were always small. For operating reasons, however, the plants had to be far larger than the market initially required. This was also necessary in order to allow for exports at a later date, something that was promoted increasingly by the respective governments. On the other hand, we always had to be in a position to withstand the competition of imports from third countries.

Trevira – A World Name

The other great field in which we had to unfold an international activity was our polyester fibre, Trevira. All the polyester producers of the world, particularly those in the United States and Europe, were licensees of I.C.I. Production and selling were geographically limited in the first years by the patent situation and licence agreements. All the producers therefore awaited the expiry of the patents in order to operate outside the regions to which they had hitherto been confined.

During the years 1963 to 1968, the moment came. The patents expired at long last although the date of expiry in the various countries differed considerably. We had to expect competition from the other large companies, not only overseas but also in Europe and especially in Germany itself. It was, therefore, important for Hoechst to prepare the various markets as soon as possible and to find the most suitable sites for polyester manufacture.

The first such plant was set up in Lenzing in Austria as a joint undertaking with a spun rayon factory there. Two further plants were built soon afterwards in Chile and South Africa. These first polyester factories abroad were comparatively small and were supplied with primary products and polymers from our German plants in Offenbach and Gersthofen. In the last few years, we have erected a larger plant in Northern Ireland, where the government offered us special terms.

The most important and significant decision, however, had to be made in the United States. The U.S.A. was one of the largest users of textiles including synthetic fibres. We could not ignore this important market.

It quickly became known that, apart from I.C.I., all the powerful fibre producers of the United States, particularly Du Pont, intended to set up manufacturing plants in the Federal Republic. Du Pont placed its plant near Unna in Westphalia. I.C.I. erected a production unit in Östringen near Bruchsal. It therefore became imperative that we, too, should look out for a base in America. In view of the great financial resources of our American competitors, we had to avoid at all cost a situation in which – as I once said at a press conference – we would sell in India and Africa while the Americans supplied the European market and our own.

The jump into the American lion's den, as I once called it, was a risky undertaking. The plant had to be large enough to secure a worthwhile share of the polyester sales in the huge American domestic market. To achieve this, ignoring the supply of starting products for the moment, investments of more than 100 million dollars were necessary. Moreover, a sales organization had to be set up that could spread the name of Trevira throughout the U.S.A.

While in Europe you usually deal with a few hundred textile customers, in the United States the textile industry consists of only a few vast concerns which, measured by European standards, process huge amounts of materials. These large customers are extremely demanding, insisting on almost unlimited supply capacities. However, we felt we could only slowly introduce Trevira, a new and foreign product.

We decided to realize the project in partnership with an American company. Hercules, the chemical complex in Wilmington, Delaware, seemed to be the most suitable. We already enjoyed excellent cooperation with Hercules in the field of low pressure polyethylene. One of the greatest attractions about Hercules was that it was the largest producer of dimethylterephthalate, the polyester starting product, and declared itself ready to incorporate its modern DMT plant into the new company.

The first negotiations were carried out during an American trip in 1965. The final decision was by no means easy because we were talking about an engagement on a scale that was quite new to us as far as foreign projects were concerned.

During my stay in the U.S.A., incidentally, I was lucky enough to go to Cape Kennedy, with my companions and my two grown-up sons, to watch a Gemini launching. We also took time off to pay a subsequent visit to NASA in Huntsville, Alabama. Wernher von Braun and his colleagues gave us detailed information about the Apollo programme. We saw the huge rockets at close proximity with their 200 metre high platform and even entered a prototype model of the later lunar landing craft.

It was very impressive to meet so many German scientists. They had come to Huntsville after the war and had later brought over many of their young colleagues. It is regrettable that these capable physicists and engineers can find interesting jobs in the space industry only in the U.S.A. because in Europe it has not been possible to develop a joint space programme of significance. This is another example of the unfortunate lack of European integration.

After our visit to NASA, each of us followed the first moon flight of the Americans in 1969 with particular interest.

Setting the Points in the U.S.A.

The Trevira factory was erected in Spartanburg in South Carolina, the heart of the American textile industry. It was ceremoniously opened in 1968. On this occasion, Hoechst held its first press conference in America in the New York Plaza Hotel. Until then we had had a certain aversion to press conferences in the U.S.A. because we knew that American journalists were in the habit of asking very pointed and at times awkward questions. This, of course, also happens in Germany but the long and continuous contact with reporters in the Federal Republic has created a mutual confidence that was as yet absent in New York.

We found, however, that it was possible to have fruitful discussions with American journalists, too. Since then we have met the press once a year and have conducted numerous interesting conversations with these journalists during small press receptions and interviews.

These years saw many other important decisions in the United States. We founded a film factory in Delaware together with Stauffer Chemicals in order to utilize the experience of Kalle and Gendorf.

As a result of all this, when we inaugurated our new administrative complex in Bridgewater, New Jersey, in 1970, a comprehensive and promising business had been set up in the United States.

Since the economic position in the States had in the meantime become more difficult, and since the starting-up costs of the new plants were greater than we and our partners had originally calculated, we came to a friendly agreement both with Hercules and with Stauffer. Hoechst acquired their interest in the joint undertakings and became the sole owner. It was found in these negotiations that in spite of every readiness to cooperate, American and German partners follow different business principles in a joint project.

These decisions during the last two years extended our foreign engagements to such a degree that business abroad grew at a quicker rate than at home. These investments also tied up large funds and involved us in very high starting costs. It will take a long time yet before all these undertakings are self-supporting and can develop from their own resources. It was, however, the only way of securing Hoechst's competitive position abroad in rapidly growing world chemistry.

The domestic organization with its research and administration and the extensive sales apparatus can be supported only if it is based in Europe on adequate and rational operating plants from which it can profitably export. On the other hand, such exports must be secured by a world-wide multi-national potential which, in the countries concerned, is closely linked to the economy of those countries through substantial production units.

Encounter with the East

Our international activities and their growing success could not hide the fact that the world in which we live today has become far smaller than before the Second World War. At that period, and even more so before the turn of the century, the German chemical industry had good relations in areas now not readily accessible to us, particularly Russia, China and the countries of the former Austrian-Hungarian monarchy. Even before 1900 there was a Hoechst dyestuffs factory in Moscow.

Today, the frontiers run right across Germany, not only in the political field but also in the scientific and economic area. The most modern chemical plants of the former I. G. Farbenindustrie were located in what is now the German Democratic Republic. The Buna factory in Schkopau and the huge Leunawerk near Halle; the modern plants for light metals in Bitterfeld; the artificial silk factory and the dyestuffs plant in Wolfen, were amongst the most efficient plants in the world, and during the period of re-armament and the war they had swallowed the major part of the I. G. investments. Their value at the end of the war was far higher than that of the largely antiquated works available in the west.

I paid my last visit to the I. G. plants in central Germany in February 1945. Since then, I have had hardly any contact with these former I. G. works especially since their leading chemists all chose to go to the west. At one time, colleagues from the G.D.R. still attended our scientific meetings but then even those visits became less and less frequent.

Nevertheless, we did not regard this as an obstacle to starting an exchange of goods with the D.D.R. As a result of meetings at the Leipzig Fair, personal contacts between people of Hoechst and East German colleagues were formed. They were, however, mainly confined to the sales organization or to Uhde and its design engineering offices. Twenty-five years of separation had left their mark, particularly since the two German chemical industries developed along such different political tracks.

Surprisingly, contact with almost all the other countries of the eastern bloc, in so far as it concerns technicians and scientists, was far more extensive than that with the D.D.R. For all of us, relationships in these countries in the scientific and technical fields were the most interesting and the easiest to establish, apart from commercial transactions. My activities in the field of chemical technology and my collaboration in Dechema and the meetings of Achema, provided the starting points for these contacts. An important mediator role was also played by Uhde.

In 1964, I had an opportunity to visit Warsaw. In 1965 I was in Bucharest, 1966 in Budapest, and 1967 in Prague. All these trips became memorable events. After detailed and thorough preparation by our sales people and the Bonn authorities, these visits proved to be very stimulating. I was usually asked to give a lecture on such occasions, which I gladly did, as I also did during my trips in the west. The subject of the lecture was usually the most recent technical developments in chemistry. There was always something new to report, particularly since many eastern colleagues had only a few connections with the western world and publications from the west were not readily accessible to them.

These lectures gave me a great deal of pleasure, even during the preparatory stage, and they provided many a starting point for protracted discussions. The reception I had from the government, colleagues, and the public, in so far as one had contact with it, was always extremely cordial, and resulted in non-political but enjoyable and lasting personal relationships.

During these visits I quickly realized once more that I was in European capitals with which we were linked through century-old cultural bonds. I had never seen these cities before and could not therefore judge properly the extent to which they had changed. It is, however, noticeable that the east European countries have preserved many of their own characteristics and have all reacted quite differently to the communism to which they are all subjected. It is consoling to note that the differences in people can limit even levelling ideologies.

In Warsaw in 1964, the effects of the war and of the misery that it had brought to Poland could still be seen and felt everywhere. The old city of Warsaw, rebuilt with the help of generous donations from all over the world, still presented a slightly artificial appearance. The streets had been straightened and enlarged and for this purpose a famous church had been hydraulically moved sidewards and turned around. For the remainder, however, the frontages had been authentically reconstructed as they looked before the war, using contemporary pictures of Canaletto, the Merian of Poland, as reference.

Early in the morning, the population crowded into the churches which still wield considerable influence. Foreign newspapers could be bought on the kiosks. Many of the treasures from old art collections, which had survived the war, had been brought together in the royal castle at Wilamowitz on the outskirts of Warsaw. The paintings exhibited there provided proof of the stormy history of Poland which is characterized particularly by its conflicts with Russia.

The main subject for discussion in Warsaw, as in all the other countries of the eastern bloc, was the establishment of a national chemical industry and our possible participation in it. Poland had taken over modern chemical works in Upper Silesia which had formerly belonged to the German chemical industry. Also, a start had been made in Galizia by opening up a considerable deposit of elemental sulphur.

A year later, I visited Romania, a country which, because of its plentiful crude-oil deposits, has been able to secure for itself a certain amount of freedom of action within the eastern bloc and also a reasonable standard of living. Certainly, the standard of living in Romania, at least in the towns, was noticeably higher than in the neighbouring countries.

During our journey, we visited Brasov, the former Kronstadt, and Sibiu, the former Hermannstadt. In these towns, one can still see some of the former German Siebenbürgen people, whose numbers have been decimated as a result of war and subsequent emigration. Nevertheless, they have been able to maintain throughout the centuries much of their German protestant culture. The capital, Bucharest, retains the atmosphere of a generous, French-orientated metropolis. My lecture at the university was received with a great deal of interest. Next to the speaker's desk was the Romanian translation of the *Chemical Technology*, a touching gesture.

This visit led to extensive cooperation with Romanian industry. Unfortunately, however, trade has been impaired to this day by the foreign currency problems of the country. This is particularly important in the case of Romania because we are not able to buy much there that could help to restore the balance through an exchange of goods. At the end of 1970, there was a meeting in Bucharest between representatives of Hoechst and the Romanian chemical industry when a Trevira factory in Romania was started up. In 1971, the Romanian Minister for Chemistry, Mihail Florescu, visited the Federal Republic and Hoechst.

In 1966, I got to know Hungary. From Vienna, we travelled by car through the beautiful Burgenland to the Platten lake and, from there, to Budapest. There, in the evening, we enjoyed the wonderful view from the citadel of the town below, whose war and post-war wounds, visible during the day, are easily overlooked because of its tremendous charm. In meetings with the Hungarians, who are fully conscious of their special characteristics within the eastern bloc, we found great interest in modern chemical developments and cooperation with western chemical industry.

All relationships between these east European countries and the western world necessarily remain modest because the population has only inadequate opportunities of travelling to the west. Economically, the states of the eastern bloc are closely linked to the COMECON organization. The scale of the exchange of goods and experience within this community cannot, however, be compared with that within the western world. Everything points to Moscow, where all the important threads are gathered. But the road to the Kremlin is a long one and the possibilities of direct trade between the individual eastern bloc states without the participation of Moscow are limited. This also applies to the relationships between Hungary and the Balkan countries.

We appreciated the world-famous Hungarian hospitality, complete with gypsy music, specially provided for us one evening. In Budapest, too, our visit resulted in encouraging scientific and technical cooperation, which drew its strength from the roots of the former relationships and affinities between Hungary and Germany.

In September 1967, I undertook a further trip to Prague via Eger and Karlsbad. I had never seen the 'Golden City' before. History is encountered at every step here, and Prague provides strong evidence of the close connection with western and particularly German history. I know of hardly another place where these historical ties are so vividly reflected in such concrete terms. I remember above all a visit to the castle in Prague and a splendid demonstration of the ancient art of fencing using medieval weapons. The evening was spent in the historic Wallenstein Palace.

As yet, there was no indication of the internal political events that were about to happen and that were to make the world hold its breath. Wenceslaus Square, the old town hall, and the noble bridge across the Moldau offered a picture of solid tradition that pulsated with life. There was no longer any sign of antipathy to the Germans which we might well have experienced previously. In contrast to the other countries of the eastern bloc, Czechoslovakia had extended its contacts with the west through the exchange of scientific information and reciprocal participation at meetings. These were further strengthened through the influx of tourists.

In any case, industrial technology in Czechoslovakia had reached a high level even before the German invasion of 1939. This was maintained and even raised. I had participated at that time on a number of occasions in an exchange of technical experience which comprised I.C.I., the Belgian Solvay Group, I. G. Farbenindustrie and the Aussiger Verein. For us inorganic chemists, the name Aussig represents a wealth of valuable technical developments which started there.

Of course, there now existed in Czechoslovakia, too, a need to continue the former exchange of goods and experience. During my visit, interesting initial contacts were made. We are happy that it was possible to continue this cooperation even after the Soviet invasion.

I did not visit Belgrade until 1971, on the occasion of an international congress of chemical engineers where I had been asked to give a lecture.

Hoechst has excellent relations with Yugoslavia, which cannot, of course, be regarded as part of the eastern bloc proper. Here the future promises well. The extensive German tourist traffic to the Adriatic coast and the large number of excellent Yugoslav workers in Germany are contributory factors in the development of greater understanding between our two peoples.

The last of the eastern bloc states that I visited was the Soviet Union, where I went in May 1969 at the invitation of the Moscow Chemistry Ministry. Many German industrialists, and even colleagues from Hoechst had preceded me. We had maintained good relations with Russian chemistry for many years. I frequently met Russian chemists and engineers at the Achema in Frankfurt. In 1964, the chemical industry of the Soviet Union and Farbwerke Hoechst had exchanged delegations. The result of these contacts was the award of a large Russian contract to Uhde for the construction of several phosphorus furnaces in Tschimkent in the vicinity of Taschkent. At the time of my trip, Uhde had already completed part of this work. Many German engineers, chemists and foremen spent a great deal of time there.

Before I set out on my two weeks' journey, we asked the Ministry for the Chemical Industry in Moscow to provide us with as versatile a picture as possible of life in the Soviet Union, of its science and culture, quite apart from the actual field of chemistry itself. As a result, an unusually comprehensive programme was provided by the Russians and this was carried out with the aid of a charter plane.

The journey led from Moscow via Kiev and Tiflis to the Uhde site in Tschimkent, and from there, via Samarkand, back to Moscow, where final discussions were held. Finally, we travelled via Leningrad and Helsinki back to Germany. Before I set out, I had read a description by Alexander Dumas, the author of *The Count of Monte Cristo*, of his travels in Russia and the Caucasus in 1860. I quickly noticed that our Russian companions knew Dumas' description very well indeed. Of course, our trip was far more comfortable and rather less dangerous than the adventures of Dumas a hundred years before.

In Moscow, we visited the Kremlin and all the other famous sites. We saw some first-class ballet at the Bolshoi Theatre and in the huge new congress hall of the Kremlin. We also listened to an excellent concert given by the Leningrad Philharmonic Orchestra, which happened to be in Moscow at the time.

One trip was made to Dubna, the Russian nuclear research centre, where the nuclear physicists of the eastern bloc countries work closely together like their western colleagues in CERN in Geneva. We were also shown a modern cancer research centre with an adjacent clinic that had been erected in the vicinity of Moscow.

After a lecture at Moscow University on chemical technical problems, we proceeded to Kiev, where we were warmly received by Gennady Vilesov, the Minister of Ukrainian Chemical Industry. After my lecture I was subsequently entertained in the Ukrainian manner with a sumptuous meal and excellent drinks. In the evening, we attended 'Rigoletto' in the town's theatre, sung in Ukrainian.

Next morning, we were transported by hydrofoil to a chemical combine in Tschernigov. There we were received by the Minister of Chemistry who, incidentally, was very familiar with Germany and had visited Hoechst and spent quite some time in Schkopau at the end of the war. As I had been there when Schkopau was erected, we had a great deal to talk about.

On the way back to Kiev, the Minister arranged a great surprise. After a meal in Tscherkassy, we were given presents. In a short, serious speech, the Minister recalled that Tscherkassy had been the centre of one of the bloodiest and unhappiest battles of the Second World War. Then he presented us with a beautifully carved pipe with the request that it might serve as a symbol for a lasting peace.

During this trip to Russia, we had many opportunities for

intensive talks. There was never a wrong note, even when we came to speak of those important and still unsolved political problems between the Soviet Union and the Federal Republic which have achieved considerable topicality as a result of the German-Soviet agreement.

During the weekend in Tiflis, we gained a deep impression of the old cultures indigenous to this area of the Black Sea, and enjoyed the beauty of the foothills of the Caucasus. Subsequently, overwhelmed by the vastness of the country, we flew to Tschimkent which was near Taschkent, and therefore not far from the Chinese frontier. In the phosphorus factory there, we met colleagues from Uhde and Hoechst who for some years had been engaged in the erection of modern chemical plants together with the Russians. The large order, which related to one of the most difficult chemical processes, namely electrothermal production of phosphorus, was executed with absolute precision and in complete harmony.

In Samarkand, the capital of Mongolia, which in 1400, under the Grand Khan Tamburlaine had exercised a rule of terror right up to the frontiers of Europe, we found the unique oriental mosques alongside the evidence of modern Soviet pioneering work.

A year previously, and only a few hundred kilometres further south, on the other side of the Hindukush mountains, I had spent a few days in Kabul, the capital of Afghanistan. There I discovered the really picturesque Orient, and saw camel caravans which were travelling to Russia and over the Khyber Pass to West Pakistan. Kabul was an intricate melée of different cultures and ways of life.

This rewarding visit to Tschimkent provided us with an opportunity to discuss further possibilities of collaboration in Moscow.

The journey, prepared by the Russians with great care, had greatly deepened our understanding of the problems of this huge and powerful country. The sheer size of Russia makes special demands upon its economy. Distances, transport routes, the exchange of goods within Russia and with countries abroad, have to be looked at in a totally different light. On the other hand, the great wealth of raw materials of all kinds, and the tremendous need for consumer goods offer prospects that even in earlier decades had led to close economic relationships with Germany.

Such a powerful economic bloc is an interesting partner for a company like Hoechst. An exchange of goods, such as takes place between the western industrialized nations, is complicated because of payment problems, especially as the different economic systems, with their totally different type of planning, require a great deal of mutual understanding. At that time in Moscow we came to the conclusion that with goodwill on both sides there could be many further opportunities of cooperation, not only in the exchange of commodities but also in the technical and scientific sphere. The discussions that followed our visit have led to a welcome intensification of negotiations. The possibility, opened up in May 1971, that we might be able to inaugurate a branch in Moscow will no doubt greatly promote these aims.

After many discussions, we eventually took our leave of the Soviet Union in Leningrad, where we had an opportunity of inspecting many historic buildings and seeing the unique collections in the Winter Palace. We returned home to Germany via Helsinki. It was my last trip as chairman of the board of management of Farbwerke Hoechst. Shortly afterwards, I presented the annual report in this capacity to the annual general meeting on 3 June 1969. I then resigned from the chairmanship which I had held for more than seventeen years, since 1952.

11

The Generation Change

24 JANUARY 1969 was a Friday. As usual, I left my office on the third floor of our building at about six-thirty, and took the lift downstairs where my car was waiting for me at the entrance. It was a Friday evening like any other. At any rate that was what the young colleagues whom I met thought and they wished me the obligatory 'Have a nice weekend'. It was to become a weekend in which my feelings of satisfaction were to be mixed with a little sadness.

For the 24 January 1969 had not been a day like any other. The supervisory board and board of management of the company had taken an extraordinarily important decision. The succession of the Hoechst management had been agreed upon and a whole number of new appointments had been decided. Soon, a large part of the people who, with me, since 1952 had managed the affairs of the company, would be replaced by a younger generation. For me, too, my days as chairman of the board of management were numbered. In a little more than four months, I would resign my office.

The plans for a smooth transition had been set out on this 24 January. After the decisions had been taken, we did not hesitate to make them known to the public. On the following Monday, 27 January, we gave the press the names of six new members of the board of management who were to be appointed during the year. They were: Erhard Bouillon for social questions; Enrique Hartung and Willi Hoerkens for sales; Hubertus Müller von Blumencron for foreign production; Josef Max Nowotny for fibres; and Klaus Weissermel for science. It was unusual to nominate such a large number of new members to a board of management publicly, although some of them were not going to take up office for a year.

At the same time, we announced a fundamental reorganization of the company. Its quick growth in the last few years had caused it to burst through the organizational framework that we had given it in 1951.

The generation change had been prepared carefully for a long time. We knew that in 1968 and 1969, no less than six colleagues would reach the age limit of sixty-five, and, according to the rules of the company, that they would then have to leave the board of management.

Three board members had retired in the preceding years: in 1965 my deputy and works' manager Erich Bauer; in 1966 the head of the pharmaceutical division, Fritz Lindner; and also the financial chief, Robert Hegels. Lindner had been replaced by Wolfgang von Pölnitz, and Hegels by Hans Reintges.

This meant, of course, that within a space of four years, more than half of the board of management had been replaced. Fortunately, during this period, not one member of the board had been seriously ill, or had died. Nevertheless, the accumulation in the management of people of roughly equal age, who would retire about the same time, was presenting the company with important problems. Any generation change can have its dangers if it takes place too suddenly and too drastically.

Similar situations arise almost everywhere in public life. In Germany, the generation that just missed the First World War is particularly strong. On the other hand, the Second World War has torn great gaps in the succeeding generation. There is therefore a particular gap in manpower between the ages of fifty to sixty years.

These legacies of an unhappy past mean that suddenly people who have borne the brunt of successful reconstruction have to resign. Many uncertainties and tensions in our present situation and also the impossibility in many respects of properly solving this succession problem, are related to this age gap. There is a temptation to bridge the gap by allowing the older generation to stay on longer. However, and this is particularly noticeable in politics, this leads to over-ageing and to dissatisfaction amongst those who, now forty or fifty years old, are seeking greater responsibility. We should not make the mistake of letting them wait too long. They have the experience and they are, in every respect, able to take over leading positions.

They will also find it easier to make contact with youth which, throughout the world, is demanding new approaches, especially in the social field.

Indecision over the timing of transfers of power may result in attempts to solve the problem by postponing the retirement of those eligible for it. In such a large undertaking as ours, however, everyone has to be subject to the same regulations if we are not to be unjust and give rise to friction. For this reason, we were always agreed on the board that we would follow the rules of the house and that no board member, just as any employee, would remain on the active list when he celebrated his sixty-sixth birthday.

Because we had foreseen this for a long time, we had also made every effort to train young people and had thought continuously about the question of succession on the board of management. When the moment came, therefore, we had available a large number of suitable people and we hoped that we would be able to overcome the critical phase without any difficulty. We had also ensured that the management included some younger people who had been able to collect a few years of board experience. Such times of personnel change provide a company with opportunities for carrying out fundamental organizational changes.

If such reorganization goes hand in hand with the redistribution of responsibility, it always gives rise to unrest and can impair the initiative and the activities of a company. It is therefore best carried out by those people who are just about to retire from active management, since they have the necessary experience and the required authority to impose the changes without difficulty. They have, of course, to seek the advice of the new generation. For this reason we thought it necessary to know who these successors would be in good time before we made any changes in the old order.

Individual Decisions

The hire and fire system as it is still practised to some extent in the U.S., may promote mobility of people and may protect an organization against premature ageing. But these enforced changes also have disadvantages. I have demanded such intervention and approved it when demanded by others, only if the situation rendered such steps inevitable. Even then, it is essential that the dignity of the person and his material rights are maintained. There are no ideal solutions to all these questions or to the problems of human cooperation within an organization, although such solutions are today frequently proposed on a scientific or rather methodical basis. There are, in my view, only individual cases for which an individually correct decision has to be found.

We had had to concern ourselves with questions of management and the attendant organizational problems even during the difficult period of re-constitution. At Hoechst we probably had to do so more than any other company. The system upon which we agreed at that time proved its worth during seventeen years. Now, however, the time had come to adapt it to the requirements of a volume of business that had increased tenfold during that period. The problem was to find a reasonable compromise between continuity and essential modernization.

As early as 1952, we had learnt how difficult it is in such a traditional company as ours, which for a very long time had been denied its freedom of action, to advance beyond the confines of traditional fields and find new ones. A complex like Hoechst engenders considerable inertia. But this is not only a negative quality. Rather, it is based on the significant intellectual and material values present in a large company. The expensive research facilities and manufacturing plants alone represent a vast item in the balance sheet of a chemical company.

Particularly valuable, however, are the people who work in it. Research, production, sales and planning, and extensive investment, indeed company policy as such, can be realized only through these people.

But neither the highly qualified specialists nor the material assets can be moved around at will. The great inner reserves that they represent are assets that cannot be evaluated in terms of money. Their usefulness depends upon the extent to which they can be adapted to the continuously changing world and its requirements. All these potentials and values are always characterized by the original purpose for which they were once designed, that is to say, by the past. They cannot be modified indefinitely. What can be done with them in the future therefore varies for any company at any given time. It simply is not possible to keep changing direction or to apply a stop-go policy to such a situation.

At moments of great decisions, therefore, especially in the chemical industry, you face special problems for which there simply are no universal solutions. One always has to remain conscious of this individual inheritance. In this context inheritance and tradition must not be understood in the sense of a burdensome historical charge with sentimental bonds, but as the realization that an industrial company simply cannot deny its character. The tremendous values inside that company must be applied specifically and individually.

The history of Hoechst, and that of the other large German and international chemical companies, show this very clearly. Twenty years after the formation of the I. G. Farbenindustrie, the individual differences in the company structure of the I. G. members, as well as the attitude and the aims of the people working in these companies, was still so pronounced that even an outsider had little difficulty in determining which of the founder companies – Bayer, BASF or Hoechst – had been responsible for a certain development or activity. Indeed, it was precisely these differences that presaged the form of dismemberment of the company more or less in the way in which it was finally carried out by the Allies. Whether this was due to understanding on the part of the Allies, or whether they were forced to take this course as a result of the inherent conditions, is irrelevant to the issue.

In 1970, twenty years later, these differences can still be clearly seen. The three large German chemical companies have behaved and developed in quite a different way. Even today, each of them exhibits the traditional characteristics, which it once brought into the I. G. Farbenindustrie. The only things they have in common is an approximately equal volume of business, their world importance, and their progress. However, what they undertook in order to regain their place amongst the great international companies is as different as the beginning of their more than one-hundred-year-old history.

With most other established chemical companies in the world, whether large or small, it is also not difficult, even today, to determine their beginnings. They, too, react quite differently, and characteristically, to new situations and problems, whether these arise in science and technology, or in the commercial field.

Such experience and knowledge has to be taken into account when the moment comes to make personal or organizational decisions, especially at a time when the chemical industry, and therefore also Hoechst, is faced with the problem of expanding over the next ten years by about two and a half times or about 10 per cent a year.

This, at any rate, is the current estimate for the requirement of chemical products throughout the world. Naturally, this growth will not take place at the same rate in the case of every product. Hoechst has had to take into account which of its fields would be particularly involved if it wanted to maintain the position achieved in the meantime amongst its major competitors. It also had to take into account the fact that the Federal Republic has largely caught up with its requirements and that the conditions for chemical production in Germany have been rapidly deteriorating because of restrictive legislation and particularly because of the lack of sufficient labour.

During the years 1967 to 1969, significant decisions had been taken at Hoechst. These concerned not only the further development of current programmes but also some fundamentally new departures. They were a further example of the fact that a company is not completely free in its actions but dependent upon development trends that derive from its past. Also, if we did not want to overreach ourselves, we had to forgo many tempting propositions.

For example, Hoechst took the deliberate decision to continue its previous policy in petrochemistry and not to engage in the crude oil business. During the re-orientation of the German crude oil companies, the opportunity of mergers with Wintershall or with GBAG arose. These ideas were by no means secret, and were in fact, discussed fairly openly. During friendly discussions with the possible partners, we expressly declined, however, to realize such mergers. The two oil companies concerned later joined BASF and the Rheinisch-Westfälisches Elektrizitätswerke. Hoechst secured its supplies of crude oil through long-term contracts with UK Wesseling and Gelsenberg.

Clearing Up

The agreement with Bayer concerning the Hüls problem was based on similar considerations. In the course of time, Hoechst had complemented its plastic range through the production of polyvinylchloride and the acquisition of a polystyrene plant in Holland. As a result, our interest in Hüls had lessened. On the other hand, Bayer was particularly interested in these plastics fields, which had not until then formed part of its production programme. Moreover, the synthetic rubber production of Hüls was a traditional Bayer interest.

Eventually, this situation was resolved and as a result Bayer, together with VEBA, took over Hüls. Apart from a substantial cash payment, Hoechst was awarded a majority holding in Cassella with which it had long been connected, even before the I. G. era.

The cash that became available to us partly as a result of this arrangement and partly through our decision not to participate in a refinery, could now be devoted to specific fields with which Hoechst was especially familiar and in which it wanted to intensify its activities, not only in Germany but also abroad. We therefore decided to collaborate in the pharmaceutical sector with the French group of Roussel-Uclaf and Nobel. Pharmaceutical activity was also intensified in the United States, and the Trevira business was greatly enlarged. The same happened in England. Moreover, Hoechst decided to devote considerable funds to opening up the cosmetic field, and to intensify its efforts in the field of paint raw materials. These were all tremendously important decisions. Whether they were right will be seen only after many years. At any rate, in the prevailing situation and in view of the tradition of the company, they seemed to us the most sensible things to do.

New Leaders at Hoechst

Following my sixty-fourth birthday in September 1967, I informed the supervisory board that I would resign from my post as chairman of the board of management at the annual general meeting in 1969. In a most collegial gesture, Hermann Richter, chairman of the supervisory board, offered to make his post available to me. Gustav Ehrhart, who was approaching his seventy-fifth birthday, had already previously declared that he wished to retire from the supervisory board. Thus it was possible for me to be proposed at the general meeting for election to the supervisory board. Readers will readily understand that I was not only interested in but derived a great deal of pleasure from the prospect of being able to continue my activities there. I was therefore most grateful for the generous decisions that had been taken.

After many discussions, the board of management agreed unanimously at its official meeting on 11 June 1968 to propose to the supervisory board that Rolf Sammet should be the future chairman. In its constituting meeting after the annual general meeting in June 1968, that is to say before my sixty-fifth birthday, the supervisory board, as the appropriate body, took the decision, at my request, to award the office to Sammet one year later. The announcement of this decision, a year before my departure, greatly facilitated all further decisions and also the ensuing consultations.

That our choice fell upon Rolf Sammet did not cause too much surprise within the company. I had met Sammet, who joined us in 1949, and who first of all worked in a scientific laboratory, quite early on.

He played a significant part in the equipment of the new Trevira plant in our Bobingen factory. Later on, he was in charge of the technical directorate. When he was appointed to the board in 1962, his particular responsibility was the film and foil division. Rolf Sammet was also works manager in Hoechst for a number of years and a kind of 'Minister of the Interior' for the group. It was this arrangement that enabled me to make so many trips with our 'Foreign Minister', Kurt Lanz.

The appointment of Kurt Lanz as deputy chairman of the board of management seemed an equally obvious choice. In the present international competitive situation, which did not exist before, the commercial man is as important as the scientist. Kurt Lanz had taken on the organization of the foreign trade office in Hoechst in 1949. Later he was appointed sales director and head of the commercial directorate. In 1956, at the age of thirty-seven, he was appointed to the board of management and has since then carried the main responsibility for sales and the extension of our important business abroad.

The decision concerning one's successor, and the timing of this decision, is probably the greatest responsibility that one has to fulfil in professional life. The future fate of the company to a large extent depends upon this decision and I was never in favour of taking it too early. The pretender to the throne should not have to wait too long, because this would only lead to stress and premature wear. On the other hand, it is absolutely vital for a company of our size to have in its top management a body of people that can be called into the front line at the right moment.

It is not solely a matter of scientific and technical qualifications, a matter of intelligence or gifts which are taken for granted. What is equally important is the mental and physical capacity of the people about to be appointed. Top management must be in top condition because otherwise it would not be able to withstand the continuous professional exertions and above all the strain of tough and extended negotiations.

Apart from mental and physical condition, home background can often also play an important part. The person who has a quiet and harmonious atmosphere at home can concentrate all his energy upon his professional tasks. These factors therefore must not altogether be ignored when it comes to the selection of candidates for top management positions.

Family Celebration on the Rhine

I spent my sixty-fifth birthday with my family at the 'Krone' in Assmannshausen on the Rhine. It was at this hostelry that my parents had celebrated their silver wedding, shortly before my father died in 1913. My wife, my son Albrecht, my daughter Lotte, and I had a pleasant evening here, and we talked a great deal about the history of our family. Unfortunately, my son Ernst-Ludwig was not present. He had recently departed for California with his wife, where, following his graduation, he wanted to spend two years at the Biochemical Institute of the University of California in Berkeley.

All my children had a secure career before them. Albrecht, the physicist, had started his doctorate work and was involved with a Heidelberg group of scientists in the FR 2, the first reactor in Karlsruhe built by the Federal Republic. Now, following the successful conclusion of his studies, he, too, is at Berkeley. Lotte was an enthusiastic medical student, already concentrating on her preliminary examinations.

When, on the evening of the next day, we returned from a steamer trip on the Rhine, we found our room filled with greetings and presents. Later on, there was another family celebration, on a somewhat larger scale, in Eltville.

Shortly after my birthday, there was another meeting of the supervisory board which at that time of the year looks into the investments and financial plans for the coming year. The recession of 1967 had been overcome and the business situation was satisfactory. We therefore turned to far-reaching plans which we discussed with a great deal of self-confidence and every hope for a successful 1969.

Following this meeting, there was a birthday celebration in the old restaurant, to which the supervisory board, the board of management, and some friends from the scientific and commercial worlds, as well as some close collaborators from the works, had been invited. There were fewer people than five years ago on my sixtieth birthday, but they were more intimate friends. Hellmut Bredereck congratulated me on behalf of the Society of German Chemists and Hermann Richter and Werner Schultheis on behalf of the supervisory board and the board of management.

I was particularly delighted by the invitation of the Mayor of Frankfurt, Willi Brundert. He had arranged a small birthday party in the 'Römer' in Frankfurt. Unfortunately, after this party, I did not see Brundert on many more occasions. He had assumed office in 1964 in succession to Werner Bockelmann. He was a serious and convinced Social Democrat whose many pleasant attributes were quickly appreciated by Frankfurt's citizens. But his sad personal fate – many years' imprisonment in East Germany – the tough political conflicts, and the sheer administrative burden had left its mark. He died in the spring of 1970 at the age of fifty-eight.

Collaboration with the city of Frankfurt and its representatives has always been extremely fruitful. It is not always easy to reconcile the interests of a large city with that of a large-scale industrial undertaking which has located in that city not only its central administrations but also many factories and certainly a large number of its employees. I have always been happy that most of our problems were discussed in a friendly atmosphere and satisfactorily resolved. The personal understanding shown by many of the leading officials of the city of Frankfurt have made this task very much easier for me.

After all these celebrations, the problems of everyday life reasserted themselves and with them the need to design organizational plans for the future. I had thought about this a great deal in recent years and had discussed it with my colleagues. There are many views and theories about the way a company should be managed. Naturally, we had our own ideas and we attempted to arrive at solutions that would do justice to the character and size of the company.

A Younger Board

Of course, in view of impending change in the leading generation, we had to have a close look at our past experience. This applied to the board of management as much as to the other administrative bodies who were, of course, subject to the same changes.

The personnel composition of such a board of management cannot be based on universal rules. It is governed by the specific character of the company and the structure of its operational programme. In accordance with their importance in a chemical company, science and technology must be represented by a number of people who can do justice to the breadth of the company's operation. The important scientific engagement in research and development work requires this management to be of an international standard. The international sales programme throughout the world must also properly be taken into account. In addition, there must be expert administration of finance and accounts.

Naturally, the social requirements of the company must also be represented on the board of management. Particularly in a chemical firm, with its complex employee structure, social policy requires a great deal of sensitivity and care. Moreover, management must be in a position to cope with the many legal problems presented by our complicated economic and social system.

The size of the board of management is governed by these needs. The vital factor is always that every important area of responsibility is properly represented and that the rights and duties are clearly distributed and arranged so that everyone knows what is going on. Every employee of a company should know that there is someone on the board of management who is fully competent in his field, even if he is not familiar with its every detail.

In Hoechst we had always been resolved not to be afraid of having a large number of people on the board. The requirements, as we saw them, dictated approximately fifteen to sixteen board members. Of course, the people on the board must not represent only individual interests. They must assume collective responsibility and this must manifest itself both internally and externally.

To forge such a corporate purpose, superseding any individual functions, is not easy in a board with so many members. This is particularly the case where important decisions have to be made requiring high investments or laying down the main development lines of the company for many years ahead, or, indeed determining the future of the company for even longer periods. At such moments, different temperaments and interests, as well as differently orientated qualifications, are bound to collide. It is not always possible then to apply exclusively parliamentary methods. In such situations, people are not equals, and their voices cannot have the same weight.

Naturally, no one will ever decide upon a new pharmaceutical development against the advice and opinion of the representatives of the pharmaceutical division. And nobody would ever agree to an investment plan for the coming year if the finance department did not support it. It is always a question of style and skill, of finding the precise moment when a subject is right for final decision, even if this decision is not necessarily unanimous. A precondition for such an approach, however, is that the management not only has the powers of final decision but is also capable of exercising them.

At the moment of an important final decision, a moment that doesn't arise all that often, the management should meet on its own and should not transfer responsibility to experts. Incidentally, there have only been rare instances in Hoechst where the management did not arrive at unanimous decisions. When matters were really difficult, we often adjourned the discussions repeatedly until we all managed to agree on the same course at some future board meeting.

New Divisions are Created

In order to leave the board of management free for fundamental discussions and decisions, it was decided to delegate many of its functions to a far greater extent than before, and to have these tasks far more clearly defined. A new level of responsibility was created beneath the board of management. The entire business of the company was divided into fourteen divisions. These were to have complete world-wide responsibility for the extent of the business with which they were concerned. The management of each division consists of a group of scientists and technicians, sales people and economists constituted in such a manner that the business policy of the field for which they have assumed responsibility is readily understood by them. The responsibility of these divisions is enormous. Their annual sales volume is between 500 and 1,000 million DM.

The responsibility of the board of management was so arranged that, in conformity with earlier procedures, one half of the board members looked after the new divisions, and the other half after the coordinating departments. The whole system is shown in diagram form on page 424. The system means that, in principle, two members of the board are able at any one time to make individual decisions in the overall field of the company, and thus to take over special functions from the management, within the framework of overall responsibility.

Of course, such decentralization is subject to the risk of internal divergence in company policy, and of individual interests beginning to predominate. This danger is all the more acute because each division is responsible for its own profits and it is of tremendous importance that they invoice inter-company deliveries at reasonable prices which very often cannot be market prices.

The operation of this whole system can be guaranteed only if there are many bodies in which those involved are almost forced to discuss their problems with one another. Directorate meetings and commission meetings on fixed dates are ideal institutions to promote such discussions. It has always seemed important to us that these committees should not be *ad hoc* groups adapted to particular requirements. To exclude any arbitrariness, they are appointed as permanent institutions by the board of management or its chairman.

In this interplay of the various bodies, the staff departments fulfil an important role. They are the preparatory link for all the working committees, and at the same time a good training ground for all those who pass through these departments. The danger of these staff departments is, however, that in view of their ready access to comprehensive information they become too powerful and are eventually concerned more with themselves than anything else.

Moreover, human understanding will always be necessary to keep such a form of management vital and effective. People have to be found, at every level, who fulfil not only the tasks allocated to them under the organization plan but who, with intelligence and tact, aim for cooperation and agreement beyond the confines of their particular responsibilities.

In the first few months of 1969, the board of management had repeated joint meetings with their future colleagues. In this way, we were able to decide on the final details of the design of the new organization which we then announced in May 1969. The personnel decisions concerning the management of the various divisions were also undertaken then. The designated leaders were then instructed to plan the organization of their divisions in such a way that all the change-over operations would be completed by the end of the year. This particularly affected the accounts department, which was faced with an immense task, because the entire distribution of accounts and the presentation of the results had to be adapted to the new organization.

Harmonious Farewell

On 3 June 1969 I presented the report of the board of management to the annual general meeting for the last time. The year 1968 had been highly satisfactory and the current year 1969 looked equally promising. We were therefore able to allow the shareholders to participate in the improved profit position through the issue of bonus shares from the reserves. We had proposed such a measure to the shareholders three years previously, and had found then that they preferred this to an increase in the dividend. The employees, too, participated in these benefits which were equivalent to a 1 per cent increase in the dividend.

On the evening before the annual general meeting, a small but original exhibition had been opened in the centenary hall under the theme 'Years of Decision'. It showed all that had happened in Hoechst since its re-birth. The public relations and advertising departments had produced a film under the same title and they surprised me with this when the exhibition was opened. During this period and the succeeding weeks and months, the board of management and its colleagues had thought up many gestures of appreciation for me which gave me a great deal of pleasure. The television people were preparing a feature, and for this a reporter came to see me at seven o'clock one morning at home, and then filmed my complete working day, including my trip to the works.

The annual general meeting, too, became a kind of farewell celebration. I was very pleased with the speeches of recognition that were given by the supervisory board represented by Hermann Richter and by many shareholders at the meeting. Subsequently, the supervisory board elected me as chairman; Rolf Sammet was appointed chairman of the board of management, and Kurt Lanz deputy chairman. A long series of anxious discussions, exchanges of views, and important decisions had thus been concluded. In the dry

and business-like manner with which these proceedings were transacted, one could sense the confidence and self-assurance with which
Hoechst was now looking into the future.

On the evening of the annual general meeting, we met, as always,
at Eltville, together with the supervisory board and board of management. The new chairman of the board of management had to make
his first speech in that capacity. Next morning, I left with my wife
for a trip by car through Scandinavia, passing through Denmark,
Sweden, and Finland up to the North Cape, and along the Norwegian coast to Oslo. I had saved up this experience for the weeks
immediately after my retirement since previously there had been no
opportunity for such a trip at that time of year.

New Obligations

When I returned a month later, the new organization was already
operating. I had now gained the necessary perspective and took over
the rights and obligations of the chairman of the supervisory board.
My colleagues made this change-over easy for me. We all took it
for granted that the cordial relationships that had previously existed
would continue.

It was during this period of transition in particular that I could
see for myself the wisdom of the provision of the German company
law which deliberately separates the active responsibility and
executive power of the board of management from the activities
of the supervisory board. I believe that this is better than the English
and American system in which the executive sits together on the
same board with non-executive members. The division practised in
Germany leads to valuable discussions between the people from
outside, who are able to provide a good deal of sound advice to the
company, and those who wield the actual executive power. The
horizons of the company are enlarged in this way and responsibilities
are more clearly defined.

At the meeting of the supervisory board of September 1969, we
decided to call an extraordinary general meeting in order to ask
for approval for a convertible loan. The extraordinary high investments and expansion of our business demanded such an improvement
in our capital resources. This general meeting took place in January
1970. At this meeting we also said farewell to W. Alexander Menne,
Robert Zoller, and Hans W. Ohliger, who had left the board on

31 December 1969. Their successors were presented. In place of our great friend Erich Bauer, who had died, the general meeting elected Werner Schultheis to the supervisory board. Schultheis had represented research on the board of management for many years, and had retired in the summer of 1969.

The preliminary report that we were able to present to this general meeting gave an outstanding result for 1969. It was clear that the dividend would be maintained and that a considerable amount could be placed in reserve. For the first time, the distributed dividend and the amount placed in reserve, which serves for self-financing, bore a proper ratio.

But there were already threatening clouds on the horizon. The DM revaluation of 9·3 per cent upon which the new Federal government had so quickly decided, affected our exports and its profits. Even at that time, it was to be expected that we would have to suffer considerable losses during the following months. Moreover, the terms of the convertible loan upon which we had decided six weeks previously when we invited our shareholders to the general meeting, were no longer in line with the general situation. To contain the boom, the Federal bank had greatly increased the discount rate so that the shareholders were very critical of our conditions although we were able to improve on them at the last moment. We could only point out that in such uncertain times, strong company management was necessary to take its decisions in such a manner that the policy of the company was not endangered. Fortunately, and in spite of much criticism, the shareholders on the whole showed understanding for this attitude.

Prospects

WHEN THIS book was concluded in June 1971, the chemical industry was once again a centre of economic interest. Its situation has greatly deteriorated in all industrial countries. In the expectation that the considerable growth rates of the past would continue or even increase, new capacities were set up in some countries which are simply not adequately utilized at the present time. As a result, prices for chemical products are dropping, while almost all other investment and consumer goods are becoming more expensive and are thus falling into line with the general trend of increasing costs. The chemical companies have suffered greatly reduced profits for 1970. It would appear that this branch of industry is once more in a critical phase. And we can hear the sceptics with their prompt Cassandra warnings that the optimistic forecasts of the chemists were wrong and that the heady days and growth of chemistry are coming to an end.

The recession is particularly pronounced in the Federal Republic. But it must be seen against the background of the unusual rise that the German chemical industry experienced after the Second World War. The three I. G. successor companies, Bayer, BASF, and Hoechst, were able to catch up with the great chemical leaders in the world. Between 1961 and 1970, chemical production in the Federal Republic increased from 24 thousand million DM to almost 50 thousand million DM. The sales of Farbwerke Hoechst, unfortunately not quite comparable by normal statistical methods, increased during the same period from 3,200 million DM to 12,200 million DM, almost four times. At the time of re-constitution in 1952, sales were 760 million. And even in 1971 the increase in sales is of the order of 8 to 10 per cent.

Many concerned with the problems of chemical industry feel distinctly uncomfortable. In view of the obvious difficulties, shareholders are concerned about their dividend. Labour in the Federal

Republic of Germany is in short supply so that the number of foreigners among the employees is continuously increasing. Because of the necessary economy measures, employers are becoming concerned about their jobs. Nevertheless, they all join in the claim for increased wages and improvements in social conditions, especially as the cost of living rises.

But among the general public, too, there are many voices raised in criticism of the chemical industry. The world-wide discussion about environment protection appears to be aimed, in the first place, at chemistry. Chemists are accused of polluting air and water with their production processes. They are accused of flooding the market with products that are harmful to health, or even toxic. On the other hand, chemistry is accused, in areas where it is admittedly indispensable such as in pharmaceuticals, of exploiting monopoly positions and charging excessively high prices. Merger controls and anti-trust laws have been applied to prevent concentrations and price agreements within chemistry. Because the economic situation is becoming more difficult, the industry is advised at the same time to avoid excess capacities through investment agreements. But the one excludes the other.

General confusion has therefore arisen. Anyone who has been concerned with the developments of the past decades is bound to ask himself whether chemistry, which has provided the world with so many advantages, is really suffering from so many defects and whether the industrial and economic utilization of chemical knowledge has, after all, exceeded its limits. Even in the field of research, it is being asked whether there are too many chemists. Doubts are expressed whether enough new discoveries are likely now that the great inventor's epoch of plastics and man-made fibres, which gave rise to the expansion of the last decades, has passed.

At such critical moments, a sober analysis is very necessary of all the possibilities and conditions that determine the fate of chemistry and of the chemical industry.

It will generally be agreed that mankind cannot exist without the products of chemistry. Fertilizers and agro-chemicals have made possible a better harvest, and have thus preserved millions of human beings from starvation, at least in those areas where organizational or political obstacles have not prevented adequate supplies. The requirements for fertilizers and agro-chemicals have by no means yet been met. In 1965–6, some 40 million tons of fertilizers were used throughout the world. The World Food Organization estimates that by 1980 requirements may be as high as 80 million tons. Every year, one-third of world crops is destroyed by animal and vegetable pests.

Man-made fibres have made it possible for mankind to dress better and more cheaply. In the last twenty years, plastics have opened up entirely new opportunities and have improved our way of life. Without synthetic rubber, the car could never have been mass produced.

But perhaps most significant of all is the performance of the pharmaceutical industry. Because of its scientific and economic successes, health and life expectation have been greatly improved. Life expectation alone, compared with the last century, has doubled from thirty-five years of age to seventy. The modern pharmaceuticals, especially the sulphonamides and antibiotics, have played a significant role in this development. They have drastically reduced the dangers of infectious disease. Over and above this, treatment of pain is probably one of the most outstanding successes of the pharmaceutical industry.

There are, however, still many parts of the world that do not participate in this progress because they have to import chemical products of all kinds until they are able to produce these in their own country in the same way as the industrialized countries. For this reason, the expansion of the chemical industry is one of the most urgent economic needs in many countries, including those of the eastern bloc.

The German chemical industry has played an outstanding role in the successes of the past. At home, it was quickly able to fill the post-war gap in demand so that the consumption of chemical products rapidly exceeded that of most other countries. Moreover, through its increasing exports, it succeeded not only in opening up markets in the competitive industrialized countries but also in supplying the rest of the world with chemical products. Once the chemical industry of Germany had consolidated its internal structure, it could think in terms of erecting larger production units abroad.

It is German chemical exports in particular that are liable to suffer most because of declining profits. In the countries of the eastern bloc, and in many other parts of the world, free trade is considerably restricted so that the possibilities of an exchange of goods remain small. On the other hand, isolation trends have again sprung up in the industrialized countries. In particular, continuous, and in recent years accelerating, inflation, which has frequently changed monetary relationships, has made international trade more difficult. The repeated revaluation of the Deutschmark, devaluation in other countries, and the clinging to out-of-date exchange rates, have put the chemical industry in great difficulties. In the long term, it will have to forgo part of its exports and replace it with production abroad.

Fundamentally, chemistry in the last two to three decades has achieved a considerable economic success. Based on petrochemistry, it has supplied the markets with valuable new consumer goods and at the same time it has not only economically utilized and financed all its developments in open, free competition but it has also, contrary to the general trend, reduced the prices of its products. Here are some examples from the list of products newly-developed by Hoechst since 1952.

In 1961, a few years after it had been introduced, Hoechst Trevira fibre cost 14 DM per kilogram. By 1970, this price had been reduced to 3.80 DM per kg. In 1961, a kg. of Hostalen still cost 3.20 DM while the price at the end of 1970 was 1.70 DM. In 1961, the price of 1 kg. of the newly developed Remazol turquoise was 31.80 DM while by the end of 1970 the price had been reduced to 22.70 DM. A box of Rastinon, the oral antidiabetic first marketed in 1956, cost 6.90 DM in 1961 and 5.75 DM in 1970.

The price index of all chemical products dropped from 100 in 1961 to 91.8 in 1970. During the same period, almost all other costs increased. The fixed assets of 1.300 million had to be increased to 7,000 million DM at increased rates of interest.

During the same period, the labour cost per hour worked increased from 5.82 DM to 12.54 DM.

The development of the chemical industry is based on healthy economic conditions. It will solve its problems through adapting itself to the prevailing world conditions.

That all this progress at times produced undesirable effects or was even misused could hardly be prevented altogether. But it must generally be recognized that every one of us has gained far more advantages than disadvantages from the versatile products of chemistry.

When man has so greatly changed the look of the world through his habits and consumer demands in a relatively short span of time, he must not be surprised if he changes the environment at the same time. Surely nobody dreams of abolishing the car, the washing machine, the oil-fired central-heating or so many other comforts that we now have come to take for granted. On the other hand, it is true that our standard of living and our consumer habits make new demands on the environment which must be satisfied by the state and the civil authorities, by industry and consumers and, in the final resort, by us all.

There can be no doubt that the problems of traffic, noise, air, and water pollution are far more difficult for state and public to solve than the environment problems of chemical factories.

Public discussions sometimes give the impression that it is primarily the chemical factories that are responsible for environmental pollution. But there is in fact little question that it was the chemical industry which first saw the dangers. The chemical industry is concerned most intensively with the protection of the environment, and can point to the greatest successes in this field. It will be far more difficult to maintain the general standard of living of a civilized and, not surprisingly, technological society, and to improve it further while maintaining a tolerable environment. This requires organizational measures that will probably intervene significantly in the life of each individual. Towns and parishes will have to make considerable investments and provide expensive services to meet these needs.

But chemistry, too, will have to learn from the economic situation and from the opposition that it is meeting. In the field of the exact sciences, chemistry is concerned with changing matter. Chemistry produces numerous products from the raw materials that occur on earth and from natural substances. These products help to make life better for mankind. When sufficient knowledge has been gained in certain fields, chemistry will have to turn to new problems. In the field of plastics and fibres, it looks as though the great fundamental inventions belong to the past. But even here, many problems remain whose solution will enable us to lead still more comfortable lives.

With modern methods of preparative and analytical chemistry, the chemist is able to produce an almost infinite number of chemical compounds and to establish their precise structure and composition in a short period of time.

He has to turn increasingly to a study of the functions of such new compounds and the question of how they can be used successfully, without causing harm. The greater the possibilities of chemical synthesis, the more difficult and more expensive the selection and critical evaluation of their use.

This requires exact scientific knowledge of the mode of action in the human and animal organism and in the plant world. In molecular biology and in biochemistry generally, wide prospects are opening up which, once we understand the mechanism better, will create new conditions for the treatment of disease and pests.

But in many technical spheres, too, for example in communications, in information, in transport, and in the building industry, new problems are arising continuously which cannot be solved without the creative contribution of the chemical industry.

Since chemistry has been able to make such a significant contribution to protecting mankind from hunger and disease and increasing its life expectancy, it will surely also be able to help in future to overcome the misuse and mistakes that have arisen as a result of excessively quick industrialization of our world. That, too, is a new scientific task that must be realized in teaching and research.

Wars and economic crises have placed chemistry in repeated difficulties during the last decades and have presented it with big new problems. The reverses and criticisms that chemistry now has to suffer will have to be overcome through fresh efforts and new opportunities. My own industrial experience has shown me clearly that those periods in which industry was able to mould its own fate without excessive intervention by the state were the happiest times, not only for the chemical industry, but also for the economy as a whole. Intense competition has always been a characteristic of the chemical industry. It does not worry me, for it serves progress. I have no doubt that the people who are fashioning the fate of our industry will not lose courage even under the present difficult conditions and will lead their companies into a healthy future.

Bibliography

Bäumler, E.: *A Century of Chemistry*, Düsseldorf 1963.

Duisberg, C.: *Meine Lebenserinnerungen*, edited by J. v. Puttkamer, Leipzig 1933.

Flechtner, H.-J.: *Carl Duisberg. Vom Chemiker zum Wirtschaftsführer*, Düsseldorf 1959.

Holdermann, K.: *Im Banne der Chemie – Carl Bosch, Leben und Werk*, Düsseldorf, 1953.

Howard, F. A.: *Buna Rubber. The Birth of an Industry*, New York 1947.

Knieriem, A. v.: *Nürnberg. Rechtliche und menschliche Probleme*, Stuttgart 1953.

Ter Meer, F.: *Die I. G. Farbenindustrie Aktiengesellschaft*, Düsseldorf 1953.

Festival brochure of Badische Anilin- & Soda-Fabrik AG: *Im Reiche der Chemie*, published on the centenary of BASF, Düsseldorf/Vienna 1965.

Festival brochure of Farbenfabriken Bayer AG: *Revolution im Unsichtbaren*, published by the management of Farbenfabriken Bayer AG on the centenary on 1 August 1963, Düsseldorf/Vienna 1963.

Appendix

Address on the occasion of the re-constitution of Farbwerke Hoechst on 27 March, 1953

Honoured Guests, Friends,
Colleagues, Ladies and Gentlemen,

After Farbwerke Hoechst AG, formerly Meister Lucius & Brüning, had been founded on 7 December 1951 with a share capital of 100,000 DM, there took place today the transfer of the works and participations from the assets of the I. G. Farbenindustrie in Liquidation allocated to Hoechst by the Allies. As a result of the dismemberment measures carried out by the Allies, Farbwerke Hoechst AG has taken over, with effect from 1 January 1952:

1. Farbwerke Hoechst
   Chemische Fabrik Griesheim
   Naphtol-Chemie Offenbach
   Lech-Chemie Gersthofen
with a total of 14,867 employees.

2. The total capital of the following companies:

	Capital	Employees
Knapsack-Griesheim AG	36,000,000 DM	5,748
Kalle & Co. AG	20,400,000 DM	3,487
Bobingen AG für Textilfaser	8,500,000 DM	1,857
Behringwerke AG, Marburg	5,000,000 DM	510
Sperr- und Fassholzfabrik	Stock capital	
Goldbach GmbH	750,000 DM	196

The total number of employees therefore is 26,665.

3. In addition, our company has acquired:
49 per cent of Wacker-Chemie, which has a stock capital of 40,000,000 DM and 3,975 employees, and 30 per cent of Duisburger Kupferhütte, whose capital is 24,000,000 DM, and which employs 3,362 people.

4. A number of smaller concerns have also been acquired.

On the basis of the assets made over to us, the capital of Farbwerke Hoechst AG has been determined, by resolution of the annual general meeting, at

285,700,000 DM.

Our works and subsidiaries, without the participations, achieved sales in 1952 of 760,000,000 DM.

As of today, Allied control has ended. The company has regained its full rights and responsibilities in accordance with German law. When some eight years ago, on 23 March 1945, we gave the order for the complete stoppage of all plants in view of the advancing battle front, all life ceased in our ninety-year-old works. During those weeks we saw in our country, as the fearful consequence of a war conducted with inhumanity to the point of disintegration, the destruction of all that had been created during centuries of tradition. Economy, state and law collapsed.

In mute resignation, we experienced the end of our statehood. If today, after the first years of reconstruction, we have regained full jurisdiction over our company, which is again in full operation, this shows that we overestimated the power of destruction.

Under the shadow of impending disaster, we forgot that somehow life always continues. It has continued, in spite of death and destruction. If the fight for our existence and the efforts involved in our reconstruction have left us little time for reflection, then on this day of joy our first duty is to recall those friends and collaborators who have not survived this most fearful catastrophe in the history of our people.

In the companies and works now belonging to Hoechst, 1,933 employees were killed either in battle, or by bombs, or are missing. Our thoughts are with them and their kin. Let them remind us at all times that we must never again gamble with the precious gift of peace.

We commemorate all the friends and employees that have died since the end of the war and were not able to witness today's new start. Our thoughts are expecially with Johannes Moser whom we buried only this week.

One of the most far-reaching steps that the Allies took in consequence of their victory, was the Control Commission Law No. 9 of 30 November 1945 which sanctioned the confiscation of the I. G. Farbenindustrie on 5 July 1945 and which formed the basis of the dismemberment of the I. G. in conformity with the later law No. 35 of the Allied High Commission. Almost unnoticed by the majority of the people, who were preoccupied with the fight for their existence, this meant the destruction of the most important undertaking that German science, technology and enterprise had ever developed.

In a trial fought with great bitterness, the responsible leaders of the I. G. Farbenindustrie AG, and thus our entire company, were able to rebut all the charges of war crimes, robbery and plunder levied against them. We feel closely linked with all the former leaders of the I. G.

Farbenindustrie AG, and with all the old friends of this company, and we are happy that a number of them are able to be with us today.

Up to now, rebuilding the old works has been carried out under Allied control. These works had been partly destroyed by bombs and their organization had been completely upset by dismissals. Their links with subsidiaries, on whom they had come to rely for all stages of manufacture as a result of twenty years of collaboration, had been completely severed. The central selling organization no longer existed and a provisional system had to be established in the individual works. With untiring effort, the employees of our factories, under their new management, have achieved an admirable feat of reconstruction.

We thank the staff and workers who helped us in this task and who stayed loyal to their former works. We also thank the managers and trustees who succeeded, within the limitations of narrow and stringent regulations imposed by the Allies, in bringing the works back to full production and making them competitive once more.

The work of reconstruction in the various plants was accompanied by a bitter fight concerning the future economic organization of the I. G. successor companies. As both victor and vanquished slowly drew back from the atmosphere of hate and destruction, they became more reasonable and the plans for rebuilding what remained were put on an economically sounder footing.

We have succeeded in preventing complete disintegration of the I. G. and in confining the division of the I. G. Farbenindustrie to the minimum number of companies so as to maintain viable units. This has largely been due to the control authorities who had been charged by their countries with the dismemberment of the I. G. Farbenindustrie AG and who could, in many cases, be persuaded to take another view and to accept our plans for the foundation of economically practicable units.

The German government intervened in these arguments at an early date and used its authority to help ensure that instead of an infinite number of uneconomic plants, three large successor companies were formed. In tough diplomatic negotiations the basis of the present arrangement was hammered out, the arguments in respect of each company frequently extending over many months.

We should like to take the opportunity to thank the Federal government, led by Chancellor Dr Adenauer, who at the decisive moment, intervened personally in the negotiations, and especially in matters concerning the Hoechst works. We also thank the Federal Minister of Economics, Professor Dr Erhard, and Secretary of State Westrick and his colleagues, particularly Dr Prentzel, who have effectively supported us in the protracted negotiations. Hoechst also offers its thanks to the government of Hesse and in particular to Dr Zinn, its Minister-President. He displayed at all times a considerable interest in our many special problems and he has often intervened personally, with great determination and considerable success, on behalf of Farbwerke Hoechst.

Our thanks are also due to the Bavarian government with whom we are closely linked through our plants and interests in Bavaria. The negotations extended over many years and involved considerable differences of opinion. That they have nevertheless led to a reasonable and economically viable result, is due mainly to the valuable part played by the press and radio.

I am pleased to welcome the representatives of press and radio here today. We thank you for your past support and hope that we may enjoy your goodwill also in the grave times ahead of us.

We also thank the I. G. liquidators, Dr Brinckmann, Dr Reuter and Dr Schmidt, for their efficient support and helpful mediation.

Finally, I feel I must thank all those members of our company, at whatever level, who have tried to find a practical solution to our problems. Above all, I must thank our founders who have given practical expression to the solution at which we arrived. Re-constituted and freed from Allied control at last, Farbwerke Hoechst AG thus sets out on its future. Its companions are Leverkusen, Ludwigshafen, Cassella Farbwerke Mainkur, and Chemische Werke Hüls, who have now also been re-constituted. All these companies are linked by an association that has lasted over many years. Their dissection after the war has left many wounds. We are closely linked with regard to the supply of starting products and intermediates and we also supplement our respective selling ranges. We shall be able to face future economic competition and we shall be able to fulfil our economic obligations only if competition – which can have beneficial effects – is honest and reasonable. The close, and in many cases personal, friendship between management and employees, which has linked us over a long period of common history, will help us in this.

In this sense I heartily welcome the boards of Leverkusen, Ludwigshafen, Hüls, and Cassella. At this moment, we also greet the works in the eastern zone who have suffered their own fate and whom we do not wish to forget.

The company that we have christened today may be a complex not readily understood by the outsider. Those, however, who have followed our struggle for enlargement from a knowledge of the old Farbwerke Hoechst and the relationships of the old I. G. Farbenindustrie will know that these efforts were not merely concerned with an increase in sales or the acquisition of additional interests, but that they aimed at completing the intricate pattern of our activities.

One of the most important divisions of Hoechst continues to be the dyestuffs division which has now been supplemented by Naphtol-Chemie Offenbach. Hoechst dyestuffs manufacture is based on our intermediates' production which has now been supplemented by Griesheim and Lech-Chemie.

The pharmaceuticals division has regained its traditional complement, namely Behringwerke. To be economic, our sulphuric acid production relies to a large extent on collaboration with the Duisburger Kupferhütte and for this reason, we warmly welcome the re-establishment of the former close relationship. An important contribution to the fertilizer and plant protection field are the calcium cyanamide production of Knapsack and the pesticides produced in Gersthofen.

The solvents and plastics divisions developed at Hoechst have long been based on Knapsack carbide and acetaldehyde. This field, too, has now been extended in important respects by the Perlon factory in Bobingen.

The Kalle plants, which are concerned with the processing of plastics, will closely collaborate with Hoechst's plastics division and we believe that this collaboration will provide a fresh and strong impetus for both. In this field, the old link with Wacker-Chemie GmbH is also of great value. Together, we have promoted the development of acetylene chemistry for more than thirty years. We have a large stake in the electrochemical field. There are the phosphorus and ferrous alloys from Knapsack, carbon from Griesheim, graphite from Sigri, common salt electrolysis at Hoechst, Gersthofen and Wacker, and sodium production in Gersthofen. There is, finally, the important field of welding techniques, with carbide production at Knapsack and the manufacture of oxygen and welding equipment in a number of widely scattered plants. It is not possible, on this occasion, to follow these relationships more closely. The prerequisite for progressive development in all these extensive fields is adequate research. After great initial difficulties, some 992 chemists, engineers, doctors and pharmacists are now once more employed in our scientific laboratories and in our plants. We hope that we shall succeed in filling the gaps of the past and in helping the German chemical industry to get back on its feet. We must, however, be clear that we shall find it difficult to realize the large vision that the former I. G. Farbenindustrie pursued.

One of our most rewarding tasks will be the promotion of a spirit of cooperation throughout our establishments. We believe that the form of organization that we have chosen will, for historical and factual reasons, be particularly conducive to this end. While the basic production is concentrated in the Hoechst, Griesheim, Offenbach, and Gersthofen complex, the structure of the subsidiaries is based on specific, self-contained fields that have a worthwhile sales potential.

The involuntary long separation faces us with tremendous organizational tasks that will require outstanding human qualities.

We shall all have to show a great deal of confidence and understanding so that we derive the maximum effect from the merger of the companies in the Hoechst group.

In the hope that we shall succeed in this, we welcome today, with cordial affection, the boards of the companies associated with us, and especially the gentlemen of Wacker-Chemie GmbH and Duisburger Kupferhütte.

At this moment of satisfaction over our regained freedom and the chance for a new start, we should remain conscious of the responsibility that we assume. Our shareholders have had to bear heavy sacrifices as a result of the dissolution of the I. G. Not only the large shareholders but tens and thousands of small savers who supported the I. G. Farbenindustrie with confidence and loyalty for many years have been hard hit during these times. Worries about the future fate of their hard-earned assets were re-awakened during the discussions concerning the nominal capital of the new companies. The opening DM balance sheet of the I. G., published in spring 1952, created many misunderstandings concerning the actual capital situation among those savers not familiar with all the details of these intricate financial questions. If the current rate of exchange of 10:9 causes dissatisfaction amongst some, we beg them to realize the seriousness of our present circumstances. The successor companies and plants that are now going to look after the former I. G. capital together own no more than 36 per cent of the assets of the I. G. Farbenindustrie: 14 per cent have been lost abroad and 50 per cent in the eastern zone and beyond.

The loss of all our patents and trademarks abroad, the publication of all our trade secrets, the extensive damage suffered during dismantling and the curtailment of many important and profitable industrial activities have caused us serious harm. In contrast, the rest of the world has used the post-war era to build up its industries and to lay the foundations for a successful future.

We must therefore ask you to understand why we have evaluated so soberly the assets that have been made over to us. We were not guided by any desire to make life easy for ourselves. In fixing the nominal capital, we were conscious of our great responsibility towards our former I. G. shareholders. Once the transition period of the share exchange has passed, our shares will again become the classic, safe investment in the German stock market, an investment in which shareholders can have faith, even in times of crisis, because it is based on a long-term, balanced and sustained dividend policy.

Now that the shareholders' committee has signified its support of our decisions, we propose to remain faithful to our shareholders if they continue to be faithful to us. After the most careful examination of our business prospects, we are confident that we can accept the responsibility under present conditions. We hope, of course, that the government will facilitate our fulfilment of this obligation by a forward-looking financial and fiscal policy so that, apart from meeting our dividend obligations, the expansion of the company remains safeguarded.

We should like to assure our pensioners that we shall extend the same loyalty to them also. For some years after the end of the war we were not allowed to resume pension payments and it was later still before we were permitted to make up the payment arrears that had accrued meanwhile. The pension regulations now decreed by the Allies have as their main purpose the distribution of the pension liabilities of the I. G.

Farbenindustrie AG over the successor companies. They also safeguard the present pension of all I. G. pensioners, including those that did not work in any plants of the successor companies. But even more important than this regulation is the firm resolve of management and employees to continue the personnel policies initiated by the former I. G. Farbenindustrie.

We shall regard the fate of our pensioners as our own – as indeed it is – for a cardinal principle of any personnel policy is care for the aged and the infirm. It must, of course, be realized that this duty imposes great responsibilities on our works. Just how great a burden this represents is strikingly illustrated by the fact that for every two active employees in our company, there is one pensioner.

In this hour of rebirth of Farbwerke Hoechst, I appeal on behalf of the management to all employees to extend to us their wholehearted cooperation. There has for many years been understanding and friendship between us and these have survived even the greatest calamities. We are accustomed to close collaboration with the works councils. If we wish to solve the tremendous personnel problems ahead of us, this collaboration will have to be closer than before.

At this moment of our re-creation, we must realize that our work for the company imposes upon us great and serious duties. Unsparing devotion and a sense of responsibility at all levels – in the plants, the workshops, the offices, the management – deep understanding of the human factor – whether in the boardroom or on the shop floor – these are the foundations of our new, and yet so old, company. If we accept these obligations, seriously and conscientiously, we shall be able to evolve that social pattern for which our people, chastened by catastrophe, so earnestly strive. Then our company will prosper; then we shall find security for our families both during active life and in retirement; then we shall find satisfaction and happiness in our work without which no life is worth living.

In this sense, I welcome you all on behalf of Farbwerke Hoechst AG, vormals Meister, Lucius & Brüning.

Address on the occasion of the centenary of Farbwerke Hoechst AG on 11 January 1963

Your Excellencies, Magnificences,
Presidents, Ladies and Gentlemen,
my dear Colleagues—

In this solemn hour, when we are assembled on the occasion of the hundredth birthday of Farbwerke Hoechst, I warmly welcome all our guests and friends. We thank you all, ladies and gentlemen, for according us the honour of celebrating this birthday in our midst. We felt that on this important day we wanted to have with us representatives from all the walks of life in which the company and its people are involved: from politics and public life, government bodies, science, industry and commerce.

I should like to thank you also for all the greetings and presents that you have sent to us in such overwhelming numbers.

Perhaps you will allow me to pick out one name from our vast circle of friends and another from the large number of our employees and their families, of whom, in spite of the size of our new hall, we could accommodate only a few: Firstly, the grand old lady of our founder families, Frau Else v. Meister, whom we were able to congratulate only a few weeks ago on her ninetieth birthday, and who at the last minute had to decline the invitation to be present on the grounds of ill-health. And secondly, Karl Kunz who started his job with Hoechst fifty years ago today, on 11 January 1913, when he entered the despatch department of Hoechst as a messenger boy.

They symbolize the loyalty and support which the company has been accorded for the past hundred years by the many thousands of people who have worked for it, and for which we are truly grateful.

The hundred-year-old history of Farbwerke Hoechst began as the scientific developments of the nineteenth century, in particular those of chemistry, entered a decisive phase.

August Wilhelm von Hofmann, the famous pupil of Liebig, had been recalled from England, and had started work in Berlin. In England, Perkin had synthesized the first organic dyestuff. In 1865, Kekulé proposed the structural formula of the benzene ring, and thus created a revolutionary concept whose consequences no one could foresee at the time and which has significantly influenced the development of synthetic organic chemistry to this very day.

In the field of physics, Helmholtz was at the zenith of his career and Werner v. Siemens developed the dynamo, thus ushering in the industrial production of electric energy.

Smelting technology had gained vital impulses through the coming of the railways. With the establishment of the first coking ovens, those by-products that made possible the major developments of chemistry later on, became available. A new chapter in agricultural chemistry began with the production of potassium salts in Stassfurt in 1863. At the same time, the production of crude oil began in Pennsylvania and in the Caucasus. Today, after a hundred years, crude oil looks like replacing coal as the raw material of the chemical industry.

This decisive period which, during only two to three years, established the foundations of the whole of Germany's large-scale chemical industry was also of fundamental importance for the political, economic and social development of the country.

Shortly before, in the autumn of 1862, Bismarck, well known to the Hoechst founder families of Meister and Lucius as ambassador of the Deutsche Bund, had been appointed Minister-President of Prussia. This opened a long and fruitful period of German unification which, in turn, heralded a prosperous economic development. The same period, however, also saw fundamental social changes. While in 1861, Russia abolished serfdom as a first move away from the medieval feudal system, industry in Europe was suffering its first upheavals and reversals. Karl Marx, living in poverty and resignation in London, was writing his provocative essays and laying the cornerstones of the social revolution.

In the year that Hoechst was founded, Lassalle published his study on the 'Unbreakable Wage Law' and founded the General Association of German Workers.

All these events were the distant flashes of lightning announcing one of the stormiest periods in human history that was to influence the development of Farbwerke Hoechst during all its phases. The fate of Hoechst during its rise to one of the largest companies in the world was governed by the interaction of extraordinary technological and economic possibilities with the revolutionary trends of public life. In the same way, it moulded and ruled the life of the people linked with this company. When the first jubilee was celebrated twenty-five years later in 1888, the founders Meister, Lucius and Brüning – the co-founder Müller had long since withdrawn – had already converted the private company into a public one. The turbulent expansion of the dyestuffs range, which had been enlarged by many new groups, for example alizarin, had been supplemented by the beginnings of a scientific pharmaceutical chemistry. Hoechst had acquired Antipyrin from Knorr. In 1897, Pyramidon, developed by Hoechst's own research, was added. The foundation stone of a pharmaceutical chemistry based on science had been laid.

Developments were beginning to transcend the frontiers of Germany. For similar reasons as today, plants had to be erected abroad. In 1878, a Hoechst dyestuffs factory was established in Moscow, and in 1883 another at Creil, near Paris. A few years later, a plant was set up near Liverpool in England. The worries attending foreign production plants were frequently the same as those we experience today. Germany had gained great power politically and economically. During the congress of Berlin, Bismarck had acted as the mediator of the world. The jubilee year of 1888, however, was the year of three German Kaisers. After the death of the aged Wilhelm the First, the influence of Bismarck waned. A great uncertainty came over Germany. In the socio-political field, revolutionary events had taken place. The first social legislation ever enacted by a modern industrial state had not resulted in the internal peace that the country had hoped for. The famous old Chancellor no longer understood the world. Society and the state did not understand the inexorable progress of industry and the problems that this brought with it. At first, however, there was still a long period of peace for Germany during which technology and industry developed in an undreamt-of manner.

In 1913, at the height of its success, Farbwerke Hoechst celebrated its fiftieth jubilee. Herbert v. Meister proudly presented the company report in place of Gustav v. Brüning whose approaching death was already imprinted upon his features.

The dream of the organic chemists, the synthesis of indigo, had been realized. Years of tireless effort to achieve this synthesis had almost consumed the resources of the company for a time. Other precious dyestuffs had been added to the range.

The discoveries of the immortal Robert Koch, especially that of tuberculin, had not provided Hoechst with the hoped-for big success. Even today, tuberculin recalls the first biochemical work and the hopes that had been placed upon it. Laubenheimer, who was then in charge of the pharmaceutical activities of Hoechst, did not lose faith. Through Robert Koch, he came in contact with the latter's pupil, Behring. The birth of immuno-biology was imminent. In 1894, Hoechst marketed the first diphtheria serum which was followed in 1896 by the tetanus serum. The scientists, however, did not rest on their synthetic laurels. Pyramidon was followed by other important pharmaceuticals such as Melubrin. In 1905, Einhorn had developed Novocain in Hoechst. At the same time, Suprarenin was discovered, the first synthetic hormone identical to the circulation-promoting adrenalin present in the suprarenal gland. Together with Paul Ehrlich, the company developed Salvarsan, one of the major discoveries of the early twentieth century.

Ostwald, Haber and Nernst had helped physical chemistry to achieve its breakthrough. The time was ripe for technical catalytic processes. Duden had prepared the foundation of acetylene chemistry and Klatte had polymerized the first plastics, a decade too early for technology to use the value of his invention. This development could prosper only because electrochemistry had created the conditions for it.

In the search for nitrogen as a fertilizer, Albert Frank had found calcium cyanamide which, in turn, aroused great interest in the carbide process. Interest in carbide and calcium cyanamide brought Hoechst in contact with Knapsack.

Pistor, who was a member of our supervisory board until quite recently, and who had come from Griesheim, promoted electrochemistry. Together with Stroof, he had worked on perfecting an industrial method of chlorine-alkali electrolysis. Griesheim then decisively promoted aluminium to which it later added electrothermal phosphorus and magnesium, developments that have gained world-wide significance.

The founder period of industrial chemistry had given rise to serious economic problems. The German dyestuffs factories had to get together, but their tremendous success did not generate in them a positive attitude to make the necessary sacrifices for such a merger.

Partial solutions had to be accepted. During the jubilee in 1913, A. v. Weinberg of Cassella and Wilhelm Kalle transmitted the congratulations of the companies that had merged in 1906. The other group, headed by Leverkusen and Ludwigshafen, had long been linked in scientific and technical competition with Hoechst.

After a long period of peace, political life had reached boiling point. The Balkan wars and political power blocs in Europe gave some warning of tensions to come. Internally, the problems of social policy had not been solved. True, the founders of German industry had quickly recognized that they were responsible for the life of their employees and had introduced far-reaching social measures. Hoechst, for example, had established a sickness benefit and housing scheme as well as many other social facilities. But none of these was sufficient to meet the demands of the time. Landowners and merchants, citizens and workers had joined in powerful parties and were facing each other in rigid blocs, kept together only by the imperial throne, itself no longer an entirely secure institution.

At the seventy-fifth jubilee in 1938, Ludwig Hermann gave the festive address. During the bloody period of the First World War and the changing years of the post-war period, science had progressed and the chemical industry had assumed gigantic proportions. At the same time, tremendous competition had grown up throughout the world. The needs of the post-war period had overcome the stubbornness of the giants. Hoechst had been merged with them in the I. G. Farbenindustrie. A proud concern had been forged, unsurpassed throughout the world in its magnitude and its scientific and technological performance. It was based on a strong individual life of its constituent members who were proud of their history and perpetuated it, but who were nevertheless prepared to participate in a larger, common task.

In 1938, on the day of its seventy-fifth birthday, Hoechst was still bearing the scars of the First World War. They could be healed only slowly even during the I. G. era. Much, however, had been achieved. The progress of the pharmaceutical division had been maintained. In 1921, Novalgin had been developed. In 1923, Insulin was for the first time prepared on a technical scale. Carl Ludwig Lautenschläger, who died only a few weeks ago, was closely linked with this important epoch in diabetic therapy. Hoechst was also taking its first steps in organic fluoro-chemistry with its promising future.

In competition with the sister companies, Hoechst had developed important parts of the Indanthren range. Hoechst's acetylene chemistry had helped to lay the foundations for plastics and synthetic rubber. A broad system of joint research in the I. G. Farbenindustrie had created a new era, the chemistry of plastics, synthetic fibres and foils and films the oldest of which, Cellophane, was developed by Kalle.

Largely self-sufficient, Germany was already shut off from the world. Its scientific research and its economic measures were all influenced by these self-sufficiency aspirations. Internal cohesion had been rendered extremely difficult in the post-war world and had been regained only to a limited extent, even though the products of the company were being exported throughout the world.

The company and its people had kept pace with developments in the world. The 1918 revolution had resulted in many social changes: the eight-hour day, the works council law and many other improvements. The development of democratic order and stability, however, had not been completed because of a lack of political freedom, and as a result of continuous interruptions through a succession of economic crises from which only force and a dictatorship seemed to offer escape.

In 1938, the sceptics were still in a minority. They were uniformly distributed among the old and the young, and at all levels of public life. The majority, however, were carried along by a wave of optimism and activity and overwhelmed by many superficial successes. It was a great gathering-in of all the forces but confined too closely to the German economic area, and therefore, crowded with problems of national ambition and, in the long run, worthy of a better fate.

But quiet progress had been made even then. In a tragic succession of severe depressions, resolute application and deep human disappointment, the social climate in our factories had changed. Through the camaraderie of a war conducted with equal ferocity both at the front and at home, and resulting in such a terrible end, there arose a community that provided the sole basis for the future existence of our fatherland.

Today, twenty-five years later, on our hundredth birthday, we look back upon all this as though it was a dream. After a tremendous effort during the war when incredible achievements and sacrifices were matched by boundless injustice and inhumanity, everything collapsed – Germany, the German people as such, and our former company the I. G. Farbenindustrie. For many years, the life of the state, of science and technology, of domestic and foreign trade, almost stood still. It took a long time before life began to reassert itself once more. Many lost their belief in a future because, in their humanity, they forgot that life always continues. The fate of many whom we remember today with sadness because they are no longer with us was fulfilled through desperation, human and economic misery and infinite hardness. In spite of all this, the company has been re-born on a scale that, on its hundredth birthday, we note with astonishment and joy, but also with the appropriate degree of modesty.

Detachment from the I. G. Farbenindustrie and the re-constitution in 1953 could not restore the situation in which Hoechst had once merged in the I. G. Human factors, economic and technical developments as well as political aspects dictated that the company should be completely redesigned, by grouping new developments around the old core, which in any case was not the same, to form a viable new whole. In spite of all the mistakes and difficulties, the success of the measure resided in the fact that it really had been possible to create such an organism which was then able to prove its viability and force right up to the present day. In such an hour one looks with satisfaction at the development that the company has achieved thus far. The components of the company had to be organized in a new form. After the first expansion, science and technology had to be put on an international footing once more.

The old fields derived attractive new developments from the new impetus. The growing chemistry of plastics had to be based on a new foundation, the field of petro-chemistry, which had now become accessible. Synthetic fibres were developed and films were produced for the first time on a large scale. Our sales people travelled throughout the world and created a selling organization that once more provided our product with international repute.

Farbwerke Hoechst has regained its place in the world. History will have to judge the value of these achievements and decide whether they will last. This has been a period when much lost ground had to be made up in respect of goods of all kinds, and, of course, this greatly promoted the reconstruction of the company. But ground also had to be made up in the application of the intellect and the performance of fruitful work which enabled people, after such a long period of inactivity, to perform outstanding achievements in their regained jobs.

This development will not stop after today. It is a development that is expressed less in large sales figures, investment figures, or the number of employees, than in uninterrupted technological and economic reorientation. Theoretical economic policy likes to conjure up a succession of boom conditions against the background of past experience which usually disregards scientific and technical developments. These developments, however, will not stand still and will also affect the life of society in the future.

The 2,200 natural scientists in Hoechst who are being provided with the appropriate facilities in the new laboratories now under construction, will guarantee this future. The fields of our research are expanding and will make more demands. Biology is giving us a greater insight into the world around us, and physics and mathematics are providing us with new problems and new answers that are reflected in the work of our factories, and that provide us with new fields of activity.

We thank our scientists for the impressive demonstration of their research as it is orientated at present and as documented in a volume containing seventy-eight scientific papers covering all parts of our research activities.

Our scientific progress is closely linked to the fate of the teaching and research institutes of our German universities, scientific institutions and societies, particularly the Max Planck Society. They provide us with the scientists of tomorrow. They provide us with the vital bloodstream that links the intellectual life of the company with that of our age. In deep gratitude, we, the natural scientists at Hoechst, appreciate the friendly and traditional links with all these mainsprings of our scientific endeavours which will never stand still for as long as we are prepared to recharge them through human contact, the friendly exchange of ideas and ready help whenever it is needed.

The scientists in our laboratories, the technicians and sales people that make up our company, as well as the many other gifted and diligent people that work with us, can succeed only on the basis of a broad and appropriate education imparted to them from early youth. The foundation of our economic future and of our entire future social order is being prepared in our German schools. The past has taught us that all progress, especially in the field of science and technology, can prosper only where it is not confined in a national strait-jacket, but where it is embedded in the affairs of a far-reaching world policy.

The First World War had put an end for a long time to the age of free trade and free movement throughout the world. National frontiers became economic frontiers and often even human frontiers. The resulting self-sufficiency necessarily provided many a transient impetus for science and technology. It meant, however, that industrial policy could no longer be operated according to generally valid economic points of view. From 1913 to 1951, production of goods in Europe almost doubled, while inter-European trade increased by only a few per cent.

Today, seventeen years after the end of the Second World War, the world seems to polarize into two halves, of which one has once again reverted to Slav and Asiatic isolation. It is painful for us, especially in this festive hour, that this divide should cut right across the middle of our German fatherland. It separates economic areas that belong together organically, and it separates people that want to be together. Nevertheless, on the hundredth birthday of Farbwerke Hoechst, it looks as though a new era has begun. It appears that the European people have once more recognized their task. They are beginning to tear down the frontiers whose continued existence, at any rate in so far as they are of economic importance, can only be a matter of years. Europe and North America have again opened their frontiers to more liberal policies.

In the remainder of the world, too, a fundamental change faces people with the choice of continuing their emancipation and returning to a free world, or, having been given this freedom, of returning into the seclusion of regressive isolation. It depends on us which way the decision will fall.

On the basis of a joint cultural heritage hammered out through the centuries, the peoples of Europe once found their way to liberal thinking. In bloody conflicts and crises, an intellectual attitude developed that once permeated the world with the courageous commercial enterprise of the great merchant venturers and the scientific journeys of discovery by such people as Alexander v. Humboldt. However, the connections then were severed. Europe set out on its victorious technological forward march that swept the entire western world and raised the standard of living of the people in this admittedly small part of the earth to undreamt-of heights. The tensions of today are due basically to the fact that the remainder of the world did not follow along this course, either in the achievement of freedom or in the intellectual re-birth of the early nineteenth century and the technological developments of the last hundred years – the period that coincides almost wholly with the history of our company.

The free and open economic relationship between the countries will also make new demands upon our concern. As raw material requirements and the economic connections are continuously changing with technological progress, the former agrarian countries cannot do without their own industrial development. Technology has become common property and is no longer the preserve of only a few, secured by patents and an intellectual lead.

The task of selling our products in the outside world in competition with others has now been complicated by the competition in our domestic markets. But we need to have our own plants abroad. We must make our contribution, even in less industrialized countries, to the establishment of an organically growing industrial structure if we wish to participate in the newly-opened markets.

In the last years, we have had to make great financial efforts in many countries to establish these plants as well as the appropriate sales organization. The external evidence of this newly-formed world organization are the 7,500 people that work for us outside Germany in all parts of the world and whose leading men I am glad to welcome amongst us today.

In the future, technological development will determine peoples' mode of living and their social order. To the extent that people are changing their environment as a result of scientific and technical achievements, they are also changing, both consciously and unconsciously, their own relationship to this environment, to the state and to society.

The initiative and enterprise of the founders, and the scientific urge of the period have attracted, decade after decade, a growing number of people linked to one another through their common task. Local factors governing life in the factories and human affinities ensured that families from every professional level remained linked to the company for generations. But there was also a continuous influx of new people from different areas, with a different and more modern education and style of life.

The people that become fused in such a factory community will always differ in their intelligence and training, their inclinations and abilities. The demands made upon them and the values created by the individual are not all the same. Together, however, they serve a common task and in their differences they are essential for the prosperity of the company.

Working in a large community – in factory, workshop, office and administration – makes considerable calls upon discipline, self-control, and consideration for others. It requires as much devotion as the technical realization of a major discovery in production and sales. It is, of course, possible to be all alone in such a company with one's notions of duty and responsibility. During shiftwork, walking through the extensive plant which operates day and night, at the control desk watching the colourful permutations of the indicators and control instruments, this loneliness can be as pronounced as that of the distant sales office, the inventive calm of the study, the solitude of the hour of decision. A company and cooperation between a large number of people will thrive only if one succeeds in wisely placing people of different abilities with their varying tasks, without prejudice, and solely on the basis of suitability and character.

In this festive hour, we wish to thank all those who, in the past, have placed their life in the service of the company. Let us include in our greetings and good wishes all those who belong to us today and who are discharging their duties in the large complex of Farbwerke Hoechst.

We had to travel a long road before we could accomplish this form of collaboration. At the time of our foundation, the old social order in Germany was collapsing. This applied both to the geographically controlled feudal system and the bourgeois system of civic commerce and crafts. A new social order evolved gradually from a random industrial population, based on fundamentally new principles. Wise and far-seeing industrialists, also in our company, strove from an early date to apply the patriarchial benevolence of the landowner or master of the guild to the new situation and to provide the uprooted people with a new feeling of security. It soon became clear, however, that matters could not rest here. Out of the persistent striving of all the classes of society and the professions, and especially the organizations representing them, there arose an entirely new order. The collapse following two lost wars and the consequent changes in people's way of life made a considerable contribution to this new order.

A system had to be found for salaries and wages, for working hours and leisure. People had to be given security in all the likely situations of need – accidents, illness, old age and other personal misfortunes. The position of the people in the factory had to be defined through a self-governing body and its participation in the general works measures.

This development has not yet been concluded. Individual wishes and the continuously changing position of man in our technical age, force us to pursue it all the time. We shall probably always have to concede that there is no final solution. The harder the state tries to establish this order, the clearer it becomes that this is not the end of the matter. Human fate cannot be regulated and shaped through legal and state measures alone. It needs the continuous participation of the individual in our environment in which he can still recognize the impact of his activities. At the moment when our homes become far-flung organizational structures, when work or family can no longer be reached on foot or by bicycle, when the human voice needs a loudspeaker to make itself heard even in the immediate vicinity, people need comprehensible dimensions within which they can still act out their own potentialities unless they wish to exist with the anonymity of the ant-heap.

Family and property, a home of your own, are steps towards this goal which provides man with a first basis of security. This is why our company has – rightly – spent increasing amounts for these purposes. To own assets and to accumulate savings is possible only if there is a guaranteed minimal existence. It will, of course, also always depend on the personal attitude to life. To render the relationship closer to the job has been a subject of constant endeavour on our part. Guaranteed participation in the net profit of the company has been aimed at from an early date and our company has long since practised it. The issue of shares to employees is another step in this direction. They provide the individual not only with a modest basis for acquiring personal assets and a feeling of belonging to the property-owning classes, but they also promote interest in an understanding of commercial thinking and the unfortunately limited knowledge of the German public of the bases of our economic and social order.

Such developments will help to strengthen the self-confidence of the individual, and his ability to judge, and will convince him that he is not the mindless, soulless member of the modern industrial society that the sceptics at the beginning of the industrial era feared. Such material progress cannot by itself ensure self-confidence, optimism or *joi de vivre*. At the height of an almost unbelievable economic boom, it is often forgotten that man does not live by bread alone but that his inner strength and self-confidence depend upon the realization that he is fulfilling his place in life. We have learnt from the unemployment of earlier economic crises and from the enforced inactivity after the war that factory and job also have an idealistic value. Our young people are subjecting themselves to further education at evening institutes, company courses and universities not only for the sake of earning more money, but because, with sound instinct, they feel that satisfaction in life is achieved only if man is able to use all his talents and if he enjoys his work. One day, he has to exercise these abilities in a sphere to which he has an inner link. Apart from holidays and the use of leisure time, there is, as a prerequisite for a self-assured attitude to life, the responsibility in family and job which provides man with his real attitude.

To believe in this, and to deepen this conviction, is the most reliable guide to the further improvement of our social order.

Belonging to a company, especially one with such a long tradition as ours, will promote a healthy factory egoism which holds the people together in a community that is moulded not only by state laws and ensured rights but also by an inner tradition of human friendship, welfare and enjoyment of success.

We hope that this hall, where we are joined for the first time today, is a symbol of such a community. In spite of its tremendous dimensions, it is small in relation to the buildings that the company erects every year, and it looks modest by the side of the proud plants in which we work together. Let us thank all those who have helped in the construction of this hall, including the pension fund which made the money available. We hope to discuss our affairs in this building with dignity and mutual respect, and we hope also that this hall will allow us to enjoy art and culture during our leisure hours, thus providing us with relaxation to compensate for the strains and stresses of everyday life.

The large Farbwerke Hoechst family is not a state within a state. We cannot mould it according to our own aims alone. In the many wide fields in which we are engaged, we are responsible for many. The growth of the company during past decades caused it to outpace the ambitions of the original owners. Today, more than 230 thousand shareholders own the company to which, in part for many decades, they have entrusted their savings and their possessions.

To all those, without whose confidence in our company and without whose funds we would not have been able to carry out reconstruction, we owe a debt of gratitude in this festive hour. They also help us to anchor our concern, far beyond its immediate boundaries, in the public and to provide a link with the large masses of our people. In this they are joined by the hundreds of thousands of suppliers and customers who remind us daily of our obligation to the whole through our economic and business policy.

Just as each individual can live his life only within a parish, town or country, so our concern with all its responsibility is embedded in the economic life of its people. Close contact with economic and other organizations that share our interests also help to integrate us into a common state organism with which each one of us and also the company as a whole is linked for better or for worse. Therefore, no one in our concern can escape these general obligations.

This applies equally to collaboration in the field of communal policy and self-administration, participation in professional and industrial societies, and active involvement in the cultural life of our time. We are striving for new forms and laws in all these spheres of our life, especially since technology and industry – like ourselves with the products of our company – are continually changing the external aspects of our life and our position in it. It will therefore be readily understood that following a stormy period of reconstruction in which there was little time for emotional considerations, the discussion of a new order continues. These discussions exceed the frontiers of our country and concern the fundamental question of the structure of our industrial life and our social order. At such times, when so much is in the melting pot, the state assumes a high degree of responsibility. It has to watch trends together with the democratically elected representatives of the people, and has continuously to re-examine the principles upon which law and order are based in order to establish whether these still remain valid for our present age. The state cannot perpetuate what is out of date and it cannot suppress what its citizens are promoting as the result of the success of their work. To be progressive in such an era without violating fundamental principles of right and equality requires confident cooperation from all, and cannot be ensured either through the interest of individual people or classes or through an abstract state authority. At the end of the day, the forces of order can achieve lasting success only if they are based on the sense of responsibility of all the citizens.

Today, at the beginning of the second century of Farbwerke Hoechst, we find ourselves once more in the centre of the problems of our age. We shall overcome them so long as there are people willing to devote to our cause their intellect, their ability to work, and their personal faith. We pay homage to all those who walked this road before us and who did not allow themselves to be deflected from their work through human disappointment. Originally, it was a small family that knew each other and held together in times of need. Our new, much larger family, can also exist only on the basis of human relationships. May the spirit of common aspiration, mutual respect, and a loyal sense of duty show the company the road to a happy future.

ORGANIZATIONAL STRUCTURE

Chairman, Board of Management					

Technical Directorate	Commercial Directorate				

Divisions / Co-ordinating Departments	I	II	III	IV	V
Finance and Accounts					
Legal Department and Patents					
Sales					
Research					
Engineering					
Works Management Personnel Purchasing					
Technical Manager*					

* Abolished after appointment of the chairman of the board

424

Chairman or Deputy Chairman of Board of Management

Administration of Divisions through six technical or commercial members of the Board of Management

Staff functions

Divisions

A	Inorganic Chemicals
B	Organic Chemicals
C	Agriculture
D	Dyestuffs and Starting Products
E	Tensides and Auxiliaries
F	Fibres and Starting Products
G	Synthetic resins and paints
H	Plastics and waxes
J	Films and foils
K	Reprographic materials
L	Pharmaceuticals
M	Cosmetics
N	Plant Construction
P	Low temperature technology, welding techniques, industrial gases

Co-ordinating Departments of Management

Technical Works Management
Domestic
Foreign Production
Sales
Research
Application Techniques
Engineering
Finance and Accounts
Legal, Patent and Tax Departments
Purchasing
Personnel & Social Services/Works Administration

Indexes

NAME AND SUBJECT

Indexes

NAME INDEX

SUBJECT INDEX